ENVIRONMENTAL PROTECTION
AND THE COMMON LAW

For
Gwen and Ivor Edmunds

Environmental Protection and the Common law

Edited by
JOHN LOWRY and ROD EDMUNDS

OXFORD – PORTLAND OREGON
2000

Hart Publishing
Oxford and Portland, Oregon

Published in North America (US and Canada) by
Hart Publishing c/o
International Specialized Book Services
5804 NE Hassalo Street
Portland, Oregon
97213-3644
USA

Distributed in the Netherlands, Belgium and Luxembourg by
Intersentia, Churchillaan 108
B2900 Schoten
Antwerpen
Belgium

© The contributors severally 2000

The contributors have asserted their rights under the Copyright, Designs
and Patents Act 1988, to be identified as the authors of this work

Hart Publishing Ltd is a specialist legal publisher based in Oxford, England.
To order further copies of this book or to request a list of other
publications please write to:

Hart Publishing Ltd, Salter's Boatyard, Oxford OX1 4LB
Telephone: +44 (0)1865 245533 or Fax: +44 (0)1865 794882
e-mail: mail@hartpub.co.uk
www.hartpub.co.uk

British Library Cataloguing in Publication Data
Data Available
ISBN 1 901362–93–0 (cloth)

Typeset by Hope Services (Abingdon) Ltd.
Printed in Great Britain on acid-free paper
by Biddles Ltd, Guildford and King's Lynn.

Foreword

Environmental Law, as such, is not a subject known to the Common Law. It is indeed only in the last thirty years that we have had a Government Department specifically responsible for the "Environment". It is not perhaps surprising, therefore, that the present law in this area exhibits what one of the papers calls "structural malaise". Unfortunately, new cases do not come before the courts in a structured way, and there are few opportunities to develop a more coherent approach. My own experiences as a Judge of the Chancery Division and of the Crown Office List (some of which are referred to in this book) have illustrated the variety of issues which may arise under the general heading of "Environmental Law", and the necessary intermingling of Common Law and statutory sources (both English and European). I have for some years been advocating the desirability of a form of "Environmental Court", as a means of providing more order and direction. Professor Malcolm Grant's recent study on this subject for the DETR will, I hope, stimulate further debate. However, he recognises that "It is in Civil Law that the greatest difficulties arise in identifying any distinctly 'environmental' actions."

The present collection of essays will provide fascinating reading, and a valuable working tool for that continuing debate. To my mind, the depth of the discussion and the variety of subjects covered are themselves testimony to the continuing vigour of the Common Law.

Robert Carnwath
Law Commission
May 2000

Preface

Tort law as a means of protection against environmental harms is seemingly on the wane. The decision of Buckley J. in *Gillingham* that planning permission ought to be determinative of the "neighbourhood standard" against which a particular harm is to be judged, served to rekindle the debate surrounding the continued effectiveness of nuisance as an instrument for environmental protection. The debate was further invigorated by the reaffirmation in *Hunter* of *Malone* v. *Laskey* (exclusive possession being the prerequisite for locus standi), thereby dashing the optimism which had fleetingly followed on the heels of *Khorasandjian* v. *Bush*. Looking towards the rule in *Rylands* v. *Fletcher* as holding the true potential of the common law in the overall regime of environmental protection will also bring little joy following the decision in *Cambridge Water* which wedded *Rylands* to the fate of nuisance.

The essays contained in this volume do not purport to offer a single or, indeed, a comprehensive theoretical solution for the future development of the property-based torts as a means of continuing to play an effective environmental role. The shadow of *Cambridge Water* and *Hunter* loom too large for that. But rather, the essays are intended to contribute to the wider debate. They highlight some of the principal areas of contention within UK law and the EU in which responses to environmental harm are deserving of further thought.

In compiling this collection, we have incurred many debts. First, to the contributors themselves who willingly sacrificed their time to support this project. Equally, we owe a debt of gratitude to Jenny Steele who gave us the benefit of her experience in bringing a work of this type to fruition. Her advice proved invaluable. We are grateful to John Murphy for helping us formulate the idea at its initial conception and staying with us through its metamorphosis and contributing to the final volume. We have also incurred debts of gratitude to many others including, David Cowan, Philip Rawlings and Linda Clarke. Lynne O'Meara gave us both constant support in maintaining the organisation of this project and the sheaf of correspondence generated. Finally, we wish to thank Richard Hart, Hannah Young and all at Hart Publishing for their encouragement, perseverance and enduring patience going beyond that which should be decently expected.

John Lowry and Rod Edmunds
All Saints Day 1999.

Contents

Table of Cases   ix
Table of Legislation   xix

1 VICTORIAN FOUNDATIONS?   1
Professor Raymond Cocks, Keele University

2 NUISANCE, THE MORALITY OF NEIGHBOURLINESS, AND
ENVIRONMENTAL PROTECTION   27
James Penner, London School of Economics and Political Science

3 NOXIOUS EMISSIONS AND COMMON LAW LIABILITY:
TORT IN THE SHADOW OF REGULATION   51
John Murphy, University of Manchester

4 FROM THE INDIVIDUAL TO THE ENVIRONMENTAL:
TORT LAW IN TURBULENCE   77
Professor Robert G Lee, Cardiff Law School

5 TORT AND ENVIRONMENTAL PLURALISM   93
Professor Keith Stanton and Christine Willmore, University of
Bristol

6 STATUTORY LIABILITY FOR CONTAMINATED LAND:
FAILURE OF THE COMMON LAW?   115
Owen McIntyre, The Law Society of Ireland, Dublin (formerly of
the University of Manchester)

7 NUISANCE AND ENVIRONMENTAL PROTECTION   139
Karen Morrow, University of Durham

8 MARKING THE BOUNDARY: THE RELATIONSHIP
BETWEEN PRIVATE NUISANCE, NEGLIGENCE AND FAULT   161
Paula Giliker, Queen Mary and Westfield College, London

viii   *Contents*

9 STIGMA DAMAGES, AMENITY AND THE MARGINS OF
ECONOMIC LOSS: QUANTIFYING PERCEPTIONS AND
FEARS   179
*John Lowry, University of Warwick and Rod Edmunds, University
of Sussex*

10 TOWARDS A EUROPEAN TORT LAW ON THE
ENVIRONMENT? EUROPEAN UNION INITIATIVES AND
DEVELOPMENTS ON CIVIL LIABILITY IN RESPECT OF
ENVIRONMENTAL HARM   201
*Martin Hedemann-Robinson, Brunel University and Mark Wilde,
University of Hertfordshire*

11 ENVIRONMENTAL PROTECTION AND THE ROLE OF THE
COMMON LAW: A SCOTTISH PERSPECTIVE   239
*Professor Jeremy Rowan-Robinson and Donna McKenzie-Skene,
University of Aberdeen*

Index   267

Table of Cases

EC

Aktien-Zuckerfabrik Schoppenstedt v Council Case 5/71 [1971] ECR 975 ...231
Banks v British Coal Case C-128/92 [1994] ECR I-1209 230
Bowden v South West Water Services Limited, Secretary of State for the
    Environment and Director-General of Water Services [1998] 3 CMLR
    330..234
Brasserie de Pecheur SA v Germany Case C-46/93 [1996] ECR I-1029 231
Commission v Council (Generalised Tariff Preferences) Case 45/86[1987]
    ECR 1493..206
Commission v Council (Titanium Dioxide) Case C-300/89 [1991]
    ECR I-2867 ....206, 207
Commission v Council (Waste Management) Case C-155/91 [1993]
    ECR I-939 207
Commission v Germany Case C-131/88 [1991] ECR I-825 232
Commission v Germany Case 361/88 [1991] ECR I-2567 232
Commission v Germany Case C-58/89 [1991] ECR I-4983 232
Dillenkofer v Germany Cases C-178-179, 188-190/94 [1996] 3 CMLR 469 ...231
European Parliament v Council (Shipment of Waste) Case C-187/93 [1994]
    ECR I-2874 207
Francovich and Bonifaci v Italy [1991] ECR I-5403 ....204, 229, 233, 237
Marleasing SA v La Comercial Internacional de Alimentacion SA Case
    C-106/889 [1992] ECR I-4135..230
Marshall v Southhampton and South-West Hampshire Area Health
    Authority Case 152/84 [1986] ECR 723 230
R v HM Treasury, ex p. BT plc Case C-392/93 [1996] 2 CMLR 217...............231
R v Secretary of State for Transport, ex p. Factortame Case C-48/93 [1996]
    ECR I-1029 231
Rheinmuhlen-Dusseldorf v Weinfuhrh und Vorratsstelle fur Getreide Case
    166/73 [1974] ECR 33 234
Srl CILFIT and Lanificio di Gavardo SpA v Ministry of Health Case 283/81
    [1982] ECR 472 234
Van Gend en Loos v Netherlands Case 26/62 [1963] ECR 1..................230, 233
Von Colson and Kamann v Land Nordrhein Westfalen Case 14/83 [1984]
    ECR 1891..230

x *Table of Cases*

United Kingdom

AB v South West Water Services Ltd [1993] 1 All ER 609 ....70, 71
Abbey National Mortgages plc v Key Surveyors Nationwide Ltd [1996]
  1 WLR 1534 106
Adkins v Thomas Solvent Co 487 NW2d 715 (Mich. 1992) 192, 193
Albery-Speyer v BP Oil Ltd and Shell Oil Ltd 1980 PCR 586......................252
Allan v Barclay (1864) 2 M 874...254
Allen v Gulf Oil Refining [11980] QB 156 ....38, 39, 110, 153
Alphacell Ltd v Woodward [1972] AC 824 (HL) 132
Anderson v Dickie 1915 SC (HL) 79; 1915 1 SLT 393 256
Andrae v Selfridge Co Ltd [1938] Ch 1 ....33, 72
Attia v British Gas plc [1988] QB 304...191
Attorney-General v Gastonia Coaches [1977] RTR 219................................55
Attorney-General v Manchester Corporation [1893] 2 Ch 407..............102, 104
Attorney-General v Mayor of Preston (1896) 13 TLR 14 33
Attorney-General v Nottingham Corporation [1904] 1 Ch 673 104
Attorney-General v PYA Quarries [1957] 1 All ER 894 ....52, 100, 112
Attorney-General v Rathmines and Pembroke Joint Health Board [1904]
  1 IR 161 ....102, 104
Attorney-General v Tod-Heatley [897] 1 Ch 560......................................167
Avon County Council v Millard [1985] 274 EG 1025 258
Ballard v Tomlinson (1885) 29 Ch D 115 154
Bamford v Turley (1862) 3 B&S 66; 122 ER 25 ....7, 31, 33, 143
Bank of New Zealand v Greenwood [1984] 1 NZLR 525 ....42, 190
Barker v Herbert [1911] 2 KB 633 167
Barrett v Enfield LBC [1997] 3 All ER 171 108
Ben Nevis Distillery (Fort William) ltd v The North British Aliminium Co
  Ltd 1948 SC 592 248
Berry v Armstrong Rubber Co., 989 F 2d 822 (5th Circ. 1993) 182
Best v Samuel Fox & Co Ltd [1952] AC 716..195
Bixby Ranch Co v Spectrol Electronics Corp. No BC052566
  (Cal. Sup Ct, 15 Dec 1993) 182, 197
Blackburn v ARC Ltd [1998] Env. LR 469.........................87, 150, 151, 156, 189
Blair v Lochaber District Council 195 SLT 407.......................................258
Blue Circle Industries v Ministry of Defence [1998] 3 All ER 385 .....97, 99, 100,
                                        182, 183, 184, 185, 186, 198, 200
Bolam v Friern Hospital Management Committee [1957]
  2 All ER 118 ....78, 107, 147
Bolitho v City & Hackney Health Authority [1998] AC 232 147
Bolton v Stone [1951] AC 850..153, 171
Bone v Seale [1975]1 All ER 787...172
Bonnington Castings Ltd v Wardlaw [1956] AC 613................................146
Bourhill v Young 1942 SC (HL) 78...249

Table of Cases xi

Bowden v Southwest Water Services Ltd [1998] Env LR 445.........................135
Bower v Peate (1876) 1 QBD 321 164
Bradford Corporation v Pickles [1895] AC 587 63
Brand v Hammersmith and City Railway Co (1867) LR 2 QB 223 162
British Celanese v Hunt [1969] 1 WLR 959 ....176, 196, 199
British Railways Board v Herrington [1972] AC 877 176
Broad v Brisban City Council and Baptist union of Queensland [1986]
    2 Qd R 317...190
Brown v Rolls Royce Ltd 1960 SC (HL) 22...251
Budden v BP Oil Ltd and Shell Oil Ltd 1980 PCR 586...................................252
Burgess v M/V Tamano (1973) 370 F Supp 247 (USDC)...............................101
C & G Homes Ltd v Secretary of State for Health [1991] 2 WLR 715 180
Caledonian Railway Co v Greenock Corporation 1917 SC (HL) 56......244, 245
Cambridge Water Co v Eastern Counties Leather plc [1994]
    AC 264.........................34, 36, 43, 44, 45, 48, 62, 64, 65, 66, 79, 80, 81, 87, 88,
                    97, 98, 107, 112, 116, 118, 119, 135, 143, 146, 152, 154,
                    155, 156, 158, 165, 166, 173, 186, 195, 198, 242, 245, 247
Campbell v F & F Moffat (Transport) Ltd 1992 SCLR 551............................255
Cassell v Broome [1972] AC 1027 71
Cattle v Stockton Waterworks Co (1875) LR 10 QB 453................................195
Cavanagh v Ulster Weaving Co [1960] AC 145..251
Central Motors (St Andrews) Ltd v St Andrews Magistrates, 1961
    SLT 290 242
Chalmers v Dixon (1876) 3R 461 245
Chasemore v Richards (1859) 7 HLC 349 33
Christie v Davey [1893] 1 Ch 316 ....33, 63
Clifford v Holt [1889] 1 Ch 598 55
Clippens Oil Co v Edinburgh and District Water Trustees (1897) 25 R 373 248
Coventry City Council v Cartwright [1975] 1 WLR 845 57
Cowan v National Coal Board 1958 SLT (Notes) 19 255
Crisculoa v Power Authority of New York, 621 N E 2d 1195 (NY 1993)......181
Cummnock & Doon Valley District Council v Dance Energy Associates Ltd
    1992 GWD 25-1441 242
Cunard v Antifyre Ltd [1933] 1 KB 551 171
Cunliffe v Bnakes [1945] 1 All ER 459...152
Davidson v Kerr 1996 GWD 40-2296 242
De Keyser's Royal Hotel v Spicer Bros. Ltd (1914) 30 TLR 257 33
Delaware Mansions Ltd v Westminster City Council [1999] 46 EG 194 188
Department of Transport v North West Water Authority [1984] AC 336.....247
Dollman v Hillman [1941] 1 All ER 355 (CA) 166
Donoghue v Stevenson [1932] AC 562 ....162, 249
Doughty v Turner [1964] 1 QB 518..156
Earl of Ripon v Hobart (1843) 3 M & K 169 102
Eastern & SA Telegraph Co v Cape Town Tramways [1902] AC 381..........153

xii *Table of Cases*

Edinburgh Railway Access and Property Co v John Ritchie and Co
(1903) 5 F 299 245
Elliot Steam Tug Co v Shipping Controller [1922] 1 KB 127 195
Empress Car Company (Abertillery) Limited v National Rivers Authority
[1998] 1 All ER 481..........127, 133
Exxon Corp. v Yarema 516 A 2d 990 (Md Ct Spec App 1986) 193
Fleming v Hislop 13 R (HL) 43 242
Fletcher v Bealey (1885) 28 ChD 688 102
Friends of the Earth, Re [1988] JPL 93..........58, 60
Fritz v Hobson (1880) 14 ChD 542..........33
Frost v King Edward VII Welsh Memorial Association [1918]
2 Ch 180..........103
G & A Estates Ltd v Caviapen Trustees Ltd (No. 1) 1993 SLT 1037 .....245, 248
Gateshead Metropolitan Borough Council v Secretary of State for the
Environment and Northumbrian Water (1994) 71 P & CR 3350 150
Gaunt v Finney (1872) 8 LR Ch App 8..........64, 145
Gillingham BC v Medway (Chatham) Dock Co Ltd [1993]
QB 343 ....38, 39, 97, 110, 118, 150
Golden Sea produce Ltd v Scottish Nuclear plc 1992 SLT 942 259
Goldman v Hargrave [1967] 1 AC 645 ....45, 152, 168, 169, 170, 177
Graham and Graham v Re-Chem International Ltd [1996]
Env LR 158..........67, 141, 142, 143, 144, 145, 147, 148,
149, 151, 156, 242, 246, 250, 252, 263
Griffiths v British Coal Corporation QBD, 23 Jan 1998 ....82, 136
Gunn v Wallsend Slipway an Engineering Co Ltd (1989) *The Times*,
23 Jan 1989 116
Hadley v Baxendale (1854) 9 Exch. 341..........261
Halsey v Esso Petroleum Ltd [1961] 1 WLR 683..........98
Hanrahan v Merck Sharp & Dohme (Ireland) Ltd [1988]
ILRM 629 ....141, 142, 143, 144, 145, 146, 149, 252
Harris v Evans [1998] 3 All ER 522..........109
Harrison v Southwark and Vauxhall Water Co [1891] 2 Ch 409 ....33, 72
Hedley Byrne & Co Ltd v Heller & Partners Ltd [1964] AC 465..........185
Hickey v Electric Reduction Co of Canada Ltd (1971) 21 DLR (3d) 368
(Newfoundland)..........100
Hill v Chief Constable West Yorkshire Police [1989] AC 53 108
Hislop v MacRitchie's Trs (1881) R (HL) 95 262
Hochester v De La Tour (1853) 2 E & B 678 260
Hole v Barlow (1858) 4 CB (NS) 334; 140 ER 1113 ....6, 7, 31, 42
Hollywood Silver Fox Farm v Emmett [1936] 2 KB 468 ....33, 63
Home Brewery Co Ltd v William Davis & Co (Leicester) Ltd [1987]
1 QB 339..........64
Hope v British Nuclear Fules plc, 1989 No 3689 (unreported)..........116
Hughes v Lord Advocate [1963] AC 837..........80, 156, 250

Table of Cases xiii

Hunter v Canary Wharf [1997] AC 655.......39, 40, 42, 45, 48, 72, 80, 87, 97, 98, 110, 112, 117, 118, 140, 142, 150, 152, 162, 163, 171, 172, 173, 174, 175, 178, 179, 184, 185, 186, 187, 188, 189, 190, 195, 198, 247, 248

Hunter v London Docklands Development Corp [1996] 2 WLR 348; [1997] 2 All ER 426...117, 183

Hussain v Lancaster City Council [1999] 2 WLR 1142.....................................175

Independent Broadcasting Authority v EMI Electronics & BICC Construction (1980) 14 BLR 1..109

Inglis v Shotts iron Co (1881) 8 R 1006 244

Invercargill City Council v Hamlin [1996] AC 624 186

Jackson v Horizon Holidays [1975] 1 WLR 1468 47

Jacobs v London CC [1950] AC 361 165

J.B.Mackenzie (Edinburgh) Ltd v Lord Advocate 1972 SC 231; 1972 SLT 204 263

Job Edwards v Birmingham Navigations [1924] 1 KB 341 ....167, 168, 177

Jones v Llanrwst UDC [1911] 1 Ch 393..102

Junior Books Ltd v Veitchi Co Ltd [1983] 1 AC 520 186

Karlshamms Oljefabriker A/B v Monarch Steamship Co 1949 SC (HL) 1; 1949 SLT 51 261

Kelvin Shipping Co v Canadian Pacific Railway Co 1928 SC (HL) 21 255

Kennaway v Thompson [1981] QB 88 ....30, 44

Kennedy v Glenbelle Ltd, 1996 SLT 1186.......................................166, 244, 246

Khorasandjian v Bush [1993] QB 727 ....45, 88, 117, 140, 142, 171, 188

Kirkham v Boughey [1958] 2 QB 338 195

Koufos v Czarnikov [1969] 1 AC 350...255, 263

Lamb v Martin Marietta Energy Syatem Inc, 835 F Supp 959 (W D Ky 1993) 182

Landcatch Ltd v International Oil Pollution Compensation Fund [1999] 2 Lloyd's Rep. 316 ....99, 100, 109

Langbrook Properties Ltd v Surrey County Council [1970] 1 WLR 161 33

Laws v Florinplace [1981] 1 All ER 659...30

Leakey v National Trust [1980] QB 485 ....38, 44, 48, 140, 152, 168, 169

Letang v Cooper [1965 1 QB 232 176

Lipiatt v South Gloucestershire County Council, 31 March 1999 (unreported)...153

Litchfield-Speer v Queen Anne's Gate Syndicate (no 2) Ltd [1919] 1 Ch 407 ....102, 103, 113

Logan v Wang 1991 SLT 580 244

Lord Advocate v North British Railway 1894 2 SLT 71 247

Lord Advocate v Reo Stakis Organisation 1982 SLT 140 243

McGhee v National Coal Board [1973] 1 WLR 1, 143 144

McKillen v Barclay Curle and Co 1967 SLT 41 255

Maguire v Charles McNeil Ltd 1922 SC 174 243

Mantania National Provincial Bank [1936] 2 All ER 633..............................33

xiv *Table of Cases*

Margereson v J.W. Roberts [1996] Env LR 304.....................................81, 136
Matania v National Provincial Bank [1936] 2 All ER 633 164
Mayor of Bradford v Pickles [1895] AC 587 33
Merlin v British Nuclear Fuels plc [1990] 2 QB 557 ....97, 99, 100, 182, 183,
184, 185, 187, 190, 198, 200
Metropolitan Asylum District Managers v Hill (1882) 47 LT 29 104
Midwood & Co v Manchester Corporation [1905] 2 KB 697 ....65, 165
Miller v Jackson [1977] 1 QB 966; [1977] 3 All ER 338 (CA) 30, 148, 162, 163
Mint v Good [1951] 1 KB 517 53
Montana Hotels Pty Ltd v Fasson Pty ltd (1986) 69 ALR 258.......................177
Morton v Wheeler *The Times*, 1 Feb 1956 166
Morton v William Dixon Ltd 1909 SC 807 251
Muir v Glasgow Corporation 1934 SC (HL) 3...249
Murphy v Brentwood DC [1991] 1 AC 398 186
National Coal Board v Thorne [1976] 1 WLR 543 57
National Rivers Authority v Biffa Waste Services Ltd, *The Times*, 21
November 1995 127
Nobles Trs. v Economic Forestry (Scotland Edinburgh Railway Access and
Property Co v John Ritchie and Co (1903) 5 F 299 Ltd 1988 SLT 662 245
Nor-Video Services v Ontario Hydro (1978) 84 DLR (3rd) 118
NRA v Yorkshire Water Services Ltd [1995] 1 AC 444 (HL) 133
O'Brien's Curator Bonis v British Steel plc 1991 SCLR 931...........................254
Overseas Tankship (UK) Ltd v Miller Steamship Co Pty Ltd, *see* Wagon
Mound (No. 2)
Overseas Tankship (UK) Ltd v Morris Dock and Engineering Co
[1961] AC 388 255
Page Motors Ltd v Epsom and Ewell Borough Council (1982)
80 LGR 337...153, 169
Paoli R R Yard PcB Litig, Re, 35 F 3d 717 (3d Cir 1994) 182, 198
Polemis and Furness, Withy and Co Ltd, Re [1921] 3 KB 560.......................255
Polsue and Alferi Ltd v Rushmer [1906] 1 Ch 234; [1907] AC 121...........37, 118
Price v Cromack [1975] 1 WLR 988 133
Pride of Derby v British Celanese Ltd [1953] 1 Ch 149.................................102
R v Dairy Produce Quotas Tribunal, ex p. Caswell [1990] 2 All ER 738 58
R v Divermoss, *The Times*, 3 February 1995...127
R v Falmouth and Truro Port Health Authority ex p. South West Water Ltd
292 ENDS 51; [1999] Env LR 833 110
R v Felixstowe Justices, ex p. Leigh [1987] QB 582 60
R v Inland Revenue Commissioners, ex p. National Federation of Self-
Employed and Small Businesses Ltd [1982] AC 617...............................60, 62
R v Inspectorate of Pollution, ex p. Greenpeace Ltd (No 2) [1994]
4 All ER 329...59, 61, 77, 112, 222
R v North Somerset District Council, ex p. Garnett [1998]
Env LR 91 ....60, 61, 62

Table of Cases xv

R v Secretary of State for the Environment ex p. Rose Theatre Trust [1990]
1 All ER 754 77

R v Secretary of State for the Environment ex p. Watson (1998)
282 ENDS 52; [1999] Env LR 310 (CA) 95

R v Secretary of State for Foreign Affairs, ex p. World Development
Movement Ltd [1995] 1 All ER 611 112

R v Secretary of State for Trade and Industry, ex p. Duddridge [1995]
3 CCMLR 231 .... 91, 95, 104

R v Somerset Council, ex p. Dixon [1998] Env LR 111 .... 60, 61, 62, 77

Rainham Chemical Works Ltd v Belvedere Fish Guano Co [1921]
2 AC 465 .... 72, 119

Rapier v London Tramways Co [1893] 2 Ch 588 55

Rattray v Daniels (1959) 17 DLR.2d 134 33

Read v J. Lyons & Co Ltd [1947] AC 156 .... 98, 119, 165, 174

Reay v British Nuclear Fuels plc, 1990 No 860. (unreported) 116

Reinhardt v Mentasti (1889) 42 ChD 685 31

RHM Bakeries (Scotland) Ltd v Strathclyde Regional Council, 1985
SLT 214 .... 142, 152, 166, 244

Rickards v Lothian [1913] AC 263 .... 66, 119

Roe v Minister of Health [1954] 2 QB 66 .... 107, 249

Rookes v Barnard [1964] 1 All ER 367 .... 69, 70

Ruxley Electronics and Construction Ltd v Forsyth [1996] AC 344 151

Ryeford Homes Ltd v Sevenoaks DC [1989] 2 EGLR 281 .... 196, 199

Rylands v Fletcher (1865) 11 Jur NS 714; 34 Ex 177; 3 H and C 774;
159 ER 737; (1866) 12 Jur NS 603; LR 1 Ex 265; 35 LJ Ex 154;
(1868) LR 3 (HL) 330 .... 9, 10, 11, 13, 17, 18, 22, 23, 24, 34, 35, 36,
38, 52, 53, 60, 62, 64, 65, 66, 67, 69, 70, 71, 72, 73,
75, 79, 80, 98, 101, 107, 135, 139, 140, 141, 142, 152,
154, 155, 158, 166, 172, 173, 174, 195, 197, 245

St Anne's Well Brewery Co v Roberts (1929) 140 LT 177

St Helen's Smelting Co v Tipping (1865) 11 HLC 642 .... 37, 99, 118, 187

SCM (United Kingdom) Ltd v W.J. Whittal & Son Ltd [1970]
1 WLR 1017 176

Sedleigh-Denfield v O'Callaghan [1940] AC 880 .... 16, 139, 154, 164, 167, 168,
169, 170, 173, 176, 177

Sevenoaks DC v Pattullo-Vinson Ltd [1984] Ch 211 103

Shelfer v City of London Electric Lighting Co [1985] 1 Ch 287 44

Shotts Iron Co Ltd v Inglis (1882) 9 R (HL) 78 .... 144, 247

Slavin v North Brancepeth Coal Co (1874) 8 Ch App 8 145

Smith v Leech Brain [1962] 2 QB 405 156

Smith v Littlewoods [1987] AC 241 .... 169, 175, 176, 177

Societe Remorquage à Helice v Bennetts [1911] 1 KB 243 195

Southport Corporation v Esso Petroleum Co Ltd [1954]
2 QB 182 .... 116, 118

xvi *Table of Cases*

Spartan Steel and Alloys Ltd v Martin & Co (Contractors) Ltd [1972] 3 All ER 557 195
Steel-Maitland v British Airways Board 1981 SLT 110................................247
Stephens v Anglia Water Authority [1987] 1 WLR 1381 33
Stewart v Kennedy (1890) 17 R (HL)1...260
Stockport Waterworks Company v Potter (1861) 7 H.& N. 160....................31
Stovin v Wise [1996] AC 175..108
Strachan and Gavin v Paton (1826) 3 W & S 19 (HL) 261
Sturges v Bridgman (1879) 11 ChD 852 ....37, 64, 118
Swaine v The Great Northern railway (1864) 4 De GJ & S 211 33
Swindon Waterworks Co v Wilts and Berks Canal Co [1875] LR 7 (HL).........3
Tailors of Aberdeen v Coutts (1840) 1 Rob App 296 256
Tetley v Chitty [1986] 1 All ER 663 30
T.H. Critelli v Lincoln Trust & Savings Co (1978) 86 DLR 3d 724 (Ontario High Court), 41
Thompson, Schwab v Costaki [1956] 1 WLR 335...190
Thompson v Smiths Shiprepairers (North Shields) Ltd [1984] QB 405 107
Three Rivers District Council v Bank of England [1999] Lloyd's Rep. Bank 283 109
Tipping v St Helen's Smelting Co 4 B and S 608; 122 ER 588; 1 Ch App Cas 66 ....4, 5, 8, 10, 11, 13, 22, 23, 24
Tophams Ltd v Earl of Sefton [1967] 1 AC 50 133
TP and KM v United Kingdom, 5 Nov 1999..108
Trecarrell, The [1973] 1 Lloyd's Rep 402 80
Tutton v A.D. Walter Ltd [1985] 3 WLR 797; [1986] QB 61 251
Vacwell Engineering Co Ltd v BDH Chemicals Ltd [1971] 1 QB 111 109
Victoria Laundry (Windsor) Ltd v Newman Industries Ltd [1949] 2 KB 528 261
Wagon Mound (No. 2) [1967] AC 617 ....34, 43, 118, 139, 140, 143, 153, 154, 165, 255
Walter v Selfe (1851) 4 de G & Sm 315 63
Watt v Jamieson 1954 SC 56..241, 243
Webster v Lord Advocate, 1984 SLT 13....................................242, 243, 247, 248
Weller & Co v Foot and Mouth Disease Research Institute [1966] 1 QB 569 196
Welton v North Cornwall District Council [1997] 1 WLR 570....................109
West v White (1877) 4 ChD 631..31
Wheeler v J.J. Saunders [1996] Ch 19 ....38, 39, 40, 118, 150
White v Chief Constable of South Yorkshire Police [1999] 1 All ER 1..........174
Whitehouse v Jordan [1981] 1 All ER 267 148
Wilsher v Essex Area Health Authority [1988] 1 All ER 871 ....144, 146
Woodar Investment Development Ltd v Wimpey Construction [1980] 1 WLR 277...47
Wringe v Cohen [1941] 1 KB 229 177

Table of Cases xvii

X (Minor) v Bedfordshire County ouncil [1995] 2 AC 633 108
Yuen Kun Yeu v Attorney-General for Hong Kong [1998] AC 175 108
Z v United Kingdom, 5 Nov 1999 108

Table of Legislation

INTERNATIONAL TREATIES AND CONVENTIONS

Convention on Civil Liability for Damage Resulting from Activities
Dangerous to the Environment 1993,
Council of Europe Convention on Civil Liability for Damage
resulting from Activities Dangerous to the Environment
(Lugano Convention) 210, 211, 214
Art 2 214
    (8) 226
    (9) 226
    (10) 215
Art 6 214
Art 8 221
    (c) 221
    (d) 221
Art 9 21
Art 10 17
Art 18 12
Art 35(1)(b) 10, 221
European Convention on Human Rights
Art 6 87
Treaty of Amsterdam 1977 ....201, 205
Treaty on European Union 1992 201
Treaty of Rome 1957 ....201, 204, 205, 235
Art 2 ....202, 205, 222
Art 3(1) 205
Art 5(2) (ex 3b(2) 233
Art 6 (ex 130r(2)) 202, 205, 233
Art 10 (ex 5) 230
Art 28 9ex 30) 230
Art 39 (ex 48) 230
Art 43 (ex 52) 230
Art 49 (ex 59) 230
Art 81 (ex 85) 230
Art 95 (ex 100a) 206, 207
    (5), ...206
    (6) 206
Art 141 (e 119) 230

xx   *Table of Legislation*

Art 174 (ex 130)..222, 233
    (2)..206
    (4)..210
Arts 174–176 (ex 130r–t)...............................205, 212, 233
Art 175 (ex 130s)...206, 207
Art 192(2) (ex 138b(2))...209
Art 226 (ex 169) 229
Art 230..206
Art 234 (ex 177) 234
Art 235 (ex 178) 231
Art 288 (ex 215(2)) 231
Art 300 (ex 228) 210
Pt I, 205

Directives

Ambient air quality assessment and management, Council Directive 96/62
    on [1996] OJ L 296/55...57
Conservation of birds, EC Directive 79/409 on [1979] OJ L 103/1.........214, 232
Conservation of natural habitats and flora and fauna Directive 92/43
    [1992] OJ L 206/7 ....214, 232
Defective Products Directive 85/374 [1985] OJ L 210/29
    Art 7
        (d) 220
        (e) 220
Drinking Water Directive 80/778/EEC [1980] OJ L 229/11 ....154, 207
Freedom of access to environmental information, EC Directive 90/313 on
    1990 OJ L 158/56 218
Groundwater Quality Directive 80/68...232
Insolvency Directive 80/987 [1980] OJ L 283/23.................................230
    Art 5 230
Integrated Pollution Prevention and Control Directive 96/61 [1996]
    OJ L 257 75
Packaging and Packaging Waste Directive 94/62/EC 86
Products Liability Directive 85/374/EEC OJ No L 210.................................89
    Art 7(e) 89
Seveso Directive 82/501/EEC [1982] OJ L 230/1...208
Shellfish Waters Directive 79/923 [1979] OJ L 281/47 234

Table of Legislation xxi

NATIONAL LEGLISLATION

Canada
Environmental Rights Act, Ontario 1994

    s 103 113

Denmark
Compensation for Environmental Damage, Act on 225/1994 235

Finland
Environmental Damage Compensation Act 737/1994 235

Germany
Environmental Liability Act 1991 235
Soil Protection Act 1983 128

Sweden
Environmental Protection Act 1969 235
Environmental Protection Act 1986 235

United Kingdom
Access to Justice Act 1999 67
Act for giving Facility in the Prosecution and Abatement of Nuisances
    Arising from Furnaces Used and in the Working of Steam Engines
    1821 18
Alkali Act 1863 ....5, 18, 141
Civil Aviation Act 1949 s 40 247
Clean Air Act 1993 ....52, 54, 55
    s 1 54
    s 4 54
    s 18 54
    s 55 54
Common Law Procedure Act 1854 ....12, 14, 15
Consumer Protection Act 1987 s 4 89
Countryside Act 1968 s 15, 258
Countryside (Scotland) Act 1967,
    s 49A, 258
Courts and Legal Services Act 1990
    s 58 94
    s 58A 67
De Sario v Industrial Excess Landfill Inc. No 89-570 (Ohio Ct C P Stark
    County, 6 Dec. 1994) 182, 196
Electricity Act 1989 s 3(3)(d) 104
Environment Act 1990, Pt III 54

xxii   *Table of Legislation*

Environment Act 1995	87, 121
s 1	55
s 2	55, 56
Environmental Protection Act 1990	52, 54, 57, 59, 60, 140, 149, 159
Pt I	54, 55, 155
Pt II	127, 155
Pt IIA	87, 120, 123, 127
Pt III	54, 103, 127
s 2(1)	5, 55
s 3(1)	55
s 4	
(2)	54, 55
(3)	54, 55
s 6	55
(1)	55
s 7	55, 56
s 13	55
s 14	55
s 23(1)	55
s 27	159
s 29	127
s 33	115
(1)	131
s 57	123
s 61	122
s 63(2)	131
s 73	
(6)	115
(6)–(9)	131
s 74	91
s 78	132
s 78A	
(2)	125
(4)	125, 127
(5)	125
(6)	125
(7)	129
(9)	123, 125, 133
ss 78A-78YC	123
s 78B	129
(1)	129
s 78C	
(8)	123
(10)	123

Table of Legislation xxiii

s 78E	129
(40)	130
s 78F,	131
(2)	131, 133
(3)	131
(4)	132
(6)	131
(7)	131
(9)	131
(10)	131
s 78H(5)	
(b)	131
(c)	131
(d)	130
s 78M	123
s 78N	123
s 78P(2)(b)	130
s 78P	123
s 78YA	125
s 78YB(2)	127
s 78YC	127
s 79	54, 57, 110, 121
(1)(b)–(d)	54, 57
(3)	57
ss 79-82	123
s 80(1)	54
s 82	67
s 85(1)	127
s 121(1)	159
s 143	121, 122, 123, 129, 130, 134, 259
s 161	127
Finance Act 1996	86, 140
Gulf Oil Refining Act 1965	110
Health and Safety at Work Act 1974	109
Housing, Town Planning etc. Act 1909	
Sch. 4, para. 13	257
Judicature Act 1873 s 24(6)	14
Judicature Acts 1873-5	12
Juries Act 1825	9
Law Reform (Contributory Negligence) Act 1945	253
Local Government Act 1972 s 222	102, 113
Merchant Shipping Act 1974	99
Merchant Shipping Act 1995	99
Merchant Shipping (Oil Pollution) Act 1971	99

xxiv   *Table of Legislation*

National Parks and Access to the Countryside Act 1949 s 16 257
Noise Act 1996 52
Nuclear Installations Act 1965..197, 198
  s 7 ....182, 183
    (1)(a) 186
  s 12 182
Occupiers' Liability Act 1957 176
Occupiers' Liability Act 1984 176
  s 1(3) 176
Pollution Prevention Control Act 1999 ....54, 75
Prescription and Limitation (Scotland) Act 1973
  s 6 253
  s 7 247
  s 8 247
  s 17(3) 254
  s 18(3) 254
  s 22B 254
  s 22C 254
Protection of Harassment Act 1997 88
Public Health Act 1848 ....19, 141
Public Health Act 1875..18
Public Health Act 1936..57
Single European Act 1986...201, 202, 205
Smoke Nuisance Abatement (Metropolis) Act 1853 141
Supreme Court Act 1981
  s 31(3) 58, 59, 222
    (6) 58
Town and Country Planning (Scotland) Act 1997
  s 75 257
    (3) 258
Town Improvement Clauses Act 1847 19
Trinity Rules 1853 14
Water Resources Act 1991................................52, 126, 140, 154, 155, 159
Pt III, Chap II...110
  s 85(1)–(5) 132
  s 161..126
    (3)..159

Statutory Instruments and Rules of the Court

Civil Procedure Rules 1998..112
  Pt 31...105
  Pt 35...105
  r 4 105

r 6–7 105
r 8 105
Environment Protection (Prescribed Processes and Substances) Regulations
    SI 1991 No 472 55
Landfill Tax Regulations SI 1996/1527 86
Producer Responsibility (Packaging Waste) Regulations SI 1997/648 86
Town and Country Planning Appeals (Determination by Inspectors)
    (Inquiries Procedure) Rules SI 1992/2039 148

United States

Equal Access to Justice Act 1980 224
Rules of the Supreme Court, Ord. 53
    r. 4(1) 58
    r. 3(7) 222

1

Victorian Foundations?

RAYMOND COCKS*

INTRODUCTION

IT WILL BE argued here that the modern relationship between the common law and environmental issues is built upon Victorian foundations.[1] Of course, the Victorian judges were not the first common lawyers to decide environmental cases. There are well-known medieval precedents and, in this important sense, there is a continuous and ancient history to the common law's concern for the environment. Equally, there are examples of medieval statutes regulating the environment. What the Victorians did was to determine how these ancient bodies of common law and statute law would be related to each other in a world which was changing rapidly through the creation of industrial hazards and the spread of pollution.

With the benefit of hindsight, the basic elements of the relationship are clear. Subject to important exceptions, the common law has had a comparatively minor role. In most cases, environmental disputes have come to be settled by reference to statutes. As a result, no leading textbook on environmental law has ever given the common law pride of place in its analysis. This part of the common law has no readily identifiable judicial champion. There is no equivalent, say, of Lord Atkin's achievement with the tort of negligence or the work of Scrutton LJ upon commercial law. Yet there was nothing inevitable about this. A moment's reflection on the social importance of environmental disputes suggests that the comparatively minor role for the common law was an unlikely outcome. The common law relating to the environment could have developed

---

* I am grateful to Tony Dugdale for his comments on a first draft of this chapter, and to Rod Edmunds for his comments on successive drafts.

[1] Use of the word "environmental" in this context is anachronistic since, as is well known, the Victorians used other words such as "public health" to refer to this area of law. For the purposes of the argument in this chapter nobody will be misled through an interchangeable use of the terms. But, more generally, it would be valuable to have a study of the uses of such words at different times. Even for the Victorians the words "public health" could mean different things from one decade to another: the words often brought to mind a vision of local government, and this could be confusing because the role of local government was often in a state of rapid change in the 19th century. There has never been a wholly stable use of words such as "public health" and "environment". Modern texts are aware of the problem: see e.g. S. Bell, *Ball and Bell on Environmental Law, the Law and Policy Relating to the Protection of the Environment* (4th edn., London, Blackstone Press, 1997), 8–11.

2   Raymond Cocks

very extensively indeed in response to the problems of pollution. But it did not do so, and an explanation is required.

Legal historians have already gone some way to accounting for this. In part it happened because the development of the common law was restricted by very practical considerations. In a detailed and pioneering study McLaren has shown that the poor often suffered most from pollution, and yet they were the people who could least afford to engage in litigation relating to pollution. Sometimes they could use local courts, but usually poor people had a simple choice: tolerate environmental problems or try to move elsewhere.[2]

However, in large part the restriction was intellectual. This was suggested over a quarter of a century ago by J.F. Brenner.[3] More recently, in a long and sophisticated analysis of changes in water law, Getzler has reminded us that "historians investigating the relationship between legal and economic change neglect the internal history of the law at their peril".[4] In his analysis he argues that:

> principles of land and water use were developed to a high level of sophistication in centuries of legal evolution before 1800. Then, in the circumstances of industrialising England, those doctrines were adapted as judges sought legal solutions to unprecedented economic problems. The confrontation of new economic and social practices with ancient laws revealed the limits of the common law as a means of governance; and this ultimately led to a shift in law-making from the courts to Parliament. Water and land-use law was one field, however, where the articulate contribution of the common lawyers always remained significant. In the court-rooms of Westminster can be found vibrant discussion of the fundamental principles of property and of civil liability, which not only had immense practical significance, but which revealed much of the common lawyers' attitudes to economic progress and its concomitant legal problems.[5]

In Getzler's view, the shift of attention from the courts to Parliament was of central significance, but both the shift and the remaining role of the common law could only be fully understood by reference to changes in the ideas of com-

---

[2] J.P.S. McLaren, "Nuisance Law and the Industrial Revolution—Some Lessons from Social History" (1983) 3 *OJLS* 155. For a study placing the changes in the context of other major themes see W.R. Cornish and G. de N. Clark, *Law and Society in England, 1750–1950* (London, Sweet and Maxwell, 1989), ch. 2, particularly at "Public Health and Amenity: The Common Law", 154–8. For the history of nuisance law as a whole see J.H. Baker, *An Introduction to English Legal History* (3rd edn., London, Butterworths, 1990), ch. 23. For an article which considers important Victorian public health issues (but without exploring the details of the common law) see B. Pontin, "Tort Law and Victorian Government Growth: The Historical Significance of Tort in the Shadow of Chemical Pollution and Factory Safety Regulation" (1998) 18 *OJLS* 661.

[3] J.F. Brenner, "Nuisance Law and the Industrial Revolution" (1974) 3 *Journal of Legal Studies* 403. Amongst other themes, Brenner emphasises the importance of a tradition of judicial restraint. His approach may be contrasted with that of the present chapter, with its emphasis on the attempt by the judges to respond to a contemporary crisis.

[4] J.P. Getzler, "Rules Writ in Water: A History of Riparian Rights and Property Use Doctrine in England to 1870", a thesis submitted in partial fulfillment of the degree of D.Phil. within the University of Oxford, 31 Aug. 1993, 346.

[5] *Ibid.*, Preface.

Victorian Foundations? 3

mon lawyers. In particular, Getzler points out that, in the course of the nineteenth century, English riparian law came to have a broad discretionary character. For example, in the 1875 *Swindon* case, Lord Cairns's judgment turned upon:

> an opaque test of "reasonableness", to be determined in the circumstances of the particular case. He did not provide indicia structuring that concept of reasonableness ... the reasonableness standard was left to be determined on the individual facts of each case.[6]

Later courts took Lord Cairns's uninformative doctrine to have settled or even codified the modern law. In his conclusion, Getzler goes on to argue that:

> The final simplification of the law comes when the courts emphasise objectivity of rights of user per se—exemplified by tests such as "reasonableness" of user, "reasonableness" in ascription of prescriptive rights—and reduce actual or presumed intentions to a subsidiary role. This allows adjudication to proceed in a more peremptory or summary mode, directly enforcing broad discretionary policy standards; and in tandem, discouraging parties from litigating chiefly on the basis of instance-specific, detailed factual pleading. Thus a tentative interpretation of nineteenth-century riparian law may be offered which does follow an explanatory thread of social engineering and efficiency maximisation—but efficiency in the operation of the legal system, not the productive economy at large. Ultimately problems of allocating water resources in the modern economy were resolved by the private bill procedure, and later by public planning legislation—in the forum of Parliament rather than the courts, where arguments of utility and communal benefit could replace the search for common-law entitlement.[7]

But note that this analysis applies only to water law. Getzler points out that in other areas of the common law the response to the problems of the industrial age was different. "In other areas of land-use law the appellate judges left more reasoned and articulate bodies of doctrine to guide the courts; water law, by contrast, was left in a state inviting a relatively intuitive style of decision".[8]

Water rights were obviously of great importance, and Getzler's analysis serves as a caution against generalisations about the whole relationship between the common law and statute law. But, to stress the point, his study has the additional merit of throwing into relief the fact that the greater part of the common law relating to land-use was more reasoned and developed than the decisions on riparian rights. As a result, this remaining and larger part of the common law was likely to have a different relationship with statute law. A full analysis of the wider response would require a long book, but it is noticeable that two particular cases figure in all discussions of the Victorian common law relating to the environment and it is reasonable to believe that they have much to tell us. In the

---

[6] *Swindon Waterworks Co.* v. *Wilts and Berks Canal Co.* [1875] LR 7 HL 697; discussed by Getzler. *supra* n.4, at 336 (and see 347).

[7] *Ibid.*, 348–9.

[8] *Ibid.*, 336–7.

4 Raymond Cocks

remainder of this chapter, these two cases, and the legal world of which they were a part, will be considered with a view to revealing the salient elements in the development of a distinctively modern relationship between statute law and case law in environmental matters.

TIPPING V. ST HELEN'S SMELTING CO.

In considering a case such as *Tipping* v. *St Helen's Smelting Co* a modern starting point may be misleading. Today's analysis of the common law often starts with a systematic exploration of legal doctrine. But to do this is to celebrate the victory of a particular way of thinking about common law problems rather than to explore the realities of legal history. From the late 1880s onwards this modern type of approach could be of central concern to a common lawyer making use of books by, for instance, Holmes, but it was of more peripheral interest to a judge of the 1860s.[9] The doctrinal disputes of the last hundred years, with their emphasis upon the uniform development of general principles, are not a safe guide to the pre-existing common law. It will be suggested that something important happened to the common law's approach to environmental issues in the mid-Victorian years and that it cannot be discovered by reference to the textbooks written after about 1880.

If we do not start with the modern concern for systematic doctrinal exposition where do we start? The alternative is to seek an understanding of what a mid-Victorian judge had in mind when he was confronted by litigants arguing about liability for alleged pollution. In other words, we may start with his view of the case "in hand". In his study, *The Common Law and English Jurisprudence*, Michael Lobban points out that the common law had difficulty in developing a coherent response to the full range of industrial pollution partly because of the importance of the facts of each particular case:

> Much nineteenth-century tort law was haphazard because judges were looking so closely at the precise allegations and precise justifications that it was hard to find a clear principle running through the cases. This can be seen, for instance, in the area of nuisance, where many of the contradictory cases reflected less a neglect by the judges of industrial pollution than the fact that the cases presented to them differed greatly.[10]

It follows that the truth is in the details of each case and it is necessary to consider examples: it is necessary to consider whether the common law in this area was to be found in precise allegations and precise justifications rather than in the creation of principles or other findings of general application. This is more dif-

---

[9] O.W. Holmes, *The Common Law* (Boston, Mass., Little Brown and Co., 1881). On the creation of textbooks, see D. Sugarman, "Legal Theory, the Common Law Mind and the Making of the Text-Book Tradition" in W. Twining (ed.), *Legal Theory and the Common Law* (Oxford, Blackwell, 1986). See, too, A.W.B. Simpson, "The Rise and Fall of the Legal Treatise: Legal Principles and the Forms of Legal Literature" (1981) 48 *University of Chicago Law Review* 632.

[10] (Oxford, Oxford University Press, 1991) 285: see also Lobban's n.114 at 285.

Victorian Foundations? 5

ficult than it may seem. For example, in one case about the preservation of the Ashdown Forest in Sussex we have a full transcript of what was said during the trial. This reveals a large gap between what was said in the course of the hearing and what eventually appeared in the law reports. Most notably, the transcript frequently reveals the extent to which environmental issues could be discussed in emotional terms in court proceedings despite the fact that there was no jury in the case in question.[11] It follows that the law reports may not give us a full picture of what was regarded as persuasive.

It is therefore fortunate that, in regard to *Tipping's Case*, Professor Simpson has recently provided an extensive historical analysis.[12] The paragraphs below are heavily indebted to his stimulating studies and the extensive accounts given in various law reports and elsewhere. The present chapter goes on to draw a radically different conclusion from that of Professor Simpson, by putting the ideas of the judges he mentions in a wider professional context, but the chapter could not have been written without reference to his valuable work.

Tipping v. *St Helen's Smelting Co.* is a major authority on the law of nuisance.[13] In the 1860s the Lancashire town of St Helens was well-known for its alkali works and copper smelting plants. About half-a-dozen smelters emitted approximately 6,000 tons of sulphuric acid annually. In July 1863 an important environmental measure, the Alkali Act, received royal assent.[14] As its title suggests, it did not relate to copper smelting and the associated creation of acids. The explanation was simple: the Select Committee on Noxious Vapours advised against regulation in this industry because "[n]o means have yet been devised of neutralising" the pollution produced by the manufacturers in question.[15] Parliament had decided that for the moment it was not much interested in sulphuric acid and litigants were left to rely exclusively on the common law.

---

[11] R. Cocks, "The Great Ashdown Forest Case" in T.G. Watkins (ed.), *The Legal Record and Historical Reality* (London, The Hambledon Press, 1989) 175.

[12] A.W.B. Simpson, *Leading Cases in the Common Law* (Oxford, Clarendon Press, 1995), ch. 7, "Victorian Judges and the Problem of Social Cost: *Tipping* v. *St Helen's Smelting Company* (1865)", 163.

[13] 4 B and S 608, 616, 122 ER 588, 591, XI HLC 642, 11 ER 1483; and see 1 Ch. App. Cas. 66.

[14] "An Act for the More Effectual Condensation of Muriatic Acid Gas in Alkali Works" (26 and 27 Vict. c. 124), and see R.M. Macleod, "The Alkali Acts Administration 1863–1884: the Emergence of the Civil Scientist" (1965) 9 *Victorian Studies* 85. At 86 Macleod argues "that the Alkali Acts administration provides a particularly suggestive and hitherto neglected frame of reference. For here was the first administratively successful and systematically applied scientific governmental policy directed towards the positive regulation of the nation's chemical industry. Here was the first instance in Victorian contractualist society of the expenditure of public funds for the scientific protection of private property; and here was one of the earliest examples of central administrative scientific control, designed from its inception to suppress an acknowledged public hazard. Finally, we see here one of the first occasions in which an expert scientific adviser, utilizing the skills of a new scientific profession, is made a Civil Servant accountable not only to Government but also to manufacturing industry and public opinion." See also discussion in Simpson, *supra* n.12, at 178.

[15] "Select Committee of the House of Lords on Noxious Vapours of 1862", British Parliamentary Papers 1862 (486) XIV 1, to be found in Irish University Press reprint in "Health: General Public Health, 1854–1862", 6–8; and see discussion in Simpson, *supra* n.12, at 183–5.

6 Raymond Cocks

In the 1860s William Tipping was the owner of land near St Helens which, in his belief, was being harmed by one particular smelting plant. In 1861 he had instructed his solicitors to write to the proprietors threatening litigation. Production was reduced, and, for a while, little harm was done to his land. In the spring of 1863 production was greatly increased and Tipping threatened litigation again. There was no response, and, on 25 May 1863, he commenced an action for damages for nuisance against the company.[16] A cynic might be forgiven for wondering if the manufacturer had increased production after it had become clear that this type of plant would not be subject to statutory regulation. It seems likely that this was so. We will see that in respect of environmental issues the use and development of the Victorian common law often can only be accounted for by reference to debates about statutes.

A final attempt at conciliation failed and, on 19 June, Tipping instructed counsel to pursue an action in which there would be a claim of £5,000 for damage caused to his property by "[n]oxious gases, vapours and other noxious matter". His declaration specified damage to trees, crops and cattle. He complained of illness to himself and his servants, and stated that the mansion and property had been "rendered less comfortable and wholesome and fit for habitation", and that "the plaintiff has been prevented from having the beneficial and healthy use of the land and premises he would otherwise have had". On top of this, he claimed that his reversionary interest in leased farms had permanently depreciated in value.

The evidence was contested on numerous points, but it became clear that damage had occurred. The substance of the dispute related to the severity of the effects and to causation. Some of the evidence (such as sick cattle and people vomiting) was likely to influence public opinion. In respect of causation the defendant argued that much of the damage had occurred before Tipping bought the property and that, in "coming to the nuisance" Tipping had deprived himself of the right to sue. Further, it was suggested that Tipping's problems had been caused by other smelting works which may not have been as near to Tipping's property but which were, allegedly, responsible.

Some of the most talented common lawyers of the day acted for the parties. They included barristers with national reputations such as William Brett QC and George Mellish QC.[17] There was a jury in the case and, in the course of hearing the contested evidence, there was argument over how they should be directed. One view was of central significance for the law of nuisance. The judgment of Sir John Byles in *Hole* v. *Barlow* (1858) could be taken to support the proposition that where a jury found that a factory was appropriately located

---

[16] *Ibid.*, at 184.

[17] Brett, William Balliol (Viscount Esher), 1815–99, Barrister, Lincoln's Inn 1846, QC 1860, MP 1866–8, Solicitor-General 1868; various judicial appointments including Master of the Rolls, 1883–97. As a practitioner he appeared frequently in the North-West: see entry in A.W.B. Simpson, *Biographical Dictionary of the Common Law* (London, Butterworths, 1984). For George Mellish QC see the entry in *Dictionary of National Biography* (Oxford, Oxford University Press, 1950 etc.): Mellish, Sir George, 1814–77, Barrister Inner Temple, 1848, QC 1861, Lord Justice of Appeal, 1870.

Victorian Foundations? 7

and operated to the normal standards for such a factory, "it did not matter how much damage or inconvenience it caused to adjacent landowners".[18] This was rejected in *Bamford* v. *Turley* (1863) in the Court of Exchequer and (by a majority) in Exchequer Chamber.[19] Plainly, this latter approach threatened the interests of industry and further litigation was likely in the near future. In *Tipping* the judge, Mellor J, a Lancashire man from a commercial family, eventually gave an interesting direction which, in substance, rejected *Hole* v. *Barlow*.[20] It was an actionable injury for a man to send: "over his neighbour's land that which is noxious and hurtful to an extent which sensibly diminishes the comfort and value of the property, and the comfort of existence on the property". This statement of principle was then somewhat obscured by reference to the need for the jury to consider "the place, the circumstances, and the whole nature of the thing". Also, the jury should remember that "the law does not regard trifling and small inconveniences".[21]

All of these words were to produce echoes in subsequent debate, and, perhaps, the distinction which is most easily missed on first reading is the reference to the comfort and value of the property *and* the reference to comfort and existence on the property.

The potential for an appeal was obvious and, before the verdict, the defendants sought to clarify the facts of the case and asked the judge to put three questions to the jury. But at this stage the questions could only be put with the consent of the plaintiff and this was refused. Later, in their verdict, the jury awarded £361 18s 41/2d by way of damages. Mellor J then asked the foreman three questions. "Was the enjoyment of the Plaintiff's property sensibly diminished?" The reply was: "[w]e think so". The foreman was then asked: "[d]o you consider the business there carried on to be an ordinary business for smelting copper?" To this the reply was: "[w]e consider it an ordinary business, and conducted in a proper manner, in as good a manner as possible". Lastly, he was asked: "and do you consider, supposing that makes any difference, that it was carried on in a proper place?" To this the reply was: "[w]ell, no, we do not".[22]

To say the least of it, the final response was inconvenient because it made it difficult for the defendants to raise the issue of "locality" on appeal. It had been treated as an issue of fact rather than law and the jury had found against them. The problem could only be circumvented for the purposes of an appeal by retrospectively limiting the role of the jury and turning what had been a question

---

[18] 4 CB (NS) 334, 140 ER 1113.

[19] 3 B and S 62, 66, 122 ER 25.

[20] Mellor J, 1809–87, born in Oldham, the son of a merchant and magistrate. Educated at the town's grammar school and by private tutor, he attended John Austin's lectures at University College and was called to the Bar (Inner Temple) in 1833. QC in 1851 and Liberal Member of Parliament 1857–9. Appointed to the Queen's Bench 1861. See Simpson, *supra* n.17, contribution by A.H. Manchester.

[21] The quotations in the three sentences preceding this note can all be found at Law J. Rep. (N S), 35 (1866) 68.

[22] The questions are recorded at *St Helen's Smelting Co.* v. *Tipping* [1865] XI HLC 644. The questions are considered in Simpson, *supra* n.12, 187–8.

8   *Raymond Cocks*

of fact into a question of law. Hence it was asserted that the suitability of the locality was a matter of law on which the jury should have been directed by the judge. It was as if there was an audible crunching of gears; the jury was, surely, reflecting what many would take to be common sense, but it was making it difficult to evolve a systematic body of law. Only after circumventing this problem could the chief issue be stated. The point taken by the defendants was: "[t]hat sensible discomfort from the carrying on of a necessary trade, in a reasonable manner and in a suitable locality, is not an actionable injury".[23]

The arguments which followed were intricate, but much of the defendant's case remained concentrated upon this assertion. As against this, on Tipping's behalf it was claimed, for instance, "that no person has a right, to the damage of his neighbour, to carry on in an improper place, or at all, any noxious trade, however conducted that trade may be". The case went from the Court of Queen's Bench to the Exchequer Chamber and then to the House of Lords. Here, as every law student knows, the direction was upheld: in effect, a properly conducted business in an appropriate location was not, as a matter of law, immune from liability in nuisance.[24]

Unfortunately, as any law student also knows, the judgments were not given in terms which were as clear as this might suggest. It is sometimes thought that Lord Westbury, the Lord Chancellor of the day, set out to create two distinct torts of nuisance. It is arguable that he discussed both "material injury to the property" and the causing of "sensible personal discomfort" in such a way as to create liability for nuisance even where a plaintiff had no proprietary interest. This observation of Westbury created the potential to argue that the tort of nuisance was severing its ancient links with interests in land. Arguably, in respect of personal suffering, a plaintiff need have no interest in land at all and a new tort of broad application had come into existence. More generally, the significance of Mellor J's qualifications to his statement of principle at the first hearing had not been adequately explored.

For present purposes it seems that the difficulty produced by ambiguities in the judgment of Lord Westbury LC (to be found in mitigated form in the decisions of Lord Cranworth and Wensleydale) may relate back to the role of the jury. In making a decision such as this, one of the audiences which a judge in the House of Lords had to have in mind at this time was that of his more junior colleagues on the Bench who had to address juries in a practical and convincing manner at the assizes. If juries could be addressed in a satisfactory manner it was highly likely that lawyers would also be able to use the judgment in an effective way when seeking to give clear advice to clients. The jury should be spoken to in terms which seemed sensible and in accordance with the expectations of everyday life, particularly the expectations of the property owners who constituted juries. True, to suggest this is to start to open up numerous other issues. It

[23] *Ibid.*, at 188.
[24] *St Helen's Smelting Co.* v. *Tipping* [1865] XI HLC 644.

requires us to acquire a full understanding of what was of concern to the judges of the day. Such an enquiry can be taken a step further by considering another case.

RYLANDS V. FLETCHER

An equally famous case of the same decade is *Rylands* v. *Fletcher*. Again we may make use of a recent analysis by Professor Simpson and accounts in a variety of law reports.[25] In 1839 the firm of John Rylands and Son purchased a mill in Lancashire. It was a small part of the industrial empire of John E. Rylands who was then in the process of becoming the biggest employer of labour in the country. (Today, scholars remain indebted to his third wife and widow for using some of his wealth to set up the John Rylands Library in Manchester.) By the late 1850s the mill in question required an increased water supply, and, with a view to providing this, a reservoir was constructed. In the course of the construction five old blocked vertical shafts were found. After completion of the reservoir, and when it was about half full, one of these shafts burst. The water filled various mine-workings, including those of Thomas Fletcher a tenant from year to year of certain mining rights in the area. He had to stop work and start pumping. The reservoir was repaired and refilled. But a second burst took place in August 1861. Now, on the advice of the inspector of mines for the area, Fletcher's mine had to be abandoned.

One can presume on Fletcher's anger, and, on 4 November 1861, he commenced an action seeking £5,000 by way of damages. The action "was framed wholly as an action for negligence" and was tried at Liverpool Assizes before Mellor J and a special jury on 3 September 1862.[26] (Special juries could be of different types. Probably this was constituted under the Juries Act 1825 and thereby contained people of the rank of "banker, merchant or esquire"; before 1870 there was no property requirement for special jurors beyond that required by other jurors[27]). "At the judge's suggestion a verdict was entered with consent in favour of the Plaintiff for £5000 and £2 costs, subject to a reference to a barrister arbitrator, James Kemplay. The function of the fictitious verdict was to give the arbitrator's award the status of a court judgment".[28]

What then happened is difficult to reconstruct. It seems that on 31 December 1864 Channell B ordered that the arbitrator should have the power to state a special case for the opinion of the Exchequer of Pleas and that the parties should be allowed to bring error on the judgment of the court. Simpson's reasonable

---

[25] (1865) 11 Jur. NS 714, 34 Ex. 177, 3 H and C 774, 159 ER 737; (1866) 12 Jur. NS 603, LR 1 Ex. 265; 35 LJ Ex. 154; (1868) LR HL 330. Simpson, *supra* n.12, chapter 8, "Bursting Reservoirs and Victorian Tort Law: Rylands and Horrocks v. Fletcher, (1868)" 195.

[26] *Ibid.,* 212.

[27] W.R. Cornish, *The Jury* (Harmondsworth, Penguin, 1971) 32.

[28] A.W.B. Simpson, *supra* n.12, at 212.

10 Raymond Cocks

explanation for this curious change is that the legal problems arising out of a disaster with a reservoir in the Sheffield area in March 1864 had suggested to the lawyers involved in *Fletcher's Case* that it had the potential to make law and provide useful guidance for the resolution of other disputes.[29] On 4 January 1865 Kemplay stated a special case and made it clear that the defendants had not been negligent. Rather, it was their contractors who had been negligent. From start to finish the identity of the latter remains unmentioned in the litigation; they may have gone bankrupt. In any event the claim had now metamorphosed into one based upon strict liability.[30]

As in *Tipping*, legislation has to be kept in mind if the common law's environmental role is to be understood. Large reservoirs were usually built after their creation had been authorised by private Act of Parliament. These Acts might or might not seek to restrict liability for damage caused by flooding, and, after some scandalous cases of neglect and consequential loss of life, there was understandable public concern about the anomalous way in which damages were awarded in some cases and not others. All this would have been well-known to the judges and the lawyers in the case. For example, Henry Manisty QC for the plaintiff and George Mellish QC for the defendants had been involved in recent "reservoir" litigation and private bill preparation.[31] In this context the attraction of *Fletcher's Case* for the legal mind is readily understood. There was no directly relevant legislation, private or public, and all the events took place on private land. It provided an unusual opportunity to clarify the common law at a time when reformers seeking public legislative reforms applicable to the country as a whole, or private Acts for specific schemes, urgently needed to know how sections should be drafted with a view to defining, enlarging or reducing common law liabilities. They needed to know what the common law was if they were to produce effective statutes.

Fletcher lost in the Court of Exchequer, but had the encouragement of a dissenting judgment from Bramwell B. In Exchequer Chamber Fletcher won. In the sole (and long) judgment, Sir Colin Blackburn was supported by Willes, Keating, Mellor (the trial judge), Montague Smith and Lush JJ. After the appeal, George Mellish QC ceased to be involved in the case and was replaced by another barrister, also with experience of reservoir law, Sir Roundell Palmer.[32] The case went to the House of Lords and was decided, according to the law report, by only two judges, Lords Cairns and Cranworth. The speech of Lord Cairns referred to "non-natural" use of property and thereby gave rise to con-

---

[29] *Ibid.*

[30] *Ibid.*

[31] Sir Henry Manisty, 1808–90, solicitor 1830, barrister Gray's Inn 1845, QC 1857, judge 1876: *Dictionary of National Biography supra* n.17; for George Mellish, QC see *supra* n.16.

[32] Palmer, Roundell (Lord Selborne), 1812–95, called to the Bar by Lincoln's Inn 1837, QC 1849, Conservative MP 1847–52, 1853–8; later Liberal MP and Solicitor-General, 1861–3 and Attorney-General 1863–6, Lord Chancellor 1872–4, 1880–5. Now remembered chiefly for his role in the judicature reforms of the 1870s. See his *Memorials Personal and Political, 1865–1895*, 4 Vols., (London, Macmillan, 1896).

Victorian Foundations? 11

siderable subsequent debate. But, in other respects, the tenor of the brief judgments was such as to suggest that it was plain that Blackburn's decision was right. Fletcher had won.

THE SIGNIFICANCE OF THE JUDGMENTS

Within a few decades the decision in *Rylands* v. *Fletcher* was to cause problems for writers such as Holmes in their attempts to expound and explain the law. How could this form of strict liability be reconciled with other elements in the law of torts?[33] By the start of the twentieth century criticism was well-established. In the case of *Tipping* v. *St Helen's Smelting*, too, the decision was seen as being both of major importance and inherently unsatisfactory. Views on the judgments have been expressed in strong terms; for example, Professor Simpson thinks the brief judgments in the St Helens case were "sloppy" and it is possible to buttress his view by pointing to matters he does not mention, such as the extraordinary political pressures to which Westbury was subject on the day he gave his judgment. (At that precise time his political problems had become unendurable and resignation had become inevitable.)[34] Many comments on the judgments in *Rylands* v. *Fletcher* have been even less charitable. All the judgments have been subject to sustained criticism.

But what if the judges were not being "sloppy"? What if the judges knew what they were doing? It is possible to imagine one judge delivering an inadequate judgment but, to put it no higher, it seems statistically improbable that all the judges would do so on two occasions. Bluntly put, we must assume either that the judges in *Tipping* and *Fletcher* were not thinking hard, or else that they were thinking about different matters from those which came to concern late-Victorian and twentieth-century commentators. To resolve the issue we need to look to the most pressing concerns confronting the judges of the day. This will include considering the two matters which have already become apparent; the importance of juries and contemporary legislation.

---

[33] Which is not to suggest that they were totally unable to do so: see Holmes, *supra* n.9, particularly at 145–63.

[34] "The waters were further muddied by the three sloppy opinions delivered by the Law Lords": Simpson, *supra* n.12, at 189. Westbury's crisis is considered in T.A. Nash, *Life of Lord Chancellor Westbury* (London and Edinburgh, R. Bentley and Sons, 1888), at, e.g., 138–42. Westbury delivered his judgment on 5 July 1865. On 6 July he made a strong resignation speech in the House of Lords in which he surveyed his numerous achievements in office and made the candid statement that: "My Lords, I believe that the holder of the Great Seal ought never to be in the position of an accused person; and such unfortunately being the case, for my own part, I felt it due to the great office that I held that I should retire from it, and meet any accusation in the character of a private person": *ibid.,* at 140. For some time Westbury had been under pressure to leave because of his conduct as Lord Chancellor in connection with a resignation and an appointment: in the words of Holdsworth, "he had shown considerable negligence in the performance of his duties"; see Sir William Holdsworth, *A History of English Law* (A.L. Goodhart and H.G. Hanbury (eds.), London, Methuen, 1973), at 79–80. 5 July 1865 was, perhaps, the worst day in Westbury's professional life.

12   Raymond Cocks

When mid-Victorian concerns have been explored it will be possible to see what was happening to the law as judges used it in their attempts to resolve environmental disputes. To put it bluntly, today's environmental lawyers often tunnel back through time looking for major cases and, as they do so, may forget that the cases in question can be understood only by looking at the nature of legal practice when such cases were decided. After all, the judges of the day did not know how their legal subject would look in the years to come. Many outcomes were possible. There was no pre-determined long-term objective for the common law relating to the environment, least of all in its relationship with statute law.

AN UNSETTLING TIME FOR JUDGES: 1840–80

Until 1854 all actions in the common law courts were tried by jury. After that date legislation allowed for trial by judge alone in civil cases where both the parties to the litigation and the court gave their consent.[35] In the mid-1850s there were doubts whether the parties would in fact take advantage of this right and there was uncertainty as to how judges would take on their new role if the parties so selected. Under the legislation which made trial by judge a possibility "the 'verdict' of the judge was to have the same effect as the verdict of a jury; and the rules made under it show that the verdict was to be drawn up and entered in the same way".[36] This gave judges a dual role which could cause difficulty. How were questions of law and evidence to be raised if judges began to find general verdicts without going through the elaborate and odd process of directing themselves? A periodical expressed concern about the matter:

> We have reason to believe that the suitors will be better satisfied, if a judge, when deciding questions of fact, will state the grounds of his decision, than if he pronounces a bare "judgment for the Plaintiff" or "judgment for the Defendant", like the verdict of a jury for the plaintiff or for the defendant.[37]

Predictably, the same periodical went on to express doubts whether the parties to litigation would in fact choose trial by judge alone. The common law was having to respond to a major procedural challenge, and the extent of the challenge was contingent upon an unpredictable change in the behaviour of litigants and trial judges. In short, trial without a jury was now a possibility, and the notion that this was possible could have disturbing consequences.

With the benefit of hindsight we know, of course, that this reform began the gradual decline in the use of juries for common law actions. But when the cases considered above were being decided this was far from apparent. As Jackson has shown, in the years before the Judicature Acts of the 1870s it is "clear that

---

[35] The Common Law Procedure Act 1854 (17 and 18 Vict. c 125): and see Baker, *supra* n.2, 109.
[36] *Ibid.*
[37] *Law Magazine or Quarterly Review of Jurisprudence* (1855) Vol. 22 NS, Vol. 53 OS, 16–17.

at common law trial was by jury in well over ninety per cent of the cases tried".[38] At the same time, lawyers knew that this might change, and rapidly so. It is not too much to say that in the 1860s there was uncertainty about the role of the judge at first instance and this challenged the way lawyers thought about their work. The transition and eventual result has been described by Baker. Today:

> the English trial judge delivers a discursive "judgment" in which findings of fact are intermingled with comment. What is now called the "judgment" combines in one piece the trial judge's notes on the evidence, a "direction" in law, a special verdict, and the court's decision, often adding for good measure the arguments of counsel as well. In a sense the trial judge is still stating a case, for potential use on appeal, but he is now doing more than was permissible under common law procedure. The substitution of one man for twelve, and the surreptitious disappearance of the formulaic concept of a verdict, have left the judge free to publish his ruminations on the evidence in a way which the common law in its wisdom forbade to juries. The effects of this change have gone far beyond procedure. . . . Now that fact and law are no longer decided separately, it is never certain to what extent judgments turn on the facts and to what extent the judge's comments on particular facts are intended to create legal distinctions.[39]

It was a significant change, and one which had to be kept in mind by a judge in the House of Lords in the 1860s when the issues were still unclear and the historical outcome uncertain. It is not too much to say that these judges had to have in mind two contrasting forms of civil litigation, one with juries and one without. In such a context it was, surely, both sensible and expedient to deliver brief judgments in cases of general public importance, particularly where a jury had been given a complicated role in responding to questions, as happened in *Tipping*. This was all the more attractive as an approach if a judge at a lower appellate level had already explored the history of the subject in some depth, as happened with Blackburn J's judgment in *Rylands* v. *Fletcher*. Such a dual approach enabled the courts to address two audiences. The judges in the House of Lords could respond to the needs of judges at assize and the more traditional practitioners. In contrast, Blackburn J in the court below could take on the fuller role of the judge brought in by the conflation of what had been distinct roles for judges and juries. Of course it is not being suggested that the judges in some sense conspired to deliver short speeches in the Lords on this occasion; it was simply a sensible response for each judge to adopt to a legal problem.

The judges had further difficulties at this time which were likely to encourage such an approach. For decades there had been unsettling debates about pleading at common law. There had been a famous attempt at the reform of the old rules in the New Pleading Rules of Hilary Term, 1834. The general issue with all its ambiguities was abolished and a form of special pleading had come to the fore. Unfortunately, this produced a strange revival of ancient pleas abstracted from their historical context. To the public it seemed that lawyers had become

[38] R.M. Jackson, "The Incidence of Jury Trial During the Last Century" (1937) 1 *MLR* 132.
[39] Baker, *supra* n.2, 110.

more interested in an almost incomprehensible game than in confronting the substance of a case.[40] Intense concern produced the Common Law Procedure Act 1852 and the Trinity Rules of 1853.[41] The use of fictions and formalities was greatly reduced, and, by consent, it became possible to avoid pleadings altogether. The latter idea haunted mid-Victorian thought about procedure, but eventually there was a compromise in the provisions of the Judicature Acts with the use of a statement of claim and defence in the context of rules which, after 1883, allowed points of law to be pleaded as well as assertions of fact. It followed that a judge of the 1860s had to guide a civil trial, with or without a jury, in such a way as to do all that was possible to relate to the substance of the case a much-criticised tradition of pleading which was not expected to last for very long. Again, brevity of judgment was surely an expedient response when there were uncertainties at the heart of common law procedure.

Another of the foundations of litigation was uncertain at this time. Precisely what section 24 of the Judicature Act 1873 did to the relationship between law and equity is still being debated. The side note stated simply: "law and equity to be concurrently administered". But, to the present writer, the section was expressed in a manner which made it at least look as if in future common law would apply by default. Subsection (6) stated that:

> subject to the aforesaid provisions for giving effect to equitable rights and other matters of equity in manner aforesaid, and to the other express provisions of this Act, the said Courts respectively, and every judge thereof, shall recognise and give effect to all legal claims and demands, and all estates, titles, rights, duties, obligations and liabilities existing by the common law.[42]

This hardly flattered the common lawyers of the day and it was a fair reflection of many of the debates which had taken place in the 1860s.[43] Reform was a popular topic in the 1860s and, amongst reformers, the common law did not have high standing. In effect Judicature Commissions were asking: was the common law at best some residual category of law? In any event, the reforms which took place in the 1870s were being much debated in the 1860s and discussions about law and equity were disturbing to common lawyers because of the impact such a change could have upon the way they worked. To take just one practical example, there were unresolved difficulties over how the common law of evidence could be reconciled with the rules of evidence in equity.[44]

Any sense of uncertainty in the correct approach to legal practice at this time was also increased by criticisms of the forms of action. At common law the relief

---

[40] *Ibid.*, at 106–7.

[41] (15 and 16 Vict., c. 76), Baker, *supra* n.2, at 107–8.

[42] (36 and 37 Vict. c. 66).

[43] R. Cocks, *Foundations of the Modern Bar* (London, Sweet and Maxwell, 1983), chs. 5 and 6.

[44] The concern is not surprising. The issues remained unresolved in important respects after the Judicature Acts. For a practical example of the need to refer to legal and equitable rules of evidence after the Judicature Acts see R. Cocks, "The Great Ashdown Forest Case" in T.G. Watkin (ed.), *The Legal Record and Historical Reality* (London, The Hambledon Press, 1989), at 187 and n.51.

for a plaintiff was fixed according to the form of action and the declaration did not include a claim. Even after reforms of 1832 and 1833 the forms of action had to be kept apart and, for the practitioners of the day, "each must be used only within its proper precedents,—trespass, case, assumpsit, trover, ejectment, debt and detinue".[45] After the Common Law Procedure Act 1852 the form of action could not be mentioned in the writ. But it was still of the first importance to a pleader because each action had its own precedents. It was only after the Judicature Acts 1873–5 that these became irrelevant. When this happened there was little surprise. It is therefore likely that many judges probably expected reform when they were hearing cases in the 1860s and sensed that here, too, the common law was in a rapid state of change. Again, in such a context it seems reasonable to suggest that what mattered most at this time was getting to the substance of the case and expressing the law in a way which was brief and intelligible to the layman. The alternative required an exploration of formidable procedural issues which were likely to become in many respects irrelevant within a few years.

The decline in respect for the forms of action and their eventual abolition reveal another matter of concern to common lawyers during these years. The notion that the forms of action would no longer be separate things inevitably raised questions about the way in which the common law would come to be expressed. In Maitland's words:

> This results in an important improvement in the statements of the law—for example in text-books—for the attention is freed from the complexity of conflicting and overlapping systems of precedents and can be directed to the real problem of what are the rights between man and man, what is the substantive law.[46]

This was written at the end of the century. But any reference to texts already touched a raw nerve for the common lawyer in the 1860s. It suggested a capacity for the law to be discussed outside its established procedural contexts. In the late 1860s a periodical observed:

> We have more than once had occasion to deplore the increase amongst us of what are called "Text-books of the Law" upon particular subjects. They are for the most part the production of young men, neither profoundly versed in the law, nor seasoned by practice.[47]

The idea of the law-book as a statement of the law, critical or otherwise, might suggest that the common law was no longer under the control of the common lawyer, in the sense that it could be discovered and criticised by having recourse to a book written by someone with little or no experience as a practitioner. There was, as yet, no textbook on the law of torts which was likely to alarm a

---

[45] A.H. Chaytor and W.J. Whittaker, (eds.), F.W. Maitland, *The Forms of Action at Common Law* (Cambridge, Cambridge University Press, 1948), 81.

[46] *Ibid.*

[47] *The Law Magazine or Quarterly Review of Jurisprudence* (1869), Vol. 26, 74 (note that the system of volume reference used in n.37 had been changed in the intervening years).

16 Raymond Cocks

traditionalist. But there was a sense that the intellectual life of the common law was no longer what it had been. There was concern about "scriblomania" in the form of the ever-increasing number of law books referring to all legal topics, not just the common law.[48] The latter were rightly seen as a threat to a way of developing the law which had relied upon oral discussion and the creation of understandings as to what was appropriate on the part of a few hundred practitioners.

Beyond the arguments about procedure and the law, it is noticeable that between about 1840 and 1880 there were radical changes in the professional setting within which common lawyers worked. In 1843 the enterprising Serjeant Cox set up the *Law Times*. This weekly periodical took advantage of the new national network of railways and was directed at provincial attorneys as well as barristers. The result was a recognition that the Bar had no monopoly over debates about legal work. Attorneys, and their new organisation, the Law Society, had increasing political influence and were prepared to use it. For barristers who had identified the common law with the Bar and judges chosen from the Bar this looked threatening and matters were made worse by the creation of the County Courts in 1846. These courts could be used by attorneys and were usually beyond the influence of the Bar, which relied on Circuit Messes which only came into existence during the assizes. The profession's difficulty in responding to change became even clearer in the late 1840s and 1850s when the educational arrangements for would-be barristers were questioned by a House of Commons select committee and a Commission on the Inns of Court. It was quite clear to the informed public that the Bar's lack of adequate training was an international embarrassment.[49]

Everywhere, there was a demand for efficiency, and common lawyers had the greatest difficulty in showing that their methods were efficient. There was no question of any judge faced with the procedural and other problems of the common law finding consolation in professional traditions. The profession was subject to as much change as the law itself. When judges confronted environmental issues in the 1860s they worked with ideas and assumptions which had no sense of permanence about them. What looks in retrospect like a "sloppy" judgment is more likely to have been one which could respond to numerous uncertainties in legal practice and the development of the law. If we are fully to appreciate the difficulties experienced by judges hearing common law cases at this time it is necessary to turn to the most significant challenge of all.

DISRUPTIVE STATUTES: 1840–80

It was in this world of changing procedures and unsettling professional debates that judges had to respond to increasing quantities of statute law. It will be

---

[48] Cocks, *supra* n.43, ch. 5; on "Scriblomania" see 116–18.
[49] *Ibid.*, chs. 3 and 4.

Victorian Foundations? 17

argued that between 1840 and 1880 the increase in statute law was sufficient, in conjunction with the other problems mentioned above, to produce a major challenge to the way in which the common law responded to problems of pollution.

Simpson's reference to private Acts has already been mentioned. It draws attention to an important area of legal activity. Certainly, private bills played a part in environmental regulation. Apart from the "reservoir bills" mentioned above, they authorised major projects such as harbours and railways. They permitted a change of landscape through enclosure. Their number reached a peak during the railway boom. In 1846, 402 special Acts came into effect. In the words of a contemporary, during the first 50 years of Victoria's reign "nearly eleven thousand Local and Personal Statutes have been passed".[50] This was also an era when there were legal reforms relating to the content of private bills. In 1829 a committee of the House of Lords gave its approval for 16 specimen bills. Under the guidance of the Earl of Shaftesbury there was a steady increase in uniformity of drafting and an associated use of standard clauses. Eventually, as legal historians have pointed out, general Acts were used to incorporate clauses into special Acts. For example, in 1845 there were Companies Clauses, Lands Clauses, Inclosures Clauses and Railways Clauses Consolidation Acts.[51] Again, there seemed to be no end to legislation and very large amounts of it related to the environment. Everywhere there was change.

In Professor Simpson's view, "the courts possessed an opportunity after the decision in *Rylands* v. *Fletcher* to impose what was now the common law theory of strict liability for bursting private reservoirs to reservoirs generally, and indeed to develop a coherent and consistent scheme of civil liability to all dangerous public and private works". But, he adds, "no sooner had the decision been taken than the opportunity was lost".[52] The law governing bursting reservoirs was reduced to a state of confusion by the House of Lords in decisions of 1869 and 1876.[53] These were linked to other cases concerned, for example, with whether particular special Acts took away liability for nuisance and, more

---

[50] F. Clifford, *A History of Private Bill Legislation* (London, Butterworths, 1885 and 1887), Preface: considered in Simpson, *supra* n.12, at 219. Clifford's research had an impact on Dicey: see A.V. Dicey, *Lectures on the Relation between Law and Public Opinion in England During the Nineteenth Century* (London, Macmillan, 1905), 30, n.2. For an interesting study of the role of the Parliamentary Bar in the passing of private bills see R.W. Kostal, *Law and English Railway Capitalism: 1825–1875* (Oxford, Clarendon, 1994), particularly at 110–43.

[51] (8 Vict cc. 16,18,20) and see O Williams, *The Historical Development of Private Bill Procedure and Standing Orders in the House of Commons* (London, Official Publication, 1948), at 107–11. It is considered in Simpson, *supra* n.12, at 220.

[52] *Ibid.*

[53] See, in particular, two cases which did not arise out of reservoir bursts but which did address the problems of statutory interpretation and the residual role of the common law: *The Directors of the Hammersmith and City Railway Co.* v. *Brand* (1865) LR 1 QB 130; (1867) 2 QB 223; (1869) LR 4 HL 171, All ER Reprint (1861–73) 60; and *River Wear Commissioners* v. *Adamson* (1876) 1 QBD 546, All ER Reprint (1874–80) 1. In a response which reflected some other reactions to Victorian legislation, most of the judges in the latter case confessed to uncertainty in interpreting what Lord Hatherley called a section "somewhat inartistically framed": *ibid.*, 6. Frequently, Victorian judges struggled with the legislation of the day.

18   Raymond Cocks

generally, with the scope of compensation in respect of statutorily authorised works. One of the cases was argued before Lords Cairns, Chelmsford and Colonsay on the same day as the first two judges heard the arguments in *Rylands* v. *Fletcher* (6 July 1868). In a full and interesting analysis Simpson points to numerous contradictory approaches on the part of the judges at all levels as they responded to statutory and common law problems. Indeed, some such as Blackburn and Bramwell became self-contradictory.[54]

But for the present writer, the significance of the evidence revealed by Professor Simpson points, once more, in a different direction. It was not so much that the judges were in some sense failing the law. Rather, they were unable to evolve consistent substantive law because of the number of "constituencies" they had to have in mind at that time. It was not the judges who produced the problem but the intellectual context within which they were working. How were they to present this area of the common law, subject as it was to so many stresses, to juries, fellow judges and the general public? Relating legislation which set contrasting standards for different projects across the country to the established common law was highly likely to produce inconsistent statements of principle as judges and juries attempted to do justice to the facts in hand. When these difficulties are considered in the context of the further procedural and professional problems mentioned above it might be suggested that the judges were well advised in not setting out to produce one coherent analysis of common law forms of liability. It would be more sensible to do justice to the facts of the case "in front of them" and leave the details of the future general shape of the law to a time when there was greater clarity about the forms of action and the like, and the major debates over the Judicature Acts had been resolved.

This argument may be taken further by considering the history of public legislation at this time. In respect of environmental law generally, the legislative mountain might be said to have begun with a molehill in the form of an "Act for giving Facility in the Prosecution and Abatement of Nuisances Arising from Furnaces Used and in the Working of Steam Engines".[55] Enacted in 1821, this Act had sufficiently limited scope to reassure the most worried of industrialists living in fear of state interference with private enterprise. However, by the 1840s legislative initiatives were of a different order. Significant Acts concerned with public health reached the statute book, and, in the decades which followed, there was legislation designed to force substantial changes in industrial practice, as with, for example, the Alkali Act of 1863 mentioned above.[56] The more general legislation became concentrated in the famous Public Health Act of 1875, and this, in turn, served as a foundation for later reforms relating to housing and, by 1909, even town planning.[57]

---

[54] Simpson, *supra* n.12, at 220–5.
[55] (1 and 2 Geo. IV, c 41).
[56] (26 and 27, Vict. c 124).
[57] (38 and 39 Vict. c 55); and see Cornish and Clark, *supra* n.2, at 179–94.

Victorian Foundations? 19

The story of this rapid production of large quantities of statute law is familiar enough. What should be emphasised in the present context is that for contemporaries there seemed to be no end to it. It is easy to forget in retrospect the extent to which the law was linked to administrative machinery in local and central government. By the 1840s it was clear that "legislation now was no longer merely declaratory of the common law or the source of new private rights".[58] There was a new group of people with an interest in the creation of public legislation in the form of commissioners, inspectorates and executive officers who had been given tasks by statutes which were, it seemed, always in need of amendment and extension:

> It would be naive to imagine that these functionaries were the mere millhands of government with no relationship to legislation other than their mechanical responsibilities. They often helped to bring legislation into existence, to revise and strengthen it, and to defend it against attack. Chadwick's initiatives in promoting factory, poor-law, police, sanitary, and local government legislation were unusually pervasive, but not unique.[59]

Anyone who doubts this expansion of the law should visit the Public Record Office at Kew and contemplate the indices for the documents to be found on 62 miles of shelving. They are a formidable record of government activity. As early as the 1860s there was a need for a regular supply of information on matters relating, say, to the local use of the Town Improvement Clauses Act 1847 and the Public Health Act 1848.[60] To take an example at random, there are large files relating to Whitehall's statutory duty to supervise the creation and implementation of local regulations. By the 1860s it was becoming clear that new arrangements would be necessary if Whitehall was to retain its influence, and in 1871 the Local Government Board was established. There seemed to be no limit to the range of the new laws which were caught within this administrative "net". To take one tiny example relating to the important environmental problem of burial, Coventry and Crewe produced by-laws relating to the permitted dimensions of new graves in Coventry or the fees and charges for Crewe cemetery and, predictably, Whitehall was told of every regulation in question.[61] The detailed nature of the laws, by-laws and regulations in this sort of context was impressive. In modern colloquial words, these laws were a growth industry. It is not too much to say that for many officials they became part of a way of life. Everywhere, Whitehall was assiduous in collecting information relating to the use of statutes, and it is noticeable, too, that it greatly improved its own capacity for drafting legislation with the creation of the Parliamentary Draftsman's Office in 1869. In brief, the legislation designed to improve the environment had already, by the mid-Victorian years, created a world of legal thought and

[58] H.W. Arthurs, "Without the Law": Administrative Justice and Legal Pluralism in Nineteenth Century England (Toronto, University of Toronto, 1985) 134.
[59] Ibid.
[60] (10 and 11 Vict. c. 34) and (11 and 12 Vict. c. 63) respectively.
[61] PRO, HLG, 27, 7.

20   Raymond Cocks

practice which could prove unsettling to the common lawyer following traditional legal ways. So much was happening, and it was happening so quickly.

For contemporaries, there was acute concern about these issues. As early as the 1850s they were of interest to the contemporary jurist, Henry Maine, who expressed doubts about the capacity of Parliament to cope with rising expectations for the making of statute law.[62] Later, in 1861, Maine published his book *Ancient Law*.[63] To the modern reader its title suggests a purely historical study, but it was far from this. In what may have been the best-selling law book of the nineteenth century, Maine explored the relevance of the legal past to the problems of the legal present. For him:

> social necessities and social opinion are always more or less in advance of Law. We may come indefinitely near to the closing of the gap between them, but it has a perpetual tendency to reopen. Law is stable; the societies of which we are speaking are progressive. The greater or less happiness of a people depends on the degree of promptitude with which the gulf is narrowed.[64]

Despite his doubts about legislation Maine saw its expanded role as all but inevitable. In advancing a "proposition of some value" he pointed to three "instrumentalities" of change in the forms of legal fictions, equity and legislation, adding that "[t]heir historical order is that in which I have placed them".[65] After the publication of *Ancient Law,* Maine went to India and devoted himself to Imperial legislative reform and, on his return at the end of the 1860s, he expressed the fashionable view that both the common law and statute law were victims of backward thinking in the legal profession and judiciary. By 1871 he was resigned to the problem. There was now little hope for the common law, or even statute law, finding an adequate response to the demands of an industrial society experiencing rapid change. For him, the explanation for the difficulties of the common law was obvious:

> Doubtless, the secret lies in the control of the English Bench by professional opinion— a control exerted all the more stringently when the questions brought before the courts

---

[62] Maine considers the subject in "Roman Law and Legal Education", first published in 1855 in *Cambridge Essays* (John W. Parker and Sons, London, 1855), 1–29, later reprinted in *Village Communities in the East and West* (3rd edn., London, John Murray, 1876), 330–83. P.G. Stein, "Maine and Legal Education" in A. Diamond, (ed.), *The Victorian Achievement of Sir Henry Maine* (Cambridge, Cambridge University Press, 1991) (at 203) points out that Maine argued that the study of Roman law would enable English lawyers to handle statutes with the same dexterity as they handle cases. Stein summarises the argument crisply: "English law lacks rules for construing statutes as a whole. As a result legislative draftsmen must 'deal not so much with principles as with applications of principles', and try 'to anticipate all the possible results of a fundamental rule' instead of trying 'to modify and shape anew the fundamental rule itself'": *ibid.,* quoting from 375 of the essay as reprinted in *Village Communities in the East and West.*

[63] (London, John Murray, 1905). The sub-title was *Its Connection with the Early History of Society and its Relation to Modern Ideas.* The quotations below are taken from the commonly found edition of 1905 which is very "close" to the edition of 1861.

[64] *Ibid.,* ch. 2, 24.

[65] *Ibid.,* 24–5. Maine's view in this matter is a nice illustration of Victorian fashionable thought; it is not suggested here that it was necessarily true: see, for comment, Baker, *supra* n.39 at 224.

Victorian Foundations? 21

are merely insulated fragments of particular branches of law. English law is, in fact, confided to the custody of a great corporation, of which the Bar, not the judges, are far the most influential part. The majority of the corporators watch over every single change in the body of principle deposited with them, and rebuke and practically disallow it, unless the departure from precedent is so slight as to be almost imperceptible.[66]

More generally, neither the common law nor legislation was being developed in a way which could fully respond to the demands of a self-consciously progressive society:

I must ask you to believe that the very small place filled by our own English law in our thoughts and conversation is a phenomenon absolutely confined to these islands. A very simple experiment, a very few questions asked after crossing the Channel, will convince you that Frenchmen, Swiss, and Germans of a very humble order have a fair practical knowledge of the laws which regulate their everyday life. We in Great Britain and Ireland are altogether singular in our tacit conviction that law belongs as much to the class of exclusively professional subjects as the practice of anatomy.[67]

In brief, Victorian lawyers were fully aware of the fact that it was possible radically to criticise the response of both the common law and statutes to industrialism and social change. In such a context it was all the more likely that in a contentious area of the law concerned with, say, pollution there were poor prospects for finding a creative relationship between common law and statute law. There was every reason for judges to proceed with caution and concentrate upon the facts of each case rather than grand pronouncements of principle.

WHAT JUDGES DID ABOUT THE PROBLEMS ENCOUNTERED IN MAKING THE LAW

The senior judges of the 1860s were fully aware of sentiments such as Maine's, and often shared them. Law Officers and Lord Chancellors did more than put forward adventurous programmes of reform relating, say, to imprisonment for debt, bankruptcy or registration of title to land. They were frustrated with the very style of both the statute book and the common law. For example, in 1866 a Royal Commission was appointed "to enquire into the expediency of a Digest of law, and the best means of accomplishing that object, and of otherwise exhibiting, in a compendious and accessible form, the law as embodied in judicial decisions". The commissioners included men from the front rank of legal practice such as Lord Hatherley, Lord Cairns, Lord Penzance, Lord Selborne, Willes J (often regarded as the pre-eminent common lawyer of his day), Lord Thring, Lord Cranworth and Lord Westbury.[68]

[66] *Supra* n.62, at 48–9.
[67] *Ibid.*, 59–60.
[68] The work of the Commission is considered in J.B. Atlay, *Lives of the Victorian Chancellors* (London, Smith Elder, 1906), ii, 283–5. In 1859 Westbury had told the reforming Juridical Society that there was a need for a Ministry of Justice which could, amongst other tasks, take on the

22   Raymond Cocks

All the judges in the House of Lords who gave decisions in the cases of *St Helen's Smelting* v. *Tipping* and *Rylands* v. *Fletcher* were involved in major programmes of law reform in the 1860s, and these programmes raised fundamental questions about the future role of the common law and its administration.[69] Westbury, in particular, never tired of telling people about the imperfections of current law and law-making. Neither case law nor statute law was an adequate vehicle for reform. In 1862 he wrote to Palmerston, the Prime Minister, about the absurdity of what he had to do as Lord Chancellor if ever he contemplated introducing a reforming measure in Parliament:

> If any amendment of the law seems to me desirable, I must beg for the approval of the Home Secretary, and, through him, the sanction of the Chancellor of the Exchequer. My secretary writes to Sir George Gray requesting him to move the Chancellor of the Exchequer to consent that the Lord Chancellor may have a small sum of money to pay the gentlemen he may employ to effect the necessary reform. After weeks of delay, an official letter comes from Mr. Peel or some subordinate, doling out some niggardly sum, as if it were a favour, and often with the most absurd stipulations.[70]

In the following year Westbury took a leading role in introducing a law to allow for the further revision of the statute-book by allowing for the removal of unused statutes. He took the opportunity to stress that law did not belong exclusively to lawyers:

> lawyers, when speaking of legislation, discourse in chains and shackles; and what are they? They are the professional prejudices, the narrow horizon within which their views are bounded, and their blunted sensibility to evils with which they have long been familiar.[71]

As for the common law, it was scarred by failings at its heart. "We have all heard the vulgar phrase, 'the glorious uncertainty of the law'. It is the common opprobrium of our system, which has passed into a proverb, and the saying has taken its rise in the fact that no man can tell with certainty whether a particular case in which he is interested, will or will not be followed by the judges."[72] Ultimately, Westbury wanted a digest of the whole law, statutory as well as case-based. In his view such a task could be properly entrusted to a Department of Justice. When this novel institution had prepared a digest it could proceed to

---

systematic reform of the law: see "Papers of the Juridical Society", i, 2, 6. Generally, see the study of Westbury's career in A.L. Goodhart and H.G. Hanbury (eds.), *A History of English Law by Sir William Holdsworth* (London, Methuen, 1973), 70–90.

[69] An example would be the debates leading up to the appointment of the First Report of the Judicature Commission, 1869 HMSO; 1868–9 British Parliamentary Papers, Vol XXV, 24. On one occasion in the early 1860s the periodical press remarked on "a competition for law reform between the noble lords": see J. Stuart Anderson, *Lawyers and the Making of English Land Law, 1832–1942* (Oxford, Clarendon Press, 1992), 108.

[70] T.A. Nash, *supra* n.34, 45.

[71] *Ibid.*, 57.

[72] *Ibid.*, 59.

use the materials within the digest as the foundation for the formation of a code.[73] The common law could be replaced.

It is easy for the lawyer of today, looking back on the Victorian era, to assume that the respect for the common law apparent in the works of Dicey and many other late-Victorian writers is a guide to the assumptions of earlier generations. In fact, Dicey's work from the mid-1880s onwards was in many ways a sustained reaction to the uncertainties of earlier decades. Dicey was seeking to provide certainty where previously there had been many doubts, not least about the capacity for the common law to adapt.[74] The earlier decades, as we have seen, were full of doubt, and it is in this context that the decisions in *St Helen's Smelting* v. *Tipping* and *Rylands* v. *Fletcher* need to be assessed. The brief judgments were not "sloppy". They were succinct attempts to cope with the facts of the case in hand, a crisis in the working of the common law and, most of all, an inability to find a constructive relationship between the common law and statute law in this area. The judicial worries of the 1860s do much to explain the brevity and approach of the judgments in the cases of *St Helen's Smelting* v. *Tipping* and *Rylands* v. *Fletcher*. The judgments responded to the needs of a distinctive phase of legal thought.

The common law has always shown remarkable resilience in the face of challenge and it survived this time of self-doubt. But it did so at the cost of leaving many of the most controversial aspects of industrial control to Parliament. The common law courts were in no position to create a novel and systematic approach to the problems of environmental regulation during this decade. Still less were they able to look for a more consistent and more principled approach to the respective roles of common law and statute law. The significance of this is nicely illustrated in the contemporary commentaries on statutory reforms.[75] To a large extent, the law of public health was one thing, the common law another. The strains within the common law in the 1860s had prevented the judges from even contemplating the common law as a vehicle for what would now be called a pro-active approach of sufficient strength to challenge the increasing importance of statutes. The judgments contained adventurous elements, but they were disruptive of the law rather than balanced attempts to address the range of problems arising out of pollution.

[73] *Ibid.*, 64.

[74] R. Cocks, *supra* n.43, ch. 9. In part, Dicey was sensitive to the problems of statute law because of his experiences at the Bar as a tax lawyer: see R. Cocks, "Victorian Barristers, Judges and Taxation: A Study in the Expansion of Legal Work" in G.R. Rubin and D. Sugarman (eds.), *Law, Economy and Society, 1750–1914: Essays in the History of English Law* (Abingdon, Professional Books Ltd 1984), 445, particularly at 463–9.

[75] For example, William Golden Lumley was a prolific author with a gift for explaining statutory reforms. A part of his work may be said to have culminated in W.G. Lumley and E. Lumley, *The Public Health Act, 1875* (London, Shaw and Sons, 1876); and this was not a work which aimed to produce a unified blend of the common law and statute law. It was very successful and went through numerous editions. We need a study of the literature which introduced reforming statutes to a Victorian audience; given the complexity of the legislation the commentaries had the potential to be influential. It seems likely that, taken as a whole, they reinforced in readers' minds the extent to which statute law could be seen as separate from common law.

24   Raymond Cocks

It is striking that after the attempts in the 1860s to bring together cases and statutes in a digest the later Victorian debates gave little attention to the *relationship* between the common law and statute law. Of course, this relationship was considered in a number of cases where particular statutes were relevant to common law issues. But there was little concern for the more fundamental question: what would be the most creative relationship between statute law and common law? There is even evidence of hostility. The extent to which late-Victorian writers could see certain types of statute law as alien to the common law is easily revealed in Dicey's analysis. The challenge of public health enactments is expressly acknowledged. It was part of "[t]he trend of collectivist legislation". For Dicey the concern was profound. In his view, the nineteenth century had produced a situation in which destructive statute law could even be self-perpetuating:

> Public opinion is, we have seen, guided far less by the force of argument than by the stress of circumstances, and the circumstances which have favoured the growth of collectivism still continue in existence, and exert their power over the beliefs and the feelings of the public. Laws, again are, we have observed, among the most potent of the many causes which create legislative opinion; the legislation of collectivism has continued now for some twenty-five or thirty years, and has itself contributed to produce the moral and intellectual atmosphere in which socialistic ideas flourish and abound.[76]

For Dicey, the individualistic values which he saw in the common law could hardly have a constructive relationship with this type of legislation. It was a case of the two systems of law being based on contrasting values.[77]

CONCLUSION

The history of this part of the common law, particularly in its relationship with statute law, is a reminder of the importance of timing. If there was to be an adventurous response on the part of the common law to the environmental degradation produced by the industrial revolution it would have been reflected in cases such *Tipping* v. *St Helens* and *Rylands* v. *Fletcher*. The judgments do reveal some minor indications of an interest in an adventurous approach. Westbury's ideas about nuisance had the potential to extend the scope of the tort. Cairns's analysis of the law in *Rylands* v. *Fletcher* did introduce a significant novelty. But, at the risk of repetition, these novelties have to be understood

---

[76] A.V. Dicey, *Lectures on the Relation Between Law and Public Opinion in England During the Nineteenth Century* (London, MacMillan and Co., 1905) 300–1.

[77] On the failure of common lawyers systematically to address the problematical relationship between statute law and common law see the important article by P.S. Atiyah, "Common Law and Statute Law" (1985) 48 *MLR* 1. Note also the article by R. Pound, "Common Law and Legislation" (1907) 21 *Harv. Law Rev.* 383. As Atiyah points out (at 7 of his article in the *MLR*), Pound suggested that common lawyers have a general tendency to refuse to receive statutes fully into the body of the law and to treat them as interlopers, and interpret them narrowly, giving them no further effect than a direct application requires.

against a background in which the senior judges of the day had little faith in the common law as an effective instrument for responding to change. They were faced with intense difficulties in developing the common law at a time when so many of its procedural and substantive aspects were being questioned. In response, some of the judges were contemplating reforms as revolutionary as the creation of a code and a Ministry of Justice. When interest in the latter type of profound change receded in the 1870s the brief judgments of the 1860s, with their undeveloped ideas, began to look like strangely defective examples of conventional common law reasoning. It was forgotten that they were in fact the product of a crisis in thought about the common law. The practical result was that the legal world was left with a restricted approach to the common law in environmental matters and, at best, a lack of interest in searching for creative links with expanding statute law.

2

Nuisance, the Morality of Neighbourliness, and Environmental Protection

J.E. PENNER

INTRODUCTION

T HE LAW OF nuisance is often, perhaps typically, described with some frustration, as an ill-defined branch of tort law with an inadequate theoretical basis which, for example, makes resolving its relationship to the tort of negligence very difficult.[1] The frustration can be eased, however, by bearing in mind that the law of nuisance is a development of the common law, as a result of which it has its own "proprietary" and "atheoretical" subject matter, terms I shall explain below.

As to the common law nature of nuisance: when a lawyer, academic or practising, is faced with sorting out any particular branch of the common law, there is a perennial tension between achieving the goal of precise definition and theoretical explanation on one hand and accommodating the reasoned decisions in actual cases on the other. I hasten to say that this is not to be confused by those under Dworkinian influences with a tension between the "fit" of one's theory of a branch of law with the cases as against the "substance" of justice, as defined by the best moral philosophical theory one can muster.[2] The tension here is one of explanation. As analysts of the common law, we naturally accord great respect to the actual decisions in actual cases and the reasons given for them. In the crucible of actual contests where the rights and fortunes of real people are at stake, we correctly suppose that, generally, judges acting in good faith will decide a case based upon reasons which will have a good deal of rational appeal to the litigants which, even if unfavourable to their cause (which will be the case for half of them), will at least express as persuasively as possible the sense or logic of the law's appreciation of the situation giving rise to the conflict. But this particular discourse of counsel and judges arguing cases and giving reasons for decisions is not philosophical or theoretical to a degree which can satisfy the

---

[1] See, e.g,. C. Gearty, "The Place of Nuisance in a Modern Law of Torts" (1989) 48 *CLJ* 214.
[2] See R. Dworkin, *Law's Empire* (London, Fontana, 1986).

28   J. E. Penner

analyst of the common law. Any analyst who wishes to speak of the character of a branch of law must show how it relates to other branches, employing definitions and abstractions that range over myriad actual decisions. In doing so, there is always a danger that certain lines of case will not fit the abstractions or definitions easily. Then the analyst is faced with a problem: either the proposed abstractions or definitions must give way, or the recalcitrant cases must be explained as anomalous or hived off as properly belonging to another branch of law. All this is perfectly familiar, and indeed is the bread and butter of blackletter legal analysis, which is paradigmatically employed when a particular case presents a significant novelty, or where the law appears to point in conflicting directions, in other words where the law might fairly be regarded as unsettled.[3]

One way of characterising all this is to say that the common law is both "incompletely theorised"[4] and "local". It is incompletely theorised in the sense that individual branches of law, and *a fortiori* the common law as a whole, are not worked-out systems of abstract rules and principles which, like an abstract moral philosophical theory of utilitarianism, can be just *applied* to any fact situation that presents itself. Partly in consequence, the common law is local in the sense that the resolution of cases is typically approached by the examination not of the purposes or nature of the law as a whole, or the purpose or nature of a specific branch of law like tort law, but in terms of the purposes or nature of the small subdivisions of cases which appear relevant to the case at hand. There are different explanations available for incomplete theorisation and locality,[5] but the one I shall mention here might be called "cognitive". This cognitive explanation holds that the development of the law is by and large a "bottom-up" rather than a "top-down" operation. In general people perceive situations of social conflict in terms of a number of basic moral concepts, which are acquired early in life (most in early childhood). It is in reference to these basic moral concepts that our moral knowledge is largely organised. Besides being fairly stable reference points for our moral knowledge, these basic concepts are resistant to displacement, in particular displacement by more global, abstract definitions and theories, because, as the fundamental building blocks of our cognition of morally significant situations, they provide us with a psychologically "real" grip on morally significant situations.[6]

The point of raising these considerations is to illuminate one perspective on trying to explain branches of the common law in an intellectually satisfying

---

[3] For one perspective on this picture of the law as a crucible in which abstract philosophical or theoretical concepts of harm and so on are tested, see B. Williams, "Afterward: What has Philosophy to Learn from Tort Law?" in D.G. Owen, *Philosophical Foundations of Tort Law* (Oxford, Clarendon Press, 1995) at 487.

[4] The term is Sunstein's: see C. Sunstein, *Legal Reasoning and Political Conflict* (New York, Oxford University Press, 1996), ch. 2.

[5] For what might be called a "political explanation" see *ibid*.

[6] See J.E. Penner, "Basic Obligations" in P.B.H. Birks (ed.), *The Classification of Obligations* (Oxford, Oxford University Press, 1997); "Cognitive Science, Legal Theory, and the Possibility of an Observation/Theory Distinction in Morality and Law" (1998) 1 *Current Legal Issues* 1–34.

Nuisance, Neighbourliness, and Environmental Protection 29

way. On this perspective, making sense of the law of nuisance is a matter of elaborating, or revealing to ourselves, the moral nature or character of a particular body of case law which seems to address a particular sort of situation of moral significance, roughly the interference with a landowner's enjoyment of his land, because in an important sense our appreciation of the moral significance of cases of nuisance is *sui generis*. It is *sui generis* because perceived/conceived in terms of a concept of interference specific or peculiar to interference with an owner's enjoyment of land. The concept of a nuisance we have is thus both "proprietary", that is, particularised to cases of nuisance and not simply some more general concept of harm which is applied to interference with an owner's enjoyment of land, and "atheoretical", that is, understood and applied by people, including lawyers and judges, even though they may not have or be able to articulate a broader theory of tort or private law into which the concept of nuisance properly and acceptably fits. On this perspective, then, there is no guarantee that we will be able to generate a theory of the law of nuisance which will fit precisely into a general framework for the law of torts, or which, for example, provides satisfying connections on all relevant matters with the law of negligence. This is not to say, not at all, that theorising about the law of nuisance is pointless or harmful for our understanding. That, after all, is what I shall do in the following. It is rather to say that in elaborating the sense of this branch of law we must be very wary of assuming that the goal of such theorising should be, or that the result will be, a fitting of nuisance law into a well-worked out theory of tort law or environmental law. Hence what I will do here will be to try to elaborate what appears to be the moral significance of those situations we appear able to cognise and classify as nuisances, without, at least initially, having in mind or indeed seeking a broader connection of nuisance law with the law of tort or environmental law. I shall then examine several recent cases from this perspective, and conclude by suggesting how this analysis sheds light on the place of nuisance in modern environmental law.

THE CHARACTER OF NUISANCE LAW

It might fairly be said that while nuisance may be very difficult to define, one can say of an instance of nuisance "I know it when I see it" in a clear range of paradigmatic cases: where the defendant causes noise, emits noxious fumes, or scatters dust in the environs of the plaintiff's land which, in some material way, makes it unliveable on, i.e. constantly filthy, impossible for sleep, conversation, or breathing, and so on. Furthermore, this appreciation of the tort sits comfortably with Newark's three-fold classification of interference with rights over land: disseisin, trespass, and nuisance.[7] In a very basically appreciable way, one can interfere with an owner of land by removing him from it, thus separating him from that over which he is to have the exclusive determination of how it is

---

[7] F.H. Newark, "The Boundaries of Nuisance" (1949) 65 *LQR* 480 at 48 ff.

30   J. E. Penner

to be used; or by trespassing, thus interfering with his exclusive right to determine who is to have access to his property; or by causing a nuisance, again interfering with his exclusive right to determine how his property is to be used, but this time by rendering impossible activities which are regarded as being within his rightful expectation of use and enjoyment of his land. Newark also accurately captures the significant defining element of the tort—that the action of the defendant occurs off the land of the plaintiff. This element is largely responsible for its somewhat nebulous character for, the action of the defendant being off the plaintiff's land and in that sense indirect, the tort of nuisance can partake of aspects both of disseisin and trespass.

Some authors focus on the similarity between nuisance and trespass.[8] True, nuisances often do have the character of "invasion", as with smoke or dust or noise (sound waves). However not all cases of nuisance can be analysed in this way,[9] and it is submitted that nuisance is more akin to disseisin despite the fact that the defendant effects the dispossessory influence on the plaintiff by activities off the plaintiff's land and though such an influence may typically be an emission by the defendant which enters or "trespasses" on the plaintiff's land.[10] It seems obvious that what counts as an unlawful dispossession of the plaintiff from his land cannot be restricted to bodily removal. Poisoning the atmosphere must be enough. Though a vaguer sense of disseisin will operate in cases of noise, smells, or the proximity of a pornography shop,[11] an interference of this character is one which reasonable persons would consider a factor materially reducing their ability to occupy the premises in the ordinary way.

Formulating the tort of nuisance in terms of a notion of disseisin will not, of course, eradicate any vagueness which characterises "nuisance", but so long as the vagueness in the explanation aligns with the vagueness of the concept explained, then we cannot ask for more. It is submitted that the description of nuisance as a particular kind of unlawful disseisin captures the essential nature of the complaint, i.e. that the defendant's conduct makes it impossible for the plaintiff to occupy his premises in the way he has a right to expect, strongly influencing, if not forcing, him to move elsewhere. The smoke or fumes make him feel ill, the noise will not let him sleep at night or make use of his garden at the weekend, the proximity of the pornography shop makes his home an unsuitable place for raising children, and so on. Obviously, evidence that an annoyance is one which induces the land occupier to go out when it is happening is strong evidence that the annoyance constitutes a nuisance.[12]

---

[8] E.g., R.A. Epstein, "Nuisance Law: Corrective Justice and its Utilitarian Constraints" (1979) 8 J of Leg. Stud. 49; T.W. Merrill, "Trespass, Nuisance, and the Costs of Determining Property Rights" (1985) 14 J of Leg. Stud. 13.

[9] E.g., *Laws* v. *Florinplace* [1981] 1 All ER 659.

[10] On the historical relation between disseisin and nuisance, see J.R. Spencer, "Public Nuisance–A Critical Examination" (1989) 48 *CLJ* 55 at 56–7.

[11] See *Laws*, supra n.9.

[12] See, e.g., *Tetley* v. *Chitty* [1986] 1 All ER 663; *Kennaway* v. *Thompson* [1981] QB 88; *Miller* v. *Jackson* [1977] 3 All ER 338 (CA).

Nuisance, Neighbourliness, and Environmental Protection   31

From this perspective, the best way of framing the basic moral question which the law of nuisance poses is this: what kinds of interference with an owner in his use and enjoyment of his land influencing him to leave the property and move elsewhere are so serious or material in this dispossessory respect that he ought to be able to enjoin them? Framing the question in this way shows why the action is typically regarded as nebulous and difficult to theorise in a satisfying way. All kinds of influences by one's neighbours may give one reason to pack up and move, and clearly not all of them can be actionable nuisances. Which ones can be regarded as so unreasonable as to be unlawful, i.e. actionable?

The answer given by the modern law was essentially established in the nineteenth century.[13] The issue of the reasonableness of the defendant's user of his land was the central issue in what is still, it is submitted, the leading case on this matter, *Bamford* v. *Turnley*.[14]

The case was preceded by four years by *Hole* v. *Barlow*,[15] in which the court appeared to hold that as long as the defendant's use of his land was itself reasonable and convenient (for example, to set up and operate a brick works where brick earth was to be found), then such use could not be a nuisance even if it interfered with the plaintiff's use and enjoyment of his land. In *Bamford* v. *Turnley* this view was firmly rejected.[16] Whether a use is unreasonable depends on whether it interferes with the plaintiff's use and enjoyment of his land to an extent beyond that which any neighbour ought to bear.[17] The court clearly adopted the view that considering the effects of a particular use of land on one's neighbours is implicit in determining whether that use is reasonable. Land is not the sort of property over which dominion can be exercised in disregard of others; it is by nature situated in a particular place and connected to the property of others. Permitting an occupier to do anything and everything reasonable on its own terms, as if what was reasonable could be determined in isolation from its effects on one's neighbours, disregards this obvious fact.

Bamford is particularly important for the judgments of Pollock CB and Bramwell B. Pollock CB gave the first formulation of the neighbourhood character rule, treating it as a relevant factor in the same way as is the duration and timing of the annoyance:

---

[13] For the history of the action leading up to the 19th century see Newark, *supra* n. 7; P.H. Winfield, "Nuisance as a Tort" (1930–2) 4 *CLJ* 189.

[14] (1862) 3 B&S 66.

[15] (1858) 4 CBNS 344.

[16] The Court of Appeal had previously confined *Hole* to its facts in *Stockport Waterworks Company* v. *Potter et al.* (1861) 7 H.& N. 160. In *Bamford*, Pollock CB dissented; while agreeing with the principle of law espoused by the majority he argued that the words "convenience" and "reasonableness" in the statement of the rule in *Hole* v. *Barlow* implicitly invoked consideration of the defendant's effect on his neighbours: *Bamford*, *supra* n.14, at 79–81.

[17] *Bamford*, *supra* n.14, at 76–8, 82–4; the decision was affirmed by the House of Lords in *St Helen's Smelting Co.*, *infra* n.46. See also *Scott* v. *Firth* (1864) 4 F&F 349, *West* v. *White* (1877) 4 Ch.D 631, and *Reinhardt* v. *Mentasti* (1889) 42 Ch.D 685, a very close decision where a hotel owner was enjoined from using a stove next to a party wall that raised the temperature of the plaintiff's room on the other side making it unsuitable as a wine-cellar.

32   J. E. Penner

> That may be a nuisance in Grosvenor Square which would be none in Smithfield Market, that may be a nuisance at midday which would not be so at midnight [sic], that may be a nuisance which is permanent and continual which would be no nuisance if temporary or occasional only.[18]

The most important statement in the case however, is Bramwell B's description of the terms of the reasonableness of the defendant's conduct:

> [T]hose acts necessary for the common and ordinary use and occupation of land and houses may be done, if conveniently done, without subjecting those who do them to an action.. . . There is an obvious necessity for such a principle as I have mentioned. It is as much for the advantage of one owner as of another; for the very nuisance the one complains of, as the result of the ordinary use of his neighbour's land, he himself will create in the ordinary use of his own, and the reciprocal nuisances are of a comparatively trifling character. The convenience of such a rule may be indicated by calling it a rule of give and take, live and let live.[19]

This passage is commonly construed to recommend that the law "balance the competing rights of neighbours, a process of compromise".[20] But notice that Bramwell B speaks not of competing rights to use land in *different incompatible* ways, for example, a right to operate a brickworks versus a right to reside in a place in comfort. Rights to annoy one's neighbours are reciprocal in the sense that every landowner has the *same* rights in this respect. Bramwell B explicitly says that a principle of reciprocality is fair because (1) the nuisances in question are comparatively trivial, and (2) they flow naturally from, in the sense that they are necessary for, the *common* and *ordinary* use and occupation of land, even when conveniently done, i.e. done with a view to minimising unpleasantness to others. Reciprocality refers to the give and take, live and let live attitude required by neighbours because they are not required to co-ordinate their activities or so arrange the enjoyment of their land that they never inconvenience or annoy each other. Nevertheless these neighbours are conceived as engaged in the same, or the same sorts of, activities, those which are common and ordinary.

If reciprocality is taken to mean compromise between *incompatible* uses of neighbouring land, then the scope of competing rights could, and presumably would, extend to uses which have nothing to do with the common and ordinary use and occupation of land. For example, the use of a cement factory which emits dust and smoke competes with the nearby residents' use of their gardens. Perhaps there ought to be some compromise regarding these uses based on the value of the cement factory as against the value of a smoke- and dust-free residence. This strikes some kind of balance, but one that has nothing in common with the reciprocality that Bramwell B's words evoke.

---

[18] *Bamford, supra* n.14, at 79.

[19] *Ibid.*, at 83–4 (italics mine).

[20] W.H. Rogers, *Winfield and Jolowicz on Tort* (15th edn., London, Sweet and Maxwell, 1998) at 497.

Nuisance, Neighbourliness, and Environmental Protection 33

Bramwell B was, furthermore, explicit about a number of other considerations. An annoyance that would not otherwise constitute a nuisance would be made so if done wantonly or with malice.[21] He also squarely rejected any defence on the ground of the public utility of the defendant's conduct.[22] Though the result might be an injunction stopping works of great value, this, in his view, was a smaller defect in the law than its permitting a defendant unlawfully to inflict injury on a neighbour. Neither did Bramwell B regard the temporariness of the nuisance as meriting any particular consideration.[23]

All these more specific points are the logical consequence of the importance Bramwell B places on the "common and ordinary use" criterion. Malice is relevant because any ordinary use, from undertaking normal repairs[24] to playing music[25] can become intolerable interference if done specifically to annoy a neighbour. Special consideration for temporariness is unnecessary, for a standard of ordinary use will incorporate it. A concern for temporariness typically arises where the defendant is undertaking building works. But though building on land is common and ordinary, that alone does not render annoyances from building works unactionable. Courts consider the work's duration, and whether the annoyance is systematic and continual, rather than merely occasional,[26] and emphasise care and consideration for one's neighbours.[27] Finally, public utility is not relevant because the common and ordinary use of land is for the private purposes of the owner; allowing individual defendants to legalise, in effect, their nuisances by citing the public utility of their activities would be to make the plaintiff owner bear a disproportionate share of the costs of that public utility for no other reason than the contingent proximity of his land to the defendant's; thus it would allow the defendant unilaterally to extinguish the private rights of his neigbours, for his own private advantage as well as the public's, without having any authority in public law to do so.

The attractiveness of Bramwell B's characterisation lies, therefore, in his elaboration in a general form of what might be called the "morality of

---

[21] *Bamford, supra* n.14 at 82–3. Malice has been found relevant in rendering behaviour which might otherwise fall below the threshold of nuisance an actionable nuisance in *Christie* v. *Davey* [1893] 1 Ch. 316; *Hollywood Silver Fox Farm* v. *Emmett* [1936] 2 KB 468; see also similar Canadian cases, reviewed in *Rattray* v. *Daniels* (1959) 17 DLR. 2d 134. The *Mayor, et. of Bradford* v. *Pickles* [1895] AC 587 is often cited in this context as a case where it was held that malice is irrelevant to the question whether a nuisance exists, however later decisions, construing *Chasemore* v. *Richards* (1859) 7 HLC. 349, upon which *Bradford* was decided, make clear that the case turns on rights in respect of percolating water: see *Langbrook Properties Ltd* v. *Surrey County Council* [1970] 1 WLR. 161 and *Stephens* v. *Anglia Water Authority* [1987] 1 WLR. 1381.

[22] *Bamford, supra,* n.14 at 84–6.

[23] *Ibid.,* at 84.

[24] See *Harrison* v. *Southwark and Vauxhall Water Co.* [1891] 2 Ch. 409, *per* Vaughan Williams LJ at 414.

[25] *Christie, supra* n.22.

[26] *Swaine* v. *The Great Northern Railway* (1864) 4 De GJ & S 211 at 215, and 216. See also *Attorney-General* v. *Mayor &c of Preston* (1896) 13 TLR 14.

[27] See *Andrae* v. *Selfridge Co. Ltd* [1938] Ch 1; *Fritz* v. *Hobson* (1880) 14 Ch.D 542; *De Keyser's Royal Hotel* v. *Spicer Bros. Ltd* (1914) 30 TLR. 257; and *Mantania* v. *National Provincial Bank* [1936] 2 All ER 633.

34   J. E. Penner

neighbourliness": comparatively trivial interferences which result from the use of land in the common and ordinary way are not actionable. But interference beyond this trivial level that arises from the defendant's activities which are not common and ordinary violate the duties of one neighbour to another, and constitute actionable nuisances. The examination of three recent cases will help elaborate in different contexts and different ways how this morality of neighbourliness is reflected in the law of nuisance.

THREE RECENT CASES

In *Cambridge Water Co.* v. *Eastern Counties Leather plc*[28] the court faced the question whether the defendant leather manufacturer was liable under the principle either of nuisance or *Rylands* v. *Fletcher*[29] for contamination of the plaintiff water company's water extraction borehole. At trial, it was found that spillages of the contaminating organic chemical onto the concrete floor of the defendant's factory occurred up to 1976, and that some of the chemical migrated through the concrete into the soil beneath, and thence over time some 1.3 miles to the plaintiff's borehole, contaminating the water and rendering it "unwholesome" under legislative standards in force from 1985. Overturning the decision of the Court of Appeal and restoring the result at trial, the House of Lords found for the defendant leather company. Although the case also concerned the issue of foreseeability of damages,[30] as regards the character and standard of liability the case is significant because the unanimous decision of the House, delivered by Lord Goff, approved, if not an assimilation of liability under *Rylands* v. *Fletcher* to liability in nuisance, then at least their close association.[31] Lord Goff appeared to accept Newark's interpretation[32] that the decision in *Rylands* v. *Fletcher* was not a turning point in establishing an entirely new tort of strict liability; rather, the general principles of common law, including those of the law of nuisance, led to the result that a defendant would be liable for an *isolated* escape of those things which he collected upon his land which were likely to cause mischief should they escape. Thus *Rylands* v. *Fletcher* demolished the notion, to the extent that it had thereto obtained, that strict liability under the law of tort (for nuisance, or akin to nuisance) applied only to a *continuing* interferences with a plaintiff's enjoyment of his land. In reaching this conclusion Lord Goff was impressed by the similar "control functions" exercise by the

---

[28] [1994] AC 264.

[29] (1866) LR 1 Ex. 265; (1868) LR 3 HL 330.

[30] Their Lordships held that liability for damages under the law of both nuisance and *Rylands* v. *Fletcher* was subject to the remoteness requirement of reasonable foreseeability under the *Wagon Mound* test (*The Wagon Mound (No.2)* [1967] AC 617, at 640, *per* Lord Reid (PC)); *Cambridge Water*, *supra* n.28, at 301–6. This issue will be of some relevance below: text accompanying n.79 *infraff*.

[31] *Cambridge Water*, *supra* n.28, at 297–300.

[32] Newark, *supra* n.7, at 487–8.

notions of reasonable user in nuisance law and non-natural user in *Rylands* v. *Fletcher* liability. He stated:

> [I]f the user is reasonable, the defendant will not be liable [for nuisance] for consequent harm to his neighbour's enjoyment of his land; but if the user is not reasonable, the defendant will be liable, even though he exercised reasonable care and skill to avoid it. Strikingly, a comparable principle has developed which limits liability under the rule in *Rylands* v. *Fletcher*. This is the principle of natural use of the land. . . . It is not necessary for me to identify the precise differences which may be drawn between this principle, and the principle of reasonable user as applied in the law of nuisance. It is enough for present purposes that I should draw attention to a similarity of function. The effect of this principle is that, where it applies, there will be no liability under the rule in *Rylands* v. *Fletcher*; but that where it does not apply, i.e. where there is a non-natural use, the defendant will be liable for harm caused to the plaintiff by the escape, notwithstanding that he has exercised all reasonable care and skill to prevent the escape from occurring.[33]

It is submitted that the association of *Rylands* v. *Fletcher* and the law of nuisance along these lines, in particular in respect of their criteria of non-natural user and reasonable user respectively, is to be commended. This is best appreciated in the context of a response to what at first glance looks like a compelling criticism of Lord Goff's speech on this issue.

In a review of the application of the law of nuisance and the rule in *Rylands* v. *Fletcher* to cases of pollution, Cross argues that the case law reveals that an occupier of land is regarded as being in a unique position to prevent injuries whose cause originates in states of affairs or activities occurring on his land. Therefore, save where the damage results from a natural hazard on the land or the activities of strangers on the land, the occupier is held strictly liable for any losses which are the reasonably foreseeable result of that state of affairs or activity. The taking of reasonable care in addressing the state of affairs or conducting the activity will not relieve the occupier of liability. Now, subject to some elaboration below, this, I would submit, is a perfectly correct statement of the law of nuisance and the rule in *Rylands* v. *Fletcher*, at least in so far as they are assimilated or associated by Lord Goff in *Cambridge Water*. Wherein, then, lies Cross's objection to Lord Goff's characterisation of these torts? Cross objects to regarding unreasonable user as a general prerequisite of liability in nuisance, and so regards associating it with the non-natural user requirement, which is a general requirement for liability under *Rylands* v. *Fletcher*, as mistaken. Cross claims that the unreasonable user requirement was only introduced to deal with those particular nuisances, paradigmatically noise nuisances, where the finding of an actionable nuisance turns on whether a threshold has been crossed.[34] We must all put up with some noise from our neighbours, but past a certain volume or frequency noise may become an actual nuisance. In cases such as this the

---

[33] *Cambridge Water*, *supra* n.28, at 299–300.
[34] G. Cross, "Does Only the Careless Polluter Pay?" (1995) 111 *LQR* 445 at 448–58.

36   J. E. Penner

essence of determination of liability consists in "a balancing of the respective interests of the parties in the context of the particular locality where their properties are situated".[35] In contrast, liability for other kinds of interference—he gives the example of the escape of poisonous gas[36]—cannot properly be regarded as subject to a balancing test: the harm to the plaintiff might be catastrophic, while at the same time the defendant's activity giving rise to the harm, say carrying out an industrial process at a reasonable level of care, may well be regarded as a reasonable user. In consequence, Cross fears that the assimilation of the two criteria might lead to the reasonable user text being subject to all the vagaries and uncertainties of the non-natural user standard, conferring upon the court "a wide and relatively unfettered discretion to exclude actions by reference to the nature of the activity carried on by the defendant",[37] and this will subject the tort of nuisance to the "same erosion of principle that has afflicted *Rylands v. Fletcher* while at the same time subverting its strict liability nature".[38]

If the association of reasonable user with non-natural user did logically lead to this result, Cross's fear would be warranted, but there is no good reason to believe that it should. The point is not merely that in *Cambridge Water* Lord Goff said that, in his opinion, "the storage of chemicals in substantial quantities on industrial premises should be regarded as an almost classic case of non-natural use",[39] so that one can be optimistic that the standard of unreasonable user/non-natural user will not be interpreted to the disadvantage of plaintiffs. Rather, the point is that Lord Goff's opinion in *Cambridge Water* that both unreasonable user and non-natural user act as control functions will not lead to the inappropriate relief of defendants from liability on the ground that they acted "reasonably" so long as the standard for reasonable use is properly appreciated. And, it is submitted, it does seem to be fully appreciated by Lord Goff, and his decision should not be read otherwise.

In the first place, it seems clear from his speech[40] that Lord Goff is treating both the unreasonable user and non-natural user criteria as *hall-marks* of *strict liability* in nuisance and under the rule in *Rylands v. Fletcher*. This indicates that Lord Goff is not pursuing the erosion of their status as strict liability torts. It is the unreasonable or non-natural user which renders the defendant liable even though, in the case of nuisance, "he may have exercised reasonable care and skill to avoid it",[41] and under the rule in *Rylands* v. *Fletcher*, "he has exercised all reasonable care and skill to prevent the escape from occurring".[42]

Furthermore, it is not clear that Cross has correctly described the unreasonable user requirement for liability in nuisance. In a footnote he states:

---

[35] *Ibid.*, at 450.
[36] *Ibid.*
[37] *Ibid.*, at 455–6.
[38] *Ibid.*, at 458.
[39] *Cambridge Water, supra* n.28, at 309.
[40] *Ibid.*, at 299–300.
[41] *Ibid.*, at 299.
[42] *Ibid.*, at 300.

Nuisance, Neighbourliness, and Environmental Protection 37

To argue that any use which causes serious interference with the plaintiff's use of his or her premises, must, *ipso facto*, be an unreasonable use would be to deny to the principle the control function which is at the centre of Lord Goff's view of it as similar to the non-natural user requirement in *Rylands* v. *Fletcher*.[43]

However, the question which must concern Cross here is not whether any use causing a *serious* interference with the plaintiff is *ipso facto* an *unreasonable* use, but whether any use which is an *unreasonable* interference with the plaintiff is ipso facto *actionable* as a nuisance, and according to traditional and orthodox definition, it is.[44] One must charitably assume that it was in this sense that Lord Goff referred to the unreasonable user requirement, i.e. as of the essence of the tort. This does not, *pace* Cross, deny this requirement its control function over liability, but it will, of course, apply differently in different circumstances. Whilst there is a distinction to be made between cases where there is a clear need for the defendant to have exceeded a threshold and cases where there is not, *that* distinction has not been characterised as one where only in the former case is the defendant's unreasonableness of the essence. The threshold/non-threshold distinction has been characterised in terms of two factors: one, whether or not actual damage to the plaintiff's property has occurred; and two, the character of the neighborhood.[45] The distinction was first drawn by Lord Westbury in *St Helen's Smelting Co.* v. *Tipping*,[46] between those interferences with the plaintiff's use and enjoyment of his property which produced "material injury to the property",[47] and those which produced "sensible personal discomfort",[48] i.e. interferences with "one's enjoyment, one's quiet, one's personal freedom, anything that discomposes or injuriously affects the senses or nerves".[49] Only in the latter sort of case is the character of the neighbourhood relevant to determining the reasonableness of the interference, and thus whether it was actionable. Thus the "threshold" nuisances are not set apart from others because only with respect to them must the defendant's conduct be found to be unreasonable. Rather, in so far as "threshold" nuisances comprise interferences with personal comfort, a particular factor which is used in determining unreasonableness will apply, i.e. the character of the neighbourhood.[50]

---

[43] Cross, *supra* n.34, at 450, n.33.

[44] M. Brazier, *Street on Torts* (9th edn., London, Butterworths, 1993), at 345: "[t]he essence of the tort of nuisance is unreasonable interference with the use or enjoyment of land"; W.V.H. Rogers, n.20 at 495: "the law repeatedly recognises that a man may use his own land so as to injure another without committing a nuisance. It is only if such use is unreasonable that it becomes unlawful'.

[45] For a detail examination of the latter, in particular with reference to the relevance of planning permission and the statutory authority defence, see J.E. Penner, "Nuisance and the Character of the Neighbourhood" (1993) 5 *JEL* 1.

[46] (1865) 11 HLC 642.

[47] *Ibid.*, at 650.

[48] *Ibid.*

[49] *Ibid.*

[50] On the contours of the character of the neighbourhood rule, see *St Helen's, supra* n.43; *Sturges* v. *Bridgman* (1879) 11 Ch.D 852; *Polsue and Alfieri Ltd* v. *Rushmer* [1906] 1 Ch. 234, [1907] AC 121.

38   J. E. Penner

It is submitted that Lord Goff's association of the unreasonable user requirement in nuisance with the non-natural user requirement in *Rylands* v. *Fletcher*, rather than tending to undermine nuisance and *Rylands* v. *Fletcher* as torts of strict liability, illuminates why they are torts of strict liability. The point is quite simple. In nuisance, once a defendant's use of his land is found to be unreasonable, in that it interferes with his neighbour's use of his land in manner or extent such that no occupier of land could be expected to put up with it, it is no answer for the defendant to say that he exercised all reasonable care and skill in conducting the activity or overseeing the state of affairs that gave rise to the interference. To do that would be equivalent to claiming that his neighbours must suffer for the sake of his activities, or the current harmful state of his land, so long as he has not been careless in his conduct.[51] The strictness of this liability is fortified, not weakened, by Lord Goff's association of the reasonable user requirement with the non-natural user requirement in *Rylands* v. *Fletcher*, so long as his discussion of the latter is carefully read. As regards the rule in *Rylands* v. *Fletcher*, the association of the two would be all to the good, for no one is satisfied that the "non-natural" use standard has been sensibly illuminated in the cases,[52] and its association with unreasonableness in nuisance will help give the standard some determinate content. Lord Goff's indication of what counts as a non-natural user does indeed seem to bring to *Rylands* v. *Fletcher* liability a standard much closer to the "common and ordinary use" standard of reasonable user standard which applies in nuisance.

The second case to be considered here is *Wheeler* v. *J.J. Saunders*,[53] which is important in light of *Gillingham BC* v. *Medway (Chatham) Dock Co. Ltd*,[54] decided three years earlier. While *Gillingham* can be interpreted to various effects,[55] at a minimum it appeared to decide that planning permission, by analogy with the defence of statutory authority,[56] could legalise what would otherwise be a nuisance, on the basis that the grant of planning permission could effect a change in the character of the neighbourhood and thus the standards of annoyance by which the plaintiff's claim in nuisance was to be judged. In *Wheeler* a unanimous Court of Appeal denied the analogy of planning permission to the defence of statutory authority.[57] The principle behind the defence of statutory authority is that the will of Parliament is not to be thwarted. Therefore, to the extent that the defendant causes a nuisance as *the inevitable result* of acting within its Parliamentary authority, no action founded upon the

[51] See also P.H. Winfield, *supra* n.13, at 199.

[52] See, e.g. *Leakey* v. *National Trust* [1980] QB 485 at 521–3 *per* Megaw LJ; S. Hedley, *Tort* (London, Butterworths, 1998), at 191–2.

[53] [1996] Ch. 19.

[54] [1993] QB 343.

[55] See Penner, *supra* n.45, for a detailed criticism of the case.

[56] Following in particular dicta of Cumming Bruce LJ in *Allen* v. *Gulf Oil Refining* [1980] QB 156 at 174, referred to on appeal to the House of Lords in the speech of Lord Wilberforce, [1981] AC 1001 at 1013–14.

[57] *Wheeler*, *supra* n.53, at 28, *per* Staughton LJ, at 34–5, *per* Peter Gibson LJ, and at 37–8, *per* Sir John May.

Nuisance, Neighbourliness, and Environmental Protection 39

nuisance can lie.[58] No similar presumption as to the extinction of private rights flows from the grant of planning permission. Staughton and Peter Gibson LJJ drew attention to the fact that planning authorities are delegated their powers for particular purposes which do not obviously include the power to extinguish civil rights, and to the difficulties of challenging planning permissions.[59] Sir John May put it this way:

> Parliament is supreme and can abolish or limit the civil rights of individuals. However, in general, planning is concerned with land use from the point of view of the public interest and as a generality is not concerned with private rights . . . Thus while the inevitability of a nuisance could well be the ground for refusing planning permission, the grant of the latter could not in my view licence such nuisance. Indeed, I think that if a planning authority were with notice to grant a planning permission the inevitable consequence of which would be the creation of a nuisance, then it is well arguable that that grant would be subject to judicial review on the ground of irrationality.[60]

Can, on the other hand, the grant of a planning permission lead to a change in the character of the neighbourhood, creating new standards by which future annoyances must be judged? Staughton LJ accepted at most that a planning authority had the power to permit a change in the character of a neighbourhood,[61] but both Peter Gibson LJ and Sir John May were more sceptical. Peter Gibson LJ read the *Gillingham* test as one where there must be an actual change in the character of the neighbourhood,[62] and Sir John May understood that "the exercise of the permission to develop granted by the local planning authority *may* have the result that the character of the neighbourhood changes".[63] Thus one can argue that, on the latter two judges' views, whilst the grant of planning permission and the consequent development *may* lead to a change in the character of the neighbourhood, this is a matter of fact; any increase in annoyance which an owner in a particular area may be forced to bear is not implicitly or explicitly authorised by a grant of planning permission, but may arise over time as a consequence of a change in the character of a neighbourhood from development, development which, of course, is only permitted by planning authorities.[64]

The decision is to be commended. It reaffirms the character of nuisance as a tort in the context of development under a planning regime. The tort of nuisance

---

[58] *Allen, supra* n.56, *per* Lord Wilberforce at 1014.

[59] *Wheeler, supra* n.53, at 28, *per* Staughton LJ, at 34–5 *per* Peter Gibson LJ.

[60] *Ibid.,* at 37–8.

[61] *Ibid.,* at 30.

[62] *Ibid.,* at 35.

[63] *Ibid.,* at 37.

[64] See also the judgment of Pill LJ writing for a unanimous Court of Appeal in *Hunter* v. *Canary Wharf* [1997] AC 655 at 669–70 (reversed in part on other grounds at 677ff.), expressing a similar view, i.e. that the question of a change in the character of the neighbourhood appears to be one of fact following the permitted development, and the speech of Lord Cooke, at 722, where his Lordship appear to regard the grant of planning permission as itself changing the character of the neighbourhood.

40   *J. E. Penner*

is not to be conceived as the common law of planning or zoning,[65] such that it is necessarily displaced by the planning regime in so far as they conflict. The protection nuisance affords for the landowner's use and enjoyment of his land, thus his reasonable expectations of his possession of it, does not arise from a concern to organise land uses so as to avoid conflicts between landowners or favour uses in the public interest, howsoever conceived. Nuisance is conservative in the sense that the underlying assumption is that no one should suffer unreasonable interference in his use and possession of land, however meritorious or in keeping with the goals of public policy the defendant's activities might otherwise be.

Finally, the House of Lords' decision in *Hunter* v. *Canary Wharf*[66] is worthy of consideration. Two issues of significance to our purposes here were addressed: first, whether interference with the plaintiff's television reception by the structural properties of the defendant's building constituted a nuisance and, secondly, whether a claim for damages in nuisance was limited to those parties having an interest in the affected land.

On the first issue, Lords Goff, Lloyd, Hoffmann and Hope decided that, even if in certain circumstances interference with television reception might constitute a nuisance, it could not do so where the interference was the result purely of the structural features of a building lawfully erected by the defendant on his own land, here the height of the building and its metal cladding and metalised windows. Put in its simplest terms, at common law (and equity) an owner of land, absent any easements or restrictive covenants, may build what he likes upon it. Lords Goff, Lloyd, Hoffmann and Hope saw no reason warranting a change in this fundamental principle given that they viewed the proposed right to television reception as analogous to a right of prospect or to a passage of air, neither of which rights is recognised at common law so as to inhibit a neighbour from building on his land as he will.[67] Lord Cooke took into consideration the fact that, given the prevalence of planning legislation, it was not true today to say of owners that their rights extended *usque ad coelum ad inferos*, and furthermore that the malicious erection of a structure purposely to interfere with a neighbour's enjoyment might well constitute a nuisance; as a result it could not be said categorically that the erection of a building could not constitute a nuisance. However in this case, because the tower was authorised under the special procedures to encourage development in an urban enterprise zone, the tower fell "within the scope of 'a strategic planning decision affected by considerations of public interest'".[68] Lord Cooke also appeared to decide that the public authorisation of the development changed the character of the neighbourhood in so far as television reception was concerned.[69]

---

[65] If there is such a common law of zoning or planning, clearly the law of restrictive covenants, though more recent in origin, is the more obvious candidate.

[66] *Hunter, supra* n.64.

[67] *Ibid.* at 685–7, *per* Lord Goff, at 699–700, *per* Lord Lloyd, at 709–11, and at 726–7, *per* Lord Hope.

[68] *Ibid.*, at 720–2, at 722 quoting Staughton LJ in *Wheeler, supra* n.53 at 30.

[69] *Ibid.*, at 722.

Nuisance, Neighbourliness, and Environmental Protection   41

With respect, the reasoning of all their Lordships is insufficient, and conflicts with the basic principles of nuisance law, at least as expressed in the "common and ordinary user" standard. It is, of course, true that erecting buildings is about as common and ordinary a use of one's land as there is. However, this simply cannot be said to encompass the erection of 800 foot towers. They are neither common nor ordinary outside a very few neighbourhoods like lower and midtown Manhattan. While there must be some height limit below which no claim in nuisance arising from the construction of the structure itself could be entertained, their Lordships give no reason why there can be no height above that at which a material interference caused by a structure could be actionable. In one Canadian case, it clearly was. In *T.H. Critelli* v. *Lincoln Trust & Savings Co.*,[70] the defendant was ordered to pay the plaintiff damages representing the latter's cost of reinforcing its roof, reinforcements required because the defendant's erection of his eight-storey building along the property boundary with the plaintiff resulted in a much increased snow load on the plaintiff's roof. While it is not clear that the case is rightly decided, since the increased snow load would have been caused equally had the defendant's building been only three storeys tall, I mention it to show that in certain circumstances the effects of a building's height *per se* might cause material interference with or even property damage to a neighbour. One can imagine other sorts of circumstances, for example the height and shape of a building causing wind effects resulting in severe discomfort and even structural damage. Would their Lordships seriously contend that cases of actual property damage could not be actionable as nuisances just because they arose from the defendant's erection of buildings rather than any other use of his land? If not, then a building or structure causing an interference with use and enjoyment which does not result in actual property damage must be actionable as well, for there is no distinction within the law of nuisance or in principle which would deny relief simply because the nuisance caused discomfort rather than property damage. And if this is so, interference with television reception is just the sort of interference of this kind that should be actionable. After all, their Lordships recognised the importance that reception of television signals has for the vast majority of residential occupiers,[71] so interference with this amenity cannot but be regarded as a very material factor influencing someone's decision to move elsewhere. As it turned out the interference was temporary, the BBC having installed a new relay station. What, though, would have been their Lordships' response if Canary Wharf had created a permanent dead zone for, let us say, both television reception and reception on cellular telephones? Could the resulting diminution in common and ordinary use and enjoyment of land and the lowering of property values which would clearly ensue really be regarded as not actionable?

---

[70] (1978) 86 DLR 3d 724 (Ontario High Court).
[71] See in particular *Hunter*, *supra* n. 64, at 684–5, *per* Lord Goff.

42   J. E. Penner

Lord Goff and Lord Lloyd both adverted briefly to *Bank of New Zealand* v. *Greenwood*,[72] in which the dazzling glare thrown onto the plaintiff's building by the glass of the defendant's building was held *prima facie* to create a nuisance, and both appeared to accept that, in principle, a nuisance might arise from the structural features of a building alone, though such cases be rare. However Lord Goff appeared to distinguish *Greenwood* on the basis that the glare emanated from the defendant's land, while here Canary Wharf tower merely prevented television signals from reaching the plaintiffs' properties.[73] This is not a distinction of principle or one found in the law of nuisance. The very fact that the court has recognised nuisances which do not "cast" anything on the plaintiff's land appears to show this,[74] and the distinction appears illegitimately to associate nuisance with trespass on the basis of some physical test, which as discussed above seems to deny the more relevant association of nuisance with disseisin.

Neither did their Lordships appear to pay any serious attention to the construction materials employed. Lord Cooke said, "it would seem hopeless to contend that the use of these materials and the design of the tower constituted any unreasonable or unexpected mode of constructing a *building of this height*".[75] Besides begging the question whether the reasonableness of materials could be assessed in relation to their suitability for very tall buildings where the dimensions of the building ought to have been one of the very matters in issue, this perspective seems to commit the mistake, often warned against and one of the principle heresies detected by Bramwell B in the reasoning of *Hole* v. *Barlow* discussed above, that the reasonableness of the defendant's conduct both in ends and means in carrying out his chosen purposes on his land is precisely not the standard to be employed in assessing whether he commits a nuisance. The reasonableness of the defendant's conduct is rather to be assessed by reference to the standard of use and enjoyment his neighbours can reasonably expect.

Before leaving this issue, one issue raised by Lord Hope deserves comment. He said:

> The prospective developer should be able to detect by inspection or by inquiry what restrictions, if any, are imposed by this branch of the law on his freedom to develop his property. He should be able to know, before he puts his building up, whether it will constitute an infringement.[76]

At first glance, this seems reasonable enough. But this sort of reasoning is quite alien to the tort of nuisance, and rightly so. Winfield broaches the heart of this matter as follows:

> [I]t must often be a pure gamble whether I act lawfully in opening a particular business in a street. If I make an error of judgment in deciding whether a business is offen-

---

[72] [1984] 1 NZLR 525; cited in *Hunter*, *supra* n.64, at 686, *per* Lord Goff, at 700, *per* Lord Lloyd.
[73] *Hunter*, *supra* n.64, at 686.
[74] E.g., *Laws*, *supra* n.9.
[75] *Hunter*, *supra* n.64, at 722 (emphasis supplied).
[76] *Ibid.*, at 726.

Nuisance, Neighbourliness, and Environmental Protection 43

sive or not, I shall not escape liability by proving that I took all reasonable care to prevent the business from being a nuisance. This is far short of saying that taking care is irrelevant in liability for nuisance. If the defendant has conducted his trade or business in a proper manner, i.e. as a reasonable man would conduct such a trade or business, he has gone some of the way towards making out a defence, but only some of the way; and conversely, he will be in danger of losing his case if he has taken no such reasonable care. But even where he has given proof of it, he will still be liable if there has been a sensible (i.e.unreasonable) amount of damage caused to the plaintiff.[77]

No principled distinction can be made between operating a business and erecting a building in so far as either might cause a nuisance. The same gamble must face the builder as it does the businessman. It may turn out, however forthright and diligent the defendant may be, that as a result of what he does he interferes with his neighbours' use and enjoyment of their property in so substantial a manner as to render him liable in nuisance. This is simply the strict liability character of the tort. As we shall discuss in a moment, it now seems clear that a defendant will not be liable for such losses which he could not reasonably have foreseen as the effect of his activities, including erecting buildings, but that will not relieve him of liability for any continuing nuisance that he causes his neighbours as soon as he is informed of it.

If all this is right, then the interference with television reception was, *prima facie*, actionable. To dispose of the plaintiff's claim for damages would require the further inquiry into (1) whether the defendant's action was legalised because it was carried out with the approval of a public authority, and (2) whether the injuries suffered were foreseeable. As regards (1), as mentioned above Lord Cooke regarded any interference with television reception to have been legalised. Unfortunately, there was insufficient discussion of the nature and purpose of the "enterprise zone" legislation, in particular the effect of the "inevitability" test applicable to the defence of statutory authority to determine whether the defendant should escape liabilty. On whether the permission resulted in a change in the character of the neighbourhood, Lord Cooke's view seems implausible. It is difficult to believe that whatever change in the character of the neighbourhood was either intended, or resulted in fact by the building of Canary Wharf tower, it was such as to make the surrounding neighbourhood one in which television reception was not an amenity to which a resident was entitled. As Pill LJ said, "I would say that the evidence does not suggest other than the neighbourhood will continue to have a substantial television-watching residential component".[78]

As regards damages, following *Cambridge Water*, it now seems clear that liability for losses suffered by the plaintiff due to the defendant's nuisance is subject to the *Wagon Mound* test of foreseeability. That is, the defendant will not be liable for any damage or suffering of the plaintiff which could not reasonably be foreseen as the consequence of his activities. While there is no record of any

---

[77] Winfield, *supra* n.13, at 199.
[78] *Hunter, supra* n.64, at 669.

44　J. E. Penner

evidence led on this issue in the proceedings, it does not seem implausible that it was within the expertise of the architects and engineers to foresee interference with the plaintiffs'television reception as a likely consequence of the erection of the tower. Although all of the plaintiffs'injuries lay in the past, the case raises the interesting hypothetical question concerning the proper remedy if the interference were permanent. If the interference were foreseeable, under traditional law the defendant would be in a very serious position, for while an injunction requiring the defendant to abate the nuisance is, strictly speaking, discretionary because it is an equitable remedy, in this area of the law injunctions seem freely to issue whatever the consequences for the defendant, and despite the social value of his activity.[79]

However, what if the interference had been unforeseeable? In *Cambridge Water* the leather company was not liable for the contamination of the plaintiff's borehole as the migration of the chemicals rendering the groundwater unwholesome was not regarded as a foreseeable consequence of its occasional spilling of the chemical on its concrete factory floor. However the facts indicated that substantial amounts of the chemical remained in the soil on the defendant's land, which would continue to migrate and contaminate the plaintiff's borehole. Was the defendant liable to prevent this ongoing contamination now that it was brought to its attention? Lord Goff thought not.[80] He reasoned, to begin with, that because the defendant brought about the current state of affairs when it could not have foreseen the consequences, it could not be liable for the plaintiff's losses, any more than it would be under liability for negligence. However he went on to say that, "at best", if the case were regarded as one of nuisance, the defendant would be liable on the principles of *Leaky* v. *National Trust*.[81] That case decided that a substantial interference with the plaintiff's use or enjoyment of land was actionable as a nuisance even though the nuisance was caused by a natural feature of the defendant's land, here a steep embankment which led to the slippage of rock and soil onto the plaintiff's land. However, one of the most important holdings of the case is that the extent of the defendant's liability to the plaintiff would turn, in part, on the *extent of the resources available to each of them to abate the nuisance*.[82] Whilst it is submitted that the judgment is defensible, it must be seen in contrast to what was regarded by many as the orthodoxy leading up to it, expressed by Shaw LJ:

> Why should a nuisance which has its origin in some natural phenomenon and which manifests itself without any human intervention cast a liability upon a person who has no other connection with that nuisance than the title to the land on which it chances to originate? This view is fortified inasmuch as a title to land cannot be discarded or abandoned. Why should the owner of land in such a case be bound to protect his

---

[79] See *Shelfer* v. *City of London Electric Lighting Co.* [1985] 1 Ch. 287 at 316; *Kennaway* v. *Thompson* [1981] QB 88; see also Penner, *supra* n. 45, at 11–13.

[80] *Cambridge Water*, *supra* n.28, at 306–7.

[81] *Supra* n.52.

[82] *Ibid.*, at 525–7, *per* Megaw LJ.

Nuisance, Neighbourliness, and Environmental Protection 45

neighbour's property and person rather than that the neighbour should protect his interests against the potential danger?

The old common law duty of a landowner on whose land there arose a nuisance from natural causes only, without any human intervention was to afford a neighbour whose property or person was threatened by the nuisance a reasonable opportunity to abate that nuisance. This entailed (1) that the landowner should on becoming aware of the nuisance give reasonable warning of it to his neighbour; (2) that the landowner should give to the neighbour such access to the land as was reasonably requisite to enable him to abate the nuisance.[83]

If *this* principle were revived, and Canary Wharf's interference with television reception was because of its unforeseeability to be regarded as akin to a naturally produced nuisance as appears to follow from the thinking of Lord Goff in *Cambridge Water*, then Canary Wharf would have no liability for the nuisance caused by the continuing existence of its tower. However, assuming that *Leakey* correctly states the law then, if Canary Wharf were liable because interference with television reception by its tower was actionable, then in terms of the relative resources of it and the local residents it appears that it might have significant liabilities. In particular, one can imagine a liability for damages measured by the cost of replacement cable or satellite service for the affected homes.[84]

In view of these considerations, it does appear something of a shame that four of their Lordships felt able to dismiss the residents'claim in nuisance for interference with their television reception so swiftly simply by reference to the fact that it was caused by the Canary Wharf tower itself.

The importance of *Hunter* does not end there. The case also decided, much against the trend of recent decisions in the Court of Appeal[85] and courts in other common law jurisdictions and much academic writing,[86] that only those who had an interest in land amounting to exclusive possession had standing to bring an action for nuisance. It is submitted that here, subject to reservations expressed below, their Lordships (Lord Cooke dissenting) were quite correct. As pointed out by all of their Lordships in the majority, the essence of a nuisance is an interference with the *rights* of use and enjoyment of land, and therefore only those with actual property rights, i.e. interests in the land, have standing to sue.[87] As Lord Hoffmann said:

> In the case of nuisances "productive of sensible personal discomfort," the action is not for causing discomfort to the person but, as in the case of [other nuisances], for

---

[83] *Ibid.*, at 528.

[84] As regards the plaintiff's claim for an injunction, it would seem to follow from the resource-balancing principles of *Leakey* that an injunction would be ruled out in all cases save those where the defendant's abatement would require fairly minimal expenditure, as in *Goldman* v. *Hargrave* [1967] 1 AC 645 (making sure a burning tree was extinguished), obviously not the case in *Hunter*.

[85] In particular, *Khorasandjian* v. *Bush* [1993] QB 727, and its decision in *Hunter*, *supra* n. 64, at 670–5, *per* Pill LJ.

[86] See the review by Lord Cooke in *Hunter*, *supra* n.64, at 714–17.

[87] *Ibid.*, at 687–8, *per* Lord Goff, at 695–9, *per* Lord Lloyd, at 705–7, *per* Lord Hoffmann, and at 724–5, *per* Lord Hope.

46   J. E. Penner

causing injury to the land. True it is that the land has not suffered "sensible" injury, but its utility has been diminished by the existence of the nuisance. It is for an unlawful threat to the utility of his land that the possessor or occupier is entitled to an injunction and it is for the diminution in such utility that he is entitled to compensation.[88]

Given that the tort of nuisance is a tort against rights in property, one must beware not to confuse actual *rights of or in property* with the mere *rightful* occupation of property, i.e. by any licensee of the owner. This is so even though the loss of amenity may be *realised in fact* not only or even through the discomfort of the owner—he may be away though his family remains—but through the discomfort of those whom he invites onto his land. However this point reveals what must be regarded as a serious flaw in the majority decision, which one day will need to be seriously broached, concerning the actual valuation of damages. Lords Lloyd, Hoffmann and Hope specifically made one rationale of their decision the argument that it would be unjust if the measure of damages against the defendant were to vary with the number of persons affected by his nuisance.[89] Thus co-owners must share any damages, and damages cannot increase as a result of the number of occupiers. This, however, follows not at all from the decision to limit standing to sue to those with an interest in the affected land.

In the first place, it seems to betray a confusion between liability for damages and the measure of damages.[90] While the defendant may be liable for nuisance only to those with an interest in land, the extent of that liability must surely depend upon the actual damages suffered. Suppose, for example, the land of two adjoining neighbours received the same unreasonable level of noise from the defendant. The defendant would be identically liable to pay damages to both. However, the measure of damages must depend on the actual discomfort suffered. If one neighbour was away on holiday the whole time, while the other was unable to complete the draft of a book at home and had to move elsewhere, there seems no reason to award the first any damages at all, while it would be perfectly just to award the latter substantial damages. In other words, the measure of the damages the defendant is liable to pay should depend upon the extent to which the unlawful interference with the plaintiff's rights was realised in fact, i.e. in actual discomfort. There is no difference here from the case of a nuisance causing actual property damage. If one plaintiff's damages lie in the destruction of plants in his garden, it is no answer to the claim by the defendant to say that the plaintiff's neighbour was not so affected because his garden was paved, but neither has the second neighbour any right to an award equal to the first's simply because rightfully, as owner, he *might* have planted a garden as well. If this is right then the number of actual occupiers on the land is a relevant considera-

---

[88] *Ibid.*, at 706.

[89] *Ibid.*, at 698, *per* Lord Lloyd, at 706–7, *per* Lord Hoffmann, and at 724–5, *per* Lord Hope.

[90] See in particular the speech of Lord Hoffman, *ibid.*, at 706–7, where he appears to conclude that because damages for "amenity" interference are not equivalent to consequential damages flowing from the an injury to land, they are to be measured only in terms of the diminution in market value of the owner's property.

tion in the measurement of damages. An owner has the right to invite others onto his land for the purposes of occupation—which is, of course, a common and ordinary use of one's land, though some may take no advantage of this right while some might do so extensively. Those that do must be able to measure their damages encompassing the distress caused to other persons who owe their intended benefits to the owner's exercise of his own rights. The problem of appreciating this and fitting it within the law is of a piece with the similar vexation in the law of contract concerning cases of breach where, for example, one person books and pays for a family holiday, as in *Jackson* v. *Horizon Holidays*.[91] Although the House of Lords in *Woodar Investment Development Ltd* v. *Wimpey Construction*[92] disapproved of Lord Denning's apparent grant of rights to sue in contract to third parties, Lord Keith said:

> There may be a certain class of cases where their parties stand to gain indirectly by virtue of a contract, and where their deprivation of that gain can properly be regarded as no more than a consequence of the loss suffered by one of the contracting parties. In that situation there may be no question of the third parties having any claim to damages in their own right, but yet it may be proper to take into account in assessing the damages recoverable by the contracting party an element in respect of expense incurred by him in replacing by other means benefits of which the third parties have been deprived or in mitigating the consequences of that deprivation.[93]

Read "licence" for contract, "owner" for "contracting party", and "licensee-occupier" for "third party" and this passage would meet the situation of damage caused by a nuisance reducing the amenity of the plaintiff's land exactly.[94] It is submitted, then, that not only did the House wrongly deny the plaintiffs' claim that interference with television reception was a nuisance, but it failed to do justice to what might be seen to be the correct essence, if not the form, of the plaintiffs' claim regarding standing, *viz.* that the measure of damages for which the defendant was liable ought to vary with the actual loss of amenity suffered by the resident owners, which in justice must include losses deriving from their perfectly rightful exercise of their power to share the occupation of their land.

CONCLUSION

The relationship between the law of nuisance and environmental law turns, of course, on the character of each. It is beyond the scope of this chapter to

[91] [1975] 1 WLR 1468.

[92] [1980] I WLR 277.

[93] *Ibid.,* at 297; see also the speech of Lord Wilberforce at 283.

[94] It is worth remarking parenthetically that the difficulty the courts have found in dealing with both third party beneficiaries in the law of contract and mere occupiers in nuisance law indicates that the problem may reveal that this sort of difficulty is not parochial to contract, to be overcome by altering the rules of privity, but may arise in any situation in which a person may exercise his own rights for the benefit of another person without at the same time creating or transferring any rights in that other person.

48   J. E. Penner

characterise environmental law, but the particularity of nuisance, with its own basic concepts understood at a local and atheoretical level, indicate something about how the two might fit together. Even conceived as directed only to the prevention and remedying of harms it appears that "environmental law" as a category is something of a grab-bag, dealing with different kinds of concern. First, environmental law might simply deal with harms to people or property operating through the physical environment which are actually or potentially so widespread in their effects as to be regarded as "environmental" in character, as opposed to being restricted in their nature to relations between a few parties. Secondly, it might address harms caused to people or property *through* an agent's effect on the environment, what one might call "environmentally embedded" harms. Thus the emission of chemicals so as to contaminate the water over a long period may be regarded as a harm under the rubric of environmental law, for the chemicals are now embedded in the environment, and the harm they cause is thus now directly the result of a newly hazardous environment. No further or continuing action by any tortfeasor is required for the harm to ensue. Thirdly, environmental law might cover harms to the environment itself, as a harm to something which is of intrinsic value to everyone, as might be the case of the destruction of forests and the extinction of species.

To the extent that nuisance fits into these categories, it might appear at first glance that it can only coincide with the first two categories. All nuisances are environmental in the first sense that they may potentially affect an indefinite number of property owners, depending upon the scope of the nuisance, the various owners' proximity to it, and the way the land is divided into individual properties. While perhaps few nuisances fall into the second category, it is clear that a nuisance may do, as in *Cambridge Water*, *Leaky* or *Hunter*. However, at first glance the law of nuisance does not seem to fit well into the third category for it is a part of private law, and the protection of values intrinsic to all must surely be a matter of public law and public regulation. True, the public law which in part concerns the protection of the environment and which has come into contact with the law of nuisance is the law of planning and, as we have seen, planning law and nuisance cannot be integrated. But it is submitted that this has less to do with the fact that planning law is concerned with public interests and nuisance law with private rights than with the fact that planning law concerns more than the protection of the environment, in particular economic growth. Despite these considerations, nuisance can be seen to serve to function to protect values intrinsic to all, and this is suggested by looking again at the issue of standing to sue raised in *Hunter*.

The importance of the restriction on standing lies not primarily in prohibiting non-owners from suing in nuisance, but in its insistence that those who do sue sue *as owners*. The most important distinguishing feature of property rights is that they are always only contingently associated with any particular person as owner.[95] This is particularly true of land, which lasts forever. What is my

---

[95] See J.E. Penner, *The Idea of Property in Law* (Oxford, Clarendon Press, 1997) ch. 5.

Nuisance, Neighbourliness, and Environmental Protection   49

land may be yours in the future, and will someday certainly be someone else's. In this respect the owner's right to sue in nuisance protects not only his interest in the land, but the interests of potential and future owners. In so far as the law's characterisation of what counts as a nuisance reflects the intrinsic values in land and living upon land, then the law of nuisance has a role to play even in the third broad category of environmental law. The law of nuisance, however, is obviously not enough, for it can do nothing whatever to prevent activities an owner may undertake on his own land which assail the intrinsic value of the environment. But then no tort protecting rights in property could, so it is difficult to fault the law of nuisance on this score.

3

Noxious Emissions and Common Law Liability: Tort in the Shadow of Regulation

JOHN MURPHY*

INTRODUCTION

OVER THE PAST few decades, there has been a steady growth in concern for the protection of the environment which has been mirrored in the corresponding evolution of environmental law.[1] This concern for the environment has been born out of a desire to protect a number of important interests including an ever-increasing number of endangered species, human life and health, and a wide range of recreational amenities available to present and future generations.[2] The fact that these environmental goods are difficult to quantify and evaluate[3] (and therefore measure against the things that must be sacrificed in order to achieve them—such as low prices and high rates of employment) has in no way muted the calls for greater environmental

---

* I am grateful to Martin Loughlin for his typically astute and helpful comments on an earlier draft.

[1] According to one study, the origins of environmental law have been traced back only as far as 1970: see R.A. Epstein, *Simple Rules for a Complex World* (Cambridge, Mass., Harvard University Press, 1995) at 275.

[2] Unlike the relatively constant worth attributed to endangered species, life and health, the value accorded to recreational amenities tends to vary much more over time according to changing preference patterns. This, in turn, can impact upon the degree of clamour for certain forms of pollution control. See further A. Ogus, *Regulation: Legal Form and Economic Theory* (Oxford, Clarendon Press, 1994) and C. Sunstein, "Endogenous Preferences, Environmental Law" (1993) 22 *JLS* 217, reprinted in C. Sunstein (ed.), *Free Markets and Social Justice* (New York and Oxford, Oxford University Press, 1997) 245 (references hereafter are to the latter source).

[3] As a crude example, noxious emissions from A's land may cause B's livestock to die (which loss is easily quantified) but may also cause environmental damage (for example, the death of a protected species, such as badgers—protected under the Protection of Badgers Act 1992—which B may regard as a pest). A further difficulty arises from the fact that an environmentalist's notion of remedying the damage does not normally mirror the common lawyer's. In our example, the environmentalist would be seeking, were it possible, to restore a badger population. The common lawyer, by contrast, would be concerned simply to make A liable to B in respect of the loss of his livestock. Further unquantifiable environmental damage might take the form of damage to the ozone layer. See further J. Steele, "Remedies and Remediation—Foundational Issues in Environmental Liability" (1995) 58 *MLR* 615.

52   John Murphy

protection.[4] In this chapter, I want first to identify just why it is that, despite the implementation of far-reaching environmental legislation,[5] such calls remain heard; and, secondly, to demonstrate that the commonplace distrust among environmentalists of the (potential) role of private law in this context is largely misplaced.[6]

It should be stated at the outset, however, that I am not concerned with all forms of pollution. Instead, as a *test case* for the inadequacies of regulation and the (possible) virtues of private law, I shall concentrate only upon noxious emissions into the atmosphere.[7] I have chosen atmospheric pollution[8] because the range of environmental issues to which such pollution gives rise—at both a local[9] and international[10] level—is suitably wide to allow my observations in respect of it to be applied, *mutatis mutandis*, to other forms of pollution. In other words, the claims I shall make about the potential of private law in respect of air-borne pollutants could just as easily be made in relation to, say, poisonous discharges into watercourses or the contamination of land. More particularly, my enterprise shall be to show that there are sufficiently important gaps in the regulatory regime, or at least in its enforcement, for the properly understood, strict liability torts of private nuisance and *Rylands* v. *Fletcher*[11] to fill.[12] In the course of this exercise I shall explain why the notions of "reasonable user" and "non-natural use"—central as they are to the juridical bases of the two torts[13]—

---

[4] According to Sunstein, this phenomenon may be attributable to "the fact that ordinary people appear to resist the use of a unitary scale and the claim of commensurability along a single metric": Sunstein, *supra* n.2, at 262.

[5] See e.g. the Environmental Protection Act 1990, as amended (hereafter "the 1990 Act"); the Clean Air Act 1993 and the Water Resources Act 1991.

[6] "One characteristic of the modern environmental movement is its manifest distrust of private law approaches to environmental protection": Epstein, *supra* n.1, at 275.

[7] It should also be noted that I do not consider private law and regulation to be alternatives, as such: regulation is essentially primarily intended to serve a preventive function, while private law, operating retrospectively, seeks primarily to secure corrective justice as between two litigants.

[8] Noise, of course, might also be viewed as a form of atmospheric pollutant (see the Noise Act 1996). However, for reasons explained in the next paragraph, noise pollution falls outside the scope of this chapter.

[9] For example, fumes and particulates that cause pulmonary diseases. Recall also the great smog of 1952 that hung over London for five days and caused the death of nearly 4,000 people.

[10] For example, destruction of the ozone layer and acid rain. For further examples see Department of the Environment, *This Common Inheritance: Britain's Environmental Strategy* (Cmnd 1200, London, HMSO, 1990).

[11] (1866) LR 1 Ex. 265.

[12] The important role of foreseeability in the two torts will, of course, continue to occlude the aspiration towards *truly* strict liability. Eekelaar captured the point succinctly when he observed that "if liability is dependent upon establishing that the defendant was, or should have been, aware of the likelihood of the events complained of, then we are outside strict liability": J. Eekelaar, "Nuisance and Strict Liability" (1973) 8 *Irish Jurist* 191, at 192. The role of foreseeability in private nuisance and *Rylands* v. *Fletcher* has been ably dealt with elsewhere: see G. Cross, "Does only the Careless Polluter Pay?—A Fresh Examination of the Nature of Private Nuisance" (1995) 111 *LQR* 445, at 458–73.

[13] Public nuisance falls outside the ambit of this study. Some public nuisances, it is true, are simply private nuisances that affect a much wider class of individuals than is usual: see e.g., *A.-G.* v. *PYA Quarries* [1957] 1 All ER 894, 908. But the only additional question that needs to be addressed in such cases is whether the class of persons affected is sufficiently wide to constitute the public

do not, as might be supposed, import the requirement of fault on the part of the defendant as a prerequisite of liability, and that as torts of strict liability they have the potential to perform an important and unique deterrent effect.

This chapter is divided into seven further sections. In the first of these, I consider the limits of the legislative framework. In this context, in so far as the relevant statutes seek to regulate noxious atmospheric emissions, I shall endeavour to establish that, in terms both of its content and its scope, the legislation is reinforced by, and (in part) dependent upon, the law of private nuisance and the rule in *Rylands* v. *Fletcher*. In the following section, I will examine the reasons why environmental judicial review is often an inefficacious means by which to hold to account the two agencies charged with administering the statutory regime.[14] In particular, my concern here will be with the problem of obtaining *locus standi* for many interested or affected parties. Taken together, these first two substantive sections provide the necessary backdrop for the central thesis of this chapter: that nuisance and the rule in *Rylands* v. *Fletcher*[15] have the potential to perform a distinctive and important environmental function, albeit in the shadow of the regulatory regime.[16]

Having established the lacunae in the regulatory web, the fourth section of this chapter will demonstrate, by means of novel analysis, the sense in which the liability in nuisance and *Rylands* v. *Fletcher* are to be understood as strict. Establishing the strictness of liability in these two torts is, of course, central to their deterrent effect: the stricter the liability, the more care prospective defendants will take to avoid causing noxious emissions. In the fifth section, I will explore two aspects of private law's under-utilised potential. Loosely, these are its capacity for exemplary damages in nuisance and *Rylands* v. *Fletcher* actions, and two prospective means of overcoming the problems faced by impecunious plaintiffs.[17] In the sixth section, I shall explain the instrumentalist justification for the recommendations I make in the fifth section. It is clearly one thing to suggest potential developments within the law, but it is quite another to supply an adequate reason for them. At the nub of this section is the fact that increased environmental protection inevitably comes at a cost, be it in higher prices,

version of the tort: the question of reasonable user (which affects the strictness of liability) will have been addressed at the earlier stage of assessing whether the interference complained of could constitute a private nuisance. The remaining class of public nuisances does not share a juridical overlap with private nuisance. Instead, it is concerned with interferences with the safety or convenience of members of the general public on the highway: see e.g. *Mint* v. *Good* [1951] 1 KB 517. Since noxious emissions into the atmosphere are seldom, if ever, highway-specific in terms of their effect, this second class of public nuisances also falls outwith the scope of this chapter. The most thoroughgoing accounts of the conceptual bases of public nuisance are to be found in J. Spencer, "Public Nuisance—A Critical Examination" [1989] *CLJ* 55 and R. Buckley, *The Law of Nuisance* (London, Butterworths, 1996) ch. 7.

[14] These are the Environment Agency and local authorities.

[15] (1866) LR 1 Ex. 265.

[16] For a valuable examination of the "potential apotheosis of nuisance into a 'Toxic Tort'" see J. Steele, "Private Law and the Environment: Nuisance in Context" [1995] *LS* 236.

[17] For a graphic literary illustration of the difficulties associated with mounting a private law action against wealthy industrial polluters see J. Harr, *A Civil Action* (Thorndike, Maine, Thorndike Press, 1998).

54 John Murphy

higher unemployment, less industrial activity or whatever. In essence, I want to show that the deterrent measures I propose achieve a better balance between the preservation of the several environmental goods alluded to earlier and the socio-economic concerns just highlighted. The chapter closes with a conclusion together with post-script that explains the absence of any references to the (not yet in force) Pollution Prevention Control Act 1999.

LEGISLATIVE LIMITS

So far as statutory regulation is concerned, the control of noxious emissions into the air falls under four separate (but inter-connected) regimes. The first is that of Integrated Pollution Control (IPC)[18] which, broadly, regulates emissions from "more polluting" processes.[19] The second is that of Local Authority Air Pollution Control (LAAPC)[20] which, in general terms, deals with "less polluting" processes.[21] Thirdly, a series of statutory nuisances—contained in Part III of the Environment Act 1990—add a further strand to the regulatory framework,[22] while, fourthly, the Clean Air Act 1993 imposes strict criminal law liability in respect of unlawful discharges of dust, smoke and fumes.[23] This last also provides protection by enabling local authorities to designate certain areas "Smoke Control Areas".[24] Yet for two reasons, detailed discussion of the 1993 Act falls outwith the scope of this chapter.[25] First, the kinds of emissions covered by that Act all constitute statutory nuisances under section 79 of the 1990 Act (albeit that the local authority's function under each of these statutes is different[26]). Accordingly, the 1993 Act raises no unique issues associated with airborne pollutants. Secondly, the major problems associated with the "policing" of statutory nuisances by local authorities under the 1990 Act arise equally (but are not greater) under the Clean Air Act. Discussion of both regimes would therefore entail needless repetition. Accordingly, my attention is directed only towards the first three regulatory mechanisms: *viz.* IPC, LAAPC and the control of statutory nuisances. And since the first two of these systems are collocated in Part I of the 1990 Act, the principal difference between them for our purposes[27] being merely one of degree, they are dealt with together.

---

[18] The 1990 Act, Part I.

[19] The language used in the 1990 Act is that of "centrally controlled prescribed processes": ss. 2(1) and 4(2).

[20] The 1990 Act, Part I.

[21] The 1990 Act refers to these as "locally controlled prescribed processes": ss. 2(1) and 4(3).

[22] S. 79(1)(b)–(d).

[23] Clean Air Act, ss. 1, 4.

[24] *Ibid.*, s. 18.

[25] A useful discussion can, however, be found in S. Bell, *Ball and Bell on Environmental Law* (4th edn., London, Blackstone Press, 1997) ch. 11.

[26] Under s. 55 of the Clean Air Act, the local authority is empowered to initiate a criminal prosecution. By contrast, under s. 80(1) of the 1990 Act the method of control is the service by the local authority of abatement notices where it is satisfied that a statutory nuisance exists or is likely to occur.

[27] Another difference is that IPC deals with *all forms* of "more polluting" processes, whereas LAAPC is concerned solely with atmospheric pollutants.

Integrated Pollution Control and Local Authority Air Pollution Control

IPC and LAAPC operate according to what is essentially a common system of regulation.[28] Notwithstanding that the former is administered by the Environment Agency[29] and the latter by local authorities,[30] they both work according to the same scheme of authorising[31] and enforcing[32] certain prescribed processes[33] which must be undertaken in accordance with specified emission limits and quality objectives.[34] Comprehensive though this licensing system may ostensibly appear, it is not without its inherent defects. Although section 6(1) of the 1990 Act prohibits carrying on a prescribed process without prior authorisation, and although section 23(1) makes it a criminal offence to contravene this prohibition, the legislation is by no means a panacea. Indeed, there are two principal problems associated with this regulatory regime. First, there are gaps in the legislation itself which means that certain forms of pollution and certain polluters are not caught. In addition, there is the problem that the regulatory system does not ensure effective enforcement of its aims and objectives.

As regards lacunae within the legislation, the most obvious example is to be found by reference to Part I of the 1990 Act. The attempts made there to control pollution operate only in respect of those who are engaged in one of the listed prescribed processes. Where noxious emissions into the atmosphere are generated otherwise than by such processes, the 1990 Act is of no moment; its provisions simply do not apply.[35] Buses left idling at a terminus, or lorries left running at a port or haulage yard are examples of sources of atmospheric pollution that lie outside the statutory prescribed list for the purposes of IPC and LAAPC. (By contrast, it has long since been established that such cases would ground an actions in private nuisance.[36])

---

[28] For a detailed and up-to-date account of IPC and LAAPC see Bell, *supra* n.25, chs. 11 and 12.

[29] The 1990 Act, s. 4(2). The Environment Agency was created under the Environment Act 1995, s. 1. It is charged thereunder, amongst other things, with the tasks formerly performed by Her Majesty's Inspectorate of Pollution and local authorities: s. 2.

[30] *Ibid.*, s. 4(3).

[31] Authorisation is granted by the relevant enforcement agency in accordance with the provisions in ss. 6 and 7 of the 1990 Act.

[32] *Ibid.*, ss. 13 and 14.

[33] These processes are not set out in the Act *per se*. Instead, the Act provides for regulations to be made which specify which processes are to be designated "prescribed processes": s. 2(1). The regulations in question are the Environmental Protection (Prescribed Processes and Substances) Regs. 1991 (SI 1991 No. 472).

[34] Again, the 1990 Act provides for regulations to be made which set the appropriate limits and objectives: s. 3(1).

[35] The Clean Air Act 1993 scarcely goes any further: that Act, aimed at factory emissions, merely covers discharges from the "chimneys of any building": s. 1. And the word "building" has been interpreted restrictively to mean the whole or part of any recognised structure: *Clifford* v. *Holt* [1889] 1 Ch. 698.

[36] See, e.g., *Rapier* v. *London Tramways Co.* [1893] 2 Ch. 588; *A.-G.* v. *Gastonia Coaches* [1977] RTR 219. Of course, "prospective environmental threats", such as the examples given here, might be caught by planning controls. But the point in the text remains valid for all existing pollutants not caught by the web of regulation.

56   John Murphy

So far as enforcement is concerned, at least three difficulties arise. To begin with, where an individual operates a prescribed process without having acquired prior authorisation,[37] the Environment Agency (or local authority in the case of LAAPC) must necessarily become apprised of this fact before it can take measures to secure compliance.[38] The problem is simply one of operating under an information deficit.[39] And since the Environment Agency is still in its infancy, this has been a fairly pronounced problem (though it may not remain so[40]). While the Agency seeks to overcome the inevitable teething troubles associated with major administrative re-organisation,[41] incomplete information presently comprises a significant obstacle to the effective implementation of IPC.

A second problem with enforcing the principles of IPC and LAAPC is that, while the Act provides powerful machinery to effect pollution control, that machinery tends to grind along rather slowly (except where the pollutant concerned is of an ultra-hazardous nature—which is more the case in the context of waste management than in relation to air-borne pollution[42]). In practice, there is often a significant time lag between the relevant enforcement agency learning of a prescribed process being operated contrary to the conditions of authorisation (or simply without authorisation) and it taking steps to deal with it.

Finally, current enforcement policy[43] allows some polluters to go completely without reprimand (when the Agency turns a blind eye to their "offence") while others may be issued with only very lenient penalties. To an important degree, such enforcement policy undermines the extent to which the regulatory regime

[37] Authorisations are usually granted subject to conditions: s. 7. Typically, these will include the duty to prevent or reduce emissions by employing the best available techniques not entailing excessive cost (BATNEEC). For a suggested legal interpretation of this phrase, and for discussion of other conditions that might be imposed under the Act, see M. Purdue, "Integrated Pollution Control in the Environmental Protection Act 1990: A Coming of Age of Environmental Law?" (1991) 54 *MLR* 534, at 540–5.

[38] This problem is compounded by the fact that the Environment Agency's pollution inspectors have hitherto concerned themselves more with ensuring that the terms of authorisation are being met at recognised IPC sites than with discovering unlicensed sites: see the *Environment Agency Annual Report and Accounts 1996–97* (Bristol, Environment Agency, 1997) at 45.

[39] The problem is not confined to an absence of notification, but stretches to an inability to garner sufficient detailed information to substantiate claims made about polluting activities. During 1996–7, e.g., only 852 out of 1,952 reported incidents were substantiated by the Environment Agency, *ibid.*

[40] The extent to which there is scope for an information deficit will also be reduced by the fact that the Environment Agency is invested with extensive investigative powers under s. 2 of the Environment Act 1995. Equally, the system of planning control can assist local authorities to detect the would-be operation of potentially polluting operations.

[41] Recall that the Agency was invested with a myriad of functions, some new, and some formerly performed by bodies as disparate as Her Majesty's Inspectorate of Pollution and the National Rivers Authority.

[42] C. Abbot, *The Scope and Impact of the Waste Management Licensing Regime* (Unpublished PhD thesis, University of Manchester); Friends of the Earth, *Friends of the Earth Fingers Filthy Factory* (London, Friends of the Earth, 1998) (press release of 1 Apr. 1998).

[43] Environment Agency, *Enforcement and Prosecution Policy* (Bristol, Environment Agency, 1998).

ensures compliance with the specified maximum emission limits.[44] It also does little to deter other would-be polluters from similar contraventions.

Statutory Nuisances

The statutory nuisances with which we are concerned—smoke; fumes or gases; dust or other effluvia emitted from industrial premises[45]—provide a useful additional means of controlling noxious emissions. But, just as with IPC and LAAPC, there are serious limits to the scope of the statute. In respect of each type of pollutant, the 1990 Act specifies that it shall be a statutory nuisance only if it is "prejudicial to health or a nuisance".[46] To be prejudicial to health, the statutory nuisance must be "injurious, or likely to cause injury, to health".[47] The alternative basis for qualifying as a statutory nuisance is that the emission concerned must be capable of supporting a common law action for nuisance, whether public or private.[48] In this latter context, the continuing importance of the common law is self-evident: the statute is in part dependent upon it for meaning. But the common law's role is not confined merely to that of an interpretational aid. Leaving aside the several exemptions to the statutory nuisance regime for which the Act provides,[49] two more serious limitations inherent in section 79 provide scope for the abiding usefulness of the common law. The first is that only emissions that are (potentially) injurious to health fall within the statutory nuisance scheme. Emissions that pose a threat to other natural resources—such as land or watercourses—are not covered. The second shortcoming is that even where the particular emission does threaten health, it must also be an *emission from premises* to qualify as a statutory nuisance.[50] As such, the examples of the bus and lorry with their engines left idling, that we observed to fall outside IPC and LAAPC, are equally beyond the statutory nuisance scheme. In short, section 79 is restricted in two main ways: it is both pollutant-specific and polluter-specific.

ENVIRONMENTAL JUDICIAL REVIEW

A further problem which is intricately related to the ones we have already

---

[44] These limits are specified in a series of "Daughter Dirs." made under the auspices of European Council Dir. 96/62 on ambient air quality assessment and management [1996] OJ L 296/55.

[45] The 1990 Act, s. 79(1)(b)–(d).

[46] *Ibid.*

[47] *Ibid.*, s. 79(7). The second part of this definition (which appeared also in the Public Health Act 1936) has been narrowly interpreted to require the likelihood of causing disease: *Coventry City Council* v. *Cartwright* [1975] 1 WLR 845.

[48] *National Coal Board* v. *Thorne* [1976] 1 WLR 543.

[49] The 1990 Act, s. 79(3).

[50] *Ibid.*, s. 79(1)(b)–(d).

58   John Murphy

considered, but nonetheless distinct, is the availability of what I shall call environmental judicial review. The problem stems from what are perceived to be unlawful administrative decisions on the part of the relevant enforcement agency. For the most part, the scope for judicial review arises from the broad statutory discretions afforded to the Environment Agency and local authorities.[51] For present purposes, judicial review might lie (at least in theory) in respect of their decisions to authorise the undertaking of prescribed processes, and from their decisions not to prosecute offenders (or, in the context of statutory nuisances, serve abatement notices).[52] Yet it is clear that current enforcement practice leaves much to be desired. With respect to the Environment Agency, the recent publicity concerning the chemical industry giant, ICI, provides a useful example. In relation to its factory at Runcorn—allegedly one of Britain's filthiest[53]—it has been reported that:

> [T]he Environment Agency has failed to control the factory properly—it has insufficient staff and has failed to force ICI to improve its plant. Even when it secures a conviction against the company, penalties are too light to act as a deterrent.[54]

As regards local authorities, they too may be disinclined to take a rigorous approach to their function as an enforcement agency. Because they are often concerned to attract inward industrial investment (which might also generate employment within the region), and because they would also be chary of closing down a large industrial plant that was a vital existing source of local employment, local authorities have every reason to take a lenient rather than strict approach to the exercise of their enforcement powers.

Naturally, the familiar problems associated with judicial review—such as applying for leave within a three month time limit[55] and avoiding delay[56]—apply equally, and just as problematically in relation to environmental matters as they do to any other. But, because they are not particularly germane to this context, and because of limitations of space, I do not discuss them here.[57] Instead, my chief concern is with the problems relating to *locus standi* that are particularly pertinent in respect of environmental judicial review. Essentially,

---

[51] As Lord Woolf observed, "it is not difficult to identify provisions [of the 1990 Act] which will be a fruitful source of judicial review": H. Woolf, "Are the Judiciary Environmentally Myopic?" (1992) 4 *JEL* 1, at 1.

[52] Note here that the Environment Agency operates its enforcement powers in conformity with the principal of proportionality, which means that "action taken by the Agency to achieve compliance should be proportionate to any risks posed to the environment and to the seriousness of any breach of the law or relevant licence or consent": Environment Agency, *supra* n.43, para. 13.

[53] See Friends of the Earth, *supra* n.42, at 1.

[54] *Ibid.*

[55] Supreme Court Act 1981, s. 31(3); RSC Ord. 53, r. 4(1).

[56] See e.g. *Re Friends of the Earth* [1988] JPL 93. A further problem is that of adequately establishing the merits of the case: see P. Craig, *Administrative Law* (Oxford, Oxford University Press, 1994) ch. 13.

[57] For a general account of principles covering delay see *R. v. Dairy Produce Quotas Tribunal, ex p. Caswell* [1990] 2 All ER 738. See also Supreme Court Act 1981, s. 31(6).

Noxious Emissions and Common Law Liability   59

they are twofold. To begin with, following the decision in R. v. *Inspectorate of Pollution, ex p. Greenpeace Ltd (No 2)*,[58] there arises the question of which factor or factors are essential prerequisites to obtaining standing for interested (but unaffected) environmental lobbyists. Secondly, there is the question whether the test of "sufficient interest" to acquire standing is the same for all applicants (and here I am mainly concerned with the doubt that surrounds the ability of affected individuals and industrial competitors to acquire standing).

Much of the concern for the protection of the environment is voiced by interest groups rather than by private individuals or corporations. Private citizens and limited companies are, unlike such pressure groups, usually motivated only by the perceived infringement of their rights rather than by any general preoccupation with the welfare of the present or future generations. Against this background, one might expect that a broad, permissive approach would be taken with respect to the question of group standing in environmental judicial review. For, as Lord Woolf has explained extra-judicially, "the Environmental Protection Act 1990 depends upon judicial review for its control of the activities of environmental enforcement bodies".[59] To some extent this has occurred: the courts have reasonably consistently recognised a public as well as a private dimension to environmental damage. Thus, as Hilson and Cram put it, "the courts have in recent times shifted markedly from a rights-influenced model [of *locus standi*] towards a citizen action stance".[60] But in the wake of the *Greenpeace* case, the criteria according to which standing will be afforded to interest groups remains shrouded in uncertainty. In that case, Otton J held that Greenpeace did have a sufficient interest to acquire standing for the purposes of section 31(3) of the Supreme Court Act 1981; and he listed a series of factors that persuaded him of this. Initially, he drew attention to the fact that Greenpeace was a well-established pressure group with approximately 2,500 members living in the area affected by the decision on the discharge of radioactive waste from British Nuclear Fuels' plant at Sellafield in Cumbria.[61] Next, he was impressed by Greenpeace's consultative status with the United Nations Economic and Social Council.[62] He also drew attention to the relative inability of individual members of Greenpeace to challenge the decision on their own,[63] and finally placed a deal of importance upon the fact the relief sought was certiorari.[64]

What is not clear from the *Greenpeace* decision, however, is which, if any, of the factors mentioned by Otton J was critical to Greenpeace acquiring standing.

---

[58] [1994] 4 All ER 329.

[59] Woolf, *supra* n.51, at 1.

[60] C. Hilson and I. Cram, "Judicial Review and Environmental Law—Is there a Coherent View of Standing?" [1996] *LS* 1, at 12. See also O. McIntyre and T. Mosedale, "The Rise of Environmental Judicial Review" (1997) 6 *Environmental Policy and Practice* 147.

[61] [1994] 4 All ER 349.

[62] *Ibid.*, at 350.

[63] The problem with such challengers is that they do not possess "the advantage of an application by Greenpeace, who . . . is able to mount a carefully selected, focused, relevant and well-argued challenge": *ibid.*

[64] *Ibid.*, at 351.

60   John Murphy

Put otherwise, in cases where not all of these factors are present, which will be treated as crucial and which will not?[65] The only thing certain from what was said in the case is that the court would have been unprepared to confer standing had the relief sought been an order of mandamus.[66] This would seem to mark a return to the non-uniform approach to standing that had characterised the pre-1977 era[67] and, importantly for present purposes, mean that a pressure group that sought to compel an enforcement agency to exercise its powers under the 1990 Act would almost certainly be denied standing.[68] By contrast, if it is an individual whose common law rights are interfered with, he may still pursue an action at common law.[69] Should he be successful in obtaining injunctive relief, the broader interests of the environment would coincidentally receive the protection the pressure group was unable to secure. Clearly, there is a marked difference *vis-à-vis* standing for the purposes of judicial review and standing for the purposes of mounting a common law action either in nuisance or under the rule in *Rylands* v. *Fletcher*. To a large extent, this difference is explicable in terms of the fact that judicial review is designed to serve a wholly different function from a civil law action in tort. While the latter is principally concerned with effecting corrective justice as between two private individuals, the same is not true of the former. Judicial review is either concerned with the *ultra vires* doctrine—that is, entrusting to the courts the task of policing Parliament's intention in so far as Parliament has conferred specific powers or duties upon a public body—or it is concerned with providing a basis to challenge illegality that would otherwise be unchallengeable and, hence, "a more fundamental common law duty to uphold the principal of legality".[70] Either way—by reference to the *public* interest in protecting the environment or by reference to the *public* interest in making (potential) illegality challengeable—the function and object of the action is different from the private law actions in nuisance or *Rylands* v. *Fletcher*.

[65] There is a suggestion in *Re Friends of the Earth*, *supra* n.56, that being a small organisation with limited funds (and therefore unable expertly to put together *quickly* a compelling case) will be fatal to any application for leave. But here it seems that the problem is one of delay rather than one of standing.

[66] [1994] 4 All ER 329, at 351.

[67] It was in this year that the universally applicable test of "sufficient interest" was introduced: SI 1977, No 1955. But even after this reform, the judiciary displayed a concern to insist on a different test of sufficient interest according to what remedy was sought: see e.g. *R.* v. *Inland Revenue Commissioners, ex p. National Federation of Self-employed and Small Businesses Ltd* [1982] AC 617, at 633 (*per* Lord Wilberforce with whose speech Lords Roskill and Fraser agreed). For further discussion see Craig, *supra* n.56, at 489–99.

[68] Given the discretionary nature of the enforcement agency's duties under the 1990 Act, an application for mandamus would be a non-starter; the best that could be hoped for in this context would be a declaration. For an analogy, see *R.* v. *Felixstowe Justices, ex p. Leigh* [1987] QB 582 (discussed at length in P. Cane, "Statutes, Standing and Representation" [1990] *PL* 307).

[69] For the implicit view that judicial review is associated with individuals' rights, see *per* Popplewell J in *R.* v. *North Somerset District Council ex p. Garnett* [1998] Env. LR 91. Contrast the view of Sedley J in *R.* v. *Somerset Council ex p. Dixon* [1998] Env. LR 111. See also the analysis of both cases in J. Alder, "Access to the Courts: A Conflict of Ideologies" [1998] *JEL* 183, esp. at 185–6.

[70] *Ibid.* More generally in relation to this debate see C.F. Forsyth, "Of Fig Leaves and Fairy Tales: The Ultra Vires Doctrine, The Sovereignty of Parliament and Judicial Review" [1996] *CLJ* 122; cf. P. Craig, "Ultra Vires and the Foundations of Judicial Review" [1998] *CLJ* 63.

Noxious Emissions and Common Law Liability 61

The second issue can be dealt with more briefly. It concerns the question whether the standing requirements are the same for all applicants, and especially for affected individuals and industrial competitors. In relation to affected individuals, one problem is as follows. Although they may have a right that is infringed by, say, an authorisation from the Environment Agency for X to undertake prescribed process Y, they may not be able sufficiently to establish the merits of the case (which may require much technical detail) to be granted standing. The point was neatly captured by Otton J in the *Greenpeace* case when he considered the likely outcome of an application by either an employee of British Nuclear Fuels Ltd or an affected inhabitant of Cumbria. He said:

> [I]t is unlikely that either would be able to command the expertise which is at the disposal of Greenpeace. Consequently, a less well-informed challenge might be mounted which would stretch unnecessarily the court's resources and which would not afford the court the assistance it requires in order to do justice between the parties.[71]

His Lordship also doubted whether the Attorney-General could be persuaded to commence a relator action on an affected individual's behalf,[72] or whether a legally aided applicant should be granted standing for fear of leaving a successful respondent without "an effective remedy in costs".[73]

A further problem facing affected individuals is the extent to which the infringement of their private interests—*crucial* to a common law action—ought to play a part in the court's decision whether or not to grant standing. On the one hand, there is the radical view expressed by Sedley J in *R. v. Somerset Council ex p. Dixon*[74] that "public law is not at base about rights, even though abuses of power may and often do invade private rights". Rather, he thought, "it is about wrongs—that is to say misuses of public power".[75] On the other hand, there is the more citizen-friendly view of Popplewell J in *R. v. North Somerset District Council ex p. Garnett*[76] that would allow the rights of individuals to enter the equation so long as those interests were demonstrably greater than those of other members of the general public.

As regards industrial competitors—that is to say, those who wish to see that producer X meets the terms of his authorisation simply so that X's costs of production increase—it is equally doubtful that standing will be acquired.[77] Here, the problem is not one of compiling expert litigation, but rather one of showing *genuine* sufficient interest: the courts have long since declined to entertain

---

[71] [1994] 4 All ER 329, at 350f.
[72] For reasons, see Sir Karl Schiemann, "Locus Standi" [1990] *PL* 324, at 348–9.
[73] [1994] 4 All ER 329, at 350f–g.
[74] *Supra*, n.69.
[75] *Ibid.*, at 180.
[76] *Supra*, n.69.
[77] The difficulties faced by industrial competitors in acquiring *locus standi* may in part explain the fact that they are a significant source of information for the Agency in respect of those operating either without, or beyond the terms of, an official authorisation.

62 John Murphy

applications from those they have labelled "busybodies".[78] And even though the most recent case law on standing exhibits differences in approach to the question of standing, both the judges in *Garnett* and *Dixon* were resolute that busybodies should be excluded. In short, the competitor whose personal interests are not directly affected will nearly always fail to establish *locus standi*.[79]

In concluding this section, it is important to make clear that my concern is with environmental protection and with the doubt that surrounds the ability of judicial review to secure the same.[80] I am not, however, seeking to criticise the public law principles *per se*. The fact that there is a certain degree of obscurity in relation to the way in which questions of standing are intricately interwoven with the merits of a case is merely unhelpful for our purposes. I am not arguing that, while it would be more convenient for environmentalists if the merits and standing issues could be dealt with separately, it would be better in the general run of judicial review cases for them to be treated in that way. Indeed, concerning itself more broadly with the proper approach to public law, the House of Lords took quite the opposite view in the *Inland Revenue Commissioners* case.[81]

STRICT LIABILITY IN NUISANCE AND *RYLANDS* V. *FLETCHER*

Having established the various shortcomings in the draftsmanship of the environmental protection legislation and enforcement agency practice, and having adverted to the difficulties associated with obtaining environmental judicial review, it is clear that, at least potentially, an important (albeit different) role exists for the common law. Accordingly, the questions with which this section of the chapter deals centre on whether the current juridical foundations of private nuisance and the rule in *Rylands* v. *Fletcher* undermine their utility as environmental torts, or whether properly understood they are able to achieve their potential in this respect.

Probably the most important, if not (so far as nuisance is concerned) the most authoritative, judicial pronouncement on the nature of liability in *Rylands* and private nuisance is that of Lord Goff in *Cambridge Water Co. Ltd*

---

[78] See e.g., R. v. *Inland Revenue Commissioners ex p. National Federation of Self-employed and Small Businesses Ltd* [1982] AC 617, at 646 (*per* Lord Fraser). Note that while his Lordship used the term "busybodies", he failed to define them in any more clear terms than those with "the desire . . . to interfere in other people's business".

[79] Possible exceptions would be where there was great significance in vindicating the rule of law and/or immense intrinsic importance in the issue raised: see R. v. *Secretary of State for Foreign Affairs ex p. World Development Movement Ltd* [1995] 1 All ER 611, at 620 (*per* Rose LJ).

[80] Recognising this inability, Alder has argued that there may be "something to be said in favour of giving nature [i.e. an environmental interest] standing in its own right": Alder, *supra* n.69, at 187. See further, C. Stone, *Should Trees Have Standing and Other Essays in Law, Morals and the Environment* (New York, Oceana, 1996).

[81] *Supra*, n.67.

Noxious Emissions and Common Law Liability   63

v. *Eastern Counties Leather plc*.[82] There, his Lordship was of the view that liability under both torts was strict[83] so long as the loss or damage was of a kind that could reasonably be foreseen.[84] The means by which he reached this conclusion is a little perplexing and warrants closer examination. He said that "liability has been kept under control by the principle of reasonable user". He then added that:

> if the user is reasonable, the defendant will not be liable for harm to his neighbour's enjoyment of his land; but if the user is not reasonable, the defendant will be liable, *even though he may have exercised reasonable care and skill to avoid it*.[85]

The reason this *partly true* assertion[86] is consistent with strict liability in nuisance is simply this. The unreasonableness of the user is a cast-iron way of demonstrating that the interference caused is also unreasonable. But note that its accuracy is limited: it is true only to the extent that it insists that nuisance liability is associated with unreasonable interferences. And note also that an unreasonable user of land is merely *one* factor affecting the unreasonableness of the interference.[87] An otherwise reasonable use of land undertaken purely out of malice will also, for example, render unreasonable the interference thereby caused.[88] Put otherwise, in so far as it relates to the fact that nuisance is primarily concerned with eventualities—that is, with the infliction of certain forms of harm or inconvenience—Lord Goff's dictum is correct. Inherent in this, also, is the fact that private nuisance correctly understood is a tort of strict liability

---

[82] [1994] 1 All ER 53. Lords Templeman, Jauncey, Lowry and Woolf all delivered short speeches expressing their agreement with Lord Goff.

[83] *Ibid.*, at 70 (re nuisance) and 73 (re *Rylands*).

[84] See D. Wilkinson, "*Cambridge Water Company* v. *Eastern Counties Leather plc*: Diluting Liability for Continuing Escapes" (1994) 57 *MLR* 799.

[85] *Ibid.*, at 70j–71b (emphasis added).

[86] The statement is over-simplistic (and therefore inaccurate) in two respects. First, Lord Goff omits to mention that the unreasonable interference must also be a substantial one. The maxim *de minimis non curat lex* has long been recognised to be operational within the law of nuisance. In *Walter* v. *Selfe*, for example, Knight Bruce VC was forthright in requiring that the interference complained of must be "more than fanciful, more than one of mere delicacy or fastidiousness": (1851) 4 De G & Sm 315, at 322. The second inaccuracy inheres in the suggestion that a reasonable user will *never* give rise to nuisance liability. Apart from seeming to elevate the reasonable user test to the status of an inappropriate, fault-based criterion of liability, this statement is inconsistent with established authority. See *infra*.

[87] The full range of factors which affect the reasonableness of an interference (rather than the reasonableness of D's user) are discussed *in extenso* in M. Brazier and J. Murphy, *Street on Torts* (10th edn., London, Butterworths, 1999) ch. 19.

[88] *Christie* v. *Davey* [1893] 1 Ch. 316 and *Hollywood Silver Fox Farm Ltd* v. *Emmett* [1936] 2 KB 468 support such a contention. It is often thought that *Bradford Corporation* v. *Pickles* [1895] AC 587 is inconsistent with this view. The problem stems from the fact that Lord Macnaghten said there (at 601) that "it is the act, *not the motive* for the act, that must be regarded. If the act, apart from motive, gives rise merely to damage without *legal injury*, the motive, however reprehensible it may be, will not supply that element". This dictum is often interpreted to be a rebuttal of the relevance of motive. In fact it is not. It is merely an insistence that bad motive in the absence of significant harm—in his words, "legal injury"—will not give rise to liability. For the view that *Christie* v. *Davey* and the *Silver Fox* case are irreconcilable with the *Bradford* case see Cross, *supra* n.12, at 455.

64 John Murphy

because liability is harm-dependent rather than conduct-dependant.[89] I suggest that it is for this very reason that his Lordship deliberately appended the words I italicised in the passage quoted earlier.

What is unfortunate about Lord Goff's dictum, however, is that it appears to elevate to the status of necessary precondition the unreasonable user test. Were it the case, as Cross suggests, that it has become "a general prerequisite of liability in nuisance",[90] then nuisance liability would have become fault-based. But recall that these words were uttered in the context of an appeal which, by the time it reached the House of Lords, was confined to *Rylands* v. *Fletcher* liability alone. Accordingly, though what his Lordship had to say undoubtedly muddies the waters to some extent, it was still, strictly speaking, only obiter. Moreover, it was an obiter dictum that failed to conform with the orthodox juridical view. While it is true that any interference caused by an unreasonable user will, *ipso facto*, be unreasonable also, the converse is not true. Not all reasonable users of land confer immunity on the defendant. In *Sturges* v. *Bridgman*,[91] for example, the argument was not that it was *malum in se* for the defendant to have operated his pestle and mortar for the last 20 years. Instead, the contention was simply that since the plaintiff's new consulting room had been built, the interference to the plaintiff had become unreasonable; and the court was suitably persuaded by this.[92] The interference (*not the user*) had become so unreasonable as to fall outside the central "principle of give and take between neighbouring landowners".[93] According to Lord Goff's assertion, however, reasonable user and reasonable interference are co-terminus concepts, such that proof of the former ineluctably suffices to negate the imposition of liability. This is an inaccurate and regrettable over-simplification. What is worse is that, although Lord Goff was speaking obiter in the *Cambridge Water* case, a host of other judges before him, who had similarly made the assumption that there was an inevitability about the fact that a reasonable user could only give rise to a reasonable (and hence non-actionable) interference, were not.[94] Yet a moment's reflection should tell us that the operation of, say, a smelting works may well in some circumstances be a reasonable user of land which might nonetheless give rise to an actionable private nuisance.

A markedly different function from that served by the concept of unreasonable user in nuisance is performed by that of "non-natural user" in *Rylands* v. *Fletcher*. This latter, by contrast, *is* a threshold requirement of liability. In other

---

[89] For an interesting discussion of three distinct notions of strict liability within tort, based respectively on "conduct", "relationships" and "outcomes", see P. Cane, *The Anatomy of Tort Law* (Oxford, Hart Publishing, 1997) at 45–9.

[90] Cross, *supra* n.12, at 474.

[91] (1879) 11 Ch.D 852.

[92] See also *Home Brewery Co. Ltd* v. *William Davis & Co. (Leicester) Ltd* [1987] 1 QB 339 where it was held (a) that D's act in filling in an osier bed on his land was a reasonable user, but (b) that D was nonetheless liable to P in nuisance for the resulting flooding on P's land.

[93] *Cambridge Water Co. Ltd* v. *Eastern Counties Leather plc*, *supra* n.82, at 70, *per* Lord Goff.

[94] See, e.g., *per* Lord Selborne in *Gaunt* v. *Finney* (1872) 8 LR Ch. App. 8 at 12. See also Cross, *supra* n.12, at 448–51 for further examples.

Noxious Emissions and Common Law Liability 65

words, although liability may exist in nuisance even though the plaintiff cannot demonstrate an unreasonable user of the land, there can be no such liability under its sister tort—the rule in *Rylands* v. *Fletcher*—without showing a non-natural user of the land. Lord Goff was unequivocal when he stated:

> [t]he effect of this [natural user] principle is that, where it applies, there will be no liability under the rule in *Rylands* v. *Fletcher*; but . . . where it does not apply, *i.e.* where there is a non-natural use, the defendant will be liable for the harm caused to the plaintiff by the escape, notwithstanding that he has exercised all reasonable care and skill to prevent the escape from occurring.[95]

From what has been said so far in this section, it is clear that the concepts of "unreasonable user" and "non-natural use" are notionally, to some extent, related. Yet they are by no means "twins", and still less different ways of expressing the same idea. In truth, they are connected in only two ways. First, proof of either an unreasonable user or a non-natural use *may* assist a plaintiff seeking to sue, in nuisance or *Rylands* v. *Fletcher* respectively. Secondly, although proving their presence is *helpful* in both cases, in neither tort would doing so provide a *sufficient* basis of liability. The main distinction between the two concepts lies in the fact that while a non-natural user is an unavoidable precondition of liability in *Rylands*, the same is manifestly not true of an unreasonable user in nuisance.[96] As such, this casts doubt on Lord Goff's somewhat glib (and unsubstantiated) assertion that the concepts of unreasonable user and non-natural use enjoy a marked "similarity of function".[97] My suspicion is that this confusion is probably attributable to the fact that the two concepts can overlap in certain cases. The classic example occurs, of course, where the nuisance consists of an isolated injurious incident—for instance, where damage results from an explosion arising from a dangerous state of affairs on the defendant's land.[98] In such cases, the dangerous state of affairs on D's land may, at one and the same time, represent both an unreasonable user and non-natural use.

Considering the nature of the relationship between the notions of an unreasonable user and a non-natural use of land is a vital (if not novel) enterprise in order to appreciate not only the differences between *Rylands* v. *Fletcher* and private nuisance, but also just what constitutes the gist of a *Rylands* action. The *Cambridge Water* case presented the House of Lords with the first opportunity in many years to consider *directly* the basis of liability in *Rylands* v. *Fletcher*. Unfortunately, so far as the meaning of non-natural use is concerned, they did not take this opportunity. At a definitional level, the concept remains where it

---

[95] *Cambridge Water Co. Ltd* v. *Eastern Counties Leather plc, supra* n.82, at 71d–e.

[96] A second distinction is that the concept of non-natural user is necessarily broader than that of unreasonable user. A moment's reflection should tell us that a user could be unnatural (in the sense of being artificial) without necessarily being unreasonable. The example of the sewage works given earlier is equally apt in this context.

[97] *Cambridge Water Co. Ltd* v. *Eastern Counties Leather plc, supra* n.82, at 71d–e.

[98] See, e.g., *Midwood & Co.* v. *Manchester Corporation* [1905] 2 KB 697.

66   John Murphy

has always been: languishing in a cloak of obscurity.[99] In *Cambridge Water*, Lord Goff did no more than acknowledge the uncertainty of meaning afforded by the leading authority[100] before contenting himself by declaring:

> I do not think it is necessary for the purposes of the present case to attempt any redefinition of the concept of natural or ordinary use . . . I feel bound to say that the storage of chemicals on industrial premises should be regarded as an almost classic case of non-natural use; and I find it very difficult to think that it should be thought objectionable to impose strict liability for damage caused in the event of their escape.[101]

In similar vein, and without seeking to delimit the precise parameters of the concept of non-natural use, I would suggest that, measured according to any metric, environmentally polluting processes almost certainly constitute a non-natural land use. More importantly, having considered the function of the concepts of non-natural use and unreasonable user, I have sought to show that, at the level of juridical analysis, both private nuisance and *Rylands* v. *Fletcher* are torts of strict(er) liability. Having engaged in somewhat novel analysis to establish this familiar conclusion, what remains for me to do is to substantiate my central thesis that these two torts are, or could become, important complements to the regulatory regime considered earlier. It is simply not enough to assume, as many commentators do, that they are important environmental torts. Nor is it adequate merely to identify (as I have done thus far) that they *currently* have a role to play in the present state of the legislation and its enforcement. Instead, a fuller, instrumentalist account of their potential is needed. Depending on how effective a function they serve (compared with regulation) it may well be that the current gaps in the statutory framework ought better to be plugged, not by common law torts, but by yet more expansive legislation. Put otherwise, all we have so far done is identify the present role of these torts. The remaining issue is why, in contrast to other options—such as more rigorous Agency enforcement policy—they ought, as environmental torts, to be prevented from lapsing into desuetude.

The case for their retention is made in two stages. First, I consider certain distinctive advantages, for the purposes of environmental protection, that do, or foreseeably will or could, attach to a civil action in private nuisance or *Rylands* v. *Fletcher*. Secondly, and in the penultimate section of this chapter, I examine from a lawyer-economist perspective whether there ought to be a place for environmental torts in the shadow of a (purportedly) comprehensive regulatory web.

---

[99] For a useful (if somewhat dated) attempt to demystify us as to its meaning see D.W. Williams, "Non-Natural Use of Land" [1973] *CLJ* 310.

[100] Lord Moulton's famous speech in *Rickards* v. *Lothian* [1913] AC 263 is the nearest the decided cases have ever brought us to a definition of what constitutes a non-natural use of land. There, he said (at 280), "[i]t is not every use to which land is put that brings into play that principle. It must be some special use bringing with it increased danger to others, and must not merely be the ordinary use of the land or such a use as is proper for the general benefit of the community"; hardly a paragon of definitional clarity.

[101] *Ibid.*, at 79f–h.

DISTINCTIVE FEATURES OF A TORT ACTION

In this section of the chapter I consider three features of nuisance and *Rylands* actions that, over and above those already identified here and elsewhere,[102] might go a long way to clinching the argument that tort has a distinctive and valuable role to play in the protection of the environment. The first two derive from the reforms to Legal Aid provision,[103] which came into force in July 1999.[104] The third currently exists only at the level of tort theory: it is that the deterrent effect of private nuisance and *Rylands* should be enhanced by making punitive damages available for both torts. I shall argue that this can be achieved without doing violence to widely accepted foundations of tort law.

The Move Towards Conditional Fee Arrangements

The general tenor of the 1999 Legal Aid reforms is to replace Legal Aid for most damages and money actions with conditional fee arrangements.[105] Under such arrangements the plaintiff pays anything up to the full amount of a solicitor's normal bill, but only if the case is won. If it is lost, he pays nothing (except perhaps, disbursements). The fact that an impecunious plaintiff might not be eligible for Legal Aid should not, therefore, deter him from litigating under such an arrangement for he has little, if anything, to lose. In consequence, such arrangements will (in theory) enable plaintiffs of limited means, for the first time, to sue industrial polluters thereby increasing the potential to hold such entities to account in respect of unauthorised emissions.

Notwithstanding this important development in civil litigation, it is essential to sound a cautionary note as to its *practical* limitations. In short, solicitors will probably be wary of undertaking such actions against wealthy industrial corporations where technical or scientific problems associated with proof of damage or causation arise.[106] In such cases, there is little comfort to be derived in knowing that no personal outlay or expense is called for where a willing firm of solicitors

---

[102] See principally section 2 *supra*, and Steele, *supra* n.16.

[103] For a thoroughgoing account of these reforms, see M. Zander, "The Government's Plans on Legal Aid and Conditional Fees" (1998) 61 *MLR* 538.

[104] Conditional Fee Agreements Order 1998 (SI 1998 No. 1860). This extension of the ambit of conditional fee arrangements will be taken a stage further when the Access to Justice Act 1999 enters into force. By inserting a new s. 58A into the Courts and Legal Services Act 1990 such costs arrangements will be allowed in respect of all but family and criminal proceedings (other than actions for statutory nuisance under s. 82 of the Environmental Protection Act 1990).

[105] See *Access to Justice with Conditional Fees* (London, Lord Chancellor's Department, 1998) esp. paras. 3.23ff.; A. Tunkel, "Improving Access to Justice" (1997) 147 *NLJ* 1785, (1998) 148 *NLJ* 88, at 245 and 301.

[106] See, e.g., *Graham* v. *Re Chem International Ltd* [1996] Env. LR 158. In that case, Poly Halogenated Aromatic Hydrocarbons (PHAHs) emitted from a hazardous waste incinerator were alleged to have contaminated P's herd. About 90% of the judgment deals with the question of causation and the emission levels that would be required to cause the harm complained of.

68 John Murphy

cannot be found. On the other hand, all is not necessarily lost in such instances, for a second plank of the government's reforms might yet avail the plaintiff: the specially designated public interest fund.

Public Interest Litigation

One of the most welcome features of the Legal Aid reforms is the establishment of a public interest fund which makes available Legal Aid in cases where the plaintiff can establish that it is in the public interest that the case be litigated. Such monies are to be made available even though the plaintiff fails to obtain Legal Aid on the basis of the merits test, and despite the fact that his likely costs will outweigh any potential damages he might receive. Lord Irvine, the Lord Chancellor, explained the rationale underlying this element of the government's Legal Aid plans thus: "[i]n seeking reform of the Legal Aid system, I intend to focus it sharply on cases involving the social welfare of disadvantaged citizens and cases that raise the wider public interest".[107] More specifically, the criterion according to which the public interest was to be gauged for these purposes was adverted to in the Consultation Paper, *Access to Justice with Conditional Fees*,[108] in the following terms: "a case would have to demonstrate the potential to produce tangible benefits for a significant number of people in a definable category".[109]

This statement reveals that the primary function of the fund is to cover the cost of mounting test cases, in all probability, on novel or complex points of law. However, its sentiment is also capable of embracing industrial (as opposed to domestic) nuisance cases. Indeed, the Consultation Paper specifically mentioned its potential use in a case involving the pollution of a water supply.[110] Presumably, it would be equally available in respect of complaints based on air (and land) pollution caused by emissions from an industrial plant.[111]

As regards both the general shift towards conditional fee arrangements and the specific introduction of a public interest fund, the government's Legal Aid reforms have the capacity to allow a common law action to be brought where, formerly, the impecuniosity of the plaintiff would have been prohibitive of such litigation. And in particular, the availability of the public interest fund will be useful where establishing the harm caused by an industrial polluter would involve very high costs associated with necessary investigative work and acquiring expert evidence.[112] Though affected individuals might have a direct interest

---

[107] HL Debs., vol. 584, col. 43, 9 December 1997.

[108] *Supra*, n.105.

[109] *Ibid.*, at para. 3.32.

[110] *Ibid.*

[111] Such as the inhabitants of Clitheroe in Lancashire who have for years complained about the respiratory problems caused by the local cement factory.

[112] It is such costs that were fatal to the real-life case behind Harr's *A Civil Action*: see Harr, *supra* n.17.

for the purposes of seeking judicial review, the inability to compile a well-informed application (precisely because of these costs) might well, as we have already seen, prove fatal to any attempt to acquire standing.[113] As such, the private law action places the individual citizen in a stronger position to secure (albeit indirectly) a public good not achievable by an interest group or industrial competitor. Furthermore, the availability of injunctions in nuisance law will merely accentuate the utility of the civil law; for, more so than the threat of further damages, they help to secure the cessation of unauthorised polluting processes. In terms of deterring would-be polluters before any noxious emissions have been released, however, it is necessary to the consider the third potentially helpful feature of a tort action.

Punitive Damages in Nuisance and *Rylands* v. *Fletcher*?

It is most unlikely that a nuisance occasioning limited harm to only one impecunious plaintiff would entail sufficient public interest to warrant financial backing from the Legal Aid public interest fund. It is equally unlikely—because the amount of compensatory damages would be only small—that many solicitors would be willing to undertake the case on a conditional fee basis. In simple terms, to do so would be to risk more than there would be to gain. Indeed, there might be no guarantee that the lawyer's *usual* costs for the amount of work entailed could be guaranteed. What might, however, persuade the solicitor to take on such a case would be the availability of punitive damages in either private nuisance or *Rylands* v. *Fletcher*. The amount awarded by way of punitive damages might supply the requisite financial incentive for the lawyer to accept the case. If this were so, would-be polluters would be faced by a significant, additional disincintive to cause or risk pollution.

We must now explore whether there are any objections in principle to such damages being payable in appropriate nuisance and *Rylands* cases.

There are three possible objections to awarding exemplary damages in private nuisance and *Rylands*. The first is quite simply that there is no precedent for so doing. Nonetheless, I would argue that this objection is of little real substance on the footing that industrial pollution would seem to fall squarely within the second of the three recognised classes of case (identified by Lord Devlin in *Rookes* v. *Barnard*[114]) wherein such damages may be awarded. His Lordship thought such damages to be an acceptable exception to the general rule against "punishment" within tort:

---

[113] Of course, a complaint to the Environment Agency would remain an option. But on the strength of current enforcement policy, this may yield little.

[114] [1964] 1 All ER 367. The three classes of case are: (1) oppressive, arbitrary or unconstitutional conduct by government servants; (2) tortious acts designed to profit the defendant because the (compensatory) damages payable to the plaintiff will be smaller in amount than the defendant's profit; (3) where there is statutory authority for such punitive damages.

70   *John Murphy*

> [Where] the defendant's conduct has been calculated by him to make a profit for himself which may well exceed the compensation payable to the plaintiff. . . . Where a defendant with a cynical disregard for a plaintiff's rights has calculated that the money to made out of his wrongdoing will probably exceed the damages at risk.[115]

The second reason to doubt whether nuisance cases can accommodate awards of punitive damages, at least in the current state of English law,[116] stems from the Court of Appeal decision in *AB* v. *South West Water Services Ltd.*[117] There, the defendants had accidentally polluted a drinking water supply with aluminium phosphate, and had deliberately misled customers as to the wholesomeness of the water by issuing circulars declaring it to be of the right alkalinity and safe to use and drink. For two reasons the Court of Appeal refused to grant the plaintiffs exemplary damages in their action for public nuisance. First, it was held that there was a crucial difference between seeking to gain from the commission of a tort and attempting (by issuing false information) to restrict the amount they might have to pay in compensation. As Stuart-Smith LJ put it, "[an attempt] to limit the amount payable in damages to the victim . . . is an entirely different concept to that involved in the second [*Rookes* v. *Barnard*] category [of deliberately seeking to gain financially by the commission of a tort]".[118] The second reason the Court of Appeal refused to grant exemplary damages to the plaintiffs in that case was captured most succinctly in the judgment of Sir Thomas Bingham MR. He said:

> in the case of a *public nuisance* affecting hundreds or even thousands of plaintiffs, how can the court assess the sum of exemplary damages to be awarded to any one of them to punish or deter the defendant without knowing at the outset the number of successful plaintiffs and the approximate size of the total bill for exemplary damages which the defendant must meet.[119]

It is my contention that neither of the reasons given for the refusal of exemplary damages in the *South West Water* case need necessarily apply to an action in *private* nuisance or *Rylands* v. *Fletcher*. The first concerned what their Lordships considered to be a vital difference between loss-minimising conduct on the one hand, and gain-seeking conduct on the other. The second objection was confined, by definition, to *public* nuisance cases. Recalling the hypothetical of an industrial polluter who, in the course of business, causes limited damage to only one or a very few plaintiffs, it is clear that the *South West Water* case can be distinguished on both counts. As such, the decision should not necessarily be seen as prohibitive of awards of exemplary damages in private nuisance or *Rylands*. The crucial matters for the purposes of Lord Devlin's second category

---

[115] *Ibid.*
[116] For a thoroughgoing review of whether such damages ought to have any role at all in English tort law see Law Commission Consultation Paper No. 132, *Aggravated, Exemplary and Restitutionary Damages* (London, HMSO, 1993).
[117] [1993] 1 All ER 609.
[118] *Ibid.*, at 623.
[119] *Ibid.*, at 627, emphasis added.

are whether there are a finite number of plaintiffs—who are generally easier to identify in private nuisance cases—and whether the defendant was engaged in deliberate, tortious, gain-seeking conduct. It should, in principle, be of no moment that the action happens to be framed in private nuisance or *Rylands* v. *Fletcher*. Indeed, recognising just this point, Peter Cane has gone so far as to argue that even the tort of negligence should allow awards of exemplary damages if these criteria are met.[120] In sum, it is by no means settled that following the *South West Water* case "the tort of nuisance is unlikely . . . to play a greater rôle in the regulation of the environment".[121] If there is any truth at all in this remark, it holds only for cases involving *public* nuisance affecting a very large class of Her Majesty's subjects.

The final objection to granting exemplary damages in nuisance and *Rylands* stems from a more fundamental concern to keep punitive damages out of the law of tort altogether. The argument derives from the belief that the punishment of wrongdoers should be the sole preserve of the criminal law. For proponents of this line of argument, all three of the exceptional categories recognised in *Rookes* v. *Barnard* are equally untenable and anomalous. While there is much force in this argument, it should be noted that the Law Commission was ultimately unpersuaded that English tort law ought not, on occasion, to make exemplary damages awards.[122] As such, rightly or wrongly, punitive damages will probably remain a part of English tort law. That being the case, I would contend that, given the accepted bases for such damages, it would be more anomalous in the current state of the law to allow a plaintiff exemplary damages in a defamation case (where only his reputation is harmed),[123] but deny him the same in a nuisance action (where perhaps his home or health has been harmed).

The Comparative Efficiency of Common Law's Environmental Protection

So far in this chapter I have attempted to identify a valuable and unique potential role for the common law in the protection of the environment. Whether this role ought wholeheartedly to be welcomed, however, depends in significant measure on its comparative efficiency. If greater regulation that was actively policed were a more efficient means of controlling atmospheric pollution, then despite the fact that a strong case can ostensibly be made for tort's residual role, it ought ultimately to be rejected in favour of a tightening in the regulatory web. It is, then, with the comaparitive efficiency of tort that this penultimate section of the chapter is concerned.

---

[120] P. Cane, *The Anatomy of Tort Law* (Oxford, Hart Publishing, 1997) at 132–3.

[121] E. McKendrick, "Public Nuisance and the Environment" (1993) 1 *TLR* 14, at 17.

[122] The most succinct account of the various arguments for and against the abolition of exemplary damages in tort are to be found in Law Commission Consultation Paper 132, *supra* n.116, at paras. 5.1–5.38.

[123] See, e.g., *Cassell* v. *Broome* [1972] AC 1027.

72 John Murphy

How ought we to assess the efficiency of nuisance and *Rylands*? Ogus and Richardson, in their seminal study of whether nuisance provides an efficient means of protecting the environment, suggested that:

> At the general level "efficient" outcomes are those in which given increases in individuals' welfare are obtained at the least cost to society, or alternatively [those in which] a given quantity of resources is utilised in such a way as to maximise the welfare which society derives from it.[124]

To illustrate the point, let us apply their proposition to the facts of *Hunter* v. *Canary Wharf Ltd.*[125] In that case, the construction by the defendants of a huge tower caused a temporary interference to the plaintiff's television reception. At the level of corrective justice, the issue was one about competing rights: the right to construct buildings on one's own land *versus* the (alleged) right to undisturbed television viewing. But their Lordships, naturally enough, recognised that the case involved more than an acute legalistic issue; that it also bore important implications for distributive justice. Lord Hoffmann captured the point when he observed that "[t]he plaintiffs may well feel that their personal convenience was temporarily sacrificed to the national interest".[126] Expressed in terms of economic analysis, this becomes "the loss of the (alleged) right to uninterrupted television viewing represents a lesser cost to society than the non-regeneration of the London Docklands area".

Clearly, the decision in *Hunter* that the defendants were not liable accords with the economic goal of wealth maximisation. But this is not to say that all nuisance decisions are economically efficient. The law of private nuisance is essentially concerned with whether a recognised right on P's part has been subjected to an unreasonable interference for which D is responsible. Whether D's enterprise was of any social utility is not, *per se*, a defence to a suit in nuisance. It is merely one factor that must be considered in assessing whether the interference suffered by P was unreasonable or not.[127] Accordingly, it is clear that the existing law of nuisance is not especially geared to the performance of lawyer-economists' functionalist goals (though, on occasion, it may well do so incidentally). The same is true of *Rylands* v. *Fletcher*, for its gist is a formula that embraces competing *private* interests: if A brings onto his land and keeps and collects there something etc etc. which causes loss to B, then A is liable to B. Again, the fact that *Rylands* is not especially designed to serve instrumentalist

---

[124] A.I. Ogus and G.M. Richardson, "Economics and the Environment: A Study of Private Nuisance" [1977] *CLJ* 284, at 285.

[125] [1997] 2 All ER 426.

[126] *Ibid.*, at 455f.

[127] In *Harrison* v. *Southwark and Vauxhall Motor Co.* [1891] 2 Ch. 409 the useful nature of the defendants' construction work was part of the reason the plaintiff's action was dismissed. On the other hand, in *Andreae* v. *Selfridge & Co. Ltd* socially useful building work which interfered with the comfortable enjoyment of a neighbour's hotel was held to be a nuisance: [1938] Ch. 1. In *Rylands* v. *Fletcher* cases, too, the social utility of D's activities will be relevant to, but not determinative of, liability: compare *Rainham Chemical Works Ltd* v. *Belvedere Fish Guano Co.* [1921] 2 AC 465 and *Read* v. *J. Lyons & Co. Ltd* [1947] AC 156.

ends does not mean that it never will. The point is merely that when it does fulfil such goals, it does so more by accident than by design.

There are three further factors that might be thought to undermine the economic efficiency of these torts in terms of protecting the environment. First, there is the assumption that the damage in respect of which actions are brought necessarily entails environmental damage. It is true that an injunction in nuisance that prevents D from continuing a polluting process that affects P's crops will also have a beneficial environmental effect, but this is only because the damage to P's crops and the damage to the environment are, on these facts, co-extensive. They need not necessarily overlap in this way, however. If P's complaint is that D's polluting process is excessively noisy, then a nuisance action will be useless for environmental purposes because it may only result in an injunction that forces D to continue his industrial process more quietly. It need not mean that he must stop causing pollution.

Secondly, in cases where damages are sought—and this is especially the case in relation to one-off escapes that characterise a *Rylands* action—those damages might secure a common law remedy but no environmental remediation.[128] Returning to the example just given, compensation for damage to P's crops will not take into account the contribution to the erosion of the ozone layer also caused. Thirdly, there is also the assumption that the individual concerned will know of his legal rights and be prepared to sue in respect of their infringement. This assumption may well be unrealistic.[129]

To summarise, in this section I have identified four reasons why the torts of private nuisance and *Rylands* v. *Fletcher* are not especially economically efficient in their residual role in protecting the environment: when they do provide such protection—which is not always—they do so more by accident than design; injunctions that are awarded to prevent D causing certain forms of amenity nuisance (such as noise disturbance) in no way guarantee the discontinuation of any incidental environmental damage; damages awarded for these torts do not ensure any degree of remediation; their success depends on individuals being aware of their legal rights and being prepared to litigate. Ostensibly then, although I have been able to demarcate a clear and unique role for the common law, it might ultimately be rejected on the basis that it is too inefficient in fulfilling its potential. However, before we opt wholesale for the adoption of more extensive regulatory regime, we need to assess two things: the relative weight of these difficulties and whether the "greater regulation" option would be any more efficient in relation to the four problems identified.

As regards the first of these difficulties—that the common law is rather hit-and-miss in terms of dealing with cases that pose a threat to the environment—it should be noted that the new Legal Aid reforms may go a long way to remedying the problem. Of course, if an individual were sufficiently affluent not to need to rely on Legal Aid, he would almost certainly be wary of committing

---

[128] See Department of the Environment, *supra* n.10.
[129] See Ogus and Richardson, *supra* n.124, at 324.

74   John Murphy

huge sums of money to a civil action that involved a trivial interference with the enjoyment of his land. However, we might reasonably assume, I think, that he may be prepared to litigate in respect of more serious interferences such as contamination of land or the emission of poisonous fumes. In such cases, where the interference is more serious, there is also likely to be an accompanying deleterious environmental dimension. Thus, it might be said that wealthy citizens are more likely to litigate in respect of nuisances that simultaneously carry an environmental concern.

Similarly, as we saw earlier, a solicitor will be more likely to accept a case on behalf of an impecunious plaintiff where, the case involves non-trivial harm. And finally, backing from the new public interest fund will require "serious" cases which, apart from centring on the individual's private interest, also entail broader environmental concerns. In short, the economic exigencies of litigation will help greatly to eradicate the potential hit-and-miss aspect of tort law in terms of its ability to secure environmental protection.

The last three objections can be taken together, for corresponding criticisms could be made, in each case, and with equal if not greater force, in relation to the current regulatory regime. Injunctions, it is true, do not guarantee the discontinuance of environmental damage. But then neither do the enforcement records of the Environment Agency and local authorities. While common law damages do not ensure any degree of remediation, nor do penalties or authorisations (based on BATNEEC principles)[130] issued by the Environment Agency. Finally, in relation to the fact that the common law depends on the plaintiff being both aware of his legal rights and willing to sue, it is equally the case that the regulatory system depends on both the Environment Agency and local authorities being informed of "offenders" and then being prepared to put a stop to them. Put succinctly, while the common law is far from a model of regulatory efficiency, precisely the same criticism can be made of the statutory system (at least, as it currently stands).

CONCLUSION

As things stand, the consolidation of regulatory functions in the Environment Agency represents, at best, a good start. The statutory system, as I have identified, is not without significant lacunae: some are attributable to draftsmanship while others are a product of the manner in which it is administered in practice. So long as such problems continue to exist, there will be an important residual role for the common law in protecting the environment. In vindicating an individual's private law rights by publicly censuring the injurious effects of D's industrial process, tort law provides a valuable disincentive to engage in that process in the first place.[131] If, as I have argued, punitive damages were to be

---

[130] See *supra*, n.37.
[131] See A. Linden, "Tort Law as Ombudsman" (1973) 51 *Can. Bar Rev.* 155.

made available in private nuisance and *Rylands* v. *Fletcher* cases, this deterrent effect could be significantly augmented. Furthermore, the recent Legal Aid reforms—particularly the creation of a public interest fund—should, in environmentally important cases, help to make the common law's potential in this context more of a practical reality than a theoretical possibility.

On the other hand, tort could never entirely fill the gaps that exist in the present regulatory web. Nor should it aspire so to do. The common law is, primarily, a means of ensuring corrective justice:[132] it is largely backward-looking in that it operates to make available to A a legal remedy for the harms he has suffered that were caused by B.[133] A system of regulation, by contrast, is necessarily prescriptive and therefore forward-looking in nature. In view of these essentially different functions, it would be foolish to leave it to tort law to make up for the shortcomings in the regulatory web. Much more important, in practical terms, than the proper realisation of common law's potential is a more comprehensive statutory system coupled with a more rigorous (environmentally conscious) attitude towards policing it. Only where cases continue to fall outside a more tightly-drawn statutory framework[134] should we exploit the corrective potential of tort law. On the other hand, it would be remiss not to explore and maximise this potential. If this chapter has gone some way to doing that, it has served its purpose.

POST-SCRIPT

While undergraduate programmes in environmental law are now both commonplace and popular, there remains, yet, a comparative paucity of textbooks on the subject. Perhaps the best explanation of why this is so is that writing such volumes is rather like painting the Forth Bridge. Pockets of the law change so frequently (if only marginally) that presenting an up-to-date account of the whole is virtually impossible. Even in the context of this comparatively modest and self-contained chapter, this developmental tendency has been felt. Between the date of writing and the date on which I received the proofs for this chapter, the regulatory framework for IPC was supplemented by the passing of the Pollution Prevention and Control Act 1999 which was designed to give effect to the Integrated Pollution Prevention and Control Directive.[135] However,

---

[132] See E. Weinrib, *The Idea of Private Law* (Cambridge, Mass., Harvard University Press, 1995) and *idem*, "Understanding Tort Law" (1989) 23 *Val. Univ. Law Rev.* 485.

[133] On the other, forward-looking functions of tort see, e.g., G. Calabresi, *The Cost of Accidents: A Legal and Economic Analysis* (New Haven, Conn., and London, Yale University Press, 1970) esp. at 291–308.

[134] It would be both unrealistic and undesirable to put in place legislation that covered every airborne emission. For example, so to do might mean setting (meaningless) emission levels for every private household that wanted to celebrate on 5 November with a small bonfire. For reasons of common sense and practicability, regulation to such an extent ought not to be countenanced.

[135] Directive 96/61 [1996] OJ L 257.

76 John Murphy

although the new Act and the Regulations made thereunder will go much further than the existing IPC regime, it is clear that, once they come into force—which will be gradually, over the next seven years—they will only regulate large-scale installations and processes such as the energy industry, the production and processing of metals and the chemical and mineral industries.[136] As such, despite the new provisions in the Directive, the thesis advanced in this chapter—that tort law has an important interstitial role to play in this context—remains largely unaffected.

[136] See "Draft IPPC regulations set out implementation timetable' [1999] *Ends Report* 288.

4

From the Individual to the Environmental: Tort Law in Turbulence

R. G. LEE

INTRODUCTION

THE EU WHITE Paper on Environmental Liability posits a new regime described as a "restricted" form of strict liability, to remedy environmental damage.[1] In this context "environmental damage" will include property damage, death and personal injury and even damage to the unowned environment caused in the future by dangerous activities—largely those already regulated by EU environmental law. If implemented,[2] the new regime will have profound effects upon both English common law and present civil process. For example, there are likely to be increased rights for common interest groups to bring proceedings not merely in public law,[3] but also to intervene by bringing private law actions to restrict and/or remedy environmental damage. Essential elements of our tort law system will change. Thus, it is suggested that it may be sufficient for a plaintiff to point to a source of environmental damage and the type of injury likely to be triggered by that source in order to show a plausible causality. At that point the burden may shift to the defendant to rebut this presumption of causation.

This chapter does not intend to describe, or indeed, to critique the content

[1] The EU White Paper on Environmental Liability dated 9 February 2000; for a review of its content at draft stage see V.A. Jenkins, "Environmental Impairment Liability in Europe" [1999] *JBL* 378.

[2] On 13/14 December 1999, Environmental Commissioner, Margot Wallström announced that an important initiative for the year 2000 would be progress on the White Paper on Environmental Liability. It was published in February 2000.

[3] The standing of interest groups in public law has improved remarkably within the last 10 years from a low watermark of *R. v. Secretary of State for the Environment ex p. Rose Theatre Trust* [1990] 1 All ER 754, especially following the judgment of Otton J in *R. v. Her Majesty's Inspectorate of Pollution ex p. Greenpeace (No 2)* [1994] 4 All ER 329. Most recently see the position advocated by Sedley J (as he then was) in *R. v. Somerset County Council ex p. Dixon* [1998] Env. LR 111 to the effect that a person with no particular stake in an issue might have standing to call attention to the misuse of power, without being a mere meddler. This was said to be especially true where the result of the wrong was an impact upon the natural environment.

78   R. G. Lee

of the White Paper. Rather, it seeks to place this type of development within a society in which one faces increased uncertainty about the realm of the environmental and the appropriate responses to the risk thrown up in the midst of environmental change. The White Paper represents a step (no more than that) on a difficult journey. It is a necessary step, though not necessarily in the right direction. This is because it constitutes a significant move from a perception of tort law as a mechanism for compensating individual incidents of misfortune, to one in which we begin to understand the prevalence of environmental risk, demonstrate concern at environmental impairment and to seek desperately to produce some rational response. It will be argued that such a response is not forthcoming in modern tort law.

TORT LAW AND CORRECTIVE JUSTICE

Take a simple compensation claim, a workplace injury. The bilateral nature of this type of claim is instantly recognisable to the law undergraduate. It involves a claimant and a defendant; a victim and a tortfeasor. Note, however, that underpinning this bilateral relationship are certain implicit assumptions. We envisage a single injury to an unfortunate victim; by an employer not engaged in the wholesale injury of the workforce, but who, in this particular instance, fell short of the care ordinarily required (and which, it is implicitly assumed, the employer ordinarily exercises). There are strong elements of corrective justice. Thus, Rosenburg would argue that such a framework seeks to assert the individual entitlements to personal security, and to preserve individual autonomy against infringement by the tortfeasor.[4] Indeed the claim to compensation rests upon a claim that a requisite standard has been breached, and that this is out of line with established practice. This is true to the point that providing the alleged tortfeasor can demonstrate conduct which fell within that ordinarily exercised by a person of a similar calling,[5] then, however horrendous the injury of the victim, no compensation is demanded from the defendant.

It is only in the breach of what is essentially a social rule that the claim will crystallise, and only then if damage befalls the unfortunate claimant, where it can be demonstrated that it was the breach which caused the damage. Thus the starting assumption is that whatever the vicissitudes of life, disease and disability are not generally the consequences of the action of another. Where this can be shown to be otherwise, because a social rule is broken, compensation may follow. However the attribution of responsibility for serious injury to another person is not to be taken lightly, so that proof of causation is a significant barrier. That the barrier is higher still in the "beyond reasonable doubt" standard

---

[4] D. Rosenberg, "The Causal Connection in Mass Exposure Claims: A 'Public Law' Vision of the Tort Law System" (1984) 97 *Harvard L Rev.* 851.

[5] Notoriously through the *Bolam* principle: see *Bolam* v. *Friern Hospital Management Committee* [1957] 2 All ER 118.

From the Individual to the Environmental: Tort Law in Turbulence   79

of criminal law serves only to reinforce the driving force of the underpinning social roles and background notions of personal responsibility.

Notice, also, that the inquiry centres upon whether it was the defendant who was to blame for the actions that caused the injury rather than on a more open-ended investigation into what was the cause. This may be in part because we intuitively know that there are a very wide variety of factors which may contribute, also, to the accident which has become the centre of the law's scrutiny. But these are ruled out in favour of an operative cause involving human activity. Yet, not all human activity breaching the standards set will attract liability. As Cane observes,[6] "luck" or factors outside the tortfeasor's control may play a part. This is not merely because the action of the defendant does not, or cannot be shown to, cause harm but also because conduct may have caused harm ruled unforeseeable. Cane argues that tort law draws a line "in terms of the foreseeable and the unforeseeable, the normal and the abnormal, the reasonable and the unreasonable".[7]

To take an illustration from an environmental claim, in *Cambridge Water Co.* v. *Eastern Counties Leather plc*,[8] Eastern Counties Leather was found at trial to have caused, in fact, the contamination by solvents of the aquifer owned by Cambridge Water Company. But the tannery was held not to be liable by the House of Lords. This was the consequence of the judgment of Lord Goff, who asserted the necessity of foreseeability of damage within the rule in *Rylands* v. *Fletcher*.[9] At trial, and in relation to claims in nuisance and negligence, the damage arising from operational spills had been ruled unforeseeable. It is worth noting that Lord Goff accepts that some harm might result from the spillage: "somebody might have been overcome from fumes from a spillage of a significant quantity".[10] However, the particular harm ("that solvent would enter the aquifer or that, having done so, detectable quantities would be found down catchment") was thought unforeseeable, or, even if it was foreseeable, the extent of the damage ("that such quantities would produce any sensible effect on the water")[11] certainly was not.

Lines are drawn, in Cane's terms, with some vigour here. Lord Goff argues for the right to draw such lines in what many had regarded as the strict liability regime of *Rylands* v. *Fletcher*. His Lordship does so by appeal to the very language of Blackburn J in that case, the "general tenor of his statement of principle" being that "knowledge, or at least foreseeability of risk is a pre-requisite of

---

[6] P. Cane, *The Anatomy of Tort Law* (Oxford, Hart Publishing, 1997) at 170.

[7] *Ibid.*, at 178.

[8] [1994] 2 WLR 53.

[9] (1868) LR 3 HL 330.

[10] *Supra*, n.8 at 69. Ironically this now seems to have come about. Barlow, Lyde and Gilbert acted for Cambridge Water Company in this case and now report that a £150,000 study by the Environment Agency into the perchloroethylene (PCE) contamination surrounding the tannery has revealed hot spots of PCE rising through the gravels and affecting some 60 nearby homes—see *BLG Pollution and Environmental Risk Digest*, Issue 33, Summer 1999.

[11] [1994] 2 WLR 69.

80 R. G. Lee

the recovery of damages under the principle".[12] But, as Lord Goff himself acknowledges, risks do attach to the accumulation of solvents. It is not foreseeability of risk that poses the problem for the House of Lords in *Cambridge Water* but foreseeability of damage. Once risk is foreseen, then what Blackburn J advocates, surely, is that. whatever the particular consequences, liability ought to follow.

There is a distinction, then, between foreseeability of risk (which is at the heart of Blackburn J's judgment in *Rylands* v. *Fletcher*) and foreseeability of damage (which is the primary focus of Lord Goff's speech in *Cambridge Water*).[13] While Lord Goff might insist that the rule in *Rylands* v. *Fletcher* remains a strict liability principle (in that, once it can be shown that foreseeable damage resulted, notwithstanding the care taken by the operator, liability will follow) the truth is rather different. The incorporation of a requirement for foreseeable damage into the law of *Rylands* v. *Fletcher* dilutes the strict liability principle by allowing the controlling mechanism to cater for those incidents thought abnormal in Cane's terms.

This leads in a very different direction from that of the EU White Paper, and it is worth reflecting what is a stake here. In order to do so, it is necessary to return to Cane's notion of luck and to his description of how the traditional, bilateral, corrective justice of the law of tort works:

> The basic underlying idea is that human agents must take as they find in the world in which their conduct occurs and takes effect (including other agents and their conduct) except to the extent that the world exhibits features which are considered unforeseeable, abnormal or unreasonable.[14]

TOXIC TORTS

So we see an attempt to ring-fence that which is normal, reasonable, foreseeable as the domain of tort law compensation, and to exclude other elements of misfortune outside this category. The fencing is not always neat and, from time to time, the boundaries may need to be re-aligned. Nor is foreseeability the only fencing post. Other props can be used, especially in terms of defining the duty relationship and the right to bring an action, as illustrated by another decision of the House of Lords concerning environmental impacts—*Hunter* v. *London Docklands Development Corporation*.[15] Nonetheless the assumption is that the fencing can be maintained and the encroachment of whatever evil lurks outside prevented—whether this be the spectre of uninsurable loss or the ghost of long-tail historic liabilities.

---

[12] *Ibid.*, at 77.

[13] This distinction is at the heart of an earlier House of Lords' decision in *Hughes* v. *Lord Advocate* [1963] AC 837 (which does not seem to have been cited in argument in *Cambridge Water*); and see also *The Trecarrell* [1973] 1 Lloyd's Rep. 402.

[14] Cane, *supra* n.6, at 178.

[15] [1997] AC 655. This case is considered further below at n.42.

From the Individual to the Environmental: Tort Law in Turbulence 81

However there is much in here that is premised on the notion that we can isolate and judge particular events and allocate blame to a specific individual in accordance with legal classifications surrounding what is regarded as accidental. Suppose, however, that in risk society[16] there exists the potential for widespread health impairment arising out of environmental disorder. Just as no single claimant may claim injury over and above other members of the group, so, too, identifying a single defendant to bear responsibility may become problematic. The pervasive nature of environmental risk, and indeed society's own understanding of the realm of the environmental open out to contest the attribution of blame to a dominant cause and the isolation of a responsible party to compensate the innocent victim. And this is true from both sides. Just as it is more difficult to establish a causal link between individual action and ecological damage, because we are increasingly complicit in our tolerance of such damage, it is hard too to define the victim.

In addition the clear cause-in-fact links between the tortfeasor and the victim disappear. There may be little physical or temporal link between an activity (changing the feed for cattle) and its alleged effect (the onset of CJD). In contrast to the conventional tort cases of slipping and tripping or motor vehicle crashes, the disjunctive nature of incident and effect complicates the imposition of liability in any number of ways. Many toxic tort cases involve the creation of a causal link. It is no accident that the *Cambridge Water* case is set in a rural environment in which the claimant could narrow down the likely proximate users of organochlorines to two facilities. Many aquifers are polluted to a much greater degree than that beneath Sawston, but given the multitude of industrial users whose activity may have polluted ground water, chemical fingerprinting is futile and tort action is hardly likely.

Even where it is possible to isolate particular polluting activity and even identify a causal link, problems of breach of duty re-emerge. Thus, *Cambridge Water* turns in the end on the foreseeability issue. Or, to take a more obvious example, in *Margereson* v. *J.W. Roberts*,[17] it was easy enough to show that a particular condition (mesothelemia) resulted from a particular pattern of exposure (through living in proximity to the defendant's facility which produced asbestos). It is altogether more troublesome, however, to fix knowledge of the harm of this exposure such that a reasonable operator ought to have guarded against the risk. The court can, and did, engage in the entirely artificial attribution of responsibility based upon expert testimony and an exploration of scientific literature which dated back over 65 years.

There are a number of objections to this process. First one must determine a time at which the scientific debate reaches the point of closure.[18] This seems an

---

[16] This is a reference to the work of Beck which is considered below—see U. Beck, *Risk Society—Towards a New Modernity* (London, Sage Publications, 1992).

[17] [1996] Env. L R 304.

[18] This is an issue which I have explored more fully in the context of vaccine injuries: see R. G. Lee, "Vaccine Injury: Adjudicating Scientific Dispute" in G. Howells (ed.), *Product Liability, Insurance and the Pharmaceutical Industry* (Manchester, Manchester University Press, 1990).

82   R. G. Lee

improbable task since no one moment is likely, given the social process of hypothesis, debate, discussion, experimentation and publication within the scientific community. There must follow the integration of the information into another, business community such that a reasonable operator ought to have taken the precautions. Indeed increasingly the focus for the courts in toxic tort cases seems to be on the quality of the processes of risk management rather than the actual state of scientific knowledge.[19] Conditions of uncertainty in a risk society may demand action in the face of doubt rather than reaction following scientific findings.

These criticisms of *Margereson* might be countered by asserting the essential corrective justice of the award. However, in introducing this case, it was argued that it is increasingly atypical of toxic tort claims in terms of the localised and direct nature of the impact. Although the temporal link between exposure and injury is fractured in this case, the fact that the case centres around events in the 1930s illustrates its positioning in industrial rather than risk society. Indeed, it may be that almost by definition cases still reaching the courts are extraordinary, not having been settled as undeniable or rejected as hopeless. Tort lawyers need to consider what may happen in a society in which the risks which it generates pay no respect to geographical (or jurisdictional) boundaries, temporal (or limitation) links and social (duty) relationships between those creating the harm and those who are victims of it. This is a question for lawyers not merely because we might expect legal mechanisms to address or redress the onset of such risks. A fear is that it may lose all capacity to do so. In the meantime, however, the increasing tendency of tort law to resort to traditional policy mechanisms to support the refusal to attribute responsibility assists in the legitimation of conduct which is inherently risk-taking.[20] The consequences of such conduct are the fault of no-one, and there is little scope, at least through the common law, to curb hazards which become entrenched as inherent. To put this another way, the tort law domain of the normal, reasonable and foreseeable is shrinking rapidly in what Beck has called a risk society in which uncertainty becomes inherent, as little within what we might regard as the realm of the natural remains untouched by science and technology.

SCIENCE, LAW AND RISK

Beck's *Risk Society* is subtitled: "Towards a New Modernity".[21] Beck argues that just as modernisation dissolved the structures of the feudal society to herald

---

[19] For a good recent example of this see the miners' emphysema claims—see the judgment of Turner J in *Griffiths* v. *British Coal Corporation*, QBD, 23 Jan. 1998, available on-line at www.courtservice.gov.uk/qb_bcrdl.htm.

[20] This is a point made elsewhere by Beck—see U. Beck, *Ecological Politics in the Age of Risk* (Cambridge, Polity Press, 1995).

[21] *Supra*, n.16.

From the Individual to the Environmental: Tort Law in Turbulence   83

the industrial society, so too, modernity is again dissolving industrial society "and another modernity is coming into being". Earlier processes of modernisation are replaced by "reflexive modernisation". While it might be thought that an essay on tort law would focus much more on the "risk" theme rather than the "society" theme in Beck's book, this notion of modernity turning in on itself, modernising itself, is surprisingly powerful and apposite. To begin with it suggests structural change within the risk society. Much of the early part of Beck's work is concerned with the move from the distribution on wealth in the industrial society to distribution of risk—new dangers introduced by modernisation itself—or, as Beck would have it, from the allocation of "goods" to "bads".[22] Tort law theory is filled with ideas of loss distribution and risk allocation, but in risk society we may see responses by individuals to their own patterns of risk and their own place within the risk society which will challenge the social foundations of industrial society. It is idle to think that legal rules or institutions will be exempt from such restructuring.

Reflexive modernisation is very much tied to the risks that have emerged from industrial society. Indeed reflexivity is demanded in the face of risks not limited by traditional barriers of time and space. There are global and intergenerational threats. Elsewhere Beck has argued that this reflexivity may need to include the self-limitation of the development of predominant hazards and a re-definition of standards of responsibility, damage limitation and the consequences of loss.[23] However, the problem is that many of the risks "not only elude sensory perception and the powers of the imagination, but also scientific determination".[24] There are countless examples, nonetheless, of individuals reflecting upon and seeking to restructure their relationship with risk. In a society in which the genetic make-up of natural things can be changed, we can begin to question our entire relationship with the natural world. Indeed, quite how powerful this has become is demonstrated by reaction in the face of a catastrophe such as the earthquake in Turkey in the summer of 1999. The initial shock at the event quickly gave way to a desire to allocate blame—to architects, builders, government, rescue services etc. As scientists have sought to exercise more control over nature, we reach a point at which failure to control, if not nature then its consequences, cannot be easily forgiven.[25]

Giddens, in his work on risk and trust, has suggested that reflexivity is demonstrated, at least in part, by individuals choosing to place trust in, or investing

---

[22] This notion is picked up by S. Lash and B. Wynne in their introduction to the English translation (by Mark Ritter) of the book, but Beck returns to it in his later essay: U. Beck, "Risk Society and the Provident State" in S. Lash, B. Szerszynski and B. Wynne (eds.), *Risk, Environment and Modernity: Towards a New Ecology* (London, Sage Publications, 1996).

[23] In *Ecological Politics in an Age of Risk*, *supra*, n.20.

[24] In "Risk Society and the Provident State", *supra*, n.22, at 29.

[25] Another feature of the risk society is the attribution of seemingly natural events (such as hurricanes) to the effects of human intervention (such as climate change), thus increasing this sense of confusion.

84   R. G. Lee

confidence in, expert determinations in the face of competing views.[26] This seems quite a hopeful message for the tort law process, involving, as it frequently does, a determination of such conflicts. There are problems with such processes in terms of the treatment of science as value-neutral fact, and the preference of the courts for harder scientific evidence rather than other forms of observation or lay accounts of what happened. Nonetheless, there is clearly a significant role for the courts as a mediating institution. Mediating is used here in two senses: acting as a mediator between the conflicting views and acting as a media through which some more accessible account of the scientific dispute and its resolution is broadcast.

What happens, however, if those institutions which might create trust become seen as the very bodies that permit exposure to risk? As a society, and in a risk society, we may hope for processes through which we can determine the degree of risk that we are prepared to tolerate. Over time, in such a society, there is a development of social processes of evaluation which operated upon a rationality different from that of the experts, but no less powerful. Take the example of GM crops. A large proportion of people seem to form a view that, however careful and thorough the scientists claim their experiment to be, they are just that, experiments, and, whatever the supposed virtues of genetic modification, these should be rejected in the face of the risk. It might be possible here to articulate certain risks: possible toxicity of modified crops, the challenges to bio-diversity of pest resistant crops; the creation of super-weeds which cannot be controlled; the decline in nutritional values etc. But many people feel no need to identify or engage in argument about risk in this way in order to reject this step into the unknown. More and more, it is possible to identify such reaction. Environmental protest is more common and is not noticeably confined by traditional boundaries of class or social status. But it goes beyond formal protest to an emergent questioning of expert determination and the processes through which it operates.[27] It reflects a growing distrust of institutions seen to be determining the distribution of the dangers in risk society, which remain inaccessible to and remote from those affected by the determination.[28]

Lash has been critical of the work of both Beck and Giddens in exhibiting far too great a concentration on the formal and institutional at the expense of the

---

[26] A. Giddens, *The Consequences of Modernity* (Cambridge, Polity Press, 1990) and A. Giddens, *Modernity and Self-Identity: Self and Society in the Late Modern Age* (Cambridge, Polity Press, 1991). In his later work, Giddens seems to modify this position. In "Risk and Responsibility" (1999) 62 *MLR* 1 at 6, Giddens suggests that people have had to develop a "dialogic or engaged relationship with science and technology".

[27] The work of my colleague Ian Welsh considers these issues in the context of the debate on nuclear power, see I. Welsh, *Nuclear Power: Generating Dissent* (London, Routledge, 1995). *Cf.* D. Campbell, "Of Coase and Coln: A (sort of) Defence of Private Nuisance [2000] *MLR* 197.

[28] For a particularly useful account of this issue in relation to legal institutions, see S. Jasanoff, *Science at the Bar* (Cambridge, Mass., Harvard University Press, 1995).

From the Individual to the Environmental: Tort Law in Turbulence 85

grass roots.[29] For Lash, individualised responses in terms of social and cultural interactions are taking places outside formal institutional settings, and these reflexive processes need to be assimilated into our understandings of modernisation. Colleagues of Lash at Lancaster, and in particular Wynne, have undertaken much work exploring the public experience and understandings of science.[30] While it is difficult to summarise research that is broad in terms of its subject matter and deep in terms of its sociological inquiry,[31] this work has some important messages for lawyers. In particular, it demonstrates that even in the absence of any overt dispute with experts or institutions, large elements of the public have a highly ambivalent reflexive approach in which they accommodate their own dependency upon expert determinations while aware of their lack of engagement with such expertise. This relationship is problematic. Little can be done to alter the dependency upon the expertise, although there are levels of alienation such that may have continually to adapt to a situation in which individuals find themselves reliant upon institutions which, informally, they mistrust.

Wynne's work also allows consideration of the basis of this relationship as the public assesses experiences alongside those making the expert determinations.[32] As was stated earlier, scientific determinations form part of a tradition within science such that these determinations represent a social acceptance with the scientific community.[33] But this may represent a closed process with which the community, about which the determination is made, is not engaged. Further, this may allow significant social or human factors to be excluded from any risk assessment of probability. Such models refined in the laboratory do not match everyday experiences, and rather than being dialogue between scientists and the community, the interactions are stale or meaningless. Individuals may not feel free to participate in the institutions promoting determinations that defy or challenge their own experiences, but they will make judgements about their relationship to these institutions and their role or, indeed, their relevance in the face of the inherent hazards of a risk society.

REGULATION, RISK AND THE COURTROOM

The above passage makes a number of arguments. Reflexive modernisation implies structural change, driven by the individualised responses to risk.

[29] In U. Beck, A. Giddens and S. Lash, *Reflexive Modernization* (Cambridge, Polity Press, 1994).

[30] See for an overview B. Wynne, "Public Understanding of Science" in S. Jasanoff, G. Markle, J. Petersen and T. Pinch (eds.), *Handbook of Science and Technology Studies* (London, Sage, 1994).

[31] A certain summary of it is contained in B. Wynne, "May the Sheep Safely Graze? A Reflexive view of the Expert-Lay Knowledge Divide" in Lash *et al.* (eds.), *supra* n.22.

[32] This is most clearly brought out in Wynne's study of Cumbrian sheep farmers following the restrictions on sheep movements and sale in the aftermath of the Chernobyl accident: see B. Wynne, "Misunderstood Misunderstandings: Social Identities and the Public Uptake of Science" (1992) 1(3) *Public Understanding of Science* 281.

[33] For more on this see the classic work, T. Khun, *The Structure of Scientific Revolutions* (Chicago, Ill., University of Chicago Press, 1992) and H. Collins and T. Pinch, *The Golem: What Everyone Should Know about Science* (Cambridge, CUP, 1993).

86   R. G. Lee

Indeed there is much within risk society that promotes a questioning of one's relationships including the relationship with the natural world. The courts and the common law rules are important institutional instruments within risk society, not least because of their mediating role. However confidence in them is fragile. The public experience of risk is not one of unthinking acceptance of a position expounded by experts, nor is it as simple as a choice between expert positions. Rather, it involves people having to accommodate their own experience of and exposure to risk in the face of alienation from many of the institutions seen to be charged with guaranteeing their personal security or well-being.[34] If all of this is so, there is an important job to be done in re-considering the traditional model of tortious liability and its operation within a risk society.

Modern environmental law is dominated by regulation. Indeed it becomes more heavily regulated by the day as market-based instruments, often negotiated with the relevant industrial sectors, provide the primary means of modifying potentially harmful activity. Examples abound, but producer responsibility initiatives in packaging[35] and the landfill tax[36] offer two easy examples. Such developments are accompanied by a mass of detailed regulation in different forms: statutory instruments, guidance, codes of practice and working rules. These modes of regulation are chosen for a variety of reasons. Detailed technical rules are required to establish a clear basis upon which potentially polluting operations can be conducted. These are sector-specific,[37] and even site-specific. They are aimed also at protecting the environment through the minimisation of risks imposed by enterprise. Previous command and control models of regulation have proved costly and problematic in terms of relationships between the regulators and the regulated.[38] Models of self-regulation are sought through economic incentives to comply.

This is not merely a departure from the *ad hoc*, ante-natal intervention of the common law. It ought over time to reduce the scope for the operation of the common law. This is not simply because the markets become the chief regulator, but because, if successful, untoward incidents which lead to claims will be minimised. We might share a cynicism whether this will prove to be the case, but the reliance on such forms of regulation have the ironic effect of heightening the position of the courts which come to occupy a role of last resort. Their role is now truly one of corrective justice in the face of an obvious system failure. So there is a curiosity that less day-to-day dependence on the courtroom actually promotes its significance when called into play.

---

[34] See Welsh, *supra* n. 27.

[35] See the Packaging and Packaging Waste Dir. (94/62/EC) and the Producer Responsibility (Packaging Waste) Regs. (S.I. 1997/648) as amended.

[36] See the Finance Act 1996 and the Landfill Tax Regs. 1996 (S.I. 1996/1527).

[37] See e.g. a proposed Dir. on end of life vehicles (Com 97/358 [1997] OJ C337/02) and the discussions on a proposal for a Waste Electronic and Electrical Equipment Dir., both of which envisage the imposition of (differing) take-back burdens on producers of the goods.

[38] K. Hawkins, *Environment and Enforcement* (Oxford, Clarendon Press, 1983).

From the Individual to the Environmental: Tort Law in Turbulence   87

In the face of this it seems appropriate to review the response of the common law to a highly regulatory environment. One would have to describe the recent trend, at least within the House of Lords, to be both insular and timid. The first instinct is to stand aside, to argue that if wrongs must be corrected then this has become a matter for regulation rather than the common law. Yet, in so doing the courts may act in ways that are unsympathetic to, or perhaps even unaware of, modern environmental regulation. Take the *Cambridge Water* decision.[39] At a time when Parliament was developing legislative initiatives to render historic polluters liable to remedy the consequences of their actions,[40] the House of Lords took the view that "it was more appropriate for strict liability in respect of operations of high risk to be imposed by Parliament than by the courts". There follows a passage which then highlights the present conservatism of the House of Lords: "[g]iven that so much well-informed and carefully structured legislation is now being put in place for this purpose (broadly, environmental protection), there is less need for the courts to develop a common law principle to achieve the same end, and indeed it may be undesirable that they should do so".[41]

A second discernible attachment of the House of Lords is to a coherent and logical development of the common law even where it may be seen as struggling in the light of modern social conditions and in the face of obvious injustice. In *Hunter* v. *Canary Wharf Ltd*,[42] without the benefit of the usual planning constraints a community within the docklands of London was subject to two sets of interferences, said to be a nuisance: namely the interruption of its television reception and its exposure to substantial deposits of dust from the construction involved in the commercial redevelopment of its neighbourhood. The first incident was said not to constitute an actionable nuisance at common law and although the dust deposit clearly did, only those with either a freehold interest in the land or with exclusive possession of their property could sue.[43] This latter element of the judgment excluded the many people in this type of area who were flat-sharers, lodgers etc. in addition to spouses without an interest in their home. It might be added that in the event they were not deprived of a great deal since, faced with this type of mass claim, the courts took a highly restrictive view of the level of damages.[44]

However, the point of interest here lies in the approach of the House of Lords to the suggestion that there might be room to allow a remedy to mere licensees

---

[39] *Cambridge Water Company* v. *Eastern Counties Leather plc, supra* n.8.

[40] See now Part IIA of the Environmental Protection Act 1990 as introduced by the Environment Act 1995.

[41] *Supra*, n.8, at 80.

[42] [1997] AC 655.

[43] A later challenge to this decision on the basis of Art. 6 of the European Convention on Human Rights was rejected by the European Commission on Human Rights.

[44] Essentially the pegging of damages for loss of amenity to the capital value of the properties has the effect of disadvantaging those who live in low cost housing in comparison to those living in finer surroundings: cf *Blackburn* v. *ARC Ltd* [1998] Env. LR 469.

88   R. G. Lee

on the authority of a Court of Appeal case, *Kharasandjian* v. *Bush*,[45] in which the harassment of the daughter of the house by continual nuisance, even though the plaintiff's daughter had no interest in the family house. Lord Goff, consistently with his approach in *Cambridge Water*, pointed to the ability of Parliament to address such matters: "a tort of harassment has now received statutory recognition (see the Protection of Harassment Act 1997). We are therefore no longer troubled with the question of whether the common law should provide such a remedy."[46] Lord Cooke, in a vigorous dissenting speech, sought to argue that there was room for common law development in a tort which had, as its base, the notion of reasonable user:

> The principle may not always conduce to tidiness, but tidiness has not had a high priority in the history of the common law. What has made the law of nuisance a potent instrument of justice throughout the common law world has been largely its flexibility and versatility.[47]

However, the majority of their Lordships favoured, instead, the approach of Lord Hoffmann:

> There is a good deal in [*Kharasandjian*] and other writings about the need for the law to adapt to modern social conditions. But the development of the common law should be rational and coherent. It should not distort its principles and create anomalies merely as an expedient to fill a gap.[48]

The question therefore becomes: what weight do we place on the doctrinal purity of the law as against its flexibility? At the outset of this paper, tort law was examined by reference to its links to social standards of behaviour and to what Cane has described as the "acceptable and the unacceptable" or those factors which might be considered "normal and abnormal". The later parts of this chapter have argued that our notions of the "normal" are shifting rapidly in the face of bewildering technical and scientific advances which push against our understandings of the natural and unnatural. This is a turbulent world over which, as Giddens has argued, we look to exert some degree of understanding and control. As we do so, the social standards that underpin tort law are transformed. In particular the boundaries of luck and misfortune are heavily contested. This is an obvious battleground within risk society. We live in a world and face other future worlds of increasing uncertainty driven by science and technology. Beck is sanguine as to the extent to which these may be controlled, but there is no doubt that the public expects regulatory agencies at least to inform them of and generate influence over those who manufacture the risk. In other words, and by no means only in the environmental arena, our understandings of the "reasonable and the unreasonable" are shaped by regulation.

---

[45] [1993] QB 727.
[46] *Supra* n.42, at 692.
[47] *Ibid.*, at 711.
[48] *Ibid.*, at 707.

From the Individual to the Environmental: Tort Law in Turbulence 89

There is a positive danger, therefore, in a common law that closes its eyes on the regulatory world. Not only will this create dislocation between the very different processes which we label "law", but it has the capacity to create a crisis of confidence in the legal system as failures and false expectations of the regulatory mechanisms are not redressed in the courtroom. It is precisely because carefully structured legislation seeks to protect the environment that the courts need to develop a common law that acts in harmony with it. It is not merely highly desirable that it should do so. It is imperative.

THE CHALLENGE

It would be foolish, however, to underestimate the size of this task. Beck has gone as far as to argue that scientific and technological development can occur exponentially such as to go without control.[49] This is not some tired cliché of law lagging behind science, but a more profound insight that social and cultural change so rapidly follows the possibilities that science opens up that responses, legal or otherwise are difficult to formulate. Within regulation, then, the task is difficult enough. Nonetheless law has an important job to do here in formalising, at least for a moment in time, what it is that society is or is not prepared to tolerate. It follows that regulation is never really a prospective task, but it might be thought that this ongoing, frenetic activity is a more difficult task than the more leisurely responses of the common law in reviewing events, and seeking to redress matters.

Beck suggests otherwise. He argues that the spatial and geographical reaches of the risks now generated make it impossible to hold individual actors accountable.[50] More than this, as it becomes impossible to calculate the risk, it may be impossible, too, to compensate those harmed by consequent events. This is a problem not merely for lawyers, since Beck's primary audience here would seem to be the insurance industry, but it should cause lawyers to reflect on the role and purpose of courts charged with such tasks. To return to the earlier parts of the chapter, we can already see some attempts to grapple with the consequences of letting loose forces that we cannot understand let alone control. Thus product liability laws seek to regulate hazards from products by the imposition of strict liability rules.[51] Those who manufacture new technology driven products, such as, for example, the mobile phone, then press for development risk defences,[52] lest development be unduly inhibited.[53] The European White Paper

---

[49] In *Risk Society, supra* n.16. This case is made particularly in relation to modern medicine, see the text at 204ff.

[50] This concept of organised irresponsibility is reviewed in an address to lawyers by Giddens, see "Risk and Responsibility" (1999) 62 *MLR* 1.

[51] See the Products Liability Dir. 85/374/EEC OJ No L 210 7.8.1985 p. 29, and the Consumer Protection Act 1987.

[52] See Art. 7(e) of the Dir. and s. 4 of the 1987 Act.

[53] See L. Lasagna, "The Chilling Effect of Product Liability on New Drug Development" in P. Huber and R. Litan (eds.), *The Liability Maze: The Impact of Liability Law on Safety and*

90   R. G. Lee

would propose similar stricter schemes for environmental hazards, but with what likely success?

The entire edifice is ultimately built upon notions that cause and effect can be proven in accordance with an appropriate standard of proof, such as on the balance of probability. Yet increasingly there are uncertainties which will defy such resolution. And the simple truth is that reversing the burden of proof does not dispense with the difficulty, however much one might favour the development. All that we are doing here is to compensate persons in the face of uncertainty because we are sympathetic to the injury from which they now suffer. If this is the rationale, there are much more efficient processes to achieve this than long and ultimately pointless court cases. It may take considerable time to realise and respond to the inevitable, but it would seem to be this. A system of tort law built upon an industrial society model of individual claims for immediate physical injury will not prove functional in risk society. To put it another way, we need to move tort law away from its focus on the individual and consider the realm of the environmental.[54] However in so doing, we should be aware that, frequently, the environmental impacts may be so pervasive and random in their effect that, in terms of both proof and procedure, compensation will be problematic.

This should cause us to reflect upon the very domain of tort law. Giddens suggests a transformation labelled the end of nature:[55] a move from a state in which people worried about what nature could do to them to one in which they worry about what they have done to nature. Whilst initially persuasive, it is worth considering whether the transformation is quite so well defined. Many states of health disorder are, and always have been, environmentally related. In the past patterns of infectious disease spread by rats or caused by impure water were regarded as no more than fate. As such they fell outside the domain of tort law— a matter of luck rather than legal redress. More modern environmental states, such as the presence of endocrine disrupters in water or carcinogens in food, are not so regarded. Indeed it may be inherent in risk society that the law too plays its part in eroding the realm of the natural in a manner which it then finds problematic to address. There is room for social consideration of the limits to a private law model of compensation, at the same time as determining wider public responsibilities for environmental change.

In the longer term this will dictate a move towards more administratively-based systems, regulatory models in which, as part of the process of permitting activity, entail funding for the unforeseen and even uncertain possible future outcomes. We already see the seeds of this in demands for financial provision as

---

Innovation (Washington, DC, Brookings Institution, 1991). Huber has been a staunch critic of the tort law system in its dealings with product and other toxic tort claims, see P. Huber, *Galileo's Revenge: Junk Science in the Courtroom* (New York, Basic Books, 1991).

[54] My adoption of these terms was inspired by R. Gaskins, *Environmental Accidents: Personal Injury and Public Responsibility* (Philadelphia, Temple University Press, 1989).

[55] Giddens, *supra* n.50.

From the Individual to the Environmental: Tort Law in Turbulence 91

an operating condition for certain enterprises.[56] At present this is restricted in most jurisdictions to particular industrial enterprises, and is often more concerned with site re-instatement rather than the redress of personal injury. Significantly, early drafts of the White Paper looked to sectoral industrial levies to cope with the synergetic effects of pollution. There are already huge advances of public law at the expense of private law in the environmental field, even to the point that it has become the first choice in addressing problems of personal injury.[57] This move from remedies to regulation is inevitable as people seek personal security in a risk society.

Until such time as these initial developments mature, tort law finds itself in an unenviable position. More and more it will face claims in the realm of the environmental which are not susceptible to effective determination in the light of scientific uncertainty. Yet it cannot deny its responsibility to seek to respond to the claimants. It cannot leave matters to Parliament and allow the common law to deny attribution of responsibility through the courts in the event of environmental injury. The courts occupy too important an institutional position in the uncertainty of risk society. The public looks to the mediating role of the courts. Perceptions of risk drive risk society, so that the courts have a positive role in influencing feelings of personal wellbeing and security. Moreover the courts are dealing continually with manufacturers of the risk,[58] so that there is an impact on the material risk. To stand aside, to deny competence, to retract rather than maintain private law remedies may provoke a crisis of confidence by those ultimately dependent on the courts for environmental protection.

This matters considerably in a jurisdiction that has never had too rigid a divide between private and public law. Even if in the longer term there will need to be a shift to a more administratively based system of redressing environmental wrongs, in the meantime, it is important that trust and confidence is not lost through disaffection to a sterile and impotent private environmental law. There are no easy solutions, but what is needed is a realisation of the limitations and restrictions of traditional tort law when dealing with claims that are environmental in their nature and scope. Some movement is needed towards the development of private law responses that are in harmony with, not opposition to, the body of regulation that constitutes modern environmental law.

---

[56] A British example might lie in the financial provisions demanded of a "fit and proper person" under s. 74 of the Environmental Protection Act 1990.

[57] In R. v. *Secretary of State for Trade and Industry ex p. Duddridge* [1995] 3 CMLR 231, faced with the difficulties inherent in proving causation in electro-magnetic field litigation, the applicant argued unsuccessfully that the precautionary principle applied to determinations by the Secretary of State under the Electricity Acts.

[58] For an explanation of the notion of manufactured risk and external risk see Giddens , *supra* n.50.

5

Tort and Environmental Pluralism

KEITH STANTON and CHRISTINE WILLMORE*

INTRODUCTION

IT HAS BEEN said of tort that:

> For much of our legal history it [tort] served as the main protection from environmental harms.[1]

Even if that were once true, tort may never again have such a central role. Indeed, current trends suggest an underlying assumption that this is an area in which state regulation is the primary tool, tempered by judicial review, with only a limited, peripheral, role for private action. We would argue that this underrates the potential of tort. In this paper we do not wish to take a position between the free market environmentalists, with their calls for almost total reliance upon private remedial action,[2] or those who argue for enhanced regulation of various kinds.[3] There are manifest efficiencies in collective action. Our argument is not whether collective or individual action is preferable but rather it is about the importance of retaining effective mechanisms for individual action to perform specific roles.

What has been called the "unofficial" nature of private law[4] makes it a tool which can be a voice for views and priorities which may otherwise not be heard. We see two significant roles for tort actions in a pluralist society. First, they provide the primary mechanism for individuals to seek compensation for losses they have suffered. Secondly, tort can be used to assert perspectives which are unorthodox or in some way question mainstream priorities, for example challenges to established scientific wisdom or to our attitudes to risk and the allocation of loss. Law is not the only mechanism through which such diverse or

---

* We are grateful to our colleague, Caroline Sawyer, for her helpful comments on an earlier draft.

[1] C. Cranor, *Regulating Toxic Substances* (Oxford, OUP, 1993) at 57.

[2] See e.g. T. Anderson and L. Leal, *Free Market Environmentalism,* (Boulder, Pacific Research Institute, Westview Press, 1991).

[3] See J. Steele, "Assessing the Past: Tort Law and Environmental Risk" in T. Jewell and J. Steele (eds.) *Law in Environmental Decision Making* (Oxford, Clarendon, 1998); T. Hayward and J. O'Neill (eds.), *Justice, Property and the Environment* (Brookfield, Ashgate, 1997).

[4] See D. McGillivray and J. Wightman, "Private Rights, Public Interests and the Environment" in *ibid.*, at 144–67.

94   Keith Stanton and Christine Willmore

dissenting views can be aired, but the particular power associated with legal discourse can lend weight to views.

Our contention is that tort has and should continue to have this distinct role to play in environmental law, but that this role is at present hampered unnecessarily by the rules governing the torts and the limits placed on the remedies which may be obtained. The environmental torts currently suffer from a structural malaise, and there are a number of procedural and substantive obstacles to the extensive use of tort for this purpose. However, amidst the difficulties there may be opportunities to develop tort to achieve these purposes more effectively, without waiting for "an environmental *Donoghue* v. *Stevenson*".

Amongst the many obstacles to wider use of tort for these purposes, two, both associated with public nuisance, seem ripe for review. The standing rules of public nuisance, under which only the Attorney General (or local authority) can take action in the absence of particular damage, where there has been harm to a widespread area, look outmoded in the light of modern standing rules. A second barrier which may be ripe for review are the restrictions surrounding *quia timet* injunctions. Both these rules could be altered, without affecting areas outside the environmental arena, and may therefore provide an attractive, and simple, way forward whilst grander plans are awaited.

This chapter starts by analysing the reasons people may need a voice outside the state regulatory system, and then explores the structural, substantive and procedural obstacles to the use of tort to provide that voice.

THE ROLE OF ENVIRONMENTAL TORTS

The general problems which face tort when it operates in the context of environmental law have been well rehearsed, and it is not intended to re-explore that ground in this chapter.[5] The picture, however, is not wholly one-sided. Measures have been introduced in recent years to assist group actions to proceed.[6] The arrival of conditional fees[7] may have removed an important disincentive to commencing proceedings and solicitors may now be more active than they have been in the past in seeking out potential claimants.[8] Environmental pressure groups now use a wider range of techniques to further their arguments. Nonetheless, tort's further use in environmental litigation seems uncertain.

---

[5] J. Steele, "Assessing the Past: Tort Law and Environmental Risk" in Jewell and Steele (eds.), *supra* n.3.

[6] Supreme Court Procedure Committee, *Guide for Use in Group Actions*, (London, Supreme Court) 1991.

[7] S. 58 of the Courts and Legal Services Act 1990 (as amended): Conditional Fees Agreements Orders 1995 and 1998.

[8] C. Pugh and M. Day, *Pollution and Personal Injury: Toxic Torts II* 2nd edn., (London, Cameron May, 1994), ch. 2 gives detailed advice to solicitors who may be considering such a course of action.

One symptom of a possible failure in the tort system is the extent to which, instead of bringing a tortious action against the company creating the perceived environmental risk, litigants are using judicial review to challenge regulators for failure to protect them from perceived risk. This may be part of a wider social expectation of state protection, but it may also result from a lack of an effective private law remedy. Thus in *Duddridge*,[9] parents concerned about the risk to their children from a proposed high voltage power cable, lacking a basis for challenging the National Grid in a private action, challenged the Secretary of State as regulator through judicial review.

Similarly, in *R. v. Secretary of State for the Environment ex p. Watson*,[10] a leading organic farmer who wished to challenge the planting of GM crops on a neighbouring farm was forced to rely upon judicial review. Given concerns beyond that of the general public, affecting the organic farmer's property, it might seem the classic situation for which the law of tort should be available: the protection of private rights where the damage is not shared equally by the public at large. Yet Mr Watson had to resort to judicial review, challenging the regulator's decision to permit the trials to go ahead, rather than sue the farmer or the GM company. Tort has little to offer the organic farmer, at least until he suffers a form of damage recognised by tort.[11] Even were the farmer to wait until his crops had been damaged,[12] he might be considered an abnormally sensitive plaintiff. Wishing to prevent damage the organic farmer's only option is to challenge the regulator's conduct in authorising the trial of the crop. Even that avenue would be closed off, if there were not a trial authorisation scheme in place.

However, the public law route does not provide an answer either, as the *Watson* case illustrates. Whilst holding the GM authorisation to be unlawful, because of ministerial breaches of procedure, the court concluded that it had no power to order the destruction of the crops. The risk of such pyrric victory exists for applicants in judicial review: the focus of attention is the action of the administrative body, not the private sector body or the damage to the complainant. Watson was left with a GM trial site, close to his organic farm, which was outside the current authorisations, for which he had no preventive remedy. Once the state has indicated conduct is sufficiently risky to merit regulation in some form and the regulatory system has been breached, is it appropriate for the law to fail to provide a remedy?

In order to identify those factors within tort most in need of review, if it is to develop a clearer role in such cases, it is necessary to identify why people might

---

[9] *R. v. Secretary of State for Trade and Industry ex p. Duddridge and others* [1995] Env. LR 151 (CA).

[10] *R. v. Secretary of State for the Environment ex p. Watson* (1998) 282 ENDS 52 [1999] Env. LR 310 (CA).

[11] For an example of the problems of expert differences of opinion impeding access to a *quia timet* injunction see *Attorney General* v. *Manchester Corp.* [1893] 2 Ch. 87.

[12] Would removal of his soil association organic accreditation amount to actionable damage?

96 Keith Stanton and Christine Willmore

look to tort. Two key reasons would seem to underlie individual decisions to look to tort, as opposed to other legal remedies:

(1) Protection of individual health and wealth: through compensation or preventive action;
(2) A desire to provoke action by the gatekeepers of regulatory remedies whether their inaction is the result of differences of view about science and risk or differences about the exercise of regulatory discretion.

Environmental litigation may also be initiated for a whole host of other reasons, as part of wider campaign strategies, to create a suitable climate for legislative proposals, to create a focus for media attention or as part of a test case strategy. In this chapter we do not seek to analyse the specific requirements of test case strategies, or the efficacy of failed litigation in wider campaign strategies, our concern is with the individual litigant as the paradigm for tort action. If tort fails the individual litigant, then it fails in its own terms.

PROTECTION OF INDIVIDUAL HEALTH AND WEALTH

The first reason identified to invoke tort is to protect a private interest which is distinct from that of the public at large. For those who have been damaged, whether the damage is in the form of personal injury or damage to property or wealth,[13] tort remains a primary mechanism whereby compensation for those losses can be recovered. Regulatory mechanisms, as currently structured in English law, may operate to prevent losses, to limit any damage which does ensue or to compel remediation, but they have limited capacity for providing compensation for harm which has already been caused. Direct compensation for established damage flowing from the private sector wrongdoer, as opposed to the public sector body only, attracts a remedy through tortious mechanisms.

Structural Malaise

A major obstacle to the use of tort for this reason is its current structural malaise. The law concerning environmental torts is in considerable disarray. Some of the doctrines which limit tort's utility in environmental litigation are pervasive; for example its approach to evolving scientific capacity to attribute causes.[14] However, our particular concern is with the doctrinal inconsistencies

---

[13] Using the term in its widest sense to include damage to the amenity of property.

[14] Some commentators have argued that scientific capacity in this area to attribute effects to causes is advancing rapidly as considerable research effort is being directed to environmental issues, but others have concluded that scientific "advance" can create as much fresh uncertainty as it solves. Whichever view is taken on this, the process of proving causation may give rise to problems.(Pugh and Day, *supra* n.8, at 17–18.) See also R. Goldberg, *Causation and Risk in the Law of Torts* (Oxford, Hart Publishing, 1999). Much has been written about the difficulties for lay tribunals in

Tort and Environmental Pluralism   97

which create risks of litigants falling into the cracks between concepts. Despite substantial judicial attention in the last decade,[15] the overall picture remains shrouded in uncertainty: the roles of the different torts and the relationship between them remain unclear. There are simply too many bases of liability potentially available in this area and no sign of the emergence of a central governing principle which might act to unify the torts. Conceptual complexity is not a serious problem if the results obtained are both consistent and appropriate. In other areas the law has shown that it can use concurrent liability to cut through doctrinal complexity. However, our contention is that the current state of the environmental torts leaves significant gaps in the coverage of the law and that there is major scope for improvement. Much of the complexity stems from the restricted approach to the forms of damage recognised by some of the torts. Cumulatively, this limits the ability of tort to protect the "unowned" environment, or at least that part which is not deemed to be land. This has a significant effect on tort's ability to protect individual wealth and health. Actual damage to the general environment is often a prelude to injury to health. If an individual could obtain a remedy to stop conduct and remediate once the general environment suffered damage, injury to health might well be averted.

The most significant technical restraint upon the use of private nuisance to protect health and wealth stems from the requirement, re-established by the House of Lords in *Hunter* v. *Canary Wharf Ltd*,[16] that the claimant has a proprietary interest in the affected property. This leaves the tort as one restricted to the protection of private rights over land, rather than more wide-ranging public interests. Any remote possibility that the tort might have been made available to persons who were interested in protecting the general environment or particular parts of it has been firmly rejected, along with the possibility that persons directly harmed by a nuisance whilst on land in which they had no property right might be able to mount an action. *Hunter* also seems to have confirmed that damages for personal injuries cannot be claimed in a private nuisance action and added weight to the contention that it should not provide a remedy for damage to unattached property.[17]

Other technical problems also impede the operation of private nuisance. The confusion over the role of "reasonableness" as a criterion of liability under the tort and the inherent vagueness of that term is problematic because it promotes uncertainty whether liability will be established. The emphasis placed by the law

---

evaluating expert evidence concerning risk and causal links. See K. Foster and P. Huber, *Judging Science: Scientific Knowledge and the Federal Courts* (Cambridge, Mass., MIT Press, 1997); Cranor, *supra* n.1; S. Jasanoff, *Science at the Bar* (Cambridge, Mass., Harvard University Press, 1995); Goldberg, *op cit*. There is no space in this chapter to dwell upon those difficulties.

[15] *Cambridge Water Co. Ltd* v. *Eastern Counties Leather plc* [1994] 2 AC 264; *Hunter* v. *Canary Wharf Ltd* [1997] AC 655; *Merlin* v. *British Nuclear Fuels plc* [1990] 2 QB 557; *Blue Circle Industries* v. *Ministry of Defence* [1998] 3 All ER 385; *Gillingham BC* v. *Medway (Chatham) Dock Co Ltd* [1993] QB 343.

[16] [1997] AC 655.

[17] See C. Gearty, "The Place of Private Nuisance in the Modern Law of Tort" [1989] *CLJ* 214.

98   Keith Stanton and Christine Willmore

on the characteristics of the particular area when certain forms of interference are at issue weakens the ability to use private nuisance to rectify longstanding problems. Unless society as a whole has concluded that such interferences are now unacceptable generally, they may well be deemed "reasonable" activities.[18]

The future of the rule in *Rylands* v. *Fletcher*[19] is also unclear, following the mixed messages from the House of Lords in *Cambridge Water Co. Ltd* v. *Eastern Counties Leather plc*.[20] Central to that decision was the application of the reasonable foreseeability test in a way which excused a defendant for acts which had been shown to be damaging with the benefits of hindsight. However, the decision did put some teeth into the tort by reinvigorating the notion of a "non-natural" user of land. The notion that many ordinary uses of land for industrial purposes could count as natural has been exploded, even if no precise definition of non-natural use has been supplied. If a risk is foreseeable many commonplace activities may now fall within the ambit of the rule. In terms of its relationship to other torts, the House of Lords regarded the rule as a variant of private nuisance which extends to cases in which only an isolated escape has occurred. If the logic of this thinking is carried through, the tort may now be open only to those who have a proprietary interest in property onto which the escape occurs and the gist of the tort may well come to be seen as an interference with a person's use of land rather than the infliction of physical damage to it. Doubts have existed since Lord MacMillan's speech in *Read* v. *J. Lyons & Co. Ltd*,[21] about whether damages for personal injuries can be recovered under the tort. The re-established link with nuisance coupled with the decision in *Hunter* goes a long way to confirming that they are not. Indeed, Lord Goff in *Cambridge Water* argued that, given the overlap between nuisance and the rule in *Rylands* v. *Fletcher*, it would be strange if a claimant could obtain a stricter form of liability by characterising the claim as falling under the latter head. These uncertainties left by the House of Lords only add to the doctrinal confusion within environmental torts.

Negligence may well have a significant role to play in the future as an environmental tort, particularly if private nuisance and the rule in *Rylands* v. *Fletcher* cannot offer a remedy for personal injuries or damage to personal property.[22] On the current House of Lords approach, private nuisance and *Rylands* v. *Fletcher* could not handle the example of the paintwork on the car damaged by acid smuts when parked on the public highway,[23] or the bees killed by crop

---

[18] *St Helen's Smelting* v. *Tipping* (1865) 11 HLC 642.

[19] The rejection of the claim removed the possibility that the rule might be developed as either a strict liability basis requiring the owner of land to clean up contamination caused by activities in the past or a general principle of strict liability for damage caused by ultra-hazardous activities. On this see K. Stanton, "The Legacy of *Rylands* v. *Fletcher*" in N. Mullany and A. Linden, *Torts Tomorrow* (Sydney, LBC Information Services, 1998).

[20] [1994] 2 AC 264.

[21] [1947] AC 156.

[22] It is not totally inconceivable that wrongful interference with goods might also have a role.

[23] *Halsey* v. *Esso Petroleum Ltd* [1961] 1 WLR 683.

spraying when foraging away from their owner's premises.[24] Negligence, along with public nuisance, may have to plug this gap.[25] However, this possibility raises a different set of inconsistencies, in particular the likelihood of a lower standard of care and a different approach to some forms of injury, notably damage to the amenity of land. Whilst procedurally some problems may be overcome by pleading both negligence and nuisance, the potential remains for losses to fall between either. The first point raises the difference between the reasonableness of the user and reasonable care. Nuisance depends upon the reasonableness of the user. Activities, however carefully executed, may give rise to liability, if unreasonable in the locality. Negligence, in contrast, holds people liable only if they have failed to exercise reasonable care.

If negligence is the cause of action, the recoverable forms of loss under that tort create considerable problems. The common law approach to "pure" economic loss and to remoteness impedes the ability of tort to protect individual wealth from environmental harm.[26] All of the established barriers to the recovery of pure economic loss in negligence are certain to apply, with the result that loss of value and loss of turnover are certain to be excluded unless some element of physical damage exists on which to hang a claim for such losses. In addition, loss of amenity, in the form of an interference with the use and enjoyment of property, is incapable of forming the basis of a negligence claim, even if interference of this kind damages the market value of the property or reduces the amount of trade done there. Such losses are the preserve of nuisance and there is no sign of negligence, even at its most expansive, penetrating this area. The inherent complexity of biodiversity chains and economic reliance upon the environment mean that wide ripples of economic harm can result from environmental damage. The Braer oil spill prevented Shetland fish farmers from selling their fish, but also removed the market for those companies which bred young fish from eggs elsewhere, to sell to Shetland fish farmers as smolt for rearing. Applying the negligence concept of relational economic loss, in the context of a statutory regime, Lord McCluskey in the Court of Session[27] took the view that, whilst it had been rightly conceded that the fishermen themselves could recover for loss of the chance to sell their fish, the egg breeders' loss was essentially only the loss of potential supply contracts and therefore irrecoverable. In contrast, in nuisance, once property rights have been infringed, the economic consequences of inability to use the land may be recovered.

Some of the difficulties with tort could be overcome by the creation of specific statutory regimes, but the experience of such schemes to date is not entirely

---

[24] *Tutton* v. *A.D. Walter Ltd* [1986] QB 61.

[25] As it did in *Tutton*.

[26] See *Merlin* v. *British Nuclear Fuels plc* [1990] 2 QB 557; *Blue Circle Industries* v. *Ministry of Defence* [1998] 3 All ER 385.

[27] *Landcatch Ltd* v. *International Oil Pollution Compensation Fund* [1999] 2 Lloyd's Rep. 316. This was decided under the provisions of the Merchant Shipping (Oil Pollution) Act 1971 and the Merchant Shipping Act 1974. Equivalent provisions are now found in the Merchant Shipping Act 1995.

happy. Those that exist are limited in scope and have increasingly become bogged down in discussions concerning the forms of damage which they render recoverable.[28] As the recoverable forms of loss under these torts have increasingly been held to be narrower than that provided by nuisance, the common exclusion of a concurrent common law remedy[29] may result in their providing less remedial help rather than more.

In the light of these difficulties with the other causes of action, it is contended that public nuisance offers the most promising basis for developing the law. However, it, too, is beset by inherited technical and conceptual problems.[30] As a tort, public nuisance has a seriously split personality. The conventional approach[31] identifies two paradigms within the tort: the first is essentially a widespread private nuisance. It is the interference with the use and enjoyment of a lot of properties. The second concerns dangers or obstructions on or adjoining the highway.[32] The first form of the tort gives the concept of nuisance no additional definition and, as a result, the traditional approach of looking for an unreasonable interference with the use or enjoyment of property is used by default. On the one hand, public nuisance seems to serve the traditional role of protecting an individual's wealth more effectively than private nuisance, given that an interest in land need not be shown in public nuisance but, on the other hand, the definition of nuisance used makes the role of the tort still appear to be dominated by interferences with land, as opposed to injury to the person, personalty or the wider environment.

A critical difference between public and private nuisance is the scale of interference. Just how widespread does an interference need to be before it will be classified as public? Once sufficiently widespread it becomes a public nuisance,[33] with the result that the right of an individual to bring an action for his own loss will depend not on the absolute level or type of damage he suffered, but the scale of his damage as compared to the loss suffered by others. The relevant question ceases to be whether the claimant had a proprietary interest in affected property and becomes whether he has suffered particular damage, that is damage "over and above the general inconvenience suffered by the public".[34] There are three points to be made here. First, although this test is central to whether an individual can use public nuisance, without the endorsement of the Attorney General or local authority, its meaning is uncertain.[35] The second point is that there is a

---

[28] *Merlin* v. *British Nuclear Fuels plc* [1990] 2 QB 557; *Blue Circle Industries* v. *Ministry of Defence* [1998] 3 All ER 385; *Landcatch Ltd* v. *International Oil Pollution Compensation Fund, supra*, n.27.

[29] Nuclear Installations Act 1965, s. 12(1)(b) and Merchant Shipping Act 1995, s. 156(1)(b)(i) exclude concurrent common law causes of action in cases such as *Merlin, Blue Circle* ad *Landcatch*.

[30] J. Spencer, "Public Nuisance: A Critical Examination" (1989) 48 *CLJ* 55.

[31] See R. Buckley, *The Law of Nuisance* (2nd edn., London, Butterworths, 1996) at 67–8.

[32] This is a specialist area beyond the scope of this chapter.

[33] See *Attorney General* v. *PYA Quarries Ltd* [1957] 2 QB 169.

[34] *Clerk & Lindsell on Torts* (17th edn., London, Sweet & Maxwell, 1995), para. 18–02.

[35] G. Kodilnye, "Public Nuisance and Particular Damage in the Modern Law" (1986) 6 *LS* 182. Compare *Hickey* v. *Electric Reduction Co. of Canada Ltd* (1971) 21 DLR (3d) 368 (Newfoundland)

Tort and Environmental Pluralism 101

possibility that damaged individuals will fall between all of the stools: they may not have the required proprietary interest to establish private nuisance; they may be unable to prove particular damage and thus fail in public nuisance and they may not be able to show a form of damage which permits a claim to be sustained in negligence. The final point is that particular damage means damage beyond that suffered generally, it is not related to an abstract test of harm. If a pollutant discomforts everyone in an area, but kills only one individual, that person's dependents have a remedy. However, if the situation is worse and everyone dies the theory of public nuisance insists that no one can bring an action in public nuisance.

The critical issue of whether an individual has standing to bring a tort claim for damages is therefore determined by public nuisance according to a criterion which has no justification other than that individuals are not permitted to complain of widespread interferences unless particularly affected. In all other cases the responsibility for initiating such proceedings rests with public bodies which have no ability to seek compensation. It has to be questioned whether this is an acceptable approach. These rules do not permit the constraints which the law places on private nuisance claims to be circumvented in serious cases by a switch to public nuisance. This may be justified, but should the control over switching from private to public nuisance depend upon the vagaries of how many others are affected? The approach may have played a useful historical role, to avoid the danger of countless individual actions in the context of a general problem, but modern procedures for test case litigation, group actions and consolidation of related cases have surely made this an anachronism.

Preventing Harmful Conduct: Tackling Risk

Even if a path can be found through the doctrinal maze, a second critical weakness runs across tortious actions, as far as the individual facing harm is concerned; the lack of a preventive remedy. The essential tort remedy is damages, after the event, possibly coupled with an injunction to prevent future repetitions, although even that is unavailable in negligence actions.

Quia timet injunctions to prevent future injury are available only in exceptional circumstances in nuisance, and not at all in negligence or *Rylands* v. *Fletcher*. Only in public nuisance, when brought by the Attorney General or local authority, is there ready access to injunctive relief. Judges have seldom sought to justify this reluctance, although it may stem from a utilitarian unwillingness to prevent someone acting freely, unless they actually cause damage to

---

where fishermen who lost their catches because of waste from the defendant's plant were held not to have suffered particular damage with *Burgess* v. *M/V Tamano* (1973) 370 F Supp. 247 (USDC) where fishermen were held to have a sufficient interest to succeed.

another.[36] In most situations some form of balance of convenience is applied to determine whether to grant an injunction, but in the case of *quia timet* injunctions the test is much stricter. Put at its toughest, a *quia timet* injunction is available only: when substantial damage will otherwise inevitably result; when the damage is irreparable;[37] and when there is an actionable interference with property rights, even if, as yet, no damage. However judicial formulations of this test vary in their onerousness.[38] Whichever formulation is used, the injunction is available only when the action is a nuisance *per se*, and not if the incidence of damage depends upon how the action is carried out.[39] The court may decide, even if granting an injunction, to suspend its operation whilst the wrongdoer carries out remedial works.[40]

This lack of injunctive relief can be circumvented in public nuisance through a relator action—if the Attorney General is willing to participate—or if a local authority can be persuaded to bring the action. However, this procedure gives an individual no chance to seek compensation for damage to date.[41] On the other hand, an individually initiated tort claim is unable to provide preventive action and those who anticipate injury to their wealth or health are forced to seek remedies outside tort or wait for the harm to occur.

Should tort eschew responsibility in this situation and effectively force litigants into reliance upon the state, even though the harm anticipated is a personal, private loss, as opposed to damage to a general public interest? Regulatory schemes operate to prevent nuisances from arising and part of the function of public regulatory agencies is to assist where called upon in the protection of private interests. One must, nonetheless, query whether it is always appropriate for tort to force people into using the regulatory system and therefore the public purse. Lack of an injunctive remedy does precisely that: it removes the ability of a private individual to take his own private legal action to secure the prevention of harm to his property and forces him to invoke state support. Given limited public sector resources and a growing emphasis upon self-regulation rather than regulatory agency action, can this continued barrier to injunctive relief in tort be sustained? It should be remembered that statutory nui-

---

[36] J McLaren, "Nuisance Law and the Industrial Revolution—Some Lessons from Social History" (1983) 3 *OJLS* 155, argues that it derives from a desire not to hamper industry in the 19th century and from a reluctance of equitable courts to prejudge issues which would fall to a common law jury to decide.

[37] *Fletcher* v. *Bealey* (1885) 28 Ch. D 688: "a strong probability almost amounting to a moral certainty". See also *Attorney General* v. *Rathmines and Pembroke Joint Health Board* [1904] 1 IR 161.

[38] *Litchfield-Speer* v. *Queen Anne's Gate Syndicate (No 2) Ltd* [1919] 1 Ch. 407; Chitty J in *Attorney General* v. *Manchester Corporation* [1893] 2 Ch. 87 at 92: "a strong case of probability that the apprehended mischief will, in fact, arise".

[39] For example a machine which will create a noise nuisance only if operated in a particular way is not amenable to a *quia timet* injunction to prevent use: *Earl of Ripon* v. *Hobart* (1843) 3 M & K 169. Once granted, however, it may be widely worded: see *Jones* v. *Llanrwst UDC* [1911] 1 Ch. 393, where the injunction banned all discharges.

[40] *Pride of Derby and others* v. *British Celanese Ltd* [1953] 1 Ch. 149, where the nuisance resulted from growth in population overloading the public sewage system.

[41] S. 222 of the Local Government Act 1972.

Tort and Environmental Pluralism   103

sance preserves a right for individuals to pursue matters of particular concern to themselves, by way of prosecution, notwithstanding the absence of any institutional action.[42]

One way around the problem of lack of injunctive remedies is the use of the declaration. Increasingly fashionable in judicial review, the declaration may offer a useful anticipatory remedy in tort.[43] In *Litchfield-Speer* v. *Queen Anne's Gate Syndicate*,[44] the defendants were constructing new buildings. The plaintiff convinced the court that the buildings, if constructed above the height of the former buildings on the site, would cause an unacceptable interference with ancient lights. The availability of a *quia timet* injunction was disputed on the basis that the damage would not be substantial, that it was remediable in damages, and that the damage was not irremediable as the building could be demolished. P.O.Lawrence J sidestepped these difficulties by granting a declaration that the defendant was not entitled to erect buildings so as to cause an illegal obstruction to the plaintiff's music room windows, with liberty to apply for an injunction. This case exemplifies the merits of the declaration: the defendant is not precluded from continuing his course of conduct, if he wishes, but the risk allocation is explicit. The court has ruled on the central issue: when the conduct will amount to an actionable nuisance, and has given the plaintiff a quick route back into court should the nuisance arise, by granting liberty to apply for an injunction. In most cases such a declaration should provide the basis for an extra-judicial resolution of the problem. Such an approach, if applied to circumstances such as the planting of GM crops, would permit the organic farmer to seek to define the limits upon his neighbour's farming activities through private law, rather than indirectly through judicial review, in advance of suffering harm.[45]

TESTING ORTHODOXY: DIFFERENCES OF VIEW ABOUT SCIENCE AND RISK

Protection of personal interests is not the only role which can be identified for tort. Individuals may also wish to test orthodox standards themselves. Legitimate differences may exist about the issues which should be the subject of a risk assessment, the techniques of assessment to be used, the interpretation of the data and the social consequences of that data, with a resulting fragmentation of risk evaluation. In a pluralist society, risk has a plurality of meanings.

As late as 1904,[46] public nuisance was being used as a basis for testing public

---

[42] Part III of the Environmental Protection Act 1990.

[43] H. Woolf and J. Woolf, *The Declaratory Judgement* (2nd edn., London: Sweet and Maxwell, 1993).

[44] *Litchfield-Speer* v. *Queen Anne's Gate Syndicate (No 2) Ltd* [1919] 1 Ch. 407; *Sevenoaks DC* v. *Pattullo-Vinson Ltd* [1984] Ch. 211, where an injunction and declaration were granted.

[45] A remedy may be denied, however because of an inability to prove causation in the current state of environmental understanding.

[46] But see *Frost* v. *King Edward VII Welsh National Memorial Association* [1918] 2 Ch. 180 re a tuberculosis hospital.

104 Keith Stanton and Christine Willmore

concerns about the safety of smallpox hospitals. The Attorney General seemed willing to lend his name to actions in which residents challenged the orthodox scientific opinion and risk analysis that public health was best protected by putting those with smallpox in hospitals situated in relatively rural areas. So few requests are made to the Attorney General now that it is impossible to judge whether a similar open-mindedness would prevail today. It may be that where regulatory bodies exist, the Attorney General might be reluctant to facilitate actions which effectively challenge the decisions of those bodies. Local authorities may, however, be willing to sustain public nuisance actions where there is sufficient local concern, subject, however, to the financial constraints upon them.[47]

Historically, the courts adopted a relatively robust view in cases such as small pox, supporting prevailing scientific orthodoxy, nonetheless, litigation provided a platform upon which those concerns could be tested. The arrival of public health legislation removed some of the need for tort claims, and the focus of litigation turned in many areas to the scope of any applicable statutory authorisation.[48] The need for a platform upon which to test public, as opposed to state, concerns about such matters as GM crops or BSE perhaps restores the need for public nuisance to act as a safety valve once again.

The aim may be to overturn orthodoxy, or may be the more limited one of gaining an airing for alternative views.[49] Challenge to orthodoxy can involve challenge to the expert analysis of risk, and challenge to the social acceptability of that level of risk. The EMF litigation illustrates the significance of such challenges. In *Duddridge,*[50] residents sought judicial review of the Secretary of State for Trade and Industry's exercise of his licensing powers under the Electricity Act 1989.[51] Residents sought to challenge both the official analysis of the level of risk and the acceptability of that level of risk. On the second point the Duddridge family argued that in determining licensing conditions the Secretary of State should adopt the precautionary principle and therefore apply a more

---

[47] Local authorities are willing in some circumstances to invest in challenges to orthodox opinion of science or risk. See e.g. North Yorkshire Council objected to the Secretary of State for Trade and Industry's consultation on plans for new overhead high voltage power cables leading to a public inquiry in 1992:

[48] *Metropolitan Asylum District Managers* v. *Hill* (1882) 47 LT 29; *Attorney General* v. *Manchester Corporation* [1893] 2 Ch. 87; *Attorney General* v. *Nottingham Corporation* [1904] 1 Ch. 673; *Attorney General* v. *Rathmines and Pembroke Joint Health Board* [1904] 1 IR 161.

[49] Indeed the objective may be to lose, in order to demonstrate the case for legislative or regulatory intervention. C. Harlow and R. Rawlings, *Pressure through Law* (London, Routledge, 1992); D. Feldman, "Public Interest Litigation and Constitutional Theory in Comparative Perspective" (1992) 55 *MLR* 44; Comment, "The New Public Interest Lawyers" (1970) 79 *Yale LJ* 1069; T. Prosser, *Test Cases for the Poor* (London, CPAG, 1983). For examples of the misuse of such opportunities see K. Foster and P. Huber, *Judging Science: Scientific Knowledge and the Federal Courts* (Cambridge, Mass., MIT Press, 1997).

[50] R. v. *Secretary of State for Trade and Industry ex p. Duddridge and others* [1995] Env. LR 151 (CA).

[51] S. 3(3)(d) of the Act imposes a duty upon the regulator to use the licensing powers *inter alia* in the manner he considers best calculated "to protect the public from dangers arising from the generation, transmission or supply of electricity".

Tort and Environmental Pluralism   105

stringent test of acceptable levels of risk than he had done. Whilst Smith J concluded that the precautionary principle was not yet part of the legal obligations of the Secretary of State, and that the Secretary of State was entitled to conclude that the risk levels did not require action, the litigation process provided a forum in which the Secretary of State was forced to confront the evidence from other jurisdictions supportive of a link, and test the evidence leading to his conclusion. It also undoubtedly provided a focal point for media attention.[52]

Procedural Barriers

A number of particular difficulties lie in the path of using tort to test orthodoxy, some procedural, some substantive. The extent to which actions in tort can provide this platform will depend upon the approach taken by judges to the new procedure rules, regulating experts' reports[53] and disclosure of evidence.[54] The emphasis within the new rules is upon judicial pressure to identify and narrow the range of issues,[55] supported by extensive proactive judicial case-management powers.[56] Parties remain free to commission experts' reports, but cannot use them in evidence without the consent of the court.[57] The emphasis in the Practice Directions is upon use of a single expert and written as opposed to oral questioning of experts where possible.[58] Practice Directions[59] set out the form and content for experts' reports, for example, requiring the expert to set out the range of opinion on an issue, and the rules require that instructions to experts must be disclosed to the other party, along with the expert's report.[60] Although more restrictive than their predecessors, the new disclosure rules offer some opportunities to obtain information which would otherwise not be accessible.[61]

[52] Interestingly, the case was itself a result of parents seeing a television programme which alerted them to the issue.

[53] Civil Procedure Rules 1998, Part 35.

[54] *Ibid.*, Part 31.

[55] The court is under a duty to encourage the parties to co-operate with each other—including identification of what needs to be investigated (Rule 1.4) e.g. if both parties continue to have experts, the court can direct a discussion between experts for all parties with the aim of narrowing and identifying points of agreement—although the parties are not bound by any agreement their experts reach.

[56] Prior to the exercise of which it may give parties an opportunity to make representations: Rule 3.3.

[57] Rule 35.4.

[58] Rule 35.6–7.

[59] Aug. 1999.

[60] Rule 35.8.

[61] T. Prosser, *Test Cases for the Poor* (London, CPAG, 1983); most recently see the ongoing Prozac litigation in the USA, where litigation revealed information about the field trials of the drug. Outwith local government, the legal right of access to state-held information is very limited. Whilst domestic regs. implementing the Dir. on freedom of access to environmental information 90/313 OJ L375/5 and the Environmental Assessment Dir. 85/337 OJ L158/56 and numerous requirements for registers under specific regulatory regimes make information on the environment more accessible than many other forms of state and corporate information, there remain serious limitations. Disclosure of state-held information during litigation involves balancing the interests of the state in

106 Keith Stanton and Christine Willmore

How the new rules will affect the ability to use civil litigation to test regulatory wisdom is not yet known. At the time of writing no review of the initial use of the powers has been published. However a central aim of the new rules was to reduce cost and complexity in litigation. The Final Report of the Civil Justice Review [62] reserved specific, trenchant, criticism for what was perceived as an over-use of experts and disclosure rules. Given the express aims of reducing contested expert evidence and excessive disclosure, it would seem likely that the new rules will be applied to restrict both activities.[63] The rules have the potential for encouraging a clearer identification of the points of difference between different expert opinions: and for increasing the extent to which regulatory agencies have to recognise and evaluate the support for conflicting opinions in their own expert testimony. However, it would seem likely that overall the new rules will make it harder to use tort to challenge orthodoxy or to discover evidence which will assist in that challenge. Debates about the relative merits of adversarialism, in which the court is asked to adjudicate between different expert views, or single expert litigation, have tended to concentrate upon discussion about which produces the "best" scientific understanding (whatever that might be) and upon cost. Whatever the merits of that debate, if the question is phrased in terms of their effect on the ability to use courts to challenge orthodox scientific debate, the single expert solution is far weaker, even if that expert is required to refer to other schools of thought in the expert report, particularly when coupled with more limited disclosure rules.

Substantive Barriers

The extent to which tort litigation can be used to question orthodox analyses of science or the acceptability of risk will also depend upon the substantive rules of tort. Not surprisingly, given the earlier comments about the structure of tort, this will depend upon the precise formulation of the claim.

Three particular difficulties require consideration:

—reasonable foreseeability and the reasonable user tests;
—the lack of precautionary reasoning;
—subjectivity of risk.

Notions of orthodoxy are imported into nuisance by its use of a test of reasonable user in cases where there is no physical damage. The expectations which it is reasonable for a landowner to have must inevitably be determined accord-

---

secrecy against the interest in the fair administration of justice. The latter is a strong argument, particularly in the context of a constrained use of Public Interest Immunity following the Scott Inquiry. This gives civil litigation a potential use as a tool to obtain information.

[62] *Access to Justice: Final Report* (London, HMSO, 1996).

[63] See *Abbey National Mortgages plc* v. *Key Surveyors Nationwide Ltd* [1996] 1 WLR 1534 for a pre-Civil Procedure Rules example of this attitude being applied.

Tort and Environmental Pluralism   107

ing to orthodox views. For example, if overhead power cables are frequently erected close to residential properties or schools, it is unlikely that they would be held to be a private nuisance, unless they were proved to cause physical damage. Negligence is, if anything, even more explicit in incorporating orthodoxy into its theory. What amounts to reasonable care and skill in relation to such matters will be judged according to accepted standards recognised by practitioners in the field.[64] Thus if the scientific consensus is that an activity is safe or unlikely to result in significant damage it will be virtually impossible for a claimant to succeed in negligence, even though a contrary scientific view may be emerging in the literature. All the traditional rules about not judging a person's conduct with the benefit of hindsight[65] and the balancing of the advantages of the activity against the risks will apply. The point at which the contrary view should begin to be included in assessments will depend upon the court's view of the acceptable level of risk within society at the particular time. Negligence cases seem to take the view that experts will be called on to determine not only the merits of particular data, but also the acceptability of particular levels of risk. The expert will testify, as far as negligence is concerned, to when evidence about EMF and childhood cancer has become sufficiently substantial to warrant provision for the risk in the exercise of reasonable care and skill.[66] It is possible that *Cambridge Water Co. Ltd* v. *Eastern Counties Leather plc,*[67] has freed *Rylands* v. *Fletcher* from questions of normal or reasonable use of land, by insisting that the meaning of non-natural user of land is not simply governed by ordinary usage.

Orthodoxy, as defined by the relevant statutory agencies, plays a crucial role in environmental torts. A statutory authorisation to discharge into the environment will almost always be decisive in negating a negligence claim and is likely to be of strong persuasive force in a nuisance claim. Equally, in statutory nuisance, whilst the right of individual prosecution is preserved, the views of the local authority as to whether a nuisance exists is highly persuasive, albeit not conclusive.[68]

The differing definitions of damage used by tort share the common feature of constraining the nature of risk which can be explored, and the acceptability of particular levels of risk. Except in those limited cases of imminent major damage where an injunction may be available, tort is concerned with damage which has occurred, not the risk of damage. This immediately sidelines debate about precautionary action, save insofar as it can affect the reasonableness of a particular use, or an assessment of reasonable care and skill. [69]

---

[64] *Bolam* v. *Friern Hospital Management Committee* [1957] 1 WLR 582.

[65] *Roe* v. *Minster of Health* [1954] 2 QB 66.

[66] *Thompson* v. *Smiths Shiprepairers (North Shields) Ltd* [1984] QB 405.

[67] [1994] 2 AC 264.

[68] In such situations the defendant may well call the local authority officer as a witness.

[69] D. Hughes, "Analysis: The Status of the 'Precautionary Principle' in Law", (1995) 7 *Jo. Env. L* at 238–44.

108   *Keith Stanton and Christine Willmore*

One further obstacle to the use of tort to challenge orthodoxy arises from the problem of subjective risk. Expert and lay approaches to risk differ for a host of reasons, not least different evaluations of the consequences of risk, different levels of personal or professional engagement and the nature and subject matter of the risk. Margolis has identified no fewer than 19 significant differences between expert and lay perceptions of environmental risk.[70] Tort is based upon an objective assessment of risk. Whilst English law has hitherto largely avoided an over-numerical approach to risk,[71] its approach remains rooted in objectivity. Only indirectly, through the assessment of reasonableness, can wider societal concerns, or the inherent, but subjective, concern about the subject matter of risk be reflected. Numerically a 10 per cent prospect of a new animal feedstuff causing people to catch a cold may be the same in risk terms as a 10 per cent prospect of the chemical causing Creutzfeld-Jacob syndrome in small children. However much the tortious tests are seen as objective, in assessing whether reasonable care has been taken to prevent those two very differing consequences, courts will have regard to the severity of harm. To that extent, subjective assessments of risk are active in tort.

REGULATING THE REGULATOR

The task of challenging the decisions of regulators is seen as one for judicial review rather than tort. Indeed, there has been a very clear trend in recent years to restrict the role of negligence as a damages remedy against public authorities.[72] These cases have covered both authorities whose acts are alleged to have caused damage and those whose omissions are alleged to have permitted others to act and cause damage. It is the latter group of cases[73] which offer the closest analogy to the likely environmental law scenarios. A regulator might well face an action for permitting or failing to stop an activity. Whilst an application for judicial review might be possible, English law's insistence that compensation can be obtained only on proof of a tort rather than be based on a simple allegation of harm caused by unlawful administrative action effectively denies a damages remedy in the great majority of circumstances given the reluctance to recognise tort rights in these circumstances.[74] Respect for the difficulties facing

[70] H. Margolis, *Dealing with Risk* (Chicago, Ill., University of Chicago Press, 1996).

[71] But see R. Goldberg, *Causation and Risk in the Law of Torts* (Oxford, Hart Publishing, 1999) for the case in favour of numericalisation.

[72] *X (Minor)* v. *Bedfordshire County Council* [1995] 2 AC 633; *Stovin* v. *Wise* [1996] AC 175. See *Z. and others* v. *United Kingdom*; *TP and KM* v. *United Kingdom*, referred from the Commission to the European Court of Human Rights, 5 Nov. 1999.

[73] *Yuen Kun Yeu* v. *Attorney General for Hong Kong* [1998] AC 175 on regulation of financial markets, *Hill* v. *Chief Constable West Yorkshire Police* [1989] AC 53; *Osman* v. *Ferguson* [1993] 4 All E R 344 in relation to the police forces' duty to detect and prevent crime.

[74] In many of the tort cases which have been recorded in recent years, for example, those relating to the treatment of children in care (e.g. *Barrett* v. *Enfield LBC* [1997] 3 All ER 171) judicial review has not been an option: the stringent time limits are likely to have been exceeded.

Tort and Environmental Pluralism   109

those who have to make decisions on the allocation of scarce public resources, or select a course of action from equally hazardous choices, is translated into an extensive immunity from suit.

It is highly questionable whether a regulator would be liable to a negligence claim based on allegations that a permit to discharge had been given erroneously. Even if, a duty of care were established, a claimant would face an enormous burden in proving that a regulator's decision to permit a discharge was negligent in the light of scientific knowledge. The cases in analogous areas suggest that the only route to success would be proof of inadequate research into the issue.[75] Public health scares are likely induce regulators to introduce prohibitions with consequential economic losses along supply chains. But it is difficult to accept that any loss suffered by those parties should rest with the regulators, other than in the most extreme circumstances.[76] The regulator must be entitled to take emergency precautionary measures to protect public health, and there is a strong argument for recognising an immunity from action in such circumstances . However, the position of those who suffer as a result must not be ignored. The smolt supplier in the Braer oil spill case,[77] who suddenly lost his market because fish farmers could not sell any fish and therefore did not wish to buy smolt to rear, has lost income because of the use of an Emergency Exclusion Order prohibiting the sale of fish caught or reared in the affected area. Should his remedy lie against the Secretary of State by way of review of the exercise of the Secretary of State power to make an exclusion order or against the owners of the Braer? At present, he has no remedy at all: as long as the order was legitimately made to protect the public from adulterated salmon there is no remedy in judicial review; and the restrictions applied in tort will almost certainly prevent the recovery of damages.[78] It is not suggested that one would wish to make regulators reluctant to act to protect public health for fear of civil liability—indeed in the Braer case the Order was appropriate—but it is arguable that the tort remedy is too narrow and that a more widely drawn version would support both private and wider environmental interests.

[75] *Vacwell Engineering Co. Ltd* v. *BDH Chemicals Ltd* [1971] 1 QB 111; *Independent Broadcasting Authority* v. *EMI Electronics & BICC Construction* (1980) 14 BLR 1.

[76] See the analogous claim by depositors in the Bank of Credit and Commerce International against the Bank of England which seeks to invoke the tort of misfeasance in public office. The latest stage of these proceedings has failed in the Court of Appeal. See *Three Rivers District Council* v. *Bank of England* [1999] Lloyd's Rep. Bank 283. A further appeal to the House of Lords is expected.

[77] *Landcatch Ltd* v. *The International Oil Pollution Fund* [1999] 2 Lloyd's Rep. 316.

[78] As they did in the Braer case (*Landcatch Ltd* v. *International Oil Pollution Compensation Fund* [1999] 2 Lloyd's Rep. 316). The possibility of recovery of damages against a negligent regulator seemed to have been increased as a result of *Welton* v. *North Cornwall District Council* [1997] 1 WLR 570 in which an environmental health officer was alleged to have caused damage to the business of a guest house by requiring work to be done to its kitchen. However, this result was strongly criticised as being in conflict with the leading authorities (see M. Harris, "*Hedley Byrne* Applied to Public Powers—a Healthy Development?" (1998) 6 *Tort LRev* 187) and was distinguished in *Harris* v. *Evans* [1998] 3 All ER 522 which concerned the issue of improvement and prohibition notices under the Health and Safety at Work Act 1974. In this case it was pointed out that the Act provided a procedure whereby the notices could be challenged. There is, however, no statutory basis upon which a business which has been closed for a period can seek to recover its trading losses.

110   *Keith Stanton and Christine Willmore*

In some situations, however, tort has been used as a vehicle for challenging decisions of administrative bodies, notably in relation to land use planning. In *Allen* v. *Gulf Oil Refining Ltd*,[79] nuisance was used as the basis for challenging a development authorised by a private Act of Parliament,[80] in *Hunter* v. *Canary Wharf Ltd*,[81] it was used to question the consequences of activities of the London Docklands Development Corporation within a designated "enterprise zone", [82] and in *Gillingham Borough Council* v. *Medway (Chatham) Dock Co*.[83] nuisance was used to address the consequences of a planning consent. In all of these cases tort was used as a weapon against individuals whose conduct had been approved by regulators. If successful, such an approach may actually be more potent than an application for judicial review as an injunction has the capacity to block or limit the interference permanently, whereas a successful application for judicial review might only require the decision-making process to be repeated in amended form. Viewed in this way nuisance can be regarded as a tool by which regulatory mechanisms can be both supplemented and, on occasions, challenged. However, for a variety of reasons, none of these cases seems to have provided the plaintiffs with more than limited success and this route cannot be used if the loss is inherent in the exercise of the statutory power or duty.[84]

Whilst success may not be frequent, the Fal estuary case illustrates the continuing pressure for mechanisms to challenge regulatory policy. In *R.* v. *Falmouth and Truro Port Health Authority ex p. South West Water Ltd*,[85] the Environment Agency, as regulatory body, had issued a consent to South West Water to discharge fine-screened sewage into the Fal estuary. The normal statutory provisions controlling water pollution make the existence of a consent a statutory defence.[86] The Port Health Authority had objected unsuccessfully to the grant of the discharge consent and in the face of continuing public concern invoked their statutory nuisance powers.[87] This operates by reference to section 259 of the Public Health Act 1936, which deems it to be a nuisance to have "any pond, ditch, gutter, or watercourse which is so foul or in such a state as to be prejudicial to health or a nuisance". Harrison J took a narrow definition of this wording and concluded that the Fal estuary was not a "pond, ditch, gutter or watercourse". The consequence would seem to be that emitting raw sewage into a small ditch is a statutory nuisance, but polluting the entire Fal estuary is

---

[79] [1981] AC 1014.

[80] The Gulf Oil Refining Act 1965.

[81] [1997] AC 655.

[82] This designation overrode the normal requirements to obtain planning permission for developments and removed the need for a public inquiry which a development on the scale of the Canary Wharf project would normally have required.

[83] [1993] QB 343.

[84] A. Linden, "Strict Liability, Nuisance and Legislative Authority" (1966) 4 *Osgoode Hall LJ* 196.

[85] High Court, 23 Apr. 1999, 292 ENDS 51; [1999] Env. LR 833.

[86] Part III, Ch. II of the Water Resources Act 1991.

[87] S. 79 of the Environmental Protection Act 1990.

not.[88] In such cases, it is arguable that a common law remedy should be available to plug what may be an inadvertent gap in the statutory regime. However, it is difficult to see how a common law action could be brought, given the current state of the common law. Whilst there was evidence of the polluted water making people ill, there might not be an appropriate property link for an action in private nuisance to be brought, and the existence of the discharge consent would undermine an action in negligence. An individual would need to show particular damage, beyond that of the community at large, to sue in public nuisance—and the scale of the pollution may make that difficult. The best option would be an action in public nuisance, brought by the local authority, and therefore not needing the Attorney General's permission;[89] however in the case of less costly inadvertent gaps in the statutory regime, the Attorney General might be willing to act, even against public authorities.[90]

This scenario illustrates the weaknesses of the common law, and the possibility of a significant pollution incident causing demonstrable harm to health which does not give rise to an action for damages. However, it also illustrates a public desire for mechanisms to "second guess" regulatory decisions.

CONCLUSION

In this chapter we have considered the opportunities for tort to fill the interstices in regulatory systems as a voice for pluralism. Tort can fulfill a number of roles in environmental law, particularly in the protection of individual interests, but also in providing a mechanism for testing the decisions of regulators and questioning the orthodox approach to problems. Tort complements regulation: it cannot replace it. However, if effective protection of the environment is to be achieved individuals need to have a stake in the process. Tort has the capacity to be part of this.

If we are to move forward it is essential that a coherent and comprehensive network of tort remedies is developed based on clearly understood notions of the relevant forms of causation, damage and standing. However, a survey of the current state of the environmental torts leaves one wondering whether the forms of action were actually abolished in this area. This requires clarity as to the questions which tort is asked to solve, and those which are more appropriate to judicial review. In the last 15 years the House of Lords has developed the English law of tort on the basis of a conservative approach to theory. This amounts to more than just a reluctance to take on the legislative function. It is an approach

---

[88] Although both could be controlled by the Environment Agency under the Water Resources Act 1991.

[89] On the facts of the Fal estuary case, the Attorney General may not have been willing to bring a relator action, given the implications of success for the future of fine-screened sewage outlets—and the associated cost of enhancement.

[90] Historically see the smallpox cases, *supra*, at n.48.

112 Keith Stanton and Christine Willmore

which sees bodies of doctrine as having established roles and which draws firm lines between them. *Hunter* and *Cambridge Water* stand as major landmarks in this process which make it unlikely that either private nuisance or the rule in *Rylands* v. *Fletcher* will be developed significantly beyond their existing roles. Negligence carries too much baggage to be developed as an environmental tort and the statutory torts are confined to limited problems. Pervasive problems, such as the dominance of private property-based thinking in definitions of damage require a global solution: but the current approach of the House of Lords brings "an environmental *Donoghue* v. *Stevenson*" no nearer: far from it. Indeed, we sound a warning about whether the new Civil Procedure Rules will make it harder, rather than easier, for tort to operate as a voice for pluralism and the testing of orthodoxy. This offers a rather bleak prognosis for the role of tort.

However, there are some opportunities for modest improvements in tort's utility. The existing cause of action which would seem most easily adapted is public nuisance. It has a history of being used as a tool to regulate a wide range of environmental hazards, but, for a number of reasons, this feature has tended to been lost from sight. We would argue that it would not take much for the tort to be reinvigorated, so as to improve the ability of tort to meet the roles set out for it at the start of this chapter.

Two constraints in particular, merit review. At present, an action for public nuisance can be brought only by the Attorney General or a local authority, unless an individual has suffered particular damage. Lord Denning argued that these limitations exist so that citizens are not forced to take individual action to protect their community. He said the test of whether a nuisance is public is whether it:

[i]s so widespread in its range or indiscriminate in its effects that it is not reasonable to expect one person to take proceedings on his own responsibility to put a stop to it.[91]

There is a world of difference between saying individuals should not be expected to act and saying they should not be permitted to do so. If our initial argument about the role of tort in a pluralist society is accepted, then such challenges should be welcomed. Rogers, writing of American environmental law, has called the particular damage rule "an historical procedural appendage".[92] In the UK considerable liberalisation has occurred in providing access to applications for judicial review,[93] and some international developments point the way towards permitting a wider range of bodies to initiate proceedings.[94] Alongside

---

[91] *Attorney General* v. *PYA Quarries Ltd* [1957] 2 QB 169 at 192.

[92] W. Rogers, *Environmental Law* (St Paul, Minn., West, 1977) 106.

[93] R. v. *Inspector of Pollution, ex p. Greenpeace (No 2)* [1994] 4 All ER 329; R. v. *Secretary of State for Foreign Affairs, ex p. World Development Movement Ltd* [1995] 1 All ER 611.

[94] Art 18 of the Council of Europe's, Convention on civil liability for damage resulting from activities dangerous to the environment, 1993, provides that:

"Any association or foundation which according to its statutes aims at the protection of the environment and which complies with any further conditions of internal law of the Party where the request is submitted may, at any time, request:

these developments the standing rules in public nuisance look increasingly anachronistic. Ontario removed the requirement for particular damage in 1994, giving individuals the opportunity to bring public nuisance actions to protect their community, without the consent of the Attorney General.[95] England adopted a more limited liberalisation when access was extended to local authorities in 1972.[96] Whilst local authorities may sometimes be a voice of pluralist dissent, this cannot be assumed. In any event, spending constraints limit the ability of local authorities to act. It is accepted that some limitation upon access to public nuisance may be required, but an adaptation of the judicial review approach to standing, or a redefined "particular damage" rule could provide a control. We are not here arguing for a complete third party right of action: as currently defined tort is a bipolar form of action. We are simply arguing that artificial historical barriers to access by affected individuals be removed.

A more difficult, but related, issue is the current inability of tort to offer any preventive remedy. The notion of a declaration, coupled with liberty to apply for an injunction,[97] has much to commend it as a way of offering judicial guidance to support a negotiated solution, but with speedy access to the court should the worst arise. The current rules for *quia timet* injunctions are extremely strict. We are not arguing that injunctions should be available as a matter of course, but perhaps the *quia timet* rules look out of place in the context of the way injunctions have evolved in other fields. Equity has always accepted that in some cases prevention is better than cure. It is three quarters of a century since the courts had a serious look at the dividing line between prevention and cure. It is time to revisit it.

These are not offered as a panacea for solving tort's problems, but there is a danger that, for fear of not seeing a global solution, tort does nothing. If that happens, the current growth in the use of judicial review to protect private interests and challenge orthodoxy in relation to environmental concerns will continue to the long term detriment of tort.

> (a) the prohibition of a dangerous activity which is unlawful and poses a grave threat of damage to the environment;
> (b) that the operator be ordered to take measures to prevent an incident or damage;
> (c) that the operator be ordered to take measures, after an incident, to prevent damage; or
> (d) that the operator be ordered to take measures of reinstatement."

The Convention leaves domestic law to determine whether such a request is to be made to a judicial or administrative body.

[95] Environmental Rights Act, Ontario, 1994. s.103: "[n]o person who has suffered or may suffer a direct economic loss or direct personal injury as a result of a public nuisance that caused harm to the environment shall be barred from bringing an action without the consent of the Attorney General in respect of the loss or injury only because the person has suffered or may suffer direct economic loss or direct personal injury of the same kind or to the same degree as other persons". Although note that Ontario did not have a provision for local authority action.

[96] S. 222 of the Local Government Act 1972.

[97] *Litchfield-Speer* v. *Queen Anne's Gate Syndicate (No 2) Ltd* [1919] 1 Ch. 407.

6

Statutory Liability for Contaminated Land: Failure of the Common Law?

OWEN McINTYRE

INTRODUCTION

WITH THE INTRODUCTION into the UK of a statutory liability scheme for the remediation of historically contaminated land, there is inevitable debate on the merits of such a statutory regime over traditional common law actions and vice versa. This chapter seeks to examine the shortcomings inherent in the common law when applied to claims for environmental damage and, in so doing, it traces the background to the introduction of statutory provisions on liability for contaminated land. It also sets out to consider the future role of environmental tort actions in the light of statutory liability schemes and the relationship between such actions and statutory controls generally.

DEFICIENCIES OF THE COMMON LAW

The introduction of a system of statutory civil liability, which will function to allocate responsibility for the remediation of historically contaminated land, can be seen to be part of a trend. One can argue that public and administrative law mechanisms play an increasingly significant role in preventing and remedying environmental harm. Statutory regimes such as those concerned with development control or pollution licensing can be based upon common standards of environmental quality and can be enforced proactively by dedicated public agencies. Indeed, a statutory licensing mechanism may even contain explicit provisions creating a civil liability regime for any damage or loss resulting from breach of the licensing provisions.[1] Furthermore, it has long been recognised that common law tools suffer inherent inadequacies for resolving environmental disputes and remedying environmental interferences.[2] Though dealt with

---

[1] E.g., s. 73(6) of the Environmental Protection Act, 1990 imposes civil liability for damage resulting from a waste management licensing offence under s. 33.

[2] While it is recognised that tort law plays a dual role in protecting the environment, a deterrent role and a remedial role, it is intended in this chapter to concentrate on the latter as it is this role which the new statutory regime will function to supplement or supplant.

116   Owen McIntyre

more fully elsewhere,[3] it may be helpful to recount briefly the perceived deficiencies of each of the most relevant common law actions in relation to environmental disputes.

The tort of trespass appears at first glance to be a particularly appropriate action protecting, as it does, an occupier's right to enjoy land without unjustified interference. An environmental action will arise where a defendant causes polluting matter to come into physical contact with another's land. However, the courts have limited its application to "direct" interference which, in the environmental context, will often be very difficult to establish.[4] Also, the action is by definition restricted to plaintiffs enjoying legal occupation of land and suffering some interference relating to rights flowing from that occupation. As with several of the other relevant tort actions, the requirement of a recognised proprietary interest may severely restrict the class of persons eligible to seek redress.

Similarly, negligence, the most adaptable and widely applied of all tort actions, is limited in its applicability to environmental disputes. Though right of action is not based on proprietary interests but on the existence of a duty of care, it may prove very difficult to establish that the defendant's offending behaviour amounted to breach of that duty. What amounts to breach will depend on a wide variety of factors, including, *inter alia,* any accepted safety standards relating to the offending activity during the relevant period. Indeed, it may not even be possible to establish the existence of a duty of care.[5] Similarly, establishing a causal connection between a particular activity and damage or injury in environmental cases may involve hugely complex scientific or epidemiological evidence and may ultimately prove impossible.[6] Also, the resulting damage must be reasonably foreseeable, i.e. to a reasonable person in the defendant's position, for a negligence action to succeed.[7] In addition, it is a fundamental requirement of negligence that physical damage or injury results from the offending activity. Therefore, though it suits a plaintiff who has suffered actual physical injury or damage to property as a result of an identifiable negligent act, it is less suitable

---

[3] See e.g. J.P.S. McLaren, "Nuisance Law and the Industrial Revolution—Some Lessons from Social History" (1983) 3 *OJLS* 155–221; J.F. Brenner, "Nuisance Law and the Industrial Revolution" (1974) 3 *JLS* 403–33; D.N. Dewees, "The Efficiency of the Common Law: Sulpher Dioxide Emissions in Sudbury" (1992) 42 *University of Toronto Law Journal* 1–21; J. Steele, "Assessing the Past: Tort Law and Environmental Risk" in T. Jewell and J. Steele (eds.), *Law in Environmental Decision-Making: National, European and International Perspectives* (Oxford, Clarendon Press, 1998).

[4] See *Southport Corporation* v. *Esso Petroleum Co. Ltd* [1954] 2 QB 182.

[5] See e.g., *Gunn* v. *Wallsend Slipway an Engineering Co. Ltd*, (1989) *The Times*, 23 Jan. 1989, where no duty of care was established between an employer and an employee's wife who died from an asbestos related disease as a result of asbestos brought into the home on her husband's work clothes.

[6] See *Reay* v. *British Nuclear Fuels plc*, 1990 No. 860 (unreported) and *Hope* v. *British Nuclear Fuels plc*, 1989 No. 3689 (unreported). For a concise introduction to the problems of establishing causation in a class of such negligence actions, see M. Day, "Cancer: Proving the Causal Link, Tobacco, Radiation and Environmental Pollution" (1998) 66 *Medico-Legal Journal* 141.

[7] E.g. in *Cambridge Water Co.* v. *Eastern Counties Leather* [1994] 1 All ER 53, the High Court dismissed the action in negligence, having found that pollution of a chalk aquifer by ongoing, small-scale accidental spillages of a solvent was not foreseeable by a reasonable supervisor.

Statutory Liability for Contaminated Land   117

where a plaintiff objects to a continuing though less damaging interference and totally unsuitable for so-called "sensibility claims".[8]

Private nuisance, "the primary vehicle for actions in environmental cases",[9] is similarly restricted in its application to many environmental disputes.[10] As an action which arises where there is an unreasonable interference with an occupier's use and enjoyment of land, it is restricted to those situations where a plaintiff possesses a recognised proprietary interest in land which has been or continues to be affected. Recent attempts by the Court of Appeal to broaden the scope of private nuisance,[11] by extending the class of interests which would entitle a plaintiff to sue, have been reversed by the House of Lords.[12] There would now appear to be little prospect of the right to sue in nuisance ever being extended to include those who are in "substantial occupation" of property but possess no formal proprietary right. Therefore, spouses and other family members living in the family home, those who regularly enjoy the use of public parks, the countryside and other amenities, lodgers, sedentary employees and many others will continue to be disqualified from suing in nuisance for loss, injury or personal discomfort. Where the legal occupier of land is disinclined, for whatever reason, to act to protect or restore the environmental condition of that land, it is not possible for any other person, no matter how affected, to take an action in nuisance. In *Hunter*, the majority in the House of Lords were resolutely determined that nuisance should remain a tort connected with rights in land, Lord Goff stating that "the extension of the tort in this way would transform it from a tort to land into a tort to the person. This is, in my opinion, not an acceptable way in which to develop the law."[13] Addressing calls from academics and others for the tort of nuisance to be updated and adapted to changing societal needs, and to the role of environmental dispute settlement in particular, Lord Hoffmann stated that:

> There is a good deal in this case and other writings about the need for the law to adapt to modern societal conditions. But the development of the common law should be rational and coherent. It should not distort its principles and create anomalies merely as an expedient to fill a gap.[14]

[8] See M. Lee, "Environmental Blight: Liability at Common Law" [1998] *Env. Liability* 56, where a "sensibility" claim is defined as one made against a defendant for "unduly interfering with one's neighbour in the comfortable and convenient enjoyment of his or her land", at 58.

[9] R. Malcolm, *A Guidebook to Environmental Law* (London, Sweet & Maxwell, 1994), at 37. The tort of nuisance has also been described as "the environmental tort *par excellence*": see J. Wightman, "Nuisance—the Environmental Tort? *Hunter* v. *Canary Wharf* in the House of Lords" (1998) 61 *MLR* 870.

[10] For a detailed account, see G. Cross, "Does Only the Careless Polluter Pay? A Fresh Examination of the Law of Private Nuisance" (1995) 111 *LQR* 453 and C. Gearty, "The Place of Private Nuisance in the Modern Law of Torts" (1989) 48 *CLJ* 214.

[11] *Khorasandjian* v. *Bush* [1993] 3 WLR 476 and *Hunter and others* v. *London Docklands Development Corp.* [1997] 2 All ER 426.

[12] *Hunter* v. *Canary Wharf Ltd* [1997] AC 677. On the implications of this decision, see Wightman, *supra*, n. 9.

[13] *Ibid.*, at 693.

[14] *Ibid.*, at 707.

118   Owen McIntyre

Indeed, not only must the plaintiff's use or enjoyment of land be impaired but such impairment must also arise by means of the defendant's use of his land. Therefore, private nuisance is restricted to disputes concerning competing and incompatible uses of land. This was aptly illustrated in *Southport Corporation v. Esso Petroleum Co. Ltd,*[15] where the court held that "the discharge of oil [onto the plaintiff's foreshore] was not a private nuisance because it did not involve the use by the defendant of any land, but only of a ship at sea". This requirement may create problems for any party seeking redress for interferences such as those resulting from another's use of the public road network, airspace or shipping lanes.

In addition, any injury or damage or interference with the beneficial use of a plaintiff's property must have been reasonably foreseeable.[16] This will be even more difficult to establish in the case of the small-scale and continuing escapes and emanations which have traditionally given rise to environmental nuisance actions. The subjective nature of nuisance further retards its usefulness. In the absence of physical damage,[17] the so-called "locality doctrine" comes into play whereby the character of the locality is considered in determining the reasonableness of a defendant's activity.[18] Therefore, an environmental interference which amounts to an actionable nuisance in one neighbourhood may not do so in another. Also, recent judicial caution towards the progressive development of the tort of nuisance has extended beyond the question of *locus standi* to the identification and recognition of new interferences capable of amounting to nuisance. In *Hunter,*[19] the House of Lords unanimously upheld the decision of the Court of Appeal that interference with plaintiffs' television reception was not actionable in nuisance. The Lords reached this decision on a variety of grounds despite evidence showing that in the UK people watch an average of 24 hours' television weekly. Also, the growing prevalence and importance of technology involving electro-magnetic waves and of the possible implications of their obstruction, and judicial recognition of similar interference as nuisance in other common law jurisdictions,[20] could not inspire judicial innovation among the Lords. Such inflexibility is unlikely to assist the progressive development of nuisance as a modern environmental tort or to encourage reliance on nuisance to protect environmental values and interests.

---

[15] *Supra,* n. 4.

[16] See *Cambridge Water Co.* v. *Eastern Counties Leather, supra,* n. 7, where the High Court also dismissed the action in nuisance on the ground that the damage was not reasonably foreseeable. This requirement was established in nuisance in *The Wagon Mound (No. 2)* [1967] 1 AC 617.

[17] Where physical damage to property has occurred the doctrine will not apply and the character of the locality will not be considered by the court in determining whether a nuisance action will succeed: see *St Helens Smelting Co.* v. *Tipping* (1865) 11 HLC 642.

[18] See, *inter alia, Sturges* v. *Bridgeman* (1879) 11 Ch. D 852; *Rushmer* v. *Polsue and Alfieri* [1906] 1 Ch. 234, [1907] AC 121; *Gillingham BC* v. *Medway (Chatham) Dock Co.* [1992] JPL 458; *Wheeler* v. *Saunders* [1995] JPL 619.

[19] *Supra,* n.12.

[20] See e.g., the Canadian decision in *Nor-Video Services* v. *Ontario Hydro* (1978) 84 DLR (3rd) 221.

Statutory Liability for Contaminated Land 119

The doctrine of strict liability established in *Rylands* v. *Fletcher*,[21] appears almost to have been devised with environmental disputes in mind as it is concerned with escapes of potentially dangerous substances or objects from land which result in damage. Indeed, in Blackburn J's original judgment he refers to the "person . . . whose cellar is invaded by the filth of his neighbour's privy, or whose habitation is made unhealthy by the fumes and noisome vapours of his neighbour's alkali works". However, while upholding the original judgment on appeal, the House of Lords added the requirement that the defendant must have been engaged in a "non-natural use of his land" and the scope of this requirement has remained uncertain throughout the life of the doctrine.[22] It has traditionally been interpreted in such a way as to limit severely the number of activities which might be considered non-natural.[23] Therefore, the action has tended to be under-used and has been criticised on this ground by the Law Commission.[24] Also, as with nuisance, the action is restricted to plaintiffs who possess an interest in land, and no action can lie for loss or injury suffered by non-landowners as a result of the escape of dangerous substances. Furthermore, the doctrine creates strict, but not absolute, liability and it is now clearly established that the damage must have been reasonably foreseeable.[25] It is important to note that the House of Lords decision in *Cambridge Water* reintegrates the rule in *Rylands* v. *Fletcher* with the tort of nuisance, suggesting that it is merely a form of nuisance action appropriate for disputes involving escapes of dangerous substances. Therefore, its environmental application is limited by many of the same factors which limit the application of nuisance.

In addition to the specific shortcomings of each common law action listed above, there are other general factors which mitigate against the use of private tort actions to seek redress in environmental disputes. For example, the transaction costs and risks involved in an adversarial system of civil justice may prove even more discouraging where litigation is likely to prove lengthy and technically complex. Also, in environmental cases there may often be uncertainty regarding the damages to which a successful plaintiff would be entitled. Damages aim to place the plaintiff as far as possible in the position he would have been in had the wrongful act not occurred. With regard to damage to property, compensation would be calculated either on the cost of clean-up

---

[21] (1868) LR 3, HL 330.

[22] See e.g., *Rainham Chemical Works Ltd* v. *Belvedere Fish Guano Company* [1921] 2 AC 465, where the manufacture of explosives was held to be a non-natural use, and *Read* v. *J. Lyons & Co. Ltd* [1947] AC 156, where it was not.

[23] Based on the decision in *Rickards* v. *Lothian* [1913] AC 263. However, recent judicial discussion of the non-natural user test in *Cambridge Water* appears to have given a much more liberal interpretation to the test and to suggest that many activities with the potential to cause damage to the environment would constitute a non-natural user: see *infra*.

[24] *Report of the Law Commission on Civil Liability for Dangerous Things and Activities*, Law Com. No. 32, cited by Malcolm, *supra*, n.9, at 44.

[25] See *Cambridge Water*, *supra*, n.7.

120   *Owen McIntyre*

operations necessary to restore the land to its previous state,[26] or the difference between the value of the property before and after the pollution occurred. In some instances it will not be possible to reinstate property by any means, and assessing diminution in property value can prove both difficult and controversial.[27] Indeed, though physical damage is a fundamental requirement of negligence and a traditional head of damage in nuisance, it is by no means clear at what point the mere presence of pollution constitutes damage.[28]

The problems involved in attributing liability for the restoration of historically contaminated land have presented a particular challenge for the common law. Most significantly, the requirement that any damage caused must have been reasonably foreseeable at the time of the activity giving rise to the damage has now been clearly established with regard to each relevant tort action. Much industrial land will be found to be contaminated by virtue of activities carried on many decades ago when knowledge of the properties of substances employed and of the health and ecological risks associated with such substances was underdeveloped. Generally accepted standards of safety and environmental management, where they existed at all, would often be found to be hopelessly inadequate, thereby creating difficulties for the plaintiff seeking to establish fault in negligence. Common law principles alone would be inadequate to dictate the level of remediation required with regard to the particular circumstances of individual sites whilst ensuring an efficient allocation of scarce environmental resources. Also, any regime for the allocation of responsibility for the remediation of contaminated land would require sophisticated arrangements for the apportionment of liability where multiple wrongdoers have been identified. Finally, where the activities resulting in the contamination of land have occurred in the distant past, it becomes increasingly likely that the party responsible under common law principles will have ceased to exist. Even where it would still be possible to take an action against that party's erstwhile insurer, the practical and evidential difficulties would be considerable. In the light of these inherent problems in the common law in relation to disputes over contaminated land, the need for legislation has been obvious for some time.

ENVIRONMENTAL PROTECTION ACT 1990, PART IIA

In recent years, a number of high-profile incidents in the UK involving contaminated land have highlighted the need for legislative measures which clearly impose responsibility and allocate costs for the remediation of such contamina-

---

[26] However, while liability in tort may require payment towards the cost of restoration of the land, it does not necessarily require that the land be restored to the *status quo ante*, even though that may be possible. See J. Steele, "Remedies and Remediation: Foundational Issues in Environmental Liability" (1995) 58 *MLR* 615.

[27] For example, on the vexed issue of liability at common law for "environmental blight", see Lee, *supra*, n.8.

[28] *Ibid.*, at 58.

tion. These include those at the Chemstar solvent recovery works at Stalybridge, the Laporte Works at Ilford and the Ministry of Defence site at Lumsden Road in Portsmouth. After the failure and abandonment of initial measures intended to establish public registers of potentially contaminated land and to provide for the remediation of closed landfill sites causing pollution, the UK government eventually introduced a statutory regime imposing liability initially on the polluter with residual liability falling on the innocent landowner or occupier. This regime, in common with UK statutory nuisance provisions,[29] requires the identification of contaminated land through local authority inspection and provides for remediation of the most dangerously polluted sites, i.e. those causing or likely to cause further harm. Such sites are to be remediated to the extent necessary for particular specified uses. As with many recent statutory environmental measures, much of the substance and detail of the provisions are to be contained in guidance notes, some binding and some merely advisory, which are to be issued after extensive consultation. Despite the regulatory character of the provisions, it seems likely that their most important function will be to provide certainty regarding potential liability for those involved in transactions for the sale or development of contaminated land, thereby making it easier for parties to negotiate warranties and indemnities. In this way the provisions can give effect to the government's preferred policy of harnessing market forces to remediate contaminated land.

The Environment Act 1995 represents the UK government's second attempt to get to grips with the problem of contaminated land. Section 143 of the Environmental Protection Act 1990 was adopted to establish registers of potentially contaminated land but, on 24 March 1993, Michael Howard, then Secretary of State for the Environment, announced the withdrawal of the provision and a general review of the legal powers of regulatory public bodies to control and tackle land pollution. Section 143 had many critics, and thus a turbulent, if brief, existence. This criticism was well founded.[30] First, it required registration of all land that had been subjected to contaminative uses irrespective of whether actual contamination had occurred. The government realised that, throughout the UK, an enormous amount of land was potentially contaminated and would thus be "blighted" by the registers and, therefore, reduced the number of suggested categories of contaminative use from 40, in its first consultation paper on the subject,[31] to eight, in its second such paper.[32] Secondly, the legislation contained no procedure for deregistering land once it was found to be free of all contamination or once it had been adequately cleaned up. Therefore, many "brownfield" sites would be likely to remain blighted

---

[29] Under s. 79 of the Environmental Protection Act 1990.

[30] See S. Tromans, *The Environmental Protection Act 1990: Text and Commentary* (2nd edn., London, Sweet & Maxwell, 1993), at 296–8; R Lewis, "Contaminated Land: The New Regime of the Environment Act 1995" [1995] *JPL* at 1087–8.

[31] *Public Registers of Land Which May Be Contaminated* (London, DoE, May 1991).

[32] *Environmental Protection Act: Section 143 Registers* (London, DoE, July 1992).

122   *Owen McIntyre*

indefinitely, thus discouraging the development of such sites and increasing development pressures on greenfield sites. Indeed, by failing to provide for deregistration of sites on clean-up, it effectively discouraged market forces from becoming involved through redevelopment. Thirdly, section 143 had only ever offered an incomplete policy solution to the problem of contaminated land as it did not stipulate, once contaminated sites were identified, what, if any, remedial action was to be taken or who would be liable for the cost of such action.

Similarly, section 61 of the Environmental Protection Act 1990 was to have placed a duty on Waste Regulation Authorities to inspect closed landfill sites and detect whether they were in such a condition that they may cause pollution of the environment or harm to human health. Where this was the case the authority would have been under a duty to carry out such remedial works as appeared to it to be reasonable to avoid such pollution or harm and it would have been entitled to recover the costs incurred from the person who was for the time being the owner of the land. However, this section was never implemented and the Department of the Environment (DoE) announced in November 1994 that "special arrangements will be put in place for monitoring and controlling any closed landfill sites which come within the definition of contaminated land, replacing the unimplemented provisions of section 61 of the 1990 Act".[33]

The vacuum existing in UK law and the resulting need for a comprehensive statutory response to the problem of contaminated land has been highlighted in recent years. In *Cambridge Water Company* v. *Eastern Counties Leather*,[34] Lord Goff suggested that legislation would be required when he stated that it would be more appropriate for any system of strict liability for environmental damage to be introduced by Parliament than by the courts:

> I incline to the opinion that, as a general rule, it is more appropriate for strict liability in respect of operations of high risk to be imposed by Parliament, than by the courts. If such liability is imposed by statute, the relevant activities can be identified, and those concerned can know where they stand. Futhermore, statute can where appropriate lay down precise criteria establishing the incidence and scope of such liability.[35]

Also, with regard to retrospective liability for historical pollution, he stated that "it would be strange if liability for such pollution were to arise under a principle of common law".[36]

The deficiencies in the English law were further highlighted by the work of the Commission of the European Community in its embryonic attempts to formulate a Community-wide regime of civil liability for environmental damage. The debate surrounding the publication of the 1993 Commission Green Paper on remedying damage to the environment,[37] and the UK government's obstructive

---

[33] *Framework for Contaminated Land* (London, DoE 1994), para. 4.3.6.

[34] *Supra*, n.7.

[35] *Ibid.*, at 76.

[36] *Ibid.*, at 78.

[37] Communication from the Commission to the Council and Parliament on Environmental Liability, COM(93)47. See O. McIntyre, "European Community Proposals on Civil Liability for Environmental Damage—Issues and Implications" [1995] *Environmental Liability* 29.

Statutory Liability for Contaminated Land 123

response, inevitably drew attention to the fact that the UK, almost alone among its European counterparts, had, as yet, no dedicated statutory liability system covering contaminated land.

The new contaminated land provisions are contained in section 57 of the Environment Act 1995 which inserts a new Part IIA into the Environmental Protection Act 1990 (EPA), consisting of sections 78A to 78YC. After much delay, these provisions are due to enter into force in April 2000. The adoption of section 57 meets the DoE's objective of establishing a "modern, specific contaminated land power",[38] and provides, for the first time in UK law, a specific definition of contaminated land and separate procedures for its control and remediation. It replaces, as regards contaminated land, the statutory nuisance provisions contained in sections 79–82 of the 1990 Act. The section 57 provisions were conceived with the criticism of section 143 very much in mind.[39] The new provisions establish a system which provides for the identification of contaminated sites by reference to the risk posed by contaminants actually present on the site in the context of that site's intended use. Therefore, land would not automatically be blighted by virtue of its having been subjected to potentially contaminating past uses or even by the mere presence of contaminants. They also provide for the level of remediation to be carried out, requiring the cost of clean-up to be balanced against the risk of harm, that risk again being measured in terms of further harm and intended use. The various persons on whom liability may be imposed for the cost of clean-up are identified and a hierarchy of liability established. The duty to identify contaminated land and the person or persons responsible for remediation, as well as that of determining what remediation is to be undertaken, is placed on the local authority,[40] or in the case of a site designated a "special site",[41] on the Environment Agency. The legislation provides for the enforcing authority to undertake remedial measures itself in the case of an emergency or where no responsible party can be found.[42] Where the party identified as responsible fails to undertake the required remediation, the enforcing authority may act and recover its costs from that party.[43] The defaulter will also be criminally liable.[44] Each enforcing authority is placed under a duty to maintain a public register of contaminated land identified within its jurisdiction. Consistent with government policy, the provisions allow market

[38] *Framework for Contaminated Land*, (London, DoE, 1994), para. 3.4.4.

[39] For the new government policy, see *ibid*. See also P. Lane and M. Peto, *Blackstone's Guide to the Environment Act 1995* (London, Blackstone Press, 1995), at 137.

[40] Under s. 78A(9), a local authority in England and Wales is any unitary authority, any district council so far as it is not a unitary authority, or the Common Council of the City of London.

[41] Under s. 78C(8), a contaminated site is to be designated as a special site by the relevant local authority if it is of a description prescribed by regs. to be made by the Secretary of State. Under s. 78C(10), the regulations may, in particular, have regard to whether the harm or pollution concerned is serious or whether the Environment Agency is likely to have expertise in dealing with that harm or pollution.

[42] S. 78N.

[43] S. 78P.

[44] S. 78M.

124   *Owen McIntyre*

forces and pressure for development to play a role in the remediation of contaminated land while preserving the *caveat emptor* principle. In this way much of the burden of inspecting potentially contaminated land will fall, at the transactional stage, on parties contracting for land. To ameliorate the harsh application of the new provisions, the enforcing authority may, when deciding whether or not to order remediation, have regard to hardship that would be caused to the liable party.

Contaminated Land

An all-embracing definition of contaminated land would be very difficult to formulate and might cast a very wide net, placing a sudden and unacceptably onerous burden on the economy. This concern was first voiced in the government's 1990 White Paper which stated that "[a]ction on the environment has to be proportionate to the costs involved and to the ability of those affected to pay them. So it is particularly important for Governments to adopt the most cost-effective instruments for controlling pollution and tackling environmental problems."[45] The government again alluded to this concern in 1994 when it stated that "[i]t would be neither feasible nor sensible to try to deal with all land contaminated by past activities at once—the wealth-creating sectors of the economy could not afford to do so" and that contaminated land problems should be dealt with "in an orderly and controlled fashion with which the economy at large and individual businesses and land-owners can cope".[46]

The potential scale of the problem and of the costs involved is enormous. A 1988 survey undertaken by Liverpool University on behalf of the Welsh Office identified 746 potentially contaminated sites in Wales with an estimated area of 4,080 hectares.[47] Friends of the Earth have estimated that there may be as many as 100,000 contaminated sites in England,[48] which, according to the Confederation of British Industry, might cover as much as 200,000 hectares of land and cost up to £20 billion to investigate and, where appropriate, remedy.[49] Therefore, the government has opted for a loose definition which leaves room for further policy guidance which may take account of advances in scientific understanding of the risks associated with contamination to identify priority contaminants and sites. In this way "the overall expenditure on investigation or remedial work can be spread over many years, even decades".[50]

---

[45] 1990 White Paper, *This Common Inheritance: Britain's Environmental Startegy* (Cmnd. 1200, London, HMSO, September 1990), para. 1.24.

[46] *Supra*, n.38, para. 2.6.

[47] *Paying for our Past* (London, DoE, March 1994), para. 2.8.

[48] *Buyer Beware: A Guide to Finding Out about Contaminated Land"* (London, FoE, July 1993). See *Paying for Our Past* supra, n.47, para. 2.10.

[49] *Firm Foundations: CBI Proposals for Environmental Liability and Contaminated Land* (London, CBI, October 1993). See *Paying for Our Past, supra,* n.47.

[50] *Ibid.*, para. 2.13.

The new statutory definition of "contaminated land" is contained in section 78A(2) of EPA which provides:

> Contaminated land is any land which appears to the local authority in whose area it is situated to be in such a condition, by reason of substances in, on or under the land, that—
> (a) significant harm is being caused or there is a significant possibility of such harm being caused, or
> (b) pollution of controlled waters is being, or is likely to be, caused.

This definition is sufficiently wide to include much of the land covered by the derelict land grant provisions as well as contaminated land still in beneficial use. For derelict land grant purposes the DoE has defined "derelict land" as "land which is so damaged by industrial or other development that it is incapable of beneficial use without treatment". For the purposes of the new provisions, "harm" is, in turn, defined as: "harm to the health of living organisms or other interference with the ecological systems of which they form part and, in the case of man, includes harm to his property".[51] "Substance" is widely defined to mean "any natural or artificial substance, whether in solid or liquid form or in the form of a gas or vapour".[52]

Contaminated land will be land which "appears" to be such to the enforcing authority. This implies that, rather than acting on the basis of mere speculation, the authority would need to justify the designation of land as contaminated. In making such a determination an authority must have regard to guidance to be issued by the Secretary of State, in accordance with section 78YA, as to:

(a) what harm is to be regarded as "significant";
(b) whether the possibility of significant harm being caused is "significant"; and
(c) whether pollution of controlled waters is being, or is likely to be, caused.[53]

Section 78A(6) provides that such guidance may assign different degrees of importance to:

(a) different descriptions of living organisms or ecological systems;
(b) different descriptions of places; or
(c) different descriptions of harm to health or property, or other interference.

Furthermore, the guidance may make provision for different degrees of possibility to be regarded as "significant" in relation to different descriptions of significant harm. For consultation purposes, the DoE has issued very detailed draft guidance on determination of whether land is contaminated.[54]

---

[51] S. 78A(4).
[52] S. 78A(9).
[53] S. 78A(5).
[54] *[Draft] Guidance on Determination of Whether Land is Contaminated Land under the Provisions of [Part IIA of the Environmental Protection Act 1990]* (London, DoE, 5 May 1995). Discussion on the guidance is ongoing and the latest discussion draft was issued by the DETR in October 1998.

126   *Owen McIntyre*

Significant Harm

In order for a site to fall within the statutory definition of "contaminated land", harm caused by contamination on the site must be "significant" or there must be a "significant possibility of such harm being caused". This qualification was included by amendments introduced at the Report Stage by the House of Lords which, according to Viscount Ullswater, "meet many of the concerns as to the scope of these provisions raised by noble Lords in our debate on this clause in committee".[55]

The qualification of "significant harm" involves consideration by the enforcing authority of the extent of any harm and of the nature of what might be affected, i.e. the target. The test relating to the "significant possibility" of significant harm being caused requires the enforcing authority to strike a balance between the probability of any harm arising, and the consequences if it does. Such consideration will involve the application of risk assessment techniques to be contained in binding guidance to be issued by the Secretary of State.[56] For example, with regard to effects on human health arising from an intake of pollutants, the possibility of harm would be "assessed in relation to appropriate, authoritative and scientifically based information on the toxicological properties of those pollutants".[57] This would require the preparation, in turn, of technical documents on the toxicological properties of a wide variety of substances occurring on land. The possibility of significant harm being caused to ecological systems or living organisms in protected habitats would be significant where it was likely that there would be a breach of any relevant provision under which the habitat is protected.[58]

Pollution of Controlled Waters

The other test for determining whether land is contaminated for the purposes of the new provisions, that of causing "pollution of controlled waters" is defined as meaning "the entry into controlled waters of any poisonous, noxious or polluting matter or any solid waste matter".[59] This definition uses the terminology employed in section 161 of the Water Resources Act 1991 and is not intended to create any additional liability for pollution of controlled waters but to provide a single process for dealing with contaminated land problems.[60] One advantage with this approach is that the terminology employed in the Water Resources Act

---

[55] HL Debs., vol. 562, 7 March 1995, cols. 137–8.

[56] See papers prepared by the DoE for an informal consultation meeting between DoE officials and representatives of interested bodies (London, DoE, 16 February 1996). It is stressed that these papers are merely early working drafts, that the DoE is not committed to the texts as they stand and that a draft for consultation will be issued once these drafts have been further developed.

[57] *Supra*, n.54, Ch. I, para. 14.

[58] *Ibid.*, Ch. I, para. 16.

[59] S. 78A(9).

[60] Viscount Ullswater, *supra*, n.55.

Statutory Liability for Contaminated Land   127

has benefited from a wealth of judicial attention and has, therefore, been rendered relatively certain in scope and application.[61] Indeed, there would appear to be a conscious effort to maintain the overall coherence and uniformity of UK environmental controls. In 1994, the government listed as one of its overall policy aims that "UK policy towards land contamination fits within an overall environmental policy".[62] To this end, the new section 78YB(2) of the EPA 1990 provides that the new contaminated land provisions will not apply to any land in respect of which there exists a waste management licence under Part II of the EPA 1990. Where a waste management licence exists, civil liability for damage caused as a result of any activity authorised under the licence, whether or not in breach of a licence condition, will only arise under Part II. Also, section 78YC provides that the new measures will not apply to land contamination caused by radiation, unless this is expressly provided for in regulations. Similarly, "harm", as defined in section 78A(4), does not, as in section 29 of the EPA, include offences to the senses. Land shall not be regarded as contaminated on the basis of escaping smells which may be offensive, though not harmful. Smells will continue to be dealt with under the statutory nuisance provisions in Part III of the EPA.[63]

In fact, the government has consistently maintained that Part IIA will not impose any new liabilities but will, instead, consolidate and clarify existing requirements with regard to contaminated land. Viscount Ullswater has argued that "[it] was the position under the statutory nuisance powers in Part III of the EPA and also reflects the position of the common law"[64] and that "our intention is not to increase existing liabilities under the legislation".[65] Commentators have, however, criticised this reading of the provisions.[66] The recent working draft guidance states that "the new controls will complement other regimes" and that "although the regime itself is new, its overall structure and the nature of the controls it can apply broadly reflect existing, more general, powers under 'statutory nuisance' legislation. These other powers will cease to apply to contaminated land."[67]

---

[61] Examples of cases which have involved the interpretation of s. 161 terminology (though in the context of s. 85(1) offences) include *Empress Car Company (Abertillery) Limited* v. *National Rivers Authority* [1998] 1 All ER 481; *R.* v. *Dovermoss, The Times*, 3 February 1995; and *National Rivers Authority* v. *Biffa Waste Services Ltd, The Times*, 21 November 1995. See also O. McIntyre, "The Concept of Causing in Environmental Offences" (1998) 5 *Irish Planning and Environmental Law Journal* 57–61. On what amounts to "poisonous, noxious or polluting", see W. Howarth, "Poisonous, Noxious or Polluting: Contrasting Approaches to Environmental Regulation", (1993) 56 *MLR* 171–87.

[62] *Supra*, n.47, para. 2.1.

[63] *Per* Viscount Ullswater, HL Debs., vol. 560, 31 January 1995, col. 1440.

[64] *Ibid.*, at col. 1461.

[65] HL Debs., vol. 562, No. 52, col. 143.

[66] See A. Layard, "Contaminated Land: Law and Policy in the United Kingdom" [1995] *Environmental Liability* 56.

[67] *Supra*, n.54, Introduction, paras. 7–8.

128   *Owen McIntyre*

Suitable for Use Approach

The new harm-based definition of contaminated land reflects the government's adoption of a "suitable for use approach". The new definition depends on a specified or proposed use of the land as opposed to the section 143 definition which only had regard to a past use. This approach would require restoration of contaminated land to a level suitable for certain predetermined purposes and contrasts with a "multi-functional approach" which would require restoration of the land to a level suitable for any purpose, i.e. to the pristine state in which it existed before any damage occurred.[68] The adoption of a "suitable for use approach", which concentrates on future rather than past land use, marks, as regards the identification and remediation of contaminated land, a shift in emphasis in government thinking. In a 1987 circular, the DoE advised local planning authorities that: "knowledge of the previous uses of a site is therefore essential before deciding whether further investigation is needed, and if it is, to assist in designing suitable programmes of sampling and analysis".[69] The circular then lists examples of past industrial uses likely to be associated with contamination, including, *inter alia,* asbestos works, chemical works, gasworks, landfills, oil refineries and tanneries. More comprehensive lists of potentially contaminative uses were then included in consultation papers issued as part of the process intended to lead to the preparation of the section 143 registers.[70] The shift in emphasis to future land use was apparent throughout the consultation exercise. *Paying for Our Past* expressly alluded to the "suitable for use approach" and stated that the government's policy was that "works, if any, required to be undertaken for any contaminated site should deal with any unacceptable risks to health or the environment, taking into account its actual or intended use".[71] The document goes on to state that the aims of this approach are:

—to deal with actual or perceived threats to health, safety or the environment;
—where practicable, to keep or to bring back such land into beneficial use; and so
—to minimise avoidable pressures on greenfield sites.[72]

The Government subsequently confirmed that it was "committed to the 'suitable for use' approach to the control and treatment of existing contamination".[73]

---

[68] As introduced in the Netherlands under the Soil Protection Act 1983.

[69] DoE Circular 21/87, *Development of Contaminated Land* (17 August 1987), replaced by Planning Policy Guidance Note 23 on Planning and Pollution (July 1994).

[70] *Supra*, nns.31 and 32.

[71] Para. 2.4.

[72] Para. 2.5.

[73] *Supra*, n.33, para. 2.3.

Statutory Liability for Contaminated Land 129

Local Authority Inspection

Critics of the new provisions point to the ineffectiveness of the Part III statutory nuisance provisions due to the vague nature of each local authority's duty to inspect its area. Others suggest that the burden of inspecting potentially contaminated land will fall on developers and others involved in transactions for the sale of such land. However, the working draft guidance suggests that the local authority duty to inspect under section 78B(1) may be quite detailed and onerous. It would be required to adopt:

> an approach which identifies these problems in an orderly and efficient manner, providing an appropriate level of vigilance and promoting confidence that any actual threats to health or the environment will be identified and dealt with.[74]

It is suggested that this would, in turn, require the local authority "to adopt, and keep under periodic review, a formal written strategy for the inspection of its area setting out a rational and ordered approach to the identification of land which merits detailed individual inspection".[75] The authority would be required to set out, in its written strategy, detailed arrangements and procedures by which it would consider, on its own initiative, the inspection of land within its area, and, by which it would respond to information or complaints from the public, businesses, voluntary organisations, and other statutory bodies.

Remediation

Under section 78A(7), "remediation" is widely defined to include assessing the condition of the site, cleaning up or containing the contamination and monitoring the site to ensure that any measures taken have been effective. Therefore, in addition to the costs of actual remedial measures, the total cost of remediation will include the costs of assessment and of on-going monitoring activities. Remediation requirements may extend beyond the contaminated site to affected controlled waters or adjacent land. Once the authority has identified land as contaminated land, in the course of its duty to cause its area to be inspected,[76] it must give notice of the identification to the owner of the land, to any person who appears to be in occupation of the whole or any part of the land and to each person who appears to be liable to have a remediation notice served on him with respect to the land.[77] A remediation notice must specify what the person on which it is served must do by way of remediation and the time periods within which each specified step must be carried out. Non-compliance with a remediation notice is a criminal offence. Sites for which remediation notices have been

---

[74] *Supra*, n. 54, ch. I, para. 25.
[75] *Ibid.*, ch. I, para. 26.
[76] Under s. 78B.
[77] S. 78E.

130   *Owen McIntyre*

served will be included on the public register, as will details of the notice. Appeals against remediation notices or charging notices and convictions for non-compliance with remediation notices are also required to be registered. There is no provision for the removal of land from the register once remediation has been carried out. This is because, under the "suitable for use" approach, the level of remediation required is determined in the context of existing or proposed use and further remediation may be required if the use of the land changes. It should be remembered that, unlike the regime envigased under section 143 of the EPA 1990, only actually contaminated land will appear on the register in the first place. Before serving a remediation notice the enforcing authority must, in accordance with regulations, enter into initial consultations with the person on whom the notice is served and the owners and occupiers of the land concerned as to what remedial measures should be undertaken. It is expected that regulations will stipulate an initial consultation period of three months.

Cost/Benefit

The enforcing authority is required to balance the interest of the environment against the cost of undertaking remediation and may require remedial measures to be undertaken only if it considers them to be "reasonable", having regard to both the costs involved and the seriousness of the harm and pollution in question.[78] In determining what is to be regarded as reasonable the authority must have regard to, but is not bound to follow, guidance to be issued by the Secretary of State.[79] Where the authority determines that remedial measures cannot be required, as the costs would outweigh the seriousness of the harm or pollution in question, it must publish a remediation declaration recording its decision. This declaration must be included on the public register maintained by the authority. Under section 78H(5)(d), the enforcing authority is precluded from serving a remediation notice on a person if it would cause "hardship" to that person to bear the cost of carrying out the remedial measures specified in the notice. In deciding whether hardship may be caused the enforcing authority must have regard to guidance to be issued by the Secretary of State.[80] This provision is intended to protect householders and small and medium-sized businesses. Where, on grounds of hardship, the authority is precluded from serving a remediation notice it must publish a remediation statement which must be included on the public register. If circumstances change so that service of the notice would no longer cause hardship the notice must be served. Other exceptional circumstances, in which the enforcing authority may not serve a remediation notice, include: "where the enforcing authority is satisfied that

---

[78] S. 78E(4).

[79] See R. Lewis, "Contaminated Land: The New Regime of the Environment Act 1995" [1995] *JPL* 1087, at 1089.

[80] S. 78P(2)(b).

Statutory Liability for Contaminated Land 131

appropriate remediation will be carried out on a voluntary basis"[81] and "where the person on whom the notice would be served is the enforcing authority itself".[82]

The new provisions do not alter the position of polluters or owners of contaminated land with regard to civil liability for environmental damage to third parties. In contrast to sections 73(6)–(9) of the EPA 1990, whereby damage caused by illegal deposits of waste in or on land contrary to section 33(1) or 63(2) of the EPA may be actionable in civil law, the new provisions do not expressly confer any right on third parties to sue for damage caused by failure to comply with a remediation notice. However, there is nothing to prevent the use of existing common law remedies where such damage occurs.

The Appropriate Person

Section 78F lays down the rules for determining who is the appropriate person to bear responsibility for any action which the enforcing authority determines is to be done by way of remediation in any particular case. Primarily, the appropriate person will be any person or persons who "caused or knowingly permitted" the substance or substances by which the land has come to be contaminated, to be in, on or under that land.[83] Each appropriate person is liable only for those remediation costs "which are to any extent referable to substances which he caused or knowingly permitted to be present".[84] However, an appropriate person is liable for all remediation costs in respect of the substance(s) he caused to be there, even if he caused only a small part of the total amount of that substance(s) to be present[85] or if remediation is needed because of the interaction between that substance(s) and another which he did not cause to be present.[86] Where more than one person is, *prima facie*, liable as a polluter, the enforcing authority must first determine, in accordance with guidance to be issued by the Secretary of State, whether any of those persons is to be treated as not being an appropriate person in relation to that remediation.[87] If after this, there remains more than one person liable for the same remedial measures, the authority must, again in accordance with guidance, apportion the cost of remediation between them.[88]

The working draft guidance refers to a person who has been identified as an appropriate person by virtue of his having "caused or knowingly permitted" the presence of pollutants as a "Class A appropriate person". It also sets out a

[81] S. 78H(5)(b).
[82] S. 78H(5)(c).
[83] S. 78F(2).
[84] S. 78F(3).
[85] S. 78F(10).
[86] S. 78F(9).
[87] S. 78F(6).
[88] S. 78F(7).

132   *Owen McIntyre*

detailed procedure and a series of tests for the exclusion from liability of some members of a Class A liability group. Grounds for exclusion from liability include, for example, where one potentially liable party has made a payment to another for the purpose of carrying out remediation, either in the course of a civil legal action or as part of a contract for sale.[89] Similar guidance is provided to assist the enforcing authority in deciding whether the different Class A appropriate persons have made differing relative contributions[90] and in the apportionment of costs between Class A appropriate persons.[91]

Where no actual polluter can be found, liability for remediation passes to the innocent owner or occupier of the land. Section 78F(4) provides:

> If no person has, after reasonable enquiry, been found who is by virtue of subsection (2) above an appropriate person to bear responsibility for the things which are to be done by way of remediation, the owner or occupier for the time being of the contaminated land in question is an appropriate person.

The actual polluter will be liable only for contaminating substances which he has caused to be present. If contamination is attributable also to another substance for which no actual polluter has been found, the owner or occupier must bear responsibility for remediation in respect of that other substance.[92] The working draft guidance refers to a person who has been identified as an appropriate person solely by virtue of his ownership or occupation of the land in question as a "Class B appropriate person" and again sets out the circumstances in which members of a Class B liability group should be excluded from liability[93] and the means of apportioning liability between other members.[94]

The key expression used in section 78, i.e. "to cause or knowingly permit", appears in other statutory environmental provisions, most notably section 85(1)–(5) of the Water Resources Act 1991, and has been the subject of considerable judicial deliberation. In *Alphacell Ltd* v. *Woodward,*[95] the phrase "to cause" had the effect of rendering the relevant offence one of "strict liability", i.e. in order to convict it is not necessary to prove intention, negligence or even knowledge. The court stated in *Alphacell*:

> The whole complex operation which might lead to this result was an operation deliberately conducted by [the accused] and I fail to see how a defect at one stage of it, even if we must assume that this happened without their negligence, can enable them to say that they did not cause the pollution.[96]

---

[89] *Supra*, n.54, Ch. III, paras. 15–18.
[90] *Ibid.*, Ch. III, para. 38.
[91] *Ibid.*, Ch. III, para. 37.
[92] S. 78F(5).
[93] *Supra*, n.54, Ch. III, para. 38, for example, where he holds "no beneficial interest in the ownership of the land".
[94] *Ibid.*, Ch. III, para. 39.
[95] [1972] AC 824 (HL).
[96] *Ibid.*, at 828.

Statutory Liability for Contaminated Land 133

This line was followed in *NRA* v. *Yorkshire Water Services Ltd.*[97] However, a mere failure to take preventive action would probably not be regarded as "causing" contamination. The House of Lords has recently delivered a definitive judgment on the very strict meaning of "causing" in environmental offences which is likely to inform practice in relation to determinations of liability under section 78F(2).[98]

In *Price* v. *Cromack*,[99] it was stated in the Court of Appeal:

> I cannot myself find it possible to say that a causing of entry of polluting matter occurs merely because the landowner stands by and watches the polluting matter cross his land into the stream, even if he has committed himself by contract to allowing the adjoining owner so to act.[100]

However, this is likely to be within the meaning of "to knowingly permit". To "knowingly permit" implies that the person concerned was aware, not only of the existence of the substance in question, but also of its harmful and contaminative properties. Once sufficient knowledge has been established, the phrase "to permit" implies that the person in question has the legal power to act. Under this construction, an occupier would only be liable if the terms of his occupation enabled him to take remedial action. This phrase may also imply that the person has the financial means to remove the substance—*Tophams Ltd* v. *Earl of Sefton*.[101] It appears therefore, that where a person responsible for land, who knows of the presence of a contaminating substance(s), does not take reasonable preventative or remedial action, he will be taken to have "knowingly permitted" the contamination.

In defining the "owner" of land, section 78A(9) includes a trustee, but expressly excludes a mortgagee not in possession. Despite pressure from the financial services sector, a mortgagee in possession is not excluded from the definition of "owner" because, in the government's view, the precautionary procedures already developed and utilised by lending institutions (ensuring that possession is not normally taken of mortgaged land) would provide adequate protection. This position is likely to ensure that, in addition to the aforementioned procedures, environmental risk assessment procedures become routine in credit assessment. A mortgagee not in possession of a contaminated site stands to lose the amount of the outstanding loan. A mortgagee in possession, however, may be liable as an "owner", and thus as a Class B appropriate person, where the actual polluter(s) cannot be found. Moreover, a lender who takes possession and learns of the contamination but fails to act may become liable as a person who has "knowingly permitted" the substance(s) to be present, and thus a Class A appropriate person under section 78F(2).

---

[97] [1995] 1 AC 444 (HL).

[98] *Empress Car Co. (Abertillery) Ltd* v. *National Rivers Authority, supra*, n.61. See McIntyre, *supra*, n.61.

[99] [1975] 1 WLR 988.

[100] *Ibid.*, at 995.

[101] [1967] 1 AC 50.

134   *Owen McIntyre*

A provision initially contained in the Environment Bill exempting a polluter from liability where he had directly or indirectly transferred that liability to the owner or occupier for the time being was subsequently removed, thereby precluding the possibility of transferring primary liability. However, a vendor of contaminated land may still negotiate indemnities in respect of his statutory liabilities which will be enforceable in contract. Also, the working draft guidance suggests that a relevant payment made for the purpose of carrying out remediation, for example as part of a contract for the sale of land, or the provision of sufficient information regarding the presence of pollutants to the purchaser of land, should be grounds for the exclusion of liability under the regime.[102]

THE FUTURE OF THE COMMON LAW

The contaminated land provisions introduced by the Environment Act 1995 are to be welcomed for finally bringing to an end a period of considerable legal uncertainty and of confusion for those involved in the property sector. They provide a more effective and more workable solution to the problem of remedying contaminated land than those available under common law or that put forward under section 143 of the EPA 1990. Also, the new regime seeks to strike a fair balance between imposing liability on the parties responsible, in line with the "polluter pays principle", and ensuring the restoration of all contaminated sites. They introduce the requirement that remedial measures ordered should be reasonable having regard to cost, and they seek to utilise market forces by preserving the *caveat emptor* principle. However, it is not yet possible to give a detailed critical analysis of the provisions as, at the time of writing, many substantive issues have yet to be clarified by guidance from the Secretary of State. Also, any attempt to comment on the practical merit or operational efficiency of the regime would clearly be premature.[103]

It seems unlikely however, that similar statutory regimes could ever usurp the role of the common law in remedying general environmental damage or even damage relating to contamination of land. As has been noted above, these provisions do not alter the position of polluters in relation to civil liability for environmental damage to third parties. They neither create a tailored statutory right to sue nor prevent the taking of existing common law actions by injured third parties. Indeed, other than resorting to public law to review a decision of the

---

[102] *Supra*, n.54, Ch. III, paras. 15–18 and 23–24. E.g. paras. 23–24 list as a ground for exclusion of liability, "where one member of the liability group has sold the site on arms length terms for an open market value to another member and has provided the purchaser with sufficient information to enable the purchaser to be aware of the presence on the site of the relevant pollutant".

[103] Though some commentators have speculated on likely practical outcomes. See e.g. O. McIntyre, "The Rise of Environmental Judicial Review" (1997) 6 *Environmental Policy and Practice* 147, where the author anticipates that the considerable discretion placed in the hands of the enforcing authority to determine whether land is contaminated and whether and to what extent to order remediation, is likely to give rise to a considerable amount of judicial review litigation, at 151.

Statutory Liability for Contaminated Land   135

enforcing authority,[104] third parties can have recourse only to common law for relief. It appears that legislation and accompanying guidance which provide so much in terms of technical and procedural detail must be, of necessity, limited in their breadth of application. Also, statutory liability regimes can only react to recognised existing problems and will then be specifically tailored to apply to such problems. Common law concepts may sometimes be applied by the courts in an inflexible and unimaginative manner, and thus fail "to absorb newer forms of environmental harm to individuals".[105] Only these concepts, however, possess the inherent ability to adapt and evolve required to continue to protect rights, and thus the environment, against ever-changing threats. As Steele correctly points out, "regulatory responses can be slow, and lag behind the activities of the risk-creators".[106]

There can be little doubt that statutory controls, and in particular those measures which set qualitative environmental standards, can complement the operation of the common law. The action for breach of statutory duty, whereby a statute imposes a duty and tort provides compensation for harm resulting from breach of that duty, exemplifies this compatibility. Many actions for breach of statutory duty have been taken in the UK by plaintiffs whose injuries arose from exposure to asbestos in regulated industries. Also, failure to abide by any qualitative environmental standards set down in legislation will usually establish the existence of environmental damage in an action in nuisance, negligence or *Rylands* v. *Fletcher*.[107] Part IIA of the EPA requires, for the purpose of identifying contaminated land, preparation of "appropriate, authoritative and scientifically based information on the toxicological properties of . . . pollutants" against which the possibility of harm to human health would be assessed.[108] It is not difficult to imagine how this information could assist the courts in determining at what point the presence of pollution on land constitutes damage for the purpose of a common law claim.

Further, it would be a mistake to understate the significance of the House of Lords judgment in *Cambridge Water* for the future role of the *Rylands* v. *Fletcher* doctrine of strict liability in environmental actions. After many years of uncertainty over the precise scope of the requirement that the defendant had been engaged in "a non-natural use of his land"[109] Lord Goff stated, obiter:

---

[104] *Ibid.*

[105] Steel, *supra*, n.3, at 124.

[106] *Ibid.*, at 128.

[107] See e.g., *Cambridge Water Co.* v. *Eastern Counties Leather, supra*, n.7, where it was accepted that damage had occurred by virtue of water intended for drinking falling foul of minimum standards for drinking water set down in an EC dir. See also the High Court judgment in *Bowden* v. *Southwest Water Services Ltd. and others* [1998] Env. LR 445, where Carnwarth J conceded that standards set under EC or domestic legislation may be relevant to common law issues, though he cautioned that such statutory provisions do not necessarily give rise to independent causes of action. See O. McIntyre, "UK Case Note" (1998) 5 *Irish Planning and Environmental Law Journal* 176.

[108] *Supra*, n.54, Ch. 1, para. 14.

[109] *Supra*, nn.22 and 23.

136   Owen McIntyre

> Indeed I feel bound to say that the storage of substantial quantities of chemicals on industrial premises should be regarded as an almost classic case of non-natural use, and I find it very difficult to think that it should be thought objectionable to impose strict liability for damage caused in the event of their escape.

This statement can only serve to include within the scope of liability under *Rylands* v. *Fletcher* a wide range of potentially hazardous activities involving chemicals or other dangerous substances.

Finally, though it is now clearly established that damage must have been reasonably foreseeable for each environmentally relevant tort action, it is by no means clear that this requirement will prove unduly onerous. In *Margereson and Hancock* v. *J.W. Roberts*,[110] the Court of Appeal upheld the trial judge's quite liberal application of the test of foreseeability. These joined cases involved claims for having contracted mesothelioma due to extensive contamination by the defendants of the district of Armley in Leeds where both plaintiffs had lived as children. The relevant period of exposure was established to be from 1925 to 1951 and, on the question of foreseeability, extensive reference was made at trial to a "seminal report" which highlighted the risks of asbestosis among asbestos workers. Despite the fact that mesothelioma was not known to medicine as a disease at any material time, the association between mesothelioma and asbestos being first noted in 1960, and that the plaintiffs had never worked with asbestos, the court had no difficulty finding that the defendant should reasonably have foreseen a risk of "some pulmonary injury", though not necessarily mesothelioma. Similarly, in *Griffiths* v. *British Coal*,[111] which involved claims by former miners for a variety of illnesses caused by fine particles of dust, the trial judge had little difficulty establishing the foreseeability of the miners' injuries. He stated that the approach taken by the defendants was "leisurely", with a long lead time between the availability of medical research and the taking of precautionary measures. Though the courts may confine this less onerous foreseeability test to so-called "toxic tort" cases, it remains to be seen whether they are prepared to apply it in cases of environmental damage generally. Where any particular class of environmental damage was foreseeable, liability might arise for any other type of damage in that class.

The statutory contaminated land provisions can be seen as an isolated response to a quite specific problem arising at a particular point in time. Much contaminated land today is the result of activities carried on in the distant past when there was little or no consideration of environmental consequences. In recent years however, there has been an exponential growth in environmental awareness and, consequently, in scientific understanding of environmental impacts and techniques of risk assessment. It appears increasingly likely that the courts could establish the foreseeability of environmental damage from more

---

[110] *The Times*, 17 Apr. 1996. See O McIntyre, "Case Note: Liability For Asbestos-Related Illness" (1997) 4 *Irish Planning and Environmental Law Journal* 83.

[111] Unreported, QBD, 28 Jan. 1998. See O. McIntyre, "Recent UK Case Law" (1998) 5 *Irish Planning and Environmental Law Journal* 123.

recent activities. Steele refers to an "escalation in awareness of environmental damage and environmental risk" and concludes that "critical debate as to the environmental effects of existing ways of living is at least more familiar, and probably more widespread, than at any previous time".[112] The implications for any test of foreseeability of damage are obvious.

---

[112] Steele, *supra*, n.3, at 111.

7

Nuisance and Environmental Protection

K. MORROW

INTRODUCTION

THE VIRTUE OF the common law—indeed one of the characteristics that gives it life and vigour—lies in its ability to adapt to the needs of society. This chapter will focus on aspects of one of the most dynamic branches of the common law—the law of torts[1]—and its relation to one of the most pressing problems facing the legal system today—environmental pollution. Such is the perceived importance of pollution-based torts impacting on both the quality of the environment and human health that they warrant a separate classification under the guise of "toxic torts".

Historical precedent reveals the law of torts being used to tackle what would now be classed as "environmental pollution". This phenomenon is particularly marked in cases involving the evolution of the flexible law of nuisance (the forms of which are often described as "protean"[2]) and the development of the rule in *Rylands* v. *Fletcher*,[3] in response to the problems engendered by the industrial revolution.[4] The twentieth century has, perhaps inevitably, given its dominant status in the law of torts generally, also seen the law of negligence coming to play a significant role in cases involving pollution.[5] Given that nuisance and the rule in *Rylands* v. *Fletcher* are intimately linked to interests in land and land-use, and that negligence is sufficiently flexible to adapt to almost any situation, such developments are not unexpected, though their effectiveness from an environmental protection perspective is much less predictable. Despite

---

[1] It is now commonplace for the role of the common law in environmental protection to feature in environmental law texts: see e.g. D. Hughes, *Environmental Law* (3rd edn., London, Butterworths, 1996), and Y. Scannell, *Environmental Law* (Dublin, Roundhall, 1995).

[2] *Sedleigh-Denfield* v. *O'Callaghan* [1940] AC 880, *per* Lord Wright at 903.

[3] (1865) 11 HL Cas. 142.

[4] Interesting perspectives on the historical development of the law of nuisance are provided by A. Ogus and G. Richardson, "Economics and the Environment: A Study of Private Nuisance" (1977) 36 *CLJ* 284 and J.P.S. McLaren, "Nuisance Law and the Industrial Revolution—Some Lessons from Social History" (1983) 3 *OJLS* 155.

[5] See, in particular, Lord Reid's oft cited speech in *Overseas Tankship (UK) Ltd* v. *Miller Steamship Co. Pty. Ltd (The Wagon Mound No 2)* [1967] 1 AC 617.

140   K. Morrow

the common observation that each of these may, in certain cases, be characterised as "environmental torts",[6] it is incumbent upon modern observers to avoid a revisionist view of the law. While is would be dubious to attribute a true "environmental protection" perspective to historic cases of nuisance, liability under *Rylands* v. *Fletcher* and negligence, at the same time, the imposition of liability under each of these torts also fits well in principle with the modern "polluter pays" ethos.[7]

Current understanding of the environment, as deserving of legal protection in its own right, and not merely as an adjunct to guarding the interests of humanity has only recently emerged in UK law,[8] and policy,[9] and is far from gaining acceptance in the echelons of the common law. That said, nuisance, liability under *Rylands* v. *Fletcher* and negligence have, in the past, provided a degree of protection to the environment as a by-product of their primary purposes, the protection of interests in property,[10] and the application of a minimum standard of care to acts or omissions affecting others. However, the impact of the common law in this area must not be overstated. Some commentators[11] suggest that, at least as far as liability in nuisance and under the rule in *Rylands* v. *Fletcher*[12] is concerned, even in its heyday, the common law played only a minor role in dealing with pollution issues. The prime limitations on the impact of such cases were seeded in the law itself and indeed are arguably returning to prominence in the most recent rulings in this area. Wider societal conditions also limited the efficacy of the law of torts in this regard, for example, since access to the courts proved both expensive and time consuming, it tended to be the preserve of the wealthy, and not the urban poor, who more often bore the brunt of industrial pollution. Litigation therefore tended to be, at best, sporadic in its occurrence and, by its very nature, localised in its impact.

It could be argued that the modern legal system has further marginalised the role of the common law in environmental matters, with well-developed land-use planning and pollution control regimes, together with simplified statutory

---

[6] See e.g. C. Gearty, "The Place of Private Nuisance in the Modern Law of Torts", (1989) 48 *CLJ* 214.

[7] The polluter pays principle plays a major role in modern environmental law. It exists in a number of forms and is demonstrated to some extent in domestic pollution control regimes, through the imposition of charges covering permitting and monitoring, fines, clean-up charges (see e.g. the Environmental Protection Act 1990 and the Water Resources Act 1991). Pollution taxes provide another manifestation of the principle (see e.g. the Finance Act 1996 which introduced the land-fill tax).

[8] See e.g. the Environmental Protection Act 1990 and the Water Resources Act 1991.

[9] See *This Common Inheritance: Britain's Environmental Strategy* (Cm 1200, London, HMSO, 1990).

[10] After a brief diversion in *Khorasandjian* v. *Bush* [1993] QB 727, the law of nuisance has returned its focus to the protection of orthodox property interests in *Hunter* v. *Canary Wharf* [1997] WLR 64.

[11] Notably McLaren, *supra* n.4.

[12] It appears that the impact of negligence on environmental issues is ripe for thorough examination in its own right. In any event, certain cases already stand out, raising important issues of responsibility for environmental damage, e.g., *The Wagon Mound (No.2)*, *supra* n.5 (with reference to man-made nuisance) and *Leaky* v. *National Trust* [1980] QB 485 (in respect of nuisances arising from natural causes).

Nuisance and Environmental Protection   141

nuisance provisions providing sufficient protection for both the environment and individual interests in it. However this proposition is fallacious on a number of grounds. In the first place, it is surely relevant that the common law continued to play an important role, and indeed became more dynamic, in tackling environmental problems during the industrial revolution, with cases such as *Rylands* v. *Fletcher* itself being decided against a background of legislative innovation.[13] Secondly, statutory regimes are geared to protecting the public interest rather than that of the individual,[14] and these cannot always, or even often, be regarded as synonymous. Thus, there appears to be good reason to conclude that it would be inappropriate for the common law wholly to relinquish a role, even if it is residual, in protecting interests impinging on the environment, and this remains, now as ever, a fertile area of rather controversial litigation. The question remains how significant tortious liability is and will be, as we enter the twenty-first century, in responding to ever more pressing and complex environmental problems. Will the common law be able to adapt, as it has done in the past, to new, indeed unprecedented, challenges, or will it become a dead letter?

THE LAW OF TORTS AND THE ENVIRONMENT

In order to illustrate some of the questions that arise when the law of torts is called upon to deal with modern environmental problems, this chapter will examine recent cases that exhibit markedly different approaches to key issues. Particular attention will be paid to the Irish Supreme Court decision in *Hanrahan* v. *Merck Sharp & Dohme (Ireland) Ltd*,[15] and the English High Court ruling in *Graham and Graham* v. *Re-Chem International Ltd*.[16] These cases, as a brief rehearsal of the facts will indicate, have much in common. The contrasting approaches adopted by the courts to their resolution disclose much about factors affecting the ability of the common law to address complex environmental damage claims.

---

[13] See e.g. the Public Health Act 1848, the Smoke Nuisance Abatement (Metropolis) Act 1853 and the Alkali Act 1863.

[14] While some argue that the common law is redundant as a tool for protecting the environment in light of modern statutory controls, this view appears to be fallacious. There seems to be ample space for systems to operate to protect the individual as well as societal interest in other areas of law, for example, in the parallel regimes of tortious and criminal liability for trespass to the person.

[15] [1988] ILRM 629.

[16] [1996] Env. LR 158. This case is one of the longest civil liability cases in modern British legal history, comprising 198 days in court over a period of 14 months. Such is the length of this case that it has been necessary on occasion to extract material from the LEXIS transcript which is omitted from the case report. Where this has occurred I have supplied a note of the relevant heading in order to aid location of the specific quotation.

142 K. Morrow

Hanrahan v. Merck, Sharp & Dohme (Ireland) Ltd

The Hanrahan family farmed land about a mile from the defendant's pharmaceutical plant in the Suir valley, Ireland, which stored, used and disposed of (by means of incineration) a range of toxic and dangerous chemicals. The plaintiffs brought proceedings in negligence, nuisance, under *Rylands* v. *Fletcher* and Article 40.3 of the Constitution[17] in respect of damage to vegetation and livestock and to their own health,[18] consequent upon the defendant's conduct of operation of its plant from 1978 to 1983. The complaints centred on emissions of hydrogen chloride and hydrochloric acidic mists. The case was dismissed in the Irish High Court by Keane J on the basis that causation had not been established. The source of the formidable list of complaints exhibited by the plaintiffs was ascribed to "poor farming practices". The Hanrahans' appeal proceeded solely on the nuisance issue. The Supreme Court allowed the appeal and sent the case for retrial on issues of causation and damages.

Graham and Graham v. Re-Chem

The plaintiffs in the *Graham* case were also farmers who alleged that, between 1980 and 1983, their land had been contaminated, their livestock damaged, their dairy business destroyed and their health[19] affected by toxic chemicals emitted by the defendants' hazardous waste incinerator. The defendants' plant was situated about two miles west of the plaintiffs' farm at Bonnybridge, Scotland.[20] The Grahams' action, after abortive reference to the rule in *Rylands* v. *Fletcher*,[21]

---

[17] Art. 40.3.2 states:
"The State shall . . . by its laws protect as best it may from unjust attack and, in the case of injustice done, vindicate the life, person, good name and property rights of every citizen."

[18] Under Irish law a claim in respect of personal injury is clearly available in nuisance. This position contrasts with that in UK law, see *infra*, n.19.

[19] While in English law damages for personal injury are recoverable in public nuisance, and statutory nuisance provisions often focus on tangentially related public health issues, it is coming to be accepted that an action for private nuisance does not allow for damages in respect such injuries. This point is discussed in some detail in Lord Goff's speech in *Hunter* v. *Canary Wharf* [1997] AC 677. However, given the relevance of personal injury in other types of nuisance, and the fact that actionable interference with the enjoyment of property includes sleep deprivation and other manifestations generating adverse health effects, confusion is perhaps understandable, though it does lead to significant overlap with negligence. Since the putative extension the protection of private nuisance to those lacking a proprietary interest in land, in *Khorasandjian* v. *Bush*, *supra* n.10, (which would readily encapsulate personal injury) has been decisively rejected by a majority in the House of Lords in *Hunter* v. *Canary Wharf*. In any event, some commentators argue that negligence provides a more appropriate avenue whereby personal injury claims may be pursued in these circumstances—see Gearty, *supra*, n.6.

[20] The case was decided under Scots law, but was heard in England, where the defendant was based.

[21] The rule in *Rylands* v. *Fletcher* has no application in Scottish law, a point clearly made in the somewhat indignant speech delivered by Lord Fraser in *RHM Bakeries (Scotland) Ltd.* v. *Strathclyde Regional Council*, 1985 SLT 214. Forbes J confirmed this as a preliminary point in his judgment in the instant case.

Nuisance and Environmental Protection 143

proceeded on the basis of nuisance[22] and negligence.[23] The chemicals implicated in this case were Polychlorinated biphenyls (PCBs) Polychlorinated dibenzoparadioxins (Dioxins) and Polychlorinated dibenzofurans (Furans), each class of which generates a variety of complex pollution effects. Scientific evidence suggests that PCBs, which are solely anthropogenic in origin, are comparatively stable and resistant to biodegradation and metabolic degradation. Furans and dioxins occur naturally as well as through incineration processes. There is a high degree of scientific uncertainty about the formation of both furans and dioxins in and as a result of combustion. Forbes J described each of these classes of chemical as ubiquitous in the environment.

Causation proved to be the dominant issue at trial,[24] that is, had the state of the defendant's property actually caused the plaintiffs' damage? The case in nuisance hinged on the question whether or not the defendant's activities amounted to an unreasonable user of land, [25] taking into account the question of the foreseeability of damage,[26] by the deposition of the chemicals mentioned above from the defendant's plant on the plaintiff's property.

A frustratingly lengthy list of intriguing issues arises in both the *Hanrahan* and the *Graham* cases. Unfortunately the confines of a chapter of this length preclude examination of many of them. Discussion will therefore focus on two of the most controversial aspects of the law in this area, the questions of causation and of foreseeability and fault in respect of nuisance actions involving damage allegedly sustained by environmental pollution.

CAUSATION

The Burden of Proof

Causation is a particularly vexed issue in environmental torts. Problems are most marked where, as is very often the case, scientific knowledge of the workings of particular causal factors is incomplete or controversial. This type of issue has proved a source of difficulty in the past in non-environmental contexts, particularly in negligence cases, notably *McGhee* v. *National Coal Board.*[27] In this case,

---

[22] The Scots law of nuisance differs from English law in some respects, though for the purposes of this chapter, these are of minor significance.

[23] The law of negligence does not differ materially from the law of delict for the purposes of this chapter.

[24] This accounts for nine-tenths of the judgment: see A. Layard, "Balancing Environmental Considerations", (1997) 113 *LQR* 254, and was ultimately the issue which determined the case.

[25] See the speech of Bramwell B in *Bamford* v. *Turnley* (1862) 3 B & S 62 at 83. In *Graham and Graham* v. *ReChem* itself the incinerator was deemed not to represent a reasonable user.

[26] This was confirmed as an ingredient of nuisance liability by the House of Lords decision in *Cambridge Water Co. Ltd* v. *Eastern Counties Leather plc* [1994] 2 AC 264 which followed the approach initiated by Lord Reid's speech in *Overseas Tankship (UK) Ltd* v. *Miller Steamship Co. (The Wagon Mound (No. 2), supra,* n.5.

[27] [1973] 1 WLR 1.

144   K. Morrow

the state of medical knowledge prevailing at the time of litigation was such that it was not possible for the plaintiff to prove, on the balance of probabilities, that his employers' alleged negligence in failing to provide washing facilities was a material cause of his damage—dermatitis. The House of Lords held that it was sufficient for the plaintiff to show instead that the defendant's conduct had materially increased his risk of contracting the disease. In addition, Lord Wilberforce stated that a defendant creating a risk of injury, which then materialised, would be subject to a reversed burden of proof, requiring him to prove that his negligence was not a cause of the injury. Such an alteration in the burden of proof has considerable potential advantages for plaintiffs, particularly in complex cases near the cutting edge of scientific discovery, as many environmental tort cases are.

The adverse implications of the *McGhee* approach for defendants swiftly became apparent in subsequent cases, providing cause for grave concern in a fault-based system of liability, particularly where complex causation arguments arose involving several possible agents of damage, some tortious, others not. The approach adopted in *McGhee* has been heavily disapproved and distinguished for such reasons (amongst others) by the House of Lords in *Wilsher* v. *Essex Area Health Authority*.[28] Does the broad approach to causation adopted in *McGhee* continue to have any relevance outside the realm of negligence, in areas such as nuisance, where fault is not always a necessary element in liability? It would appear not. For example, the attempt by the plaintiffs in *Hanrahan* to argue for a reversal in the burden of proof on causation (on constitutional law grounds) met with short shrift in Henchy J's judgment. The status of the basic issue in causation in nuisance appears not to have changed since it was succinctly expressed by Lord O'Hagan in the Scots case of *Shotts Iron Co. Ltd* v. *Inglis* in the following terms:

> We have then to determine to which of [the] causes the mischief, which was admittedly accomplished somehow, may justly be ascribed.[29]

This is not to say that causation has become a moribund issue in nuisance—for the question of "justly ascribing" causes invariably goes to the heart of the nuisance action. This factor is of particular importance in the context of the modern legal systems where environmental damage is being treated as an appropriate candidate for the application of liability based on the polluter pays principle, and rather than as an externality which allows environmental damage to lie where it falls.

"Hard" versus "Soft" Causation

It appears that the *Hanrahan* and *Graham* cases exhibit two strategies whereby the issue of causation in nuisance may be tackled. The approaches adopted in

[28] [1988] 1 All ER 871.
[29] (1882) 9 R (HL) 78, at 85.

Nuisance and Environmental Protection 145

these modern authorities have long-established historical origins. What I will term "hard causation" gives primacy to scientific evidence as the decisive basis for justly ascribing cause. An early example of this approach can be found in the speech delivered by Lord Selborne LC in *Gaunt* v. *Fynney*.[30] "Soft causation" on the other hand allows the causation issue to be determined primarily by reference to damage visible to ordinary persons conversant with the subject matter: see for example the judgments of Jessel MR and James LJ in *Slavin* v. *North Brancepeth Coal Co.*[31] The *Hanrahan* case exhibits a largely soft causation approach, whereas in *Graham* hard causation is utilised. While Henchy J was unwilling to reverse the burden of proof in favour of the plaintiffs in *Hanrahan,* he did acknowledge that the question of causation in this type of case was a difficult issue. As a result, he was prepared to adopt quite different inferences from those drawn by Keane J from the evidence at first instance. Henchy J employed a "common-sense", indeed almost a layman's, approach to causation. Evidence provided by the Hanrahan family concerning smells emanating from the plant was found amply corroborated by that provided by other people living in the locality and by plant personnel who had dealt with numerous complaints in this regard. In addition, Mr. Hanrahan's appeal on the damage he suffered to his health was allowed. Henchy J found that Mr. Hanrahan's claims were supported by the evidence provided by a medical specialist (to whom he had been referred by his general practitioner),[32] to the effect that:

> if it is shown that fumes, dust, vapours, chemicals are present in the botanical life or animal life in the area, and if appropriate environmental metrology in the evidence is compatible, and if it is shown that materials, acids, vapours are emanating from a source contiguous to the farm [the defendants' plant being the only candidate], then the balance of probabilities very much favours [the conclusion] that his lung disease can be attributed to a toxic substance.[33]

Henchy J took issue in the strongest terms with the scientific evidence produced on behalf of the defendants respecting their emissions. The judge was of the opinion that readings taken at the point of emission by the factory and used as the basis of a computer model, even when taken in conjunction with fixed time readings by state pollution control authorities, were not conclusive as to causation. The first class of evidence, he thought, lacked attention to the real physical context of the emissions and the second he deemed limited as to type and duration. The fact that the state's readings showed that emissions from the plant were within recommended guidelines was not considered to be decisive and in any event they showed that exposure levels on the Hanrahan farm were three and a half times higher than those on neighbouring properties. It is also significant that Henchy J concluded that the plant's incinerator was operating

[30] (1872) 8 Ch. App. 8.

[31] (1874) 9 Ch. App. 705.

[32] The manner in which causation was treated with regard to this aspect of the case fits closely with that advocated in *ibid.*, with scientific evidence supporting a claim framed in lay terms.

[33] *Supra*, n.15, at 642.

146   K. Morrow

at too low a temperature to achieve the results which it was designed to attain—this state of affairs constituted a breach of the planning permission under which the site required to operate. Henchy J was not satisfied that the scientific evidence was, in the circumstances, sufficient to rebut the plaintiff's case. In his opinion:

> Theoretical or inductive evidence cannot be allowed to displace proven facts. . . . It would be to allow scientific theory to dethrone fact to dispose of this claim by saying, as was said in the judgment under appeal, that there was virtually no evidence in this case of injury to human beings or animals which has been scientifically linked to any chemicals emanating from the defendants' factory.[34]

The judge concluded that the defendants' factory emissions offered the most credible explanation for the plaintiffs' damage, including that to the livestock. On the latter point he deemed further examination necessary in order to determine to what extent the emissions were legally to blame for the damage—this issue along with the question of damages was remitted to the High Court.

The approach and outcome on causation in the *Hanrahan* case could hardly contrast more strongly with that in *Graham*. In both cases copious amounts of expert evidence were provided by both parties, but in the latter instance Forbes J found that the experts appearing on behalf of the defendant were more convincing on almost every level. He formed the opinion that the emissions from the plant formed by the primary combustion process were insignificant. Interestingly, particularly given the overwhelmingly negative tone of the overall judgment, Forbes J found with respect to the more complex polluting aspects of the operation, that, even though these were not scientifically established until 1985, this did not render them unforeseeable.[35] He was of the opinion that, since the general adverse emissions aspects of incinerator operations were already well known,[36] and as such emissions were deemed to be capable of causing ill health and death in animals, this was sufficient for potential liability in nuisance. The question remained what would be determined to have actually caused or materially contributed to the damage sustained.[37] It is on this issue that a particularly clear difference of approach from that adopted by Henchy J in *Hanrahan* emerged. The question was bound to be complex both on scientific and legal grounds. The plaintiffs attempted to persuade the court that special weight should be given to eyewitness evidence. Forbes J however took the view that this type of approach was of little utility in deciding which facts had been established on a balance of probabilities, particularly where the facts in question

---

[34] *Ibid.*, at 645.

[35] Forbes J's approach to foreseeability in respect of comparatively novel pollution risks differs significantly from that adopted by Lord Goff in *Cambridge Water Co. Ltd* v. *Eastern Counties Leather plc* [1994] 2 AC 264, discussed below.

[36] The nature of the emissions from waste incinerators—dioxins and furans—was widely recognised, although the exact process leading to their formation had yet to be discovered at that time.

[37] The orthodox requirement for causation espoused in *Bonnington Castings Ltd* v. *Wardlaw* [1956] AC 613 and approved in *Wilsher* v. *Essex Area Health Authority, supra* n.28.

Nuisance and Environmental Protection   147

were disputed. He was of the opinion that expert evidence had an important contribution to make to the resolution of conflicts about the facts.[38]

Scientific evidence (especially that provided on behalf of Re-Chem) therefore held sway and the evidence of the plaintiffs themselves was viewed to be, at best, unreliable and certainly not on a par with that of the scientific experts employed in the case. Mr. Graham's firm belief that Re-Chem was responsible for the damage to his livestock was described by Forbes J as obsessive,[39] and the judge thought that his views had affected his behaviour at every stage of the case "including his ability to give accurate and reliable evidence".[40] Mr. Graham's occasionally unco-operative attitude to the various investigations into the problems with his livestock was also viewed as undermining his credibility. All in all, the Grahams underwent a considerable and very prolonged ordeal in court through detailed and drawn out cross-examination.[41] The judge was sympathetic to their plight to a degree, but considered it to be unavoidable. He made some allowances for the stress which the Grahams were placed under by the litigation, but found their evidence to be unacceptable and "very confused and confusing, contradictory and riddled with inconsistencies",[42] on a number of important points. The credibility of the Grahams' expert witnesses was also doubted, Forbes J proclaiming that they lacked objectivity.

The court's approach to the plaintiffs' evidence displays some interesting parallels with medical negligence law,[43] which often amounts to a drawn-out battle on highly technical scientific questions between the parties' expert witnesses. However, while in medical negligence cases the courts are often uncomfortable in stating a preference for the evidence of one expert over that of another,[44] such reticence does not seem to feature in toxic tort cases. The courts are often willing to take a strong line in the latter context despite the fact that the scientific

---

[38] Such were the volume and complexity of the issues under examination in this case that 27 lever arch files of scientific literature alone were collected during the course of the action—both sides eventually agreed on admissibility on the basis of a "truce letter".

[39] *Supra*, n.16, at 177 and 179.

[40] See LEXIS transcipt under the heading "The Central Issue and Some of Its Surrounding Circumstances".

[41] The case in many ways placed as much, if not more, emphasis on the Grahams and their credibility as on Re-Chem and its operations on site. In places the judgment is uncomfortably redolent of those controversial cases in criminal law where the victim seems to be placed under greater scrutiny than the alleged perpetrator.

[42] See the LEXIS transcript under the heading " The Graham Dairy Herd and the History and Management of the Farm."

[43] The test for professional negligence laid down in *Bolam* v. *Friern Hospital Management Committee* [1957] 1 WLR 582, results in the court being heavily reliant upon expert opinion in specialist fields while, at the same time, giving wide latitude to professionals acting in accordance with an accepted body of professional opinion.

[44] The central significance of deference to expert opinion in medical negligence cases is borne out in *Bolitho* v. *City & Hackney Health Authority* [1998] AC 232. This case is in many ways typical of the approach adopted by the courts in medical negligence, in that the judge felt unable to follow a personal preference for the views of one expert over those of another, judging each side to have raised valid considerations of professional judgement.

148   K. Morrow

evidence in question is just as complex as, if not more so than, that which commonly features in the former.

However the complexity of the evidence involved in toxic torts cases does not of itself provide sufficient justification for hiving them off to a specialised environmental court.[45] The fact that judges seem to regard the issues as appropriate to be addressed by reference to general principles of tortious liability seems to militate against such a step. The very real problems encountered in this area to date do however warrant swift and decisive remediation, and provide ample justification for following established practice in dealing with similarly complex issues adopted in planning law,[46] appointing expert assessors to aid the courts in evaluating complex and competing scientific evidence. This approach would do much to prevent the courts' decision-making processes from being dominated by the "hired guns" of expert witnesses and enable judges to evaluate the evidence before them on sound and objective scientific grounds.

In both established medical negligence law[47] and in the emerging area of toxic torts,[48] the courts display a marked tendency to regard the plaintiff's own contribution to the fact-finding process as at best questionable and of little utility in the court's decision-making processes. In *Graham and Graham* v. *Re-Chem*, the fact that Mr. Graham was not alone in expressing disquiet about the operation of the defendants' incinerator and its health implications was not deemed to be of any real significance by the judge.[49] More weight was given to the fact that, while there had been several official inquiries into the problems allegedly connected with the incinerator, none decisively linked the Grahams' damage with the plant.

The plaintiffs attempted to adopt a blanket approach to causation looking broadly at the overall issues. Forbes J, however, felt that this was unscientific, and observed that it was:

> an unconvincing and wholly inadequate substitute for the more appropriate approach which would have established, if it existed, detailed clinical, pathological and histological evidence of . . . toxic insult . . . which is so singularly lacking in this case.[50]

---

[45]   This idea is, however, enthusiastically advocated by many eminent in both law and the environment, particularly, Sir Harry Woolf, "Are the Judiciary Environmentally Myopic?" [1992] *JEL* 1; and R. Carnwath, "Environmental Enforcement—The Need for a Specialist Court" [1992] *JPL* 799.

[46]   Rule 9 of the Town and Country Planning Appeals (Determination by Inspectors) (Inquiries Procedure) Rules 1992 S.I. No. 2039, continues the established practice of appointing expert assessors to sit with planning inspectors on planning inquiries which raise particularly complex issues. Assessors are often used in cases focusing on environmental impacts and scientific argument features strongly in this area of law.

[47]   Medical negligence law furnishes a variety of examples of judges attributing low weight to the plaintiff's recollection or view of events: see e.g. *Whitehouse* v. *Jordan* [1981] 1 All ER 267.

[48]   It is perhaps unsurprising that toxic torts see a sceptical approach being adopted to the plaintiff's view of events, since this type of view also features occasionally in mainstream nuisance: see e.g. *Miller* v. *Jackson* [1977] QB 966.

[49]   The issue became something of an environmental *cause célèbre* both locally and nationally: see e.g. R. Allen, *Waste Not, Want Not* (London, Earthscan, 1992).

[50]   See LEXIS transcript under the heading, "Evaluation of Evidence".

The plaintiffs' animals were deemed, on the balance of probabilities, to have been damaged not by the defendants' emissions but instead by poor farming practices, and in particular a defective feeding regime—an outcome similar to that at first instance in *Hanrahan*.

The Best of Both Worlds?—Holistic Causation

The causation issue goes to the heart of the utility of the nuisance action as a means of tackling environmental damage, but it is certainly fraught with difficulty. On the one hand it is arguable that the soft causation approach such as that espoused by Henchy J in the *Hanrahan* case is highly desirable from an environmental point of view, taking an expansive view of the role of the common law in this area. This approach is superficially appealing on environmental grounds,[51] but brings with it a very real danger that judges will be tempted to eschew the security provided by established standards of scientific and legal proof, thus generating considerable uncertainty and perhaps unfairness for defendants. On the other hand, a rigid and restrictive approach to the role of the common law, as exhibited in the hard causation approach adopted by Forbes J in *Graham*, is impossible to square with modern pro-environmental opinion and arguably creates insurmountable difficulties for plaintiffs. The flexible nature of the common law can feasibly accommodate either perspective. However, it can be argued that both hard and soft causation perspectives are too extreme and fail to serve adequately the individual, the environment and the image of the common law as a dynamic and appropriate mechanism for dispute resolution where toxic torts are concerned.

While hard and soft causation may appear in principle to be irreconcilable, it is arguable that in practice the concepts may be synthesised in order to establish a viable middle ground. It is possible that, far from resulting in a muddled compromise, this approach may actually enable the law to develop a holistic approach to causation in nuisance that more closely reflects environmental realities.[52] While it is certain that the victims of pollution cannot lay claim to a full understanding of all its ramifications for the environment, they can offer detailed observation of conditions on the ground with which they are familiar. The scientific community does not therefore hold a monopoly of relevant

[51] Such an approach bears some resemblance to the emerging use of the precautionary principle in environmental legislation. The idea that environmental threats may justify a proactive action, even in the absence of firm scientific information, is inherently appealing from an environmental perspective. However, while a broad approach to scientific issues is arguably appropriate in a legislative context, it creates significant difficulties in a common law context where legal activity is largely *ex post facto*. The one situation where a precautionary approach may logically avail at common law is in cases of continuing nuisance.

[52] A holistic approach has already begun to emerge in the field of environmental legislation with the introduction of integrated pollution control in the Environmental Protection Act 1990, which seeks, in part, to fit regulation more closely to conditions on the ground than the traditional sectoral approach which it replaces.

150   K. Morrow

information, particularly in the large volume of cases where nuisance interferes with the use and enjoyment of property. In many cases, however, the current approach to causation issues adopted by the courts weighs heavily in favour of expert evidence and can disregard lay evidence almost entirely.

There are signs of the emergence of a holistic approach to causation in *Blackburn* v. *ARC Limited.*[53] This case involved an action in private nuisance, public nuisance and negligence raised by the Blackburns,[54] who lived close to a former quarry operated as a landfill site by the defendant.[55] Only the nuisance issue proceeded to full trial.[56] The interference complained of involved smell from rubbish and fumes from methane burning equipment,[57] noise from site traffic and litter escaping from the site. The claims in respect of nuisance by smell and litter succeeded, though that brought in respect of noise did not.

The plaintiffs kept a diary of the interference experienced between 1987 and 1995, their records increasing in detail following recourse to legal advice in 1991. His Honour Judge Humphrey Lloyd QC acknowledged that this record was flawed in some respects, containing extraneous and irrelevant remarks in places and also transcription errors. Nevertheless, he formed the view that it provided a reasonably accurate record of the occurrences that formed the foundation of the complaint. The evidence was evaluated on the basis that it provided an indication of conditions experienced on the ground and not as a true scientific observation. It was supplemented in examining the alleged nuisances by reference to expert opinion from a variety of sources, for example, using the statements of expert witnesses for the plaintiffs and the defendant to determine how the methane burning equipment operated in practice, in addition to considering its notional technical capabilities. Expert opinion from estate agents given on behalf of the plaintiffs and the defendant proved crucial in evaluating the diminution in the value of the plaintiffs' property through loss of amenity

---

[53] [1998] Env. LR 469.

[54] Applying the House of Lords decision in *Hunter* v. *Canary Wharf, supra* n.9, Mrs Blackburn's claim failed for lack of a proprietary interest in the property.

[55] The site was permitted by planning law and operated under a waste (disposal) licence. The relationship between such controls and nuisance is an interesting and controversial issue though, surprisingly, the interrelationship of the relevant legal regimes has been the subject of surprisingly limited and fairly inconclusive case law. See e.g. *Gillingham Borough Council* v. *Medway (Chatham) Dock Co. Ltd* [1992] 3 WLR 449 and *Wheeler* v. *J.J. Saunders Ltd* [1995] 2 All ER 697 on planning controls and nuisance. See *Gateshead Metropolitan Borough Council* v. *Secretary of State for the Environment and Northumbrian Water* (1994) 71 P & CR 350 on the relationship between planning and pollution controls and nuisance. The issue has been subject to a degree of academic discussion. See e.g. S. Ball, "Nuisance and Planning Permission" [1995] *JEL* 278; K.P. Mylrea, "Drawing the Dividing Line between Planning Control and Pollution Control" [1994] *JEL* 93; and S. Tromans and M. Clarkson, "The Environmental Protection Act 1990: Its Relevance to Planning Controls" [1991] *JPL* 507.

[56] The negligence issue was withdrawn before trial and the public nuisance claim during proceedings.

[57] A claim was made that the smells resulted in illness, but this was not established in the absence of medical evidence to support it. In any event such a claim would be unlikely to succeed in private nuisance, *supra* n. 18.

value.[58] Finally, specialist evidence provided by Kent County Council personnel also established that the defendant had "persistently flouted" the terms of its licence. Additional lay evidence also played an important role in enabling the judge to construct a full picture of the incidents in question. This proved particularly useful, because, although the events recorded by the Blackburns were seldom witnessed by anyone else, evidence taken from other people living in the area supported a finding that incidents of the types recorded were frequent.

The Blackburns' opposition to the landfill site was found not to go to their credibility. The judge characterised the plaintiffs as:

> careful and conscientious and not prone to unnecessary exaggeration and as fundamentally tolerant and patient people. I do not therefore regard their account . . . as invented, contrived, exaggerated or as the result of over-sensitivity on their part.[59]

The defendant's attempts to discredit the Blackburns' evidence on the basis of their opposition to the landfill site (and by alleging dishonesty on the part of Mr. Blackburn) failed. This rather distasteful strategy appears to be a direct and particularly undesirable manifestation of the approach taken to evaluating the plaintiff's evidence in *Graham and Graham* v. *Re-Chem*.[60] The judge was of the opinion that such tactics were "calculated to distract attention from the substantive criticisms of [the defendants'] operations".[61]

While *Blackburn and Another* v. *ARC Limited* is hardly at the cutting edge of common law strategies dealing with environmental pollution, at least in so far as it involves commonplace problems which are fairly routinely litigated, it is suggested that it has much to offer a modern appreciation of nuisance as a toxic tort. The judge's approach to evaluating the evidence and determining causation is unusually balanced and enlightened. He neither reduced the judicial task to a choice between the views of competing expert witnesses to the exclusion of the plaintiff's own contribution, nor did he allow the plaintiffs' evidence to operate to the exclusion of scientific material from the parties and the regulatory authorities. This type of synthetic approach to problems of causation and the evaluation of evidence has much to commend it in enabling the law of torts to make a positive contribution to environmental protection (subject to the use of expert assessors where the complexity of the issues requires it). It could be argued that the holistic approach adopted towards causation in *Blackburn* exhibits aspects of cutting edge environmental thinking, more usually seen in modern environmental legislation, and is to be encouraged as keeping the common law in touch with current social mores.

---

[58] Applying the House of Lords decision in *Ruxley Electronics and Construction Ltd.* v. *Forsyth* [1996] AC 344.

[59] *Supra*, n.53, at 476.

[60] *Supra*, n.16.

[61] *Supra*, n.53, at 477.

152 K. Morrow

FORESEEABILITY AND FAULT

Even if the hurdles raised by the issue of causation can be successfully overcome by the plaintiff, the chances of recovering damages in respect of environmental damage remain nil unless the foreseeability of the damage in question can be established. In the wake of the House of Lords ruling in *Cambridge Water Co. Ltd* v. *Eastern Counties Leather plc*,[62] this issue can now be viewed as the key control mechanism for the tort of nuisance and for liability under the rule in *Rylands* v. *Fletcher*.[63]

Traditionally the English law of nuisance requires neither a deliberate act nor negligence on the part of the defendant to attract liability. To this extent, liability is, in theory, strict.[64] However, in modern law it is comparatively unusual (though not impossible) for a defendant to be found liable for nuisance without also being found negligent.[65] In fact it is almost inevitable that negligence (and therefore fault in a legal as well as a technical sense) will be raised in parallel with nuisance in modern environmental pollution cases. This is because the defendant's conduct will almost always be at issue, in addition to the state of his property. This is the case even where naturally occurring nuisance is concerned,[66] though in cases of this type in particular, the lines between nuisance and negligence are blurred. Where the continuation of a naturally occurring nuisance is concerned, strict liability is tempered by the requirement of knowledge of the nuisance on the part of the defendant, coupled with a failure on his or her part to take reasonable care. These factors play a central role in determining liability. Even beyond the confines of naturally occurring interference, the law of nuisance has, in its own right and regardless of any cross-fertilisation with negligence, long required a degree of personal responsibility for the state of the property in question to ground a finding of liability. The traditional position is neatly summarised by Singleton J in *Cunliffe* v. *Bankes*:[67]

> A person is liable for a nuisance . . .
> (1) if he causes it,
> (2) if by the neglect of some duty he allowed it to arise, and

---

[62] [1994] 2 AC 264.

[63] (1865) 11 HL Cas. 142.

[64] This view is to be found in modern case law: see e.g. Lord Hoffmann in *Hunter* v. *Canary Wharf* [1997] 2 WLR 684 at 706 and academic writing, e.g. A. Ogus, "Water Rights Diluted" [1994] *JEL* 138; and R.V.F. Heuston and R.A. Buckley, "The Return of *Rylands* v. *Fletcher*" (1994) 110 *LQR* 506.

[65] In Scots law the approach adopted has been both different from and clearer than that in English law. See e.g. *RHM Bakeries (Scotland) Ltd* v. *Strathclyde Regional Council*, 1985 SLT 214 in which it was established that fault or *culpa* (though this is not synonymous with fault in negligence: see *Stair Memorial Encyclopaedia* (Edinburgh, Law Society of Scotland/Butterworths, 1988), Vol. 14 "Nuisance" paras. 2087–2108) is the basis for nuisance liability.

[66] See e.g. *Goldman* v. *Hargreave* [1967] 1 AC 645 and *Leakey* v. *National Trust* [1980] QB 485.

[67] [1945] 1 All ER 459.

Nuisance and Environmental Protection   153

(3) if, when it has arisen without his own act or default, he omits to remedy it within a reasonable time after he ought to have become aware of it.[68]

Thus, fault in a broad sense is implicitly present in nuisance and it is possible for a defendant to escape liability for the acts of third parties over which he has no control, provided that a reasonable response is made to the nuisance within a reasonable time.[69] Such an approach is not of necessity incompatible with a regime based on strict liability, since, in any situation where absolute liability is not imposed, it is perfectly acceptable to provide for exceptions to the general rule.[70]

However, it is in the progressive blurring of the lines between nuisance and negligence in more typical cases that fault-based issues have come to the fore and become problematic in the modern law of nuisance. An early example of cross-contamination appears in *Bolton* v. *Stone*,[71] a case which involved claims founded on both nuisance and negligence.[72] The court accepted the respondent's concession that a claim based on nuisance would be unlikely to succeed in the case if the negligence claim was unsuccessful. This tangential reference to a link between nuisance and negligence is not particularly enlightening of itself, nor indeed is it objectionable on the facts of the case in question. The judicial willingness to view a nuisance claim as dependant on a finding of negligence, which was evident in *Bolton* v. *Stone,* paved the way for a more overt change in the emphasis of the law. The public nuisance case of *Overseas Tankship (UK) Ltd* v. *Miller Steamship Co. Pty Ltd (The Wagon Mound (No. 2))*[73] has proved to be of profound significance for the whole law of nuisance. It will be recalled that Lord Reid stated: "although negligence may not be necessary, fault of some kind is almost always necessary and fault generally involves foreseeability".[74] Thus *The Wagon Mound (No. 2)*, in explicitly incorporating foreseeability of damage into the tort of nuisance, imported the concept of fault into all cases where the defendant has failed to prevent such damage. Although Lord Reid was speaking of foreseeability in a broad sense, and not as a technical term of art employed in the law of negligence, nevertheless his choice of terminology

---

[68] *Ibid.,* at 465.

[69] This view is implied in *Page Motors Ltd.* v. *Epsom and Ewell Borough Council* (1982) 80 LGR 337. However, the recent Court of Appeal decision in *Lipiatt* v. *South Gloucestershire County Council*, 31Mar. 1999, not yet reported, suggests that the courts will construe the leeway allowed to a defendant in this type of case rather narrowly.

[70] For example, statutory authority provides an established defence to proceedings in nuisance with respect to inevitable nuisance arising from the activities authorised: see *Allen* v. *Gulf Oil Refining* [1981] AC 1001. Even under this defence however, it is arguable that a strict liability approach is retained. *Eastern & SA Telegraph Co.* v. *Cape Town Tramways* [1902] AC 381 indicates that an individual cannot avail himself of it to increase the liabilities of his neighbour, by applying his own property to special uses (whether for business or pleasure). Liability may be imposed for a failure to adopt reasonable precautions (without prejudice to defendant's own interests) to avoid damage.

[71] [1951] AC 850.

[72] Only the negligence claim was at issue on appeal.

[73] [1967] 1 AC 617.

[74] *Ibid.,* at 639–40.

154   K. Morrow

was at best unfortunate because it has arguably facilitated the colonisation of nuisance by negligence. The logical conclusion of the line of reasoning adopted in *The Wagon Mound (No.2)* is that a defendant can act innocently or ignorantly, that is, without fault, and thus escape liability for nuisance. While appealing to intuitive fairness, this approach is highly problematic in practice for a tort notionally based on strict liability. Lord Reid's approach extends the traditional leeway for nuisances created by third parties for whom the defendant is not responsible (referred to in cases such as *Sedleigh-Denfield* v. *O'Callaghan*[75]) to all types of nuisance, including those created by third parties for whom the defendant is responsible, such as employees.

The Privy Council decision in *The Wagon Mound (No.2)* has taken a considerable time to come forward for scrutiny at the highest level in the domestic courts and has generated a degree of uncertainty in the law of nuisance in the interim. The issue of foreseeability of damage in the private nuisance context finally came to the fore in the controversial[76] litigation concerning *Cambridge Water Co. Ltd* v. *Eastern Counties Leather plc.*[77] The plaintiff brought an action in respect of contamination of part of its groundwater resource by the defendant's tanning works.[78] The claim was framed in negligence, nuisance and under the rule in *Rylands* v. *Fletcher*. Kennedy J dismissed the claims under all three heads at first instance.[79] The plaintiff succeeded on appeal where strict liability was deemed to be founded on the rather obscure authority of *Ballard* v. *Tomlinson*,[80] and the defendant appealed to the House of Lords. The case in the Lords centred on liability under the rule in *Rylands* v. *Fletcher*,[81] which was treated by the court as a species of nuisance.[82] Lord Goff was of the opinion that

---

[75] [1940] AC 880.

[76] *Cambridge Water* has generated a plethora of academic comment. See e.g. D. Wilkinson, "*Cambridge Water Company* v. *Eastern Counties Leather*: Diluting Liability for Continuing Escapes" (1994) 57 *MLR* 799; and Ogus, *supra* n.53.

[77] *Supra*, n.62.

[78] Interestingly, throughout the *Cambridge Water* litigation, the plaintiff's damage was characterised as resulting from legislative provision. Under Dir. 80/778/EEC OJ L229/11 [1980] OJ L229/11 and related provisions, water contaminated by perchloroethene, was deemed unfit for human consumption and could not therefore be sold to the water company's customers. Nowhere in the litigation trail is the damage characterised as physical, due to the peculiar position of groundwater at common law, where it has long been established that landowners do not enjoy property rights in respect of percolating water. Landowners are however entitled to extract such water at common law and have the right of access to an uncontaminated resource. This view of groundwater and pollution sits uncomfortably with a modern view of the environment generally and more specifically with statute law recognising the importance of groundwater extraction: see the Water Resources Act 1991.

[79] [1991] 1 Env. LR 116.

[80] (1885) 29 Ch. D 115 This case imposed strict liability on the defendants for the contamination of groundwater by a non-natural use of land rendering it unfit for use by the plaintiff.

[81] Lord Goff treated the Court of Appeal's decision and *Ballard* v. *Tomlinson*, *ibid.*, as simply providing a specific species of liability based on nuisance/the rule in *Rylands* v. *Fletcher*.

[82] Because Cambridge Water had appealed against Kennedy J's decision only on the basis of *Rylands* v. *Fletcher*, the case in the House of Lords was technically confined to this point. However, Lord Goff viewed the issue to be so closely intertwined with nuisance that examination of the latter formed a central theme in his decision. Lord Goff regarded the rule in *Rylands* v. *Fletcher* as representing a special species of nuisance in respect of isolated escapes.

Nuisance and Environmental Protection 155

the foreseeability of the damage in question was an essential element of liability in both nuisance and under the rule in *Rylands* v. *Fletcher*. His reasoning, confirming the role of foreseeability in this area, was based on what he termed the requirements of "common justice". Lord Goff took the view that, since foreseeability of damage must be established in claims for personal injury in negligence, it is indefensible that a plaintiff in nuisance should be in a more advantageous position with respect to claims for mere interference with the use and enjoyment of land. This "unjust" result would be inevitable if foreseeability of damage were not required as a prerequisite for liability in the latter context as well as the former. With respect, this reasoning seems to confuse the issue, particularly where toxic torts are concerned, because, first, there is no distinct dividing line between humanity and the environment and, secondly, in such cases environmental damage in itself may cause personal injury. In any event there is no justification in modern environmental thought for treating environmental damage as necessarily of lesser significance than personal injury. The decision in *Cambridge Water* on this point appears to have been reached on the basis of policy considerations whereby the concept of foreseeability is employed to temper the potential severity of nuisance in keeping with the prevalent modern negligence/fault-based perspective on liability. Despite the supposedly plaintiff-based rationale behind Lord Goff's ruling, which ostensibly brings fairness between plaintiffs utilising different branches of the law of torts, it seems clear that the result will actually be of greatest benefit to defendants in nuisance cases through the dilution, perhaps even the obliteration, of strict liability.

It is also significant that the question of foreseeability in *Cambridge Water* was based on what a reasonable site foreman at Eastern Counties Leather's plant could have been expected reasonably to foresee at the time at which spillage of perchloroethene occurred, i.e. before the end of 1976. The imposition of legal responsibility based on the knowledge of operational personnel does not sit easily with the tenor of modern pollution-control law which emphasises the need to make the knowledge of senior company personnel a central factor in determining liability for environmental pollution.[83] Further, Lord Goff's conclusion that environmental pollution would not have been reasonably foreseen as a result of the state of the company's site by ECL's foreman in the relevant period is highly debatable.[84] This is particularly so in respect of the period from 1970 onwards, since by this time environmental pollution issues had emerged into the social, political, cultural and even legal mainstream.[85]

In any event, the view of foreseeability adopted by Lord Goff in *Cambridge Water* is exceptionally narrow, particularly so when measured against the approach adopted in the law of negligence from which it is supposedly drawn.

---

[83] See e.g. Parts I and III of the Environmental Protection Act 1990 and the Water Resources Act 1991.

[84] For discussion of the site supervisor as an embodiment of the reasonable man, see Wilkinson, *supra* n.75, at 806.

[85] See e.g. J. McCormick, *British Politics and the Environment* (London, Earthscan, 1991).

156   K. Morrow

His Lordship was of the opinion that to impose liability on Eastern Counties Leather because environmental pollution *simpliciter* was foreseeable as the result of perchloroethene spillage would be to adopt too broad a basis upon which to attribute legal responsibility. Instead, he preferred an extremely narrow view of the issue, stating that it was pollution of the acquifer which would have to have been reasonably foreseen in order for liability to accrue. It is suggested that this approach appears to go beyond the notion prevailing in negligence, namely, that only the broad type of damage must be reasonably foreseeable. It is well established in negligence that neither the exact mechanism whereby damage occurs[86] nor its extent[87] need be reasonably foreseeable for the imposition of liability. However in *Cambridge Water* Lord Goff appears to apply a more stringent view of foreseeability in a nuisance/*Rylands* v. *Fletcher* context, whereby the exact type of the damage and the mechanism by which it will occur must be reasonably foreseeable for liability to be imposed.

Lord Goff's extremely narrow approach to foreseeability does not, however, appear to have found universal favour in more recent authorities which arguably take a view of the issue more akin to that adopted in negligence. The questions of fault and foreseeability were central in the *Graham* case in which Re-Chem argued that, since the details of the secondary pollution effects of its operations were not known until 1985, they were therefore unforeseeable and the company was not at fault and in consequence, not liable. Forbes J disagreed with Re-Chem's arguments on foreseeability in so far as nuisance was concerned, preferring a broad rather than the narrow approach favoured by Re-Chem to this issue:

> for the purposes of liability in nuisance, it is immaterial whether Re-Chem knew precisely how its operations could or did create the alleged toxic substances.[88]

For Forbes J it was sufficient that it was foreseeable that the emission of organic pollutants, including dioxins and furans, would occur as the result of the operation of high temperature incinerators and that it was known that some of the compounds emitted were very toxic. The actual problems of contaminant formulation as a result of secondary combustion did not therefore need to be foreseeable in order to make it possible to argue the issue. A similarly generous approach to foreseeability featured in *Blackburn* v. *ARC,* though this is perhaps unsurprising given the relatively mainstream nature of the damage complained of and the established scientific issues involved.

While a broad approach to foreseeability does give some flexibility to the notion in the context of nuisance, the question remains whether this element is appropriate at all in nuisance, particularly in cases involving pollution-based

---

[86] *Hughes* v. *Lord Advocate* [1963] AC 837. While at first sight *Doughty* v. *Turner* [1964] 1 QB 518 could be viewed as supporting Lord Goff's approach, in that case the incident in question represented an unknown danger which had never manifested itself before, whereas the same cannot be said for pollution of groundwater by surface activities.

[87] *Smith* v. *Leech Brain* [1962] 2 QB 405.

[88] *Supra*, n.16 at 168.

Nuisance and Environmental Protection   157

damage. Perhaps the problem of pollution is sufficiently serious to justify a strict approach to liability, in line with wider environmental thinking,[89] even though this contradicts the dominant fault-based negligence approach to liability in modern tort law. The wider relationship between fault and nuisance does require further clarification. The issue of whether or not importation of negligence-based concepts into the law of nuisance is desirable has yet to be adequately examined. It would seem, on the basis of complex environmental pollution cases, such as those discussed above, that importing a fault-based ideology into this area of the law is arguably at best inappropriate and at worst places an almost insurmountable burden on the plaintiff in making out a case.

CONCLUSION

The central question is: can the law of torts rise to the challenge of modern environmental pollution problems? The answer lies in the lottery of litigation and is affected by a variety of factors, including the jurisdiction in which proceedings are initiated, judicial attitude, the performance of plaintiffs and expert witnesses in court and the nature of the pollution effects complained of. While each of these issues is undoubtedly significant, underpinning the whole legal process in this area is the profound difficulty in determining the appropriate theoretical basis for imposing liability for environmental damage at common law. Such is the nature of the ascendancy of the fault-based tort of negligence that it has come to dominate the whole of the law of torts, culminating in an almost visceral rejection of alternative strategies for imposing liability. The dominance of negligence cannot be explained in purely legal or objective terms, indeed in many situations strict liability, for example, may represent a more efficient option for attributing responsibility for damage. Employing alternative approaches to liability in torts, including the extension of non-fault-oriented liability strategies into toxic torts, would certainly have serious ramifications, but this is not of itself a necessary or sufficient reason to reject them out of hand. It is clear that there are many factors to be considered in determining the most appropriate basis for liability, including risk sharing and wider considerations of social cost. These issues are particularly acute in relation to torts affecting the environment, which not only often involve practical consequences for the environment and the immediate parties to litigation, but also affect the interests of the wider community.

Unfortunately, as things stand, the courts often choose to avoid engaging with the deeper issues underlying the law in this area in a meaningful way, not

---

[89] See e.g. European Commission, *Green Paper on Remedying Environmental Damage*, COM(93)47 final and the Council of Europe's Convention on Civil Liability for Damages Resulting from Activities Dangerous to the Environment. It should however be noted that, in the latter context, future legislation on civil liability for environmental damage is however unlikely to cover historic pollution: see Wilkinson, *supra*, n.75 at 809.

158   K. Morrow

because the law of torts cannot accommodate them, but rather through an unwillingness to take decisive steps in such a controversial area. Lord Goff exhibits precisely this type of reserve in *Cambridge Water*:

> as a general rule it is more appropriate for strict liability in respect of operations of high risk to be imposed by Parliament, than by the courts. If such liability is imposed by statute, the relevant activities can be identified, and those concerned can know where they stand.[90]

While nuisance proved sufficiently adaptable, perhaps against the odds suggested by its ancient origins, to meet the challenges of the industrial revolution, recent case law in this area signals that, as currently employed, it is unlikely to be equal to the imperatives of the "environmental revolution". This may be the result of altered perceptions of the appropriate role for this branch of the law of torts during the twentieth century. There are a number of possible reasons behind this change: it may be that modern judges are less innovative than their predecessors or, more probably, that the culture of negligence has become so pervasive that it is not open for them to employ strict liability in an imaginative way.

A broader issue which arises in this context, and which raises even more serious issues than the fault/strict liability debate within the law of torts, is the fundamental question of how the judiciary perceives the role of the common law as a whole in relation to environmental pollution. The judicial response to toxic tort claims in nuisance and under the rule in *Rylands* v. *Fletcher* often demonstrates profound unwillingness to employ common law in the cause of environmental protection, and this arguably has serious implications for the role of the common law as a whole in this area. The approach adopted by Lord Goff in *Cambridge Water*, for example, certainly raises serious questions whether the common law will be allowed to make a meaningful contribution to modern environmental law:

> it does not follow . . . that a common law principle, such as the rule in *Rylands* v. *Fletcher*, should be developed or rendered more strict to provide for liability in respect of such pollution. On the contrary, given that so much well-informed and carefully structured legislation is now being put in place for this purpose, there is less need for the courts to develop a common law principle to achieve the same end.[91]

The irony is that the rule in *Rylands* v. *Fletcher* itself emerged, and the law of nuisance achieved a new lease of life, in the context of a legislative climate which both recognised environmental pollution problems and attempted to tackle them. In the nineteenth century, judges appear to have regarded themselves and the common law as having a dynamic and significant role to play in adapting existing concepts to new social conditions. By contrast, in modern law there appears to be considerable reluctance to apply even established concepts in a

---

[90] *Supra*, n.26, at 76.
[91] *Ibid.*

way that will shift the boundaries of liability. The question is not whether the common law is capable of making a meaningful contribution to environmental protection—it has proved its ability to do so in the past—but whether the judiciary is willing to allow it play a significant role in the future.

In the absence of judicial activism, it is left to the legislature to innovate, and indeed there is a trend in modern environmental law statutes to employ the concept of civil liability,[92] though very much as a subsidiary strategy, underpinning established command and control devices. The application of civil liability in this statutory context is of a special and rather limited nature, focusing on providing additional punishment for offenders and the recompense of regulatory authorities for action taken in respect of environmental damage caused in breach of statutory controls.[93] The fundamental issue of providing redress for the individual whose interests in property have been adversely affected by environmental torts is not, however, a feature of statutory pollution control regimes. It is here that the common law, far from treading over ground already covered by legislation, provides the first and last refuge of the individual—a role that will surely remain to it regardless of the evolution of more sophisticated statutory schemes promoting the public interest.

---

[92] For example, civil liability for cleanup costs is utilised in ss. 27 and 121(1) of the Environmental Protection Act 1990 and s. 161(3) of the Water Resources Act 1991 which allow for the recovery of expenditure incurred by regulatory authorities from individuals convicted of relevant pollution offences.

[93] The main offences under the Environmental Protection Act 1990 and the Water Resources Act 1991 employ civil liability as an adjunct to criminal sanctions.

8

Marking the Boundary: The Relationship between Private Nuisance, Negligence and Fault

PAULA GILIKER*

INTRODUCTION

I N ASSESSING THE extent to which the common law of nuisance is capable of offering environmental protection, its exact boundaries must be a relevant question. Yet, it is a question on which there is some confusion. This chapter will address the relationship between the torts of private nuisance and negligence which raises key issues as to the very nature of the torts and the remedies they are prepared to grant.[1] Most lawyers are familiar with the basic characteristics of these two torts. Negligence is commonly defined as "the breach of a legal duty to take care which results in damage, undesired by the defendant, to the plaintiff".[2] The tort of private nuisance, in contrast, has proven more difficult to define. Clerk and Lindsell describe it as "a condition or activity which unduly interferes with the use or enjoyment of land"[3]; alternatively, Winfield and Jolowicz describe it as "unlawful interference with a person's use or enjoyment of land, or some right over, or in connection with it".[4] The relationship between the two torts remains unclear. This is due in part to the unwillingness of the courts to address this issue, but can be largely traced to the legal development of the torts. Private nuisance is the older tort, dating back to the thirteenth century,[5] whilst the tort of negligence is a relative newcomer, but it would be

---

* This chapter is based on a paper presented at the SPTL Conference in Leeds 1999. The author wishes to express her gratitude for the helpful comments and encouragement from the Torts Section.

[1] The question of the relationship between public nuisance and negligence will not be discussed in this chapter due to lack of space. For an excellent discussion, see R.A. Buckley, *The Law of Nuisance* (2nd edn., London, Butterworths, 1996) ch. 7.

[2] W.V.H. Rogers, *Winfield and Jolowicz on Torts* (5th edn., London, Sweet and Maxwell, 1998) at 90.

[3] R.A. Buckley, *Clerk & Lindsell on Torts* (17th edn., London, Sweet and Maxwell, 1995) at 18–01.

[4] *Supra* n.2, at 494; P.H. Winfield, "Nuisance as a Tort" (1931) 4 *CLJ* 189, at 190.

[5] See *ibid.*; W. Holdsworth, *A History of English Law* (London, Sweet and Maxwell, 1942) iii, at 11; Lord Wright in *Sedleigh-Denfield* v. *O'Callaghan* [1940] AC 880, at 902–3.

162   Paula Giliker

misleading to regard the history of the two torts as distinct. Early case law does illustrate the application of certain underlying ideas of negligence and fault,[6] despite the fact that negligence was not considered as a tort in its own right until the nineteenth century,[7] although in the absence of any specific writ for negligence, it is difficult to define any overall principle. Indeed, until the landmark decision of *Donoghue* v. *Stevenson*,[8] negligence remained somewhat indistinct in character and was essentially a collection of single instances, from which no broader principle derived. It was therefore inevitable that the two actions, both being actions on the case, would be confused and overlap, a fact which was exacerbated by ongoing uncertainty about the nature of the tort of nuisance itself.[9] Without direct judicial involvement, there was no reason why such confusion should not continue into the twentieth century. The refusal of the courts to mark the boundaries between the two torts and the increasing influence of negligence and fault-based principles in this century have ensured that this question has yet to be resolved.

This chapter will consider three main questions: first, whether the tort of private nuisance has been overwhelmed by the tort of negligence and now forms a category of negligence liability, so that its environmental impact should be seen in terms of negligence; secondly, the impact of the House of Lords decision in *Hunter* v. *Canary Wharf Ltd*[10]; and thirdly, the options open to those analysing the relationship between the two torts and what conclusions should be drawn about their ongoing relationship. This discussion is not purely academic. After *Hunter*, the type of damages recoverable by the claimant is likely to differ depending on whether his or her claim is found to be in negligence or nuisance, and this is likely to result in an increasing demand for clarity. Equally, there is some authority that the remedy of an injunction is not available in negligence,[11] although this is probably in reality a pragmatic decision that negligent acts are not generally continuous and damages will therefore be an adequate remedy. Claimants will want, and should have, a clearer idea of the basis for their claim, and the time has come to examine once again the place of private nuisance in the law of torts.

---

[6] See in particular the cases mentioned in J.H. Baker and S.F.C. Milsom, *Sources of English Legal History: Private Law to 1750* (London, Butterworths, 1986) ch. 22.

[7] See P.H. Winfield, "The History of Negligence in the Law of Torts" (1926) 42 *LQR* 184. See also his "Duty in Tortious Negligence" (1934) 34 *Col LR* 41.

[8] [1932] AC 562. See A. Rodgers QC, "Mrs Donoghue and Alfenus Varus" [1988] *CLP* 1 for an entertaining review of the case.

[9] See, e.g., Erle CJ's comment in *Brand* v. *Hammersmith and City Railway* Co. (1867) LR 2 QB 223, at 247: "[t]his cause of action is immersed in undefined uncertainty".

[10] [1997] AC 655.

[11] *Clerk & Lindsell on Torts*, *supra* n.3, at 18–26; *Miller* v. *Jackson* [1977] QB 966, at 980, *per* Lord Denning.

The Relationship between Private Nuisance, Negligence and Fault   163

HAS PRIVATE NUISANCE BEEN OVERWHELMED BY THE TORT OF NEGLIGENCE?

The twentieth century has seen the great rise of the tort of negligence from an ill-defined concept to the most commonly used cause of action. It is now hard to imagine Professor Winfield justifying its existence as an independent tort in 1926.[12] It is inevitable that the growth of this tort has left its mark on other torts. Examination of this area of law reveals the impact of negligence on the tort of private nuisance to have been considerable. Courts, familiar with fault-based reasoning in negligence, have allowed it to influence their reasoning and little attempt has been made to analyse the significance of this fact, with the result that the line between negligence and nuisance has become blurred. Geoffrey Lane LJ, for example, remarks in *Miller* v. *Jackson*,[13] that "in circumstances such as these it is difficult and probably unnecessary, except as an interesting intellectual exercise, to define the frontiers between negligence and nuisance".[14] However, it is submitted that, in the light of *Hunter* v. *Canary Wharf Ltd*, this attitude can no longer be accepted. Whilst the distinction may not have been important on the facts of *Miller*, where the action was pleaded alternatively in negligence and nuisance and both torts raised similar concerns, this will not always be so. Such comments should therefore be taken to mean no more than that the defendant's conduct in such cases was such as clearly to found claims in both nuisance and negligence. As will be shown, the distinction is sometimes significant and analysis a worthwhile "intellectual" exercise.

Faced with authority which expressly refers to fault and refuses to classify the action as one of negligence or nuisance, it is inevitable that the nature of liability and the relationship between the two torts will be questioned. In our view, these issues can only be resolved by analysing the impact of negligence on the tort of private nuisance in two stages: first by examining the liability of the creator of the nuisance and, secondly, by examining the liability of the person continuing or adopting the nuisance. In so doing, it must be stressed that there is an important distinction between the impact of the tort of negligence and the impact of negligence principles, such as fault. Fault may play a part in the tort of nuisance without a merger of the two torts. It is only where fault principles operate in such a way that liability is determined in the same manner as in the tort of negligence that the very nature of the tort should be challenged.

---

[12] P.H. Winfield, "The History of Negligence in the Law of Torts", *supra* n.7.

[13] [1977] 1 QB 966, at 985.

[14] G. Williams and B.A. Hepple, in *Foundations of the Law of Torts* (London, Butterworths, 1984) at 125, cite *Bolton* v. *Stone* [1951] AC 850 in support of this argument: "[t]he claim based on negligence failed, and it was conceded that the case could not succeed for nuisance since negligence had not been established". However, this was a claim for public nuisance on the highway for which, it is submitted, there is a far closer relationship between negligence and public nuisance: see Buckley, *supra*, n. 1, at 84. It is therefore of limited assistance in relation to private nuisance.

164 *Paula Giliker*

Liability of the Creator of the Nuisance

This is the classic case of nuisance, where the unlawful interference has been caused by the defendant. Here, the division between negligence and private nuisance has long been recognised on a number of grounds,[15] of which the most important are:

 (i) the distinction between reasonable user and reasonable care; and
(ii) that negligence is not determinative of liability in private nuisance

These will be examined in more detail below.

Reasonable User

The concept of "reasonable user" lies at the heart of liability for private nuisance and determines whether the defendant's conduct is such as unlawfully to interfere with the claimant's use and enjoyment of land. This is not the same as reasonable care. "Reasonable care" in negligence is an objective standard of care, which pays little attention to the personal characteristics of the defendant. "Reasonable user", in contrast, is not a standard of conduct, but a rule of give and take by which the courts balance the respective rights of the claimant and defendant freely to enjoy their land.[16] In this sense, the torts have a different focus. Negligence assesses the conduct of the defendant utilising the yardstick of the reasonable person. Private nuisance seeks not to blame the defendant, but to protect the claimant's interest, and is therefore more concerned with the *effect* of the defendant's conduct on the claimant. An interesting way of illustrating this different focus is to look at the classic case of negligence: the road traffic accident. A negligence lawyer would seek to establish that the driver caused the accident by driving below the standard of the reasonable driver. A nuisance lawyer would weigh the right of the driver to drive the car as he or she wishes against the right of the pedestrian to cross a road safely.

Negligence is not Required

This second ground has been a point of contention for a number of years,[17] but the generally accepted view is that the creator may be liable for a nuisance regardless of whether he or she has acted deliberately, recklessly, negligently or

---

[15] Note also the different rules on liability for independent contractors between negligence and private nuisance. *Bower* v. *Peate* (1876) 1 QBD 321 and *Matania* v. *National Provincial Bank* [1936] 2 All ER 633 illustrate the more generous approach to liability adopted in nuisance.

[16] See, e.g., Lord Wright's observation in *Sedleigh-Denfield* v. *O'Callaghan* [1940] AC 880, at 903 that "[a] balance has to be maintained between the right of the occupier to do what he likes with his own, and the right of his neighbour not to be interfered with".

[17] See, e.g., R.J. Buxton, "The Negligent Nuisance" (1966) 8 *Malaya LR* 1, at 27–30; and J.M. Eekelaar, "Nuisance and Strict Liability" (1973) 8 *Ir. Jur. (NS)* 191.

The Relationship between Private Nuisance, Negligence and Fault   165

otherwise. The leading authority remains that of *Rapier* v. *London Tramways Co.*[18] The court held in that case that it is no defence to show that the defendant has exercised reasonable care if he or she has been found to have unreasonably interfered with the claimant's use and enjoyment of land.[19] Although this view has been challenged,[20] it has been affirmed recently by Lord Goff in *Cambridge Water Co.* v. *Eastern Counties Leather plc*,[21] and should be accepted as a valid statement of law.

For these two reasons, private nuisance has been said to amount almost to strict liability.[22] It is important, however, not to overstate the case. Case law indicates that the courts do take into account the nature of the defendant's conduct in deciding cases in nuisance. For example, the "reasonableness" of the defendant's conduct will influence the interpretation of reasonable user. Equally, following the Privy Council's decision in *The Wagon Mound (No 2)*,[23] the extent of damages will now be assessed in accordance with fault principles. This case, which concerned an alleged public nuisance caused by the setting alight of a quantity of furnace oil discharged by the appellants into Sydney Harbour, held that the same rules of remoteness applied to negligence, public and private nuisance. In all these cases, the extent of liability would be confined to losses of the kind which could be reasonably foreseen. Much ink has been spilt analysing the speech of Lord Reid in this case, in particular his comment that:

> Nuisance is a term used to cover a wide variety of tortious acts or omissions and in many negligence in the narrow sense is not essential . . . And although negligence may not be necessary, *fault of some kind is almost always necessary and fault generally involves foreseeability.*[24]

---

[18] [1893] 2 Ch. 588, at 590, *per* Lindley LJ.

[19] See also Lord Simonds in *Read* v. *J. Lyons & Co. Ltd.* [1947] AC 156, at 183: "[f]or, if a man commits a legal nuisance, it is no answer to his injured neighbour that he took the utmost care not to commit it. There the liability is strict, and there only he has a lawful claim who has suffered an invasion of some proprietary or other interest in land."

[20] Glanville Williams and B.A. Hepple, who argue that there is no difference between private nuisance and negligence, recognise that *Rapier* is the chief obstacle to such analysis: see *supra*, n.14, 126–7. They circumvent the authority by re-interpreting it on its facts: if it is no excuse that the defendant cannot carry out his business, even when exercising reasonable care, then the court is finding him to be at fault in failing to give up his business. One may question whether such a standard of care is "reasonable" and whether Williams and Hepple are simply asserting that one is liable for the reasonably foreseeable consequences of one's actions. See also G. Williams, "The Risk Principle" (1961) 77 *LQR* 179, at 204.

[21] *Cambridge Water Co.* v. *Eastern Counties Leather plc* [1994] 2 AC 264, at 302. See also Lord Reid in *The Wagon Mound (No 2) (Overseas Tankships (UK) Ltd* v. *Miller Steamship Co. Pty.)* [1967] 1 AC 617, at 639; *Midwood & Co. Ltd* v. *Manchester Corpn.* [1905] 2 KB 597, at 604; and *Jacobs* v. *London CC* [1950] AC 361, at 374.

[22] See G. Cross, "Does only the Careless Polluter Pay? A Fresh Examination of the Nature of Private Nuisance" (1995) 111 *LQR* 445.

[23] *Overseas Tankships (UK) Ltd* v. *Miller Steamship Co. Pty.* [1967] 1 AC 617.

[24] *Ibid.*, at 639, emphasis supplied. See R.J. Buxton, "Nuisance and Negligence Again" (1966) 29 *MLR* 676.

166   *Paula Giliker*

This statement, excellently analysed by Dias in 1967,[25] is far from clear and has caused controversy. However, in my view, such problems have been exaggerated. His Lordship does not state that fault is an essential ingredient in a nuisance claim. His comments are best explained as an attempt to recognise the impact of fault-based reasoning on nuisance. On this basis, "negligence in the narrow sense", which we may presume to mean the tort of negligence, is distinct from nuisance, although in many cases fault will be a relevant factor. This is particularly so in the examples given by his Lordship, namely highway cases in public nuisance and *Sedleigh-Denfield* v. *O'Callaghan*,[26] where fault is recognised to play a significant role.[27] This does not mean, however, that fault will play a significant role in all nuisance situations. Fault-based principles may play a role in both private nuisance and negligence, but the individual torts stand in their own right.

This approach is supported by Lord Goff in *Cambridge Water Co*. v. *Eastern Counties Leather plc*.[28] In finding that the same test of remoteness applied for negligence, nuisance and the rule in *Rylands* v. *Fletcher*, his Lordship recognised the uneasy co-existence of fault-based principles with the stricter aspects of private nuisance: "the principle is one of strict liability in the sense that the defendant may be held liable notwithstanding that he has exercised all due care to prevent the escape from occurring".[29] Nevertheless, in view of the injustice in awarding the claimant with an interest in land a higher level of damages in nuisance than in negligence, his Lordship advocated that a common test of remoteness should be applied.[30]

On this basis, fault is not determinative of liability for the creator of a private nuisance, but does exert some influence.[31] The torts of nuisance and negligence are distinct. Fault is relevant, but, in our view, this merely represents an evolution which one would hope would be expected in any legal system developing in the twentieth century.

---

[25] See R.W.M. Dias, "Trouble on Oiled Waters: Problems of the Wagon Mound (No 2)" [1967] *CLJ* 62.

[26] [1940] AC 880.

[27] The Board's decision may be criticised for limiting its examples to such cases. By relying on the specific examples of *Sedleigh-Denfield* v. *O'Callaghan* and highway cases in public nuisance such as *Dollman* v. *Hillman* [1941] 1 All ER 355, CA, and Lord Denning's judgment in *Morton* v. *Wheeler The Times*, 1 Feb. 1956, in which fault is recognised to play a significant role, there is a distinct danger that the importance of fault principles generally is exaggerated.

[28] [1994] 2 AC 264. See D. Wilkinson, "Diluting Liability for Continuing Escapes" (1994) 57 *MLR* 799.

[29] [1994] 2 AC 264 at 302. See also Cross, *supra*, n.22, at 465–8.

[30] [1994] 2 AC 264 at 300: "it is difficult to see why, in common justice, he should be in a stronger position to claim damages for interference with the enjoyment of his land where the defendant was unable to foresee such damage".

[31] This is in contrast to the position in Scotland for which *culpa* is a necessary ingredient of an action for nuisance: see *R.H.M. Bakeries* v. *Strathclyde Regional Council*, 1985 SLT 214, which also denies the applicability of the rule in *Rylands* v. *Fletcher* in Scotland. *Culpa* or fault nevertheless is distinct from negligence and may include deliberate acts with the knowledge that the action would result in harm to the other party: *Kennedy* v. *Glenbelle Ltd*, 1996 SLT 1186.

The Relationship between Private Nuisance, Negligence and Fault   167

Greater confusion, however, exists in our second category, namely that of liability for adopting or continuing the nuisance, and this will therefore be analysed in more depth.

Liability for Adopting or Continuing the Nuisance

The clearest example of the influence of fault in nuisance may be found in the group of cases on continuing or adopting a nuisance. Our starting point is the House of Lords decision of *Sedleigh-Denfield* v. *O'Callaghan*.[32] In this case, the local authority without the defendants' permission (and therefore as a trespasser) had placed a drainage pipe in a ditch on the defendants' land with a grating designed to keep out leaves. The grating had not been fixed in the correct place with the result that during a heavy rainstorm, the pipe had become choked with leaves and water had overflowed onto the claimant's land. The claimant sought damages from the defendants for his losses.

The defendants were found liable for adopting and continuing the nuisance caused by the local authority. They had used the pipe for their own purposes and so adopted the nuisance but, more importantly for our purposes, were liable for continuing the nuisance due to their failure to take reasonable steps to abate it when they should have known of the problem. Liability in both cases was founded on the fault of the defendants.

To understand the court's decision in *Sedleigh*, it is important first of all to recognise that the House of Lords had been asked to overturn the decision of the Court of Appeal below, which had adopted a narrower view of continuation. The lower court had followed its earlier decision in *Job Edwards* v. *Birmingham Navigations*,[33] in which the majority had held that the occupier did not continue the nuisance by simply failing or even refusing to abate it, even though he or she could have abated it by reasonable means.[34] In seeking to alter this position, the House of Lords was therefore required to justify the imposition of a heavier burden on a party who had no role in creating the nuisance or the state of affairs from which the nuisance arose.

The House favoured the broader definition of "continuance" utilised in a number of earlier public nuisance cases, such as *Barker* v. *Herbert*,[35] in which liability had been based on fault. Such authority had been expressly rejected by Bankes LJ in *Job Edwards*, who had held the position in public nuisance to be predicated on considerations of public interest which had no application in private nuisance.[36] The court refused to maintain this distinction and approved

---

[32] [1940] AC 880.

[33] [1924] 1 KB 341, Scrutton LJ dissenting.

[34] Although Bankes LJ did concede, *ibid.*, at 352, that where the act to abate the nuisance was of a "trifling nature" it might amount to negligence on the part of the occupier not to take that step.

[35] [1911] 2 KB 633, particularly the judgment of Fletcher Moulton LJ. See also *A-G* v. *Tod-Heatley* [1897] 1 Ch. 560.

[36] [1924] 1 KB 341, at 350.

168   *Paula Giliker*

Scrutton LJ's dissenting judgment in *Job Edwards*. The new position was stated by Lord Wright: "an occupier is not *prima facie* responsible for a nuisance created without his knowledge and consent. If he is to be liable a further condition is necessary, namely, that he had knowledge or means of knowledge, that he knew or should have known of the nuisance in time to correct it and obviate its mischievous effects. The liability for a nuisance is not, at least in modern law, a strict or absolute liability."[37]

As can be seen, the defendant's liability is wholly based on fault. Nevertheless, the court still identified liability as that of private nuisance[38] to which negligence was said to be ancillary. Whilst the analogy with public nuisance would now be questioned,[39] it proved a useful basis for extending liability in this context via the medium of fault. Subsequent case law has predictably questioned the precise nature of such liability and its effect on the future relationship of the two torts. This must therefore be examined.

The Response to *Sedleigh-Denfield*

For simplicity, our examination is confined to three main cases, namely the decisions of the Privy Council in *Goldman* v. *Hargrave*[40]; the Court of Appeal in *Leakey* v. *National Trust*[41]; and the House of Lords in *Smith* v. *Littlewoods*.[42] Other cases consider this issue, but it is submitted that these three cases are the most significant and authoritative in this area of law. These cases encapsulate the tension between nuisance and negligence, but, as will be seen, fail, despite considerable analysis, to provide any clear resolution to this problem.

All bar one were actions for nuisance. In *Goldman* v. *Hargrave*,[43] a 100-foot redgum tree growing in the centre of the defendant's land had been struck by lightning and caught fire. The defendant had quite properly cut down the tree, but had left it to burn itself out when he could have simply eliminated any risk by dousing the smouldering sections of the tree with water. The wind later picked up and rekindled the fire, which spread, causing damage to the claimant's land. Lord Wilberforce in an important judgment chose to follow

---

[37]   *Supra* n.32, at 904.

[38]   See Lord Wright, *ibid.*: "the gist of the present action is the unreasonable and unjustified interference by the defendant in the user of his land with the plaintiff's right to enjoy his property". However, Scrutton LJ in *Job Edwards* had identified such liability as being based upon negligence (see [1924] 1 KB 341, at 357).

[39]   The two torts are now generally regarded as distinct: see M. Brazier and J. Murphy, *Street on Torts* (10th edn., London, Butterworths, 1999) at 393.

[40]   [1967] 1 AC 645. See D.M. Harris, "Nuisance, Negligence and Dangers Arising Naturally on Land" [1967] *CLJ* 24.

[41]   [1980] QB 485. See R.A. Buckley, "Liability for Natural Processes: Nuisance or Negligence?" (1980) 96 *LQR* 185.

[42]   [1987] AC 241. See B.S. Markesinis, "Negligence, Nuisance and Affirmative Duties of Action" (1989) 105 *LQR* 104.

[43]   [1967] 1 AC 645.

The Relationship between Private Nuisance, Negligence and Fault 169

Sedleigh-Denfield. In so doing, he rejected the previously adopted distinction between nuisances created by third parties and nuisances created by acts of nature. On this basis, the defendant was liable for failing to act against the foreseeable risk of fire. However, in finding liability, his Lordship imposed a subjective standard of care:

> In such situations the standard ought to be to require of the occupier what it is reasonable to expect of him in his individual circumstances. Thus, less must be expected of the infirm than of the able-bodied: the owner of a small property where a hazard arises which threatens a neighbour with substantial interests should not have to do so much as one with larger interests of his own at stake and greater resources to protect them: if the small owner does what he can and promptly calls on his neighbour to provide additional resources, he may be held to have done his duty: he should not be liable unless it is clearly proved that he could, and reasonably in his individual circumstance should have done more.[44]

This is at odds with the objective test maintained by the courts in negligence, but has been applied generally in this context, for example in *Page Motors Ltd v. Epsom and Ewell BC*.[45] His Lordship declined, however, to answer "the disputable question" whether liability should be classified as nuisance or placed in a separate category. He simply commented that in this case "liability, if it exists, rests upon *negligence and nothing else*".[46] It is not difficult to see how such a statement could provoke doubts about the relationship between private nuisance and negligence. No attempt was made to resolve the uncertainty which was bound to result.

Goldman was nevertheless followed in *Leakey v. National Trust*.[47] The Court of Appeal held the National Trust liable to the claimants for damage caused by the subsidence of a hill above their properties, when there was clear evidence that it had been aware of a potential problem, but had refused to act. Megaw LJ again recognised the importance of fault:

> the duty asserted is, in effect, a duty to take reasonable care to prevent part of the defendants' land from falling onto the plaintiffs' property. I should, for myself, regard that as being properly described as a claim in nuisance. But even if that were, technically, wrong, I do not think that the point could or should avail the defendants in this case.[48]

As Shaw LJ warned, "[t]his formulation may, so it seems to me, create fresh problems, and the derivative problems may defy resolution".[49]

In the face of such *dicta*, it is interesting to note that the case in *Smith v. Littlewoods*[50] was brought in negligence and was not argued on the basis of

---

[44] *Ibid.*, at 663.
[45] (1982) 80 LGR 337.
[46] *Supra* n.43, at 657, emphasis supplied.
[47] [1980] QB 485.
[48] *Ibid.*, at 514.
[49] *Ibid.*, at 529.
[50] [1987] AC 241.

170   *Paula Giliker*

nuisance at all. The question before the court related to the liability of an occupier for the damage to neighbouring property caused by vandals setting fire to a derelict cinema on its land. Nevertheless, in reaching its decision, the court did refer to nuisance cases, particularly *Goldman* v. *Hargrave*.[51]

As is well-known, the majority of the court and Lord Goff approached the case from very different angles.[52] The majority assumed that Littlewoods owed the claimants a duty to exercise reasonable care to ensure that the cinema was not and did not become a source of danger to neighbouring buildings, and therefore decided the case on whether Littlewoods were in breach of this duty.[53] Lord Goff, in contrast, held that there was no general duty of care to prevent third parties from causing damage and it was therefore a question of establishing whether the claimants' case fell within an exception where the courts were prepared to find a defendant liable for a pure omission.[54] However, certain common principles emerge: the case is argued purely from the point of view of negligence and *Goldman* v. *Hargrave* is cited by Lords Mackay,[55] Griffiths[56] and Goff[57] as a relevant authority in negligence. It is difficult, however, to accept the views of Lords Mackay and Griffiths that, in arguing the case in terms of breach of duty, Lord Radcliffe in *Bolton* v. *Stone*[58] and Lord Wilberforce in *Goldman* express the same standard of care. Their Lordships make no comment on this point.

It is suggested that Lord Goff's speech is the more illuminating. In determining whether the *occupier* will be liable for omissions, he lists a number of situations in which the occupier is potentially liable towards visitors and trespassers (traditionally known as "occupiers' liability") and towards adjoining occupiers. This latter category embraces the situation where the occupier negligently causes or permits a source of danger to be created on his or her land and can reasonably foresee that third parties may trespass on the land and spark it off, causing damage to adjoining occupiers. This also includes *Sedleigh-Denfield* liability. All these examples have the common aim of imposing liability on the occupier by virtue of his or her exclusive control of the land in question.[59] His Lordship commented that "it is difficult to believe that, in this respect, there can be any material distinction between liability in nuisance and liability in negli-

---

[51]   [1967] 1 AC 645.

[52]   Although Lord Keith managed to agree with all four other judges!

[53]   This is understandable as Littlewoods had conceded that as owners and occupiers of the premises they had a duty to take reasonable care for the safety of the premises adjoining. However, they had strenuously denied that they owed any wider duties on which these claims are founded— see Lord Mackay, *supra*, n.50, at 254.

[54]   *Ibid.*, at 270–2.

[55]   *Ibid.*, at 269.

[56]   *Ibid.*, at 250.

[57]   *Ibid.*, at 274.

[58]   [1951] AC 850, at 868–9 See D. Lloyd, "Dangerous Sports Conducted Adjoining Highways", (1951) 14 *MLR* 499.

[59]   "I incline to the opinion that this duty arises from the fact that the defender, as occupier, is in exclusive control of the premises upon which the danger has arisen", *per* Lord Goff, *supra*, n.50, at 279.

The Relationship between Private Nuisance, Negligence and Fault 171

gence".[60] It does indeed seem arguable that the dominance of fault in this context indicates that all such liability is more appropriately classified as part of the tort of negligence.

This certainly leaves the question wide open. Despite the intervention of the highest courts in the land, the nature of the relationship between negligence and nuisance in this context is far from being resolved. In the light of the above, what has been the impact of the House of Lords decision in *Hunter* v. *Canary Wharf*?

THE IMPACT OF *HUNTER* V. *CANARY WHARF LTD*

In *Hunter*,[61] the House of Lords rejected the view of the Court of Appeal below, and earlier in *Khorasandjian* v. *Bush*,[62] that private nuisance should be extended to provide personal remedies for individuals living on the land. In *Khorasandjian*, for example, the majority of the Court of Appeal had been prepared to adapt private nuisance to protect a mere licensee of a property against persistent unwanted telephone calls. If this approach had been followed, the relationship between nuisance and negligence would indeed have become even more confused. The House of Lords, by a majority, was very keen to overturn such developments and re-establish private nuisance as a property tort.[63] *Khorasandjian* was therefore held to be incorrect and private nuisance confined to those with a right to the land affected.[64]

Although the majority's decision, which emphatically reasserted the property roots of private nuisance, is interesting for a number of reasons, this chapter is primarily concerned with its analysis of the relationship of nuisance and negligence. This was not directly in point, but in recognising that the claimant must have some interest or exclusive possession of the land, their Lordships immediately drew a line between nuisance and torts where such an interest is not required, such as negligence. More importantly, this interest is not just the qualifying test for standing; it specifies the nature of the tort and the kind of interests it seeks to protect. As a property tort, its goal must be to compensate the claimant for injury to the land, be it property damage or personal discomfort.[65] This does not logically include personal injury for which the claimant is left to

---

[60] *Per* Lord Goff, *ibid.*, at 274.

[61] [1997] AC 655.

[62] [1993] QB 727.

[63] But note the strong dissenting speech delivered by Lord Cooke.

[64] Lord Goff stressed, *supra* n.61 at 692, that "on the authorities as they stand, an action in private nuisance will only lie at the suit of a person who has a right to the land affected. Ordinarily, such a person can only sue if he has the right to exclusive possession of the land, such as a freeholder or tenant in possession, or even a licensee with exclusive possession". See P.A. Cane, "What a Nuisance" (1997) 113 *LQR* 515; S. Hedley, "Nuisance, Dust and the Right to Good TV Reception" (1997) 3 *Web JCLI*; K. Oliphant, "Unblurring the Boundaries of Nuisance" (1998) 6 *Tort L Rev.* 21.

[65] See, in particular, Lord Hoffmann's speech, *supra* n.61 at 707; and Lord Goff's approval of Professor Newark's article, "The Boundaries of Nuisance" (1949) 65 *LQR* 480. See also *Cunard* v. *Antifyre Ltd* [1933] 1 KB 551, at 556–7, *per* Talbot J.

172   Paula Giliker

pursue an action in negligence. On this basis, a division is made according to the type of injury: personal injury belongs to negligence; injury to land to nuisance. Indications to the contrary in *Bone* v. *Seale*[66] and in *Khorasandjian* were reinterpreted respectively as relating to the diminished amenity value of the property concerned or overturned. The torts are clearly regarded as distinct.

Yet, this is not a distinction without problems. One may question the legitimacy of separating two torts, not by factors relating to liability, but by remedial head. Such a rigid approach is reminiscent of the old forms of action, which may yet again be rattling their chains. Where does this leave other heads of damages such as injury to chattels or financial loss? Lord Hoffmann suggests that they are still recoverable in nuisance as consequential loss.[67] Yet, this would mean that if both my pet cat and I have breathing difficulties following an emission of smoke from your garden, I will be able to sue for the injury to my cat (consequential injury to a chattel), but not for my own injuries, thereby placing my cat in a better position than myself in nuisance. More importantly, is there really a firm and workable distinction between personal discomfort and its effect on the land?[68] Is it really legitimate to say that excessive noise affects not my ears but the amenity value of my land? If not, this distinction in itself falls apart. These are serious concerns which have already been thoroughly discussed elsewhere,[69] but are yet to be resolved.

Yet, positively, the decision gives us at long last a clear distinction. Private nuisance can only be brought (a) by a specific class of claimants who have an interest or exclusive possession of the land and (b) for a specific type of injury, namely injury to the claimant's property interest. In contrast, negligence may be brought by any claimant to whom the defendant owes a duty of care and for any injury caused by the defendant's breach, be it personal or proprietary, subject to policy restrictions on recovery. Although this distinction may be challenged, it at least recognises that nuisance and negligence are distinct torts with different roles in the law of torts. It can no longer be asserted that the two torts are in fact one and the same.

It may be noted at this stage that this is in contrast to the path taken in other jurisdictions. To take one example, in Australia the majority of the High Court of Australia in *Burnie Port Authority* v. *General Jones*[70] interpreted the rule in *Rylands* v. *Fletcher* as part of the tort of negligence, finding a non-delegable duty on the person in control of the premises under the developed law of negligence.[71]

---

[66] [1975] 1 All ER 787.

[67] *Supra* n.61, at 706.

[68] See, e.g., P. Giliker, "Whither the Tort of Nuisance? The Implications of Restrictions on the Right to Sue in *Hunter* v. *Canary Wharf*" (1999) 7 *TLJ* 155.

[69] See, e.g., J. O'Sullivan, "Nuisance in the House of Lords—Normal Service Resumed" [1997] *CLJ* 483 and articles cited at ns. 64 and 68, *supra*.

[70] (1994) 120 ALR 42.

[71] *Ibid.*, at 54: "ordinary negligence has progressively assumed dominion in the general territory of tortious liability for unintended physical damage, including the area in which the rule in *Rylands* v. *Fletcher* once held sway": *per* Mason CJ, Deane, Dawson, Toohey and Gaudron JJ.

The Relationship between Private Nuisance, Negligence and Fault   173

English law, however, as Professors Heuston and Buckley have noted,[72] chose a very different path in *Cambridge Water* and decided instead to emphasise the close tie between nuisance and the rule in *Rylands* v. *Fletcher*.

A DIFFERENT APPROACH?

This section of the chapter will examine what conclusions may be drawn from the above analysis and its relationship with previous attempts to resolve the relationship between nuisance and negligence. The House of Lords in *Hunter* assumed there to be a clear division between nuisance and negligence, thereby permitting the court to allocate remedies in the appropriate way. There was no consideration of the tension between the torts or any problems which may arise in applying this distinction. The clearest example of this problem is that of a *Sedleigh-Denfield* situation. Consider, for example, the situation if the escaping water had flooded X's land and X had fallen into the water and drowned. Could X's estate have made a claim on X's behalf? In other words, would such liability to be classified as negligence, thereby allowing a claim for personal injury, or as nuisance, where it would be rejected? In such circumstances, as can be seen, the distinction will determine whether or not the claimant will succeed in his or her claim.

It is submitted that, in light of the above, it is more important than ever to determine the question of the relationship between nuisance and negligence in the English law of torts. In our view, there are three possible techniques which may be adopted in dealing with this problem, which can be categorised as follows:

(1) Suppression
(2) Stepping back; and
(3) Surgery

This is not to say that there is an easy solution, but that it is possible to clarify this area of law. To that end these three particular options will now be considered.

Option 1: Suppression

Hunter, as stated earlier, has brought this problem to the fore by requiring that actions for personal injury must be brought in negligence. It is not, however, the *ratio* of the case, although it must be conceded that this conclusion follows logically from their Lordships' arguments. It is therefore open to the courts not to follow such *dicta* and continue to retain the power to award damages for personal injury in nuisance. This, however, is unlikely to occur. The ability of

---

[72] R.F.V. Heuston and R.A. Buckley, "The Return of *Rylands* v. *Fletcher*" (1994) 110 *LQR* 506.

174   *Paula Giliker*

private nuisance to award damages for personal injury has long been under question[73] and the case has been commonly interpreted to exclude damages for personal injury. In our view, the problem cannot be circumvented in this way.[74]

Option 2: Stepping Back

This option recognises the appeal of simply stepping back and allowing the law to settle down and resolve its own problems. In the words of Lord Steyn in *White* v. *Chief Constable of South Yorkshire Police*:

> The only prudent course is to treat the pragmatic categories . . . as settled for the time being . . . In reality there are no refined analytical tools which will enable the courts to draw lines by way of compromise solution in a way which is coherent and morally defensible.[75]

On this basis, personal injury claims must be framed in negligence; property claims must be framed in nuisance: a straightforward and pragmatic resolution of the law. On which side of the line a particular example of liability lies will thereby be decided on a case-by-case basis.

Option 3: Surgery

This is a more radical view. If one wishes a purer form of private nuisance, which is distinct from negligence law, any aspects of the tort which, through precedent, seem to blur the distinction should simply be severed.

The idea of surgery may be seen in Professor Conor Gearty's 1989 article, "The Place of Private Nuisance in the Modern Law of Torts".[76] His overriding concept, put simply, is that claims for indirect physical harm should be viewed as part of negligence.[77] Nuisance should be concerned with non-physical indirect harm, namely personal discomfort such as smells or noise. There would

[73] Although see M. Davies, "Private Nuisance, Fault and Personal Injuries" (1990) 20 *UWAust. LR* 129.

[74] It was suggested at the SPTL conference in Leeds 1999 that our view is unduly pessimistic and that the courts may simply ignore the *dicta* in *Hunter* against recovery for personal injury as they ignored such *dicta* in *Read* v. *J. Lyons & Co. Ltd* [1947] AC 156. It is submitted that the situation is different from that in *Read*. First, in contrast to the rule in *Rylands* v. *Fletcher*, there is no real line of authority supporting recovery of damages for personal injury in private nuisance. Secondly, the House of Lords has in recent case law clearly indicated its intention to limit nuisance claims, and it would take a strong Court of Appeal to ignore such express approval of Professor Newark's restrictive line, which, in the words of Lord Goff in *Hunter* v. *Canary Wharf Ltd*, "should be nailed to the doors of the law courts" (see *supra* n.61, at 688).

[75] [1999] 1 All ER 1, at 39 (a case concerning psychiatric injury which the courts also have difficulty analysing clearly).

[76] [1989] *CLJ* 214.

[77] In contrast, W. Friedmann, "Modern Trends in the Law of Torts" (1937) 1 *MLR* 39, at 45 n.8, suggests that such liability is more closely related to trespass than to the other types of private nuisance from which it is distinguished only by the archaic distinction between trespass and case.

The Relationship between Private Nuisance, Negligence and Fault 175

therefore be a general duty to take reasonable care not to cause damage to the land (or other property) of one's neighbour. Private nuisance could then concentrate on "what it does best, protecting occupiers against non-physical interference with the enjoyment of their land" allowing nuisance to "take its full place as a vital and healthy (rather than, as at present, confused and dormant)" cause of action.[78] Professor Gearty does not at any stage assert that the cases of non-physical interference should be classified as anything other than part of the tort of nuisance.

This article has been approved recently by Hirst LJ in *Hussain* v. *Lancaster City Council*,[79] who comments:

> Having regard to *Smith* v. *Littlewoods Organisation Ltd* and to Lord Goff of Chieveley's references to Professor Gearty's article in *Hunter* v. *Canary Wharf Ltd*, it seems to me clear that the law is now moving strongly in the direction favoured by Professor Gearty, *viz.*, to assimilate the law of nuisance into that of negligence in cases involving physical damage; but in view of my conclusion on nuisance in the present case, it is not necessary to decide whether Professor Gearty's goal has yet been reached.[80]

It is necessary here to consider the ideas encapsulated in this statement in more detail.

Hunter, as stated above, does seem to contemplate excluding personal injury cases from nuisance and placing them in negligence. Lord Goff cited Professor Newark's seminal article "The Boundaries of Nuisance",[81] which proposes this distinction, with approval. There is, however, little evidence that this distinction will encompass *all* physical damage, as proposed by Professor Gearty. Lord Goff simply noted Gearty's article as an idea which is "now being suggested"[82] and it is difficult to reconcile Professor Gearty's proposal with the speeches of the rest of the majority. Lord Hoffmann, viewing the tort of private nuisance as one protecting land, clearly assumes the tort to protect "material injury to property" from which he reasons by analogy in describing the nature of personal discomfort in nuisance.[83] Lords Lloyd and Hope both view nuisance to be capable of compensating for encroachment, physical injury and interference with the quiet enjoyment of land.[84] It is difficult to find any indication in favour of the idea that a tort protecting land should only protect non-physical damage to land. There are also further problems with such a comprehensive division. Private nuisance includes not only negligently committed, but also intentional indirect physical harm, which negligence will be required to absorb.[85] Equally,

---

[78] *Supra* n.76, at 218.
[79] [1999] 2 WLR 1142.
[80] *Ibid.*, at 1163.
[81] F.H. Newark, "The Boundaries of Nuisance" (1949) 65 *LQR* 480.
[82] *Supra*, n.61 at 692.
[83] *Ibid.*, at 706. See also Lord Hope, *ibid.*, at 724.
[84] *Ibid.*, at 695 and 724 respectively.
[85] Under the old forms of action, actions on the case, such as negligence and nuisance, were used to deal with actions for which other forms of action did not apply, and arguably it is justifiable to

176   *Paula Giliker*

it will be difficult to interpret cases where the courts have clearly stated that it is irrelevant that the defendant has taken reasonable care as decided in negligence *without* distorting the basic principles of negligence. Even where the courts have recognised a duty of care as the basis of liability, as in *Sedleigh-Denfield*, they have imposed the *Goldman* subjective standard of care, which is contrary to ordinary negligence principles.

In our view, a simpler approach would be to recognise that the problem lies with the *Sedleigh-Denfield* line of authority. Where the defendant has created the nuisance, the concept of reasonable user is dominant. Fault principles are relevant, but not determinative. In contrast, where the defendant has continued or adopted the nuisance, fault is determinative of liability. The defendant is being judged by his or her conduct, not by the effect of his or her conduct on the claimant. The issue is not that of continuous interference (the usual nuisance scenario),[86] but of a state of affairs which, due to the defendant's inaction, has led to a particular incident. It is submitted that such factors indicate that this line of authority is in reality a form of negligence modified to deal with omissions rather than nuisance liability. Attempts to reconcile such authority with the rest of nuisance has led to a distortion of its basic principles and is energy ill-spent. We therefore advocate that private nuisance should be confined to those cases where the defendant has created or authorised the nuisance. In contrast, where the liability is due (a) to the defendant acting as an occupier and (b) to his or her inability to exercise reasonable control over the premises, it should fall into a third category of liability between pure negligence and private nuisance into which, as suggested by Lord Goff in *Smith* v. *Littlewoods*, could be grouped the various forms of negligence-based occupiers' liability. This has a number of advantages. Lawyers are used to dealing with occupiers' liability as a separate category, admittedly at present largely in the form of the 1957 and 1984 Occupiers' Liability Acts. Secondly, again lawyers are familiar with the fact that they generally deal with a state of affairs which is due to the act or omission of the person in control of the land. There is a natural affinity between liability under *Sedleigh-Denfield* and *British Railways Board* v. *Herrington*,[87] a fact which did not escape Lord Wilberforce in the latter case.[88] Both cases concerned liability for omissions for which the courts were prepared to impose a limited duty on the occupier which took account of his or her personal circumstances.[89] Although this subjective test did not survive into section 1(3) of the Occupiers'

---

move intentional indirect harm from nuisance to negligence. Lord Denning's distinction between intentional and negligent harm in *Letang* v. *Cooper* [1965] 1 QB 232, at 239, is based primarily on the distinction between trespass and case and therefore has no direct relevance to this issue.

[86] Although not always, see *SCM (United Kingdom) Ltd* v. *W.J. Whittal & Son Ltd* [1970] 1 WLR 1017, at 1031—the point was not considered on appeal, see [1971] 1 QB 337; and *British Celanese* v. *Hunt* [1969] 1 WLR 959, at 969.

[87] [1972] AC 877.

[88] *Ibid.*, at 920.

[89] See, in particular, Lord Reid, *ibid.*, at 898–9, but contrast Lord Diplock at 941.

The Relationship between Private Nuisance, Negligence and Fault   177

Liability Act 1984, there remains an acceptance that different duties of care are owed by the occupier depending on the circumstances of the case, and that more is needed to justify imposing liability on an occupier for an omission.[90]

This analysis is not of course problem-free. Liability under the statutes relates to persons *on* the land, not adjoining landowners,[91] and of course visitors are owed an objective standard of care, but the aim of this categorisation is not uniformity but some coherent approach to the law. As noted by Lord Goff in *Smith* v. *Littlewoods*, it makes more sense to group together examples of liability for occupiers with a common fault basis. It would have the added benefit of removing the main cause of confusion and debate from private nuisance and thereby help clarify its relationship with the tort of negligence.[92]

Admittedly, this may lack the conceptual clarity and appeal of Professor Gearty's approach which neatly divides nuisance liability, but, as noted above, we believe that the distinction between physical and non-physical harm is difficult to justify in the light of *Hunter*. It is submitted that the motivation underlying *Sedleigh-Denfield* liability is not pure nuisance reasoning, but a mixture of loss distribution (the occupier is the best person to deal with the problem) and responsibility (which rests on the person controlling the land).[93] The law has in recent years recognised the occupier's duty as being of a more positive character.[94] Rather than distorting negligence and nuisance, perhaps such principles are best dealt with in their own right. Control of land carries with it responsibilities, which at times will overcome opposition to liability for non-feasance, but must be separated from ordinary principles of negligence in case they are mistakenly adopted by analogy in other contexts. This is the argument of Lord Goff in *Smith* v. *Littlewoods* and, in our view, should be seriously considered if some clarity is to be brought to this area of law.

---

[90] Omissions are not a problem under the Occupiers' Liability Act 1957 where the occupier, by giving the visitor permission to enter the premises, assumes responsibility to the visitor. On this basis, the objective standard of care should apply.

[91] There is also the problem of *Wringe* v. *Cohen* [1941] 1 KB 229, which imposed strict liability on an occupier for a public nuisance to an adjoining owner caused by an artificial structure projecting onto the highway. This case must, however, now be questioned both in terms of reasoning and authority (see, e.g., W. Friedmann, "Nuisance, Negligence and the Overlapping of Torts" (1940) 4 *MLR* 305; and *Montana Hotels Pty. Ltd* v. *Fasson Pty. Ltd* (1986) 69 ALR 258, at 263–4, PC) and should not therefore necessarily detract from our argument. In any event, recognition of valid defences of the act of a third party and latent defect largely undermine the strictness of the liability.

[92] This category should logically extend to the line of authority which finds the occupier liable for nuisance created by his or her predecessor in title. Scrutton LJ, whose dissenting judgment in *Job Edwards* v. *Birmingham Navigations* [1924] 1 KB 341 was approved by the House of Lords in *Sedleigh-Denfield*, gave a similar judgment in *St Anne's Well Brewery Co.* v. *Roberts* (1929) 140 LT 1 in which he held that the tenant would be liable if he knew or ought with reasonable care to have known of the nuisance. This has been followed in *Wilkins* v. *Leighton* [1932] 2 Ch. 106. These two cases were cited by Lord Wright in *Sedleigh-Denfield* itself, *supra* n.32, at 907, in support of his general statement of principle.

[93] See B.S. Markesinis, "The Subsidence of 'Mumps' or the Duties and Responsibilities of Landowners" [1980] *CLJ* 259, at 261.

[94] See Lord Wilberforce in *Goldman* v. *Hargrave* [1967] 1 AC 645, at 657.

CONCLUSION

Sadly, the second option is likely to prevail. However, if the line of authority dominated by Lord Goff has told us anything, it is that the courts are receptive to academic thought and will listen to constructive criticism in future formulations of the law. Perhaps, therefore, academics should not be afraid of being assertive. If future courts wish to adhere to a division between nuisance and negligence, then the cases on the boundaries must be categorised. *Hunter* at present requires a clearer division between private nuisance and negligence liability than the law now gives. As can be seen, fault principles are now well-established as part of private nuisance, thereby blurring the dividing line between the two torts. Yet, it is important to distinguish between fault principles exercising influence on the development of the law of tort, on the one hand, and dominating the question of liability, on the other. It is submitted that in relation to the creator of the nuisance, fault may assist in the determination of liability or in deciding the extent of damages, but this does not mean that all such cases should be classified as "negligence". They remain part of the evolved tort of private nuisance. Such an evolution is inevitable in the light of the growth and popularity of the tort of negligence and the changing political and economic stance of this country. However, in relation to liability for continuing a nuisance, fault is to the fore and determinant of liability. This leaves us with two main choices: stick with the current categorisation and accept its consequences, or adopt a new form of categorisation, such as that suggested above. If neither is desirable, then we are left with our first option, which is to attack the advisability of re-imposing the traditional roots of a tort on its modern developed form.

As Friedmann correctly identified in 1943, "the tort of nuisance demonstrates, in a particularly complex manner, the difficulties created by the gradual grafting of modern conceptions of negligence on older actions".[95] To demand a distinction 57 years later is bound to cause problems. It is submitted that assistance may be gathered from a more general third grouping based on occupiers' liability, which would be consistent with the case law and avoid difficult divisions according to the type of injury claimed. The resulting private nuisance would not be purified of the influence of negligence—this would be impossible in view of the parallel history of these torts and probably not a desirable step—but at least it would be rendered easier to define in the light of *Hunter* v. *Canary Wharf.* By this means, a clearer view of the environmental impact of the two torts may be achieved.

---

[95] W. Friedmann, "Incidence of Liability in Nuisance" (1943) 59 *LQR* 63.

9

Stigma Damages, Amenity and the Margins of Economic Loss: Quantifying Perceptions and Fears

JOHN LOWRY and ROD EDMUNDS

INTRODUCTION

ONE SPECIES OF loss which is problematic in private nuisance actions is the notion of stigma as a discrete head of damage. Whilst English case law to date is sparse, the issue merits consideration not least because, if experience in the United States is any guide, it is likely to gain currency in the years to come. Such claims have the potential to raise a number of difficult issues for the courts to resolve in terms of a claimant's right to recover for the depreciation in the value of his or her land. While the seminal decision of the House of Lords in *Hunter* v. *Canary Wharf Ltd*[1] answers many questions concerning the parameters of the tort of nuisance and the relationship it bears to the tort of negligence, it fails to provide clear guidance on the scope of amenity as a protected interest. Its opacity on this issue makes it less than straightforward to determine when and whether loss attributable to stigma can fall within its ambit. This conundrum is complicated further by a second uncertain legacy of *Hunter*. For whilst the decision can be seen as creating "clear blue water" between the torts of negligence and nuisance,[2] it leaves unanswered what future disposition the tort of nuisance can and should adopt in respect of claims to recover economic loss which may result from the perceived stigma which has attached to the claimant's property.

It is the purpose of this chapter both to examine the current status of the potential for the recovery of such stigma damages in English law and to probe the desirability of such compensation. This will necessitate an examination of the concept of stigma: an examination which will show how it can be applied to a diverse range of factual circumstances which do not necessarily invite a

---

[1] [1997] AC 655.

[2] The re-emphasis of the distinctive nature of the torts which can be identified within the House of Lords reasoning in *Hunter* v. *Canary Wharf Ltd* is in line with the thinking revealed in the academic contributions made by F.H. Newark, "The Boundaries of Nuisance" (1949) 65 *LQR* 480 and C. Gearty, "The Place of Private Nuisance in a Modern Law of Torts" [1989] *CLJ* 214.

180   *John Lowry and Rod Edmunds*

standard legal response. The chapter will also consider the accepted understanding of what constitutes recognisable injury to land. Here, our principal cause for concern is when, if at all, claims for compensation for diminution in value of land may succeed where the contaminating incident causes no physical damage to it. In this, it will be contended that one possible way of responding to such stigma claims is by identifying the loss as falling within the realms of amenity damage. However, the lack of a settled and clear test to determine what constitutes damage to amenity makes the analysis less than straightforward. In addition, it will be acknowledged that there are certain types of stigma claims which do (and perhaps should) fall beyond the remit of amenity. In such situations allowing a claim to succeed may be tantamount to allowing recovery for pure economic loss. Whatever the merits of acceding to this line of thinking, it will be posited that private nuisance has the potential to develop along these lines now that the tort has emerged from the shadow of negligence.

DELINEATING THE TERRAIN OF "STIGMA" IN THE TOXIC TORTS CONTEXT

Stigma is not exclusively encountered in the context of toxic torts and property damage.[3] In common parlance it is understood as some mark or stain on the character or reputation of the land, and in this the obvious comparison must lie with defamation. Yet for present purposes our focus lies with actual or potential pollution of land that results in a decrease in its value. It starts therefore with some environmental "disaster" which could be small or large in scale. The source of the pollution may be a nearby industrial plant or landfill site. Equally, toxicity may have seeped from an underground tank or leaked from overhead power cables. There is next the issue of whether or not the toxic substance released, be it dust, gas or matter of a more intangible kind (for example, an electromagnetic field) threatens or invades surrounding property. And finally there is the element of fear. This may arise from the owner's perception that the land is affected, a perception which, when shared with prospective purchasers, may be seen as making the land a less marketable commodity.

For present purposes these are the contours of stigma. As a notion, it is multifaceted and attempts at formulating an all-embracing definition necessarily become an unedifying exercise. Charting its parameters is complicated because there are subtle permutations. At the outset it is worth emphasising two of its inter-related elements. The first, which we will develop later, is the role of perception—the perception that the land is stigmatised and consequently devalued. The second element is that traditional legal reasoning predicates liability on the

---

[3] To give one example at random, the issues may also surface at least as the motivation behind attempts to enforce restrictive covenants as a means of preventing the establishment of group homes for former mental patients from being established on neighbouring land: see *C & G Homes Ltd* v. *Secretary of State for Health* [1991] 2 WLR 715.

Stigma Damages, Amenity and the Margins of Economic Loss 181

basis of the claimant being able to point to some damage which is itself legally recognisable.

In exploring the second aspect of stigma further it is instructive to refer to jurisprudential developments in the United States, where, during the last decade or so, courts in a number of states, and commentators,[4] have been considering stigma claims. Although distilling a consistent response is not easy, one common sub-division of claims is made by reference to the existence or non-existence of physical damage caused to the claimant's land by the contaminating episode. In what is perhaps the most obvious category, contamination may cause physical damage which is then remediated. And yet, because the stigma is thought to linger, the land is perceived as less saleable. This category is often referred to (as it will be hereafter) as "post-remediation stigma". However, a second category has emerged, doubtless generated in part by the expansive capacity of litigation. With instances of so-called "market stigma", stigma is said to attach to the land because there is a fear of contamination rather than some actual proven physical contamination or potential of such contamination. Market stigma cases may also occur in a more extreme situation. This is where the claim is brought by those whose land is in the vicinity of contaminated property and is, therefore, they contend, stigmatised by association. The claim is therefore made solely on the basis that a drop in value is a product of physical proximity, the claimants not contending that their land is actually contaminated or threatened by contamination.

Unsurprisingly, there is no apparent unanimity of approach to the determination of these suits by the United States courts. Not only are there jurisdictional variations in dealing with cases within one or other of the two categories identified above, the success of the action may depend upon factors such as the nature of the contamination and how objectively grounded the fear of risk is.

---

[4] See, e.g., A.N. Davis and S. Longo, "Stigma Damages in Environmental Cases: Developing Issues and Implications for Industrial and Commercial Real Estate Transactions" (1995) 25 *Envtl. LR* 10345; T.J. Muldowney and K.W. Harrison, "Stigma Damages: Property Damage and the Fear of Risk" (1995) 36 *Def. Couns. J* 525; E. Jean Johnson, "Environmental Stigma Damages: Speculative Damages in Environmental Tort Cases" (1996) 15 *Journal of Environmental Law* 185; H.B. Eisman, "*Chance* v. *BP Chemical Inc*: Changing Ohio's Perception of Stigma Damages" (1997) 45 *Cleveland State LR* 607; A. Geisinger, "Nothing but Fear Itself: A Social-psychological Model of Stigma Harm and its Legal Implications" (1997) 76 *Nebraska LR* 452. It should be noted that in one type of action other than nuisance, "eminent domain proceedings", which are broadly concerned with land compensation claims, the courts in some jurisdictions have been more amenable to allowing actions for stigma damages even where there is no suggestion that there has been physical damage to the land. The context of such actions is sometimes a dispute over the appropriate measure of damages where stigma is said to follow from the siting of power lines. Again a diversity of approach is to be found across the USA; examples of the most expansive attitude can be found in states such as Florida, Virginia, Louisiana and, more particularly, in the New York Court of Appeals decision in *Crisculoa* v. *Power Authority of New York*, 621 N E 2d 1195 (NY 1993).

It seems that the view is taken that, as the issue in eminent domain proceedings is full compensation, the reasonableness of the public's fear is irrelevant, and if there is evidence that the fear has depressed the market value, compensation will be awarded. For a detailed discussion, see A.J. Schutt, "The Power Line Dilemma: Compensation for Diminished Property Value Caused by Fear of Electromagnetic Fields" (1996) 24 *Florida State University LR* 125.

182 John Lowry and Rod Edmunds

Adding to the confused state of stigma jurisprudence in America is the variety of ways in which claims can be instituted. Actions for stigma damages may be based in nuisance or negligence or asserted by way of breach of statutory duty. Within the realms of nuisance law the confusion is compounded by the absence of any universal view among the United States jurisdictions on the requirements which underlie a nuisance action. Even states that apply similar requirements frequently differ in their interpretation of them.[5] Such reservations apart, there is a discernible trend that supports the proposition that tortious liability may depend upon the ability to establish the existence of some physical damage to the land. To this extent, this favours post-remediation stigma claims and disfavours those within the market stigma category, especially where the complaint rests exclusively on physical proximity. Such a demarcation is explicable on the basis that neither stigma nor depreciation in value is sufficient; physical impact is required before damages will be awarded.[6] Part of the underlying thinking here is to be found in one of the cardinal principles that has helped to shape tortious liability, encapsulated in the maxim *damnum sine injuria*: absent legally recognised harm to the land there is only a financial loss which is not regarded as being the basis of a valid claim.

STIGMA CLAIMS BEFORE THE ENGLISH COURTS

To date, no private nuisance claim—nor, for that matter, any other common law action—has tested whether or not either category of stigma damages is recoverable in English law. There are however two cases which, taken together, can be seen as broadly and indirectly lending support to the necessity of establishing the precondition of physical damage. In both cases, *Merlin* v. *British Nuclear Fuels plc*,[7] and *Blue Circle Industries plc* v. *The Ministry of Defence*,[8] the claim was brought under section 12 of the Nuclear Installations Act 1965. As such it raised for determination the scope of the damage recoverable for breach of the duties imposed by section 7 of that Act. In addition to compensation for loss of life and personal injury, claims are possible under the legislation where there is damage to any property.

---

[5] The point is equally applicable to the tort of negligence in US jurisdictions.

[6] As far as it is possible to discern any general trend which cuts across the jurisdictional divide in the USA, it can be said that the courts will deny recovery based on physical proximity absent actual physical harm: see, e.g., *Berry* v. *Armstrong Rubber Co.*, 989 F 2d 822 (5th Circ. 1993); and *Lamb* v. *Martin Marietta Energy System Inc.*, 835 F Supp. 959 (W D Ky 1993). *Cf.* In *Re Paoli R R Yard PcB Litig.*, 35 F 3d 717 (3d Cir 1994); *Bixby Ranch Co.* v. *Spectrol Electronics Corp.*, No BC052566 (Cal. Super Ct, 15 Dec. 1993); and *DeSario* v. *Industrial Excess Landfill Inc.*, No 89–570 (Ohio Ct C P Stark County, 6 Dec. 1994). See also Muldowney and Harrison, *supra*, n.4.

[7] [1990] QB 557. See R Macrory, "Nuclear Installations and the Statutory Duty to Compensate for Loss" (1991) 3 *JEL* 122.

[8] [1999] Env. LR 22, CA; [1997] 3 Env. LR 341, QBD. See D. Harte, "Damages Recoverable for Environmental Harm"(1999) 11 *JEL* 321; S. Tromans, "Nuclear Liabilities and Environmental Damages" [1999] *Environmental Law Review* 59; M. Lee, "Civil Liability for Contamination: *Blue Circle Industries plc* v. *Ministry of Defence*" (1999) 50 *NILQ* 403.

Stigma Damages, Amenity and the Margins of Economic Loss   183

In *Merlin*, the defendant accepted that radionuclides originating in waste emitted from the Sellafield pipeline had been brought into their house. Scientific analysis of the dust collected in the Merlins' vacuum cleaner indicated the presence of ionising radiations in the form of emitting plutonium isotopes and americium. But the court accepted the defendant's contention that this did not amount to physical damage to the fabric of the property. Gatehouse J characterised the claimant's lost sale of the house and fall in property value as being economic loss which fell outwith the terms of the statutory regime. *Blue Circle* arose out the leakage in 1989 of plutonium, when ponds at the MOD's establishment at Aldermaston overflowed onto marshland forming part of the claimant's estate. Blue Circle was not told of the contamination until four years after the incident, at which time it was in the process of selling the estate. The deal collapsed. Although MOD remediated the marshland, the action was brought under the statute to recover damages in respect of the lost sale. The claim succeeded and the first instance award of £6 million (plus interest) was upheld by the Court of Appeal.

ESTABLISHING PHYSICAL DAMAGE WITHIN THE LEGISLATIVE SCHEME:
TOWARDS A BROADER FACTUAL VIEW?

In both decisions under the 1965 Act the focus of the court's determination fell upon whether or not there was evidence of property damage. In the determination of this anterior question, there is a resonance between the respective approaches adopted in *Merlin,* on the one hand, and *Blue Circle,* on the other. In *Merlin*, Gatehouse J scrutinised the evidence presented by 12 experts. And whilst he appeared content to accept that there was some contamination of the house, in his view this did not suffice to establish liability because the contamination was not tantamount to physical damage to tangible property. Specifically, he said:

> The plaintiffs' argument that "property" included the air space within the walls, ceilings and floors of Mountain Ash [the house]; that this has been damaged by the presence of radionuclides and the house rendered less valuable as the family's home, seems to me too far-fetched.[9]

Of itself it is submitted that this is a restrictive and unfortunate interpretation of the evidence presented to the court. It is worth noting that the finding of fact and the rather literal idea of physical damage that it seems to have entailed are not echoed in the Court of Appeal's approach to the issue of physical damage in the later decision of *Hunter* v. *LDDC*.[10] It will be recalled that the Court of

---

[9] *Supra* n.7 at 570.
[10] [1996] 2 WLR 348, CA. As is well known the case went on appeal and the significant ruling of the House of Lords is discussed below. The point discussed by Pill LJ was not in issue on appeal and there is nothing in the language of their Lordships' speeches which casts doubt on his view of property damage.

184 John Lowry and Rod Edmunds

Appeal took a pragmatic view in accepting that dust can cause property damage. Pill LJ (with whom the other members of the Court of Appeal agreed) observed that:

> [I]f, for example, in ordinary use the excessive deposit [of dust] is trodden into the fabric of a carpet by householders in such a way as to lessen the value of the fabric, an action would lie. Similarly, if it follows from the effects of excessive dust on the fabric that professional cleaning of the fabric is reasonably required, the cost is actionable and if the fabric is diminished by the cleaning that too would constitute damage . . . The damage is in the physical change which renders the article less useful or less valuable.[11]

Indeed, in applying this approach to the facts in *Blue Circle,* Carnwath J found that the plutonium had become so mixed with the topsoil as to constitute physical damage to it. In determining the existence and effect of the contamination incident, the court received from four expert witnesses evidence which it regarded as objective and non-contentious. Unlike *Merlin*, therefore, there was no need for the court to review extensive or conflicting scientific analysis.[12] As Aldous LJ in the Court of Appeal observes, the physical damage was manifest by the major engineering operation which was required to remove large quantities of topsoil from the site. Carnwath J succinctly summarises the relatively clear issue of proving damage in the following terms:

> The overall conclusion of the evidence is not in dispute. The 1989 incident resulted in levels of radioactivity well above the normal background levels and above the regulatory threshold. However, even before any remedial work, and applying pessimistic assumptions, they were well below levels which would have posed any risk to health.[13]

This evaluation can also be seen as marking something of an ironic, if not unfortunate, difference in outcome between the two cases under the 1965 statute. In the latter decision the soil was damaged but the evidence did not disclose any health hazard. By contrast, whilst Gatehouse J was convinced that there was no physical damage to the Merlins' house, he seems to have recognised that the contamination did pose an increased risk of cancer to those living there.

In essence it might forcefully be objected that at one level this is little more than idle curiosity about the correctness of the factual basis for the decision

---

[11] *Ibid.*, at 366. This issue was not central to the final appeal heard by the House of Lords where the focus fell more upon the notions of *locus standi* and the nuisance potential of interference with television reception, considered *infra* at n.35 and associated text. Nevertheless, Lord Hoffmann noted, *supra* n.1 at 702, that: "[i]n the dust action it is not disputed that, in principle, activities that cause dust to be deposited on the plaintiff's property can constitute an actionable nuisance".

[12] Noting that *Merlin* had not been cited to the Court of Appeal in *Hunter*, the judge was confronted with the task of side-stepping Gatehouse J's decision. Somewhat implausibly he distinguished *Merlin* on the basis of the finding that the radionuclides emanating from waste discharge had not become so intermingled as to cause physical damage to the fabric of the property. This may be contrasted with the approach taken to the facts before the court in *Blue Circle,* property damage was found to have been caused by the plutonium this therefore led the way for an award of damages for the resulting stigma.

[13] *Supra* n.8 at 379.

Stigma Damages, Amenity and the Margins of Economic Loss 185

taken in these two modern examples of stigma actions. But our anxiety about the factual findings of the courts goes to the root of the problem. A narrow view of what in factual terms constitutes physical damage leads to the elimination of claims as purely economic, even though there may be imperceptible damage to the airspace, perhaps posing a threat to health. However, a more open-textured approach to the notion of physical damage is taken by Pill LJ in *Hunter*. This allows for a broader and therefore more inclusive view of compensatable damage. In short, the breadth of approach to the facts is a critical determinant of the claimant's chances of success. The judicial mindset here, doubtless prompted by the legislative language and context, is also trained firmly upon identifying acceptable injury to ownership rights in terms exclusively of physical damage.

DEFINING PERMISSIBLE LOSSES UNDER THE LEGISLATIVE SCHEME: A NARROW FOCUS

Put the other way round, it is interesting that an underlying anxiety pervading the judicial approach in *Merlin* and *Blue Circle* is how far the statutory regime does and should allow for recovery for pure economic loss. At first instance and on appeal in *Blue Circle* this was manifest in the judicial inclination to characterise the damage as physical and more than mere economic loss,[14] whereas in *Merlin*, Gatehouse J preferred a restrictive understanding of the phrase "damage to property". He stressed, first, that the wording of the Act did not provide for such liability and, secondly, that compensation under the statute should not extend to economic loss when such loss would not be recoverable at common law. In this respect the learned judge went further, by explaining that in the absence of a special relationship the common law exception to the economic loss embargo established in *Hedley Byrne & Co. Ltd* v. *Heller & Partners Ltd*[15] and its progeny was inapplicable to the facts before him.

It is not without interest that the issue surfaced in 1965 when the Nuclear Installations (Amendment) Bill was before Parliament.[16] At report stage, and with a corporate plaintiff particularly in mind, the Opposition renewed its earlier attempt during the Standing Committee's proceedings to put beyond doubt that it might be possible to recover loss of profits sustained when a factory was disrupted by a nuclear incident.[17] The Government, however, successfully resisted the proposed amendment, in part because such an amendment would run counter to the traditional ethos of Parliament allowing the courts to have

---

[14] [1997] 3 Env. LR 341 at 345–6 (Carnwath J); [1999] Env. LR 22 at 32 (Aldous LJ), and 52–3 (Simon Brown LJ). A similar preoccupation with characterising the damage as physical can be seen *In Re Paoli R R Yard PcB Litig.*, *supra* n.4. Strikingly, the *Paoli* court was prepared to rest its finding upon relatively small quantities of polychlorinated biphynels.

[15] [1964] AC 465.

[16] The point is well taken by Macrory, *supra* n.7 at 134.

[17] See Hansard HC Vol 706, at cols 682–685.

186   John Lowry and Rod Edmunds

recourse to the principles of remoteness in determining the scope of recoverable damage in the common law of negligence.[18]

Parliament's failure specifically to address this issue represents a missed opportunity. As is well known, the development of common law principles towards the question of liability for negligently inflicted pure economic loss has ebbed and flowed over the last 30 years or so. The high water mark in terms of liberalisation was reached in *Junior Books Ltd* v. *Veitchi Co. Ltd*.[19] As will no doubt be recalled, Lord Roskill disapproved of the "somewhat artificial distinctions between physical and economic or financial loss".[20] This in turn was roundly and robustly rejected by the House of Lords in *Murphy* v. *Brentwood DC*.[21] The judicial shift and its policy implications have attracted extensive and intense academic interest.[22] It seems unlikely that the judicial tide will turn again; at least in the near future.[23] Of itself, the unpredictable direction and force of these changes are not our main concern here. Rather, what is notable for our purposes is twofold, general and specific. At a general level is the extent to which the current disinclination of the common law to recognise, as a broad principle, liability for negligently caused economic loss formed far more than an imperceptible sub-text to setting boundaries to the recovery of stigma damages under the statute. The second and more specific point lies in the allusion to the tort of negligence as the appropriate representative of the attitude that modern tort law strikes on recoverability of damages where the loss is exclusively economic in kind.[24] If an action for stigma damages is brought at common law it is as, if not more, likely to be brought in nuisance rather than negligence.[25]

For the purposes of the statutory regime, the reasoning of the trial judge and the Court of Appeal in *Blue Circle* accords with the orthodoxy of requiring the presence of physical damage as the prerequisite for recovery for economic loss.[26]

---

[18] *Ibid.*, at col 687.

[19] [1983] 1 AC 520.

[20] *Ibid.*, at 545.

[21] [1991] 1 AC 398.

[22] See generally, J. Stapleton, "Duty of Care and Economic Loss: A Wider Agenda" (1991) 107 *LQR* 249; J. Steale, "Scepticism and the Law of Negligence" [1993] *CLJ* 437; and J. Stapleton, "Duty of Care: Peripheral Parties and Alternataive Oportunities for Deterrence" (1995) 111 *LQR* 301.

[23] Although, the Privy Council has recently decided that, as far as New Zealand law is concerned, the policy reservations concerning recovery for pure economic loss do not apply: see *Invercargill City Council* v. *Hamlin* [1996] AC 624.

[24] Although, to be fair, the tendency is not without exception: see the passing reference to nuisance by Carnwath J in *Blue Circle*, *supra* n.8, at 345. It might be contended that the tension evident in the judicial recourse to negligence rules is not inevitable. In the wake of *Hunter*'s sharp demarcation between negligence and nuisance, and the reaffirmation of nuisance as a property-based tort, the more pertinent common law analogy which would better fit those cases brought under the 1965 statute is private nuisance.

[25] And it is our contention, further explored below (at *Nuisance and Pure Economic Loss: An Open Door?*), that it is possible to mount a credible argument that, after *Cambridge Water* and *Hunter*, the tort of private nuisance may not share the same restraint in disallowing recovery for pure economic loss as is manifest in negligence.

[26] Admittedly, on the facts of the case the necessity for establishing physical damage was required by the Nuclear Installations Act 1965, s. 7(1)(a).

Stigma Damages, Amenity and the Margins of Economic Loss 187

Any diminution in property value is therefore consequential loss that may be recoverable subject to the normal rules of assessment, including principles such as foreseeability and remoteness. Absent any physical damage it appears from the decision in *Merlin* that such claims fall beyond the pale, being classified as loss that is exclusively economic in character.[27] It is our contention that, at least in the context of common law nuisance, the question to what extent stigma damage can and should be recoverable is in the first instance best approached without reference to any dichotomy between economic loss and physical damage. Rather it is more productive and theoretically sound to have recourse to determining whether or not an action lies within the realms of amenity nuisance. Such an enquiry gains fresh impetus because of the reasoning of the House of Lords in *Hunter* v. *Canary Wharf Ltd.*[28]

AMENITY: AN ENIGMA IN ENGLISH LAW?

Typically in a nuisance action the initial inquiry will generally begin with the determination of the appropriate cause of action available to the claimant seeking redress against the defendant. Lord Lloyd categorised nuisance in the following terms:

> Private nuisance are of three kinds. They are (1) nuisance by encroachment on a neighbour's land; (2) nuisance by direct physical injury to a neighbour's land; and (3) nuisance by interference with a neighbour's quiet enjoyment of his land.[29]

As between the second and third categories, Lord Hoffmann noted that following the landmark decision in *St Helen's Smelting Co.* v. *Tipping*,[30] there had been a discernible tendency to view the case as having created two separate torts of nuisance: first, one which "produces material injury to the property"[31] and, secondly, of causing "sensible personal discomfort",[32] compendiously termed amenity nuisance. His Lordship stressed, however, that such a sub-division is theoretically unsound and mistaken. He concluded that in claims for amenity nuisance "the action is not for causing discomfort to the person but, as in the case of the first category, for causing injury to the land. True it is that the land

---

[27] Professor Macrory has commented that *Merlin* is one indicator of "a distinct unease in developing consistent principles concerning compensation for pure economic damage", and he laments, as deficient, a legal system that failed adequately to provide for falls in property value through stigma: see *supra*, n.7 at 133.

[28] *Supra*, n.1. For a full analysis of this landmark decision see S. Blay, "The House of Lords and the Lord of the House: Making New Sense of Nuisance" [1999] *ALJ* 275. See also J. O'Sullivan, "Nuisance in the House of Lords—Normal Service Resumed" [1997] *CLJ* 483; P. Ghandi, "Orthodoxy Affirmed" [1998] *Conv.* 309. See further, S. Hedley, "Nuisance, Dust and the Right to Good TV Reception: *Canary Wharf* in the House of Lords" (1997) 3 *Web JCLI*.

[29] *Ibid.*, at 695.

[30] (1865) 11 HL Cas. 642.

[31] *Ibid.*, at 650, *per* Lord Westbury LC.

[32] *Ibid.*

188   *John Lowry and Rod Edmunds*

has not suffered 'sensible' injury, but its utility has been diminished by the existence of the nuisance."[33]

The impetus for much of this vigorous reappraisal lies in two inter-connected concerns which figured in the litigation. One concern resided in the need to resolve the uncertainty of who can bring an action, exclusively the property owner or others, such as an occupier with the right to exclusive possession.[34] Additionally, the House of Lords was invited to determine whether television interference resulting from the building of a tower block could fall within the ambit of private nuisance. Returning nuisance to its roots as the archetypal property-based tort designed to protect ownership rights is the unifying rationale behind the judicial response preferred by the majority. Within this context it becomes axiomatic also to reaffirm the unity of the tort and to recognise that property rights can be injured either through some physical damage or, equally, by inflicting some loss of amenity.

This begins to expose a centrally important set of questions. What exactly is amenity; and how may it be lost or damaged? In the speeches in *Hunter,* amenity is referred to in a variety of ways, including the idea of "sensible personal discomfort". But language of this ilk should not be allowed to deceive or disguise the fact that central to returning the development of nuisance to its original pathway was the need to emphasise that, to be actionable, any discomfort must affect the claimant in his or her capacity as owner.[35] This accords in part with the traditional disinclination of property law to afford protection (in the absence of some specific covenant) to rights such as a right to a view. In the context of *Hunter* the issue arose in a slightly different guise, one of the causes of action being based upon a complaint that Canary Wharf had unlawfully interfered with the television reception of neighbouring land. The claim failed. A robust statement of principle is given by Lord Hope:

> The interruption of view will carry with it various consequences. It may reduce amenity generally, or it may impede more particular things such as the transmission of visual signals to the land from other properties. *That may be highly inconvenient and it may even diminish the value of the land which is affected.* But the proprietor of the affected land has nevertheless no actionable ground of complaint.[36]

Inconvenience and reduction in value are therefore not enough to establish damage to amenity. It may, of course, be contended that impeding the flow of

---

[33] *Supra* n.1, at 706.

[34] Applying *Malone* v. *Laskey* [1907] 2 KB 141 and overruling *Khorasandjian* v. *Bush* [1993] QB 727. See further *Delaware Mansions Ltd* v. *Westminster City Council* [1999] 46 EG 194 which appears to allow an acquiring owner to be eligible to sue in relation to a continuing nuisance even where it is apparent on inspection.

[35] This analysis led Lord Hoffmann to the inexorable conclusion, *supra* n.1, at 707, that, "[o]nce it is understood that nuisances 'productive of sensible personal discomfort' do not constitute a separate tort of causing discomfort to people but are merely part of a single tort of causing injury land, the rule that the plaintiff must have an interest in the land falls into place as logical and, indeed, inevitable . . .".

[36] *Ibid.,* at 727, emphasis supplied.

Stigma Damages, Amenity and the Margins of Economic Loss 189

invisible television signals, however inconvenient in the modern world, poses far less of a serious threat or interference to the owner's comfort than the presence of some invisible toxic matter.[37] For present purposes it then becomes significant to examine how far the concept of amenity under English law may contain the potential to allow the recovery of stigma damage that attends some such environmental contamination of land.

AMENITY PERCEIVED IN NARROW AND "TANGIBLE" TERMS

It is instructive to consider an important first instance decision which applies the reasoning concerning amenity damage that held sway in *Hunter*. In *Blackburn* v. *ARC Limited*,[38] Mr Blackburn's claim in private nuisance succeeded in relation to the litter and smells produced by the quarry located close to his house, "Woodlands".[39] The allegations of nuisance were copiously catalogued in a log kept by the claimant, spanning some eight years. The learned judge accepted evidence that the defendant's "commercial priorities" had led it to create a nuisance when it breached the terms of its waste disposal licence, with the consequence that litter had escaped on to Woodlands. Similarly, a nuisance arose because the defendant persistently flouted its permission in failing to cover tipped waste and burn the gasses from the decomposing waste properly. These failures produced a nauseating smell that materially detracted from Woodlands' amenity value. The claim for compensation was thus couched in terms of a sum reflecting the diminution in the value of the land. Discounting the fall in value attributable to the permitted use of the land as a quarry, the court ultimately settled upon £25,000 as an appropriate award.[40]

In cases where amenity nuisance is consequent upon some physical damage, or indeed comprises solely of some other tangible element such as litter, noxious smells or vibrations emanating from neighbouring property, the solution posited by the majority in *Hunter*, as applied in *Blackburn*, can be readily assimilated within the orthodox common law position. Even where the amenity nuisance is transitory in effect because, for example, the defendant's activity which produced the noxious smells has sinced ceased, the court will, so as to do justice, award damages for the land's "diminution in . . . utility . . . during the period for which the nuisance persisted".[41] But the critical issue which remains is how far can stigma damage be compensatable as falling within the purview of amenity nuisance in the absence of tangible contamination, such as occurred in

---

[37] See, generally, R. Kidner, "Nuisance and Rights of Property" [1998] *Conv.* 267.

[38] [1998] Env. LR 469.

[39] Mrs Blackburn also made independent claims, but in the wake of the judicial retrenchment by the House of Lords in *Hunter* these floundered because she lacked any proprietary interest in the house.

[40] Interesting theoretical and practical issues surround the methodology of quantifying damages for diminution in value. Some of these are touched upon in the text associated with nns. 76–79, *infra*.

[41] *Supra*, n.1, at 706, *per* Lord Hoffmann.

190   John Lowry and Rod Edmunds

Merlin. There the scientific evidence was not to deny the presence of radioncules in the air which might have harmful effects for the landowner, it was to deny that that amounted to physical damage. What needs to be addressed is whether such an intangible impact can in any circumstances be regarded as damage to the amenity of the land. There are many who might consider the existence of some radioactivity, however imperceptible, to be as, if not more, unwelcome as smells or litter produced by a quarry. However, the legacy of *Hunter* does not suggest that English law is as yet prepared to go so far as to embrace all intangible violations within the notion of amenity damage. True, there is judicial language which at face value may be thought to accommodate such injury. Lord Cooke, for instance, expansively indicated that amenity might involve actions brought on the ground of some interference to "one's personal freedom, anything that injuriously affects the senses or the nerves".[42] Yet it seems unlikely that this can be understood outwith the wider concern to protect amenity from dangers that are in conventional terms more readily quantifiable. Support for this restriction can be perhaps be grounded in Lord Goff's catalogue of the general types of "emanation" from the defendant's land that may give rise to the complaint, emanations taking the form of "noise, dirt, fumes, a noxious smell, vibrations and suchlike".[43] All these amount to quantifiable, and therefore tangible, forms of injury.

Nuisance apart, the concept of amenity is encountered in a variety of contexts, some statutory, for example town and country planning legislation. It may relate to such things as the facilities present on the land, its pleasantness or convenience, and the view it enjoys. But it is not entirely easy to ascribe an agreed single meaning to the concept. Dealing with the word in *Broad* v. *Brisbane City Council and Baptist Union of Queensland,*[44] de Jersey J observed:

> There is no doubt that the concept of amenity is wide and flexible. In my view it may in a particular case embrace not only the effect of a place on the senses, but also the resident's subjective perception of his locality. Knowing the use to which a particular site is or may be put, may affect one's perception of amenity.[45]

One notable aspect of this judicial formulation is that it locates the idea as involving (at least in part) a psychological reaction to the value (and/or use) of the land, whether by the owner or other prospective purchasers. Judicial cognisance is also given to the fact that claimants may have non-economic interests in their property as well as economic interests.[46] But in assessing damage claims for such intangibles, pragmatism requires that some economic value must be

---

[42] *Ibid.*, at 712.

[43] *Ibid.*, at 685. The fact that Lord Goff acknowledged that there might be rare exceptional cases such as *Thompson-Schwab* v. *Costaki* [1956] 1 WLR 335 (prostitutes using neighbouring land) and *Bank of New Zealand* v. *Greenwood* [1984] 1 NZLR 525 (dazzling glare of the sun's rays deflected from a glass roof) seems only to bolster the thrust of the law on this point.

[44] [1986] 2 Qd. R 317.

[45] *Ibid.*, at 326.

[46] See further P. Cane, *Tort Law and Economic Interests* (Oxford, Clarendon Press, 1996) at 12–15.

Stigma Damages, Amenity and the Margins of Economic Loss   191

attached to the non-economic interest in question. Of necessity, the courts are driven to view this in much the same way as physical damage. For how else can an adequate assessment be made? This is by no means peculiar to actions in nuisance but is also discernible in claims brought in negligence for psychiatric harm consequent upon the destruction of a dwelling.[47]

While physical damage is relatively easy to assess given its tangible nature, the notion of amenity damage is at best an opaque concept and far from easy to quantify. Yet, seeking a principled approach towards the assessment of amenity damage, Lord Hoffmann stated that diminution in capital value is not the only measure of loss. He reasoned that the notion of value has an elastic quality which encompasses the fact that the value of occupying a house "which smells of pigs must be less than the value of the occupation of an equivalent house which does not".[48] Recognising that this requires placing a value on intangibles, Lord Hoffmann observed that estate agents do this all the time, and concluded that the "law of damages is sufficiently flexible to be able to do justice in such a case".[49] What therefore seems to follow is that the courts must strive to place a monetary value upon the change in the character of the affected land which, although it does not amount to some kind of physical destruction, is nonetheless to be viewed as such. Noting that damages are recoverable for injury to land and for consequential loss, Lord Hoffmann went on to add:

> But inconvenience, annoyance or even illness suffered by persons on land as a result of smells or dust are not damage consequential upon the injury to the land. It is rather the other way about: the injury to the amenity of the land consists in the fact that the persons on it are liable to suffer inconvenience, annoyance or illness. It follows that damages for nuisance recoverable by the possessor or occupier may be affected by the size, commodiousness and value of the property . . .[50]

Indeed, in applying this approach to the assessment of the damage suffered by the Blackburns' home from the litter and smells produced by the neighbouring quarry the court in *Blackburn* concluded that the amenity loss sustained should, on the basis of the expert evidence it accepted, be valued at £25,000 in respect of a property valued at £200,000.

One inference that may be drawn from this is the recognition that it is equally important to protect the amenity and the physical elements of landowning. If this is the case, then it can be argued that stigma damage can be taken to interfere with the owner's enjoyment of land. This may to some extent turn upon the willingness to see stigma as an objective phenomenon, one created by the reaction of the market. In this approach an award of stigma damages is not made to

---

[47]   *Attia* v. *British Gas plc* [1988] QB 304.

[48]   *Supra* n.1, at 706.

[49]   *Ibid*. See also the speech of Lord Lloyd, *ibid.*, at 696, who said: "[d]amages for loss of amenity value cannot be assessed mathematically. But this does not mean that such damages cannot be awarded" (applying *Ruxley Electronics and Construction Ltd* v. *Forsyth, Laddington Enclosures Ltd* [1996] AC 344 at 360–1, 374, *per* Lords Mustill and Lloyd respectively).

[50]   *Supra* n.1, at 706.

192 *John Lowry and Rod Edmunds*

compensate for the claimant's personal feelings about and reaction to the contamination. It serves to establish what the market reaction to the pollution is, and this it does by reference to the objective evidence of experts.

A BROADER US APPROACH: TOWARDS ACCOMMODATING STIGMA WITHIN THE NOTION OF AMENITY

Transatlantic support for this approach can be found in a number of judicial pronouncements. One example is to be found in the following remarks of Levin J in his dissenting judgment as part of the decision of the Michigan Supreme Court in *Adkins v. Thomas Solvent Co.*:[51]

> [A] homeowner may maintain a nuisance action to recover damages for a decline in the market value of his home that reflects interference with the use and enjoyment of his home by a condition tortiously created or maintained by the defendant on neighbouring property, and that the homeowner may do so without demonstrating interference with use or enjoyment that might result in further, separately compensable injuries to persons or property.[52]

To some extent the majority view did not differ on this statement of the operative legal principle. The unanimous view held that 22 of the 68 plaintiffs who lived near land which had suffered groundwater pollution as a result of the defendant's mishandling of toxic waste, but whose own land would never be physically contaminated, could not recover stigma damages because they were unable to show that they had suffered *significant* interference with the enjoyment of their land. The majority were content to characterise the claim in respect of the diminution in value due to the fears of third party purchasers as less than significant interference. In so doing it also identified the claimants' fears of dangers arising from negative publicity as unfounded. The Michigan Supreme Court therefore concluded that, for an actionable nuisance to arise, a legally cognisable injury must be proved and unfounded fears of diminution in property value, without more, did not amount to significant interference with the use or enjoyment of land.

To Levin J, in a vigorous dissent in which he questioned the legal basis of the majority's decision, the issue should be viewed from the perspective of causation, so that, where the defendant's tortious conduct can be demonstrated to have caused the diminution in market value, liability will follow. He doubted whether the critical issue should turn on whether or not the fears of reduction in value were demonstrably well founded. He reasoned that the defendant should be held liable if his tortious conduct can be shown to have caused the depreciation in market value—even if such conduct was not the sole cause of the plain-

---

[51] 487 NW 2d 715 (Mich. 1992).
[52] *Ibid.*, 728.

Stigma Damages, Amenity and the Margins of Economic Loss   193

tiffs' loss.[53] Although he cautioned that the majority view was clearly correct when applied to completely unreasonable fears, he went on to stress that "the relevant inquiry is not [the reasonableness of the fear or] whether the fear is factually founded, but whether [the fear] is the normal consequence of the defendants' conduct".[54]

For our purposes the dissent in *Adkins* is of obvious importance in constructing the case for stigma damages arising by virtue of non-physical interference with a claimant's enjoyment of her land. Indeed, even the majority did not rule out altogether the possibility of stigma damages being awarded where, despite the absence of tangible damage to land, the plaintiff could nevertheless show significant interference with his or her use or enjoyment of land by virtue of its diminution in value consequent upon the defendant's tortious conduct.

Indeed, this particular question came before the Michigan courts for resolution in *Exxon Corp.* v. *Yarema.*[55] The case is of significance because, at least as far as Maryland is concerned, it settled that stigma damages can be awarded for amenity nuisance and are not dependent upon proof of physical damage. In so finding, the reasoning of the court dovetails neatly with that of the majority in the House of Lords in *Hunter.* Underground gasoline storage tanks at three service stations owned by Amoco Oil Company, Gulf Oil Corporation and Exxon Corporation leaked and contaminated the groundwater near Jacksonville, Maryland. Four separate tort claims were brought by 27 parties involving some 90 claims.[56] At the time of the trial in 1983 most of the claims had either been settled or dismissed except for the claims against Exxon Corporation by Yarema, S & S, Ascot and Manor. Central to Exxon's appeal was the award of stigma damages to plaintiffs whose properties were not contaminated.

Exxon's scientific tests carried out in 1981 showed that several wells located near the service stations and certain neighbouring properties were contaminated with benzene, toluene and xylene. However, the tests also demonstrated that properties belonging to S & S and Ascot were not contaminated by the leaks. The question whether or not Yarema's property was contaminated was contentious. Nonetheless, at the trial, Exxon's own evidence revealed that its groundwater contamination was spreading.[57]

The court rejected Exxon's contentions first, that for an action in nuisance to succeed there must be "actual impact" on the claimant's land,[58] and, secondly, that with respect to the claims brought against it, diminution in property value

---

[53] Levin J stated, *ibid.*, that "[p]laintiffs should . . . be allowed to recover damages in nuisance on proof introduced at trial tending to show that the defendants actually contaminated soil and ground water in the neighbourhood of plaintiffs' homes with toxic chemicals and industrial wastes, that the market perception of the value of the plaintiffs' homes was actually adversely affected by the contamination of the neighbourhood, and thus that plaintiffs' loss was causally related to defendants' conduct."

[54] *Ibid.*, at 743.

[55] 516 A 2d 990 (Md. Ct. Spec. App. 1986).

[56] The claims were based on strict liability, negligence, trespass and nuisance.

[57] *Supra* n.55, at 995.

[58] *Ibid.*, at 1002.

194 John Lowry and Rod Edmunds

absent tangible or physical damage is insufficient to constitute actionable nuisance. Reaffirming the notion that nuisance involves interference with some right or interest in land which may or may not involve direct physical damage, the court expressed the view that, provided amenity nuisance is established, a diminution in property value is a recoverable head of damage:

> Our holding that physical impact is not necessary to sustain a tort action does not mean that plaintiffs may recover for diminution of property value without proof of harm to their property but rather that harm to property should be construed broadly to include intangible tortious interferences of plaintiffs' use and enjoyment of their properties.[59]

The court stressed that generally the reputation or perception concerning the plaintiff's property will be "inextricably interwoven in the assessment of damages".[60] There is a resonance here with the speeches of Lord Lloyd and Lord Hoffmann in *Canary Wharf*. It is also consistent with the approach taken in *Blackburn*. For although the claimant did not explicitly argue that the tortious interference with the amenity of his land arising from the excessively noxious smells caused a stigma, that in effect can be said to have been inherent in the claim for damages.

In any event it seems that showing damage of a tangible nature or in the more intangible sense of loss of amenity is an essential prerequisite to the recovery of damages. On the face of it, this excludes all claims where no such damage can be established, even though there may be compelling evidence that the property has fallen in value. Put baldly this begs the question, why is stigma not recognised as a symptom of damage to the amenity of the land? For if the owner can show that the land has become less valuable because of the defendant's actionable nuisance he or she has suffered the type of inconvenience that Lord Hoffmann seems to countenance as a legitimate type of recoverable damage. In this the focus is less upon the stigma and more upon the reason for the stigma. The owner and the market have formed the view that the land is in some way a less attractive place in which to live and which to own. Arguably this is part and parcel of the idea of amenity. At the very least it is contended that the notion is broad and flexible enough to encompass this form of damage. It can do so without doing any violence to the concept of amenity.

In all these types of cases one common element is that there is some fear that leads to the alleged drop in the market value of the land in question. The source of the fear may reside in the market concern that the property poses some risk to health and safety, or it may be that there is some less concrete sense in which owning the land is now undesirable. For present purposes, this is the element of the notion of stigma damages which is of greatest interest: the risk of the possibility of future problems. There is a difficulty here, of course, if the root of the stigma is regarded as residing in some belief that is intrinsically subjective. This

[59] *Ibid.*, at 1004.
[60] *Ibid.*, at 1005.

Stigma Damages, Amenity and the Margins of Economic Loss 195

may occur where the owner of land is unable to show that the fabric of his or her own land has suffered as a result of the contamination, perhaps because of the absence of convincing scientific evidence, or perhaps because the claimant is the owner of land that is located near to the property that has suffered the physically damage.

NUISANCE AND PURE ECONOMIC LOSS: AN OPEN DOOR?

If this is so, the logical and pressing question becomes whether or not the tort of private nuisance will accommodate claims for pure economic loss—which in this context takes the form of market stigma. This seems far from settled.[61] The scant authority on recoverability in nuisance, although inconclusive, is less than favourable in so far as the approach to the issue seems to be intrinsically tied to that of negligence which, in general terms, continues to deny liability for pure economic loss.[62]

In mapping the potential for such recognition, the modern starting point lies with the House of Lords decision in *Cambridge Water Co. Ltd* v. *Eastern Counties Leather plc*.[63] There Lord Goff stressed that the rule in *Rylands* v. *Fletcher*[64] is rooted in the tort of nuisance, and as such is no more than a species of nuisance relating to instances of isolated escape.[65] In the light of this assimilation between the two torts, the question arises whether or not pure economic loss may be recognised as a discrete head of recoverable damage under either or both causes of action. Two cases seem to suggest, albeit by way of fairly scant dicta only, that it is possible to construct an affirmative answer.[66] First, in

---

[61] Although it is certainly established that pure economic loss is recoverable in public nuisance.

[62] See generally, B.S. Markesinis and S.F. Deakin, *Tort Law* (Oxford, Clarendon Press, 1999) at 438, n.225. The traditional view pervading the tort of negligence is that all losses which are purely economic in nature and not consequent upon physical damage are non-recoverable. This general denial is rooted, in terms of principle, either by denying a legal duty of care (see *Best* v. *Samuel Fox & Co. Ltd* [1952] AC 716 at 731; *Kirkham* v. *Boughey* [1958] 2 QB 338 at 341; *Elliot Steam Tug Co.* v. *Shipping Controller* [1922] 1 KB 127 at 139); or by finding that such damage is too remote (see the example given by Blackburn J in *Cattle* v. *Stockton Waterworks Co.* (1875) LR 10 QB 453 at 457). See also *Société Remorquage à Hélice* v. *Bennetts* [1911] 1 KB 243 at 248. More often than not, however, such attempts at injecting rationalisation into the judiciary's refusal to allow recovery are unconvincing. The realistic explanation lies within the realm of so-called policy considerations, namely the perceived threat of opening the floodgates to claims, admitted as such by Lord Denning MR in *Spartan Steel and Alloys Ltd* v. *Martin & Co. (Contractors) Ltd* [1972] 3 All ER 557. With his characteristic candour, the late Master of the Rolls identified an uneasiness in understanding the basis upon which the courts determine such claims. He said, "[t]he more I think about these cases, the more difficult I find it to put each into its proper pigeon-hole. Sometimes I say: 'There was no duty.' In others I say: 'The damage was too remote.' So much so that I think that the time has come to discard those tests which have proved so elusive. It seems to me better to consider the particular relationship in hand, and see whether or not , as a matter of policy, economic loss should be recoverable."

[63] [1994] 2 AC 264.

[64] (1866) LR 1 Exch. 265.

[65] *Supra* n.62, at 298, accepting Professor Newark's view advanced in "The Boundaries of Nuisance", *supra* n.2.

[66] See M. Brazier and J. Murphy, *Street on Torts* (10th edn., London, Butterworths, 1999) at 378.

196   John Lowry and Rod Edmunds

British Celanese Ltd v. *A.H. Hunt (Capacitors) Ltd*,[67] Lawton J refused to rule out the possibility that "mere economic loss" could be recovered under the rule in *Rylands*.[68] Secondly, in *Ryeford Homes Ltd* v. *Sevenoaks DC*,[69] the issue of recovery for pure economic loss was raised as a preliminary issue, and it was no means rejected by the court. Judge Newey QC considered that the claim was, in principle at least, recoverable under the rule in *Rylands* v. *Fletcher* provided that the economic loss was a sufficiently direct result of the escape in question. The judge stated that "whether economic loss could be a sufficiently direct result of an escape of water from sewers must, I think, be a question of fact". He went on to add that "for nuisance there must be physical injury to land or substantial interference with the beneficial use of it. If economic loss results it is, I think, probably recoverable."[70] Therefore, if it can be shown that economic loss arose out of damage to the land's amenity value, there can be little objection in principle to allowing recovery.[71]

THE DESIRABILITY OF ALLOWING RECOVERY FOR STIGMA DAMAGES

Irrespective of whichever of the two possible bases of recoverability (amenity or economic loss) may be invoked, it must be recognised that allowing any such a claim may in turn raise important issues. Some of these may involve the practicalities of assessment whilst others concern policy matters. At a policy level the most likely concern may take the form of a familiar fear expressed by tort lawyers. It is encapsulated in the image of the floodgates. Such an anxiety may be particularly manifest in the market stigma context. This may be characterised by those who identify claims as "fear-driven" and potentially open to large numbers of owners with property in the vicinity of the environmental contamination. For one thing it leaves unanswered the question of what degree of physical proximity will suffice. But even where proximity is not in doubt the potential exposure to liability can be high, leading to a dramatic increase in the number of claimants. This may result in increased rates and costs of litigation, cause businesses to be exposed to damages suits that could result in bankruptcy and ultimately could interfere with the marketability of land. These risks emerge quite neatly in one United States decision, *De Sario*,[72] there being in excess of 1,700 owners who succeeded in their claim for damages. Their properties were situated within approximately 3,000 metres of the polluting landfill

---

[67] [1969] 2 All ER 1252.

[68] *Ibid.*, at 1258.

[69] [1989] 2 EGLR 281.

[70] *Ibid.*, at 284. *Cf. Weller & Co.* v. *Foot and Mouth Disease Research Institute* [1966] 1 QB 569 in which the loss of profit in question was an indirect result of the escape and therefore irrecoverable. See *Street on Torts, supra* n.66, at 402.

[71] See generally, *ibid.*, which argues that such a view is entirely consistent with Blackburn J's judgment in *Rylands* v. *Fletcher*.

[72] See *supra* n.6.

Stigma Damages, Amenity and the Margins of Economic Loss   197

site, but none had been contaminated or threatened by contamination. The jury awarded a total of $6.7 million. This might understandably set alarm bells ringing for defendants and their insurers. Yet, while the decision has been greeted as controversial, the court's reasoning should be considered with some care. The plaintiffs' fear of a 14 per cent depreciation in the value of their land was supported by a considerable weight of expert testimony.[73] To this extent the claim did therefore rest upon more than an unsubstantiated fear that the market value might have been impaired. However, even if the force of the floodgates argument is accepted, it is perhaps worth noting that the anxiety may be overstated so as to overshadow all post-remediation stigma-based claims, even those which might in English law be contained within the extended notion of amenity explored above.

Intertwined with these vexed questions of policy is the way in which the courts approach the issue of causation, both in fact and in law. Within the confines of the Nuclear Installations Act 1965 it was observed, *obiter*, by Gatehouse J in *Merlin* that, even if the plaintiff had been able to demonstrate recognisable damage, to succeed he would still have had to establish that the emission of radiancludes from the nuclear site had caused the damage.[74] Doubtless the point would rightly be echoed in a private nuisance action. As such it provides a useful check upon unmeritorious claims. Causation is, of course, an ideological quagmire.[75]

Consideration of causation prompts a general issue, to which finding an answer is less than easy. Some contend that as a matter of general principle it may well be that there is little reliable evidence to endorse a single and shared view of whether pollution ever affects the value of land.[76] There are also two related concerns. The first revolves around the practicalities of assessing the amount of any loss, not least in finding suitable sites to serve as comparators. This may unleash what was has been described as a battle of the experts.[77] However as *Blackburn* indicates it need not be an exercise that is beyond the reach of the valuers and the English courts.[78] The second is in being confident that the effect of the stigma on the value of the land is permanent. If it is not then awarding damages for the present fall in the market value of the land may unwittingly constitute providing the owner with a windfall in the event that the fall in value turns out to be transitory. At the time of the litigation it may well be that the likelihood of the property depreciation being reversed is an imponderable. It might also be argued that the focus should be estimation of the

[73] Evidence was provided by estate agents together with 5 expert economists. The case has been subjected to analysis by a number of commentators: see, e.g., Davis and Longo, *supra* n. 4, at 10347; and Geisinger, *supra* n.4, at 465 ff.

[74] *Supra* n.7, at 56.

[75] See generally, W.P. Keeton *et al.*, *Prosser and Keeton on Torts* (5th edn. Minn, West Publishing Co., 1984) ch. 24.

[76] See, e.g., surveys cited in Davis and Longo, *supra* n.4, at 10348, ns.34 and 35.

[77] See, e.g., *Bixby Ranch Co. v. Spectrol Electronics Corp.*, *supra* n.6.

[78] In that case useful guidance on some of the steps that experts should take in presenting the evidence is offered: see *supra* n.38, at 534–7.

198 John Lowry and Rod Edmunds

permanency of the risk rather than speculating upon how far the damage may continue indefinitely.[79] Whilst it may therefore provide a need to proceed with caution it does not seem that this should be seen as a bar on recovery in all circumstances.

CONCLUSION

In the latter part of the twentieth century courts across the United States of America have faced an avalanche of tortious claims posited on damage arising from the stigma that has attended a toxic episode. The central purpose of our chapter has been to go some way to anticipate how "stigma" actions might be dealt with if such a trend is replicated within our own jurisdiction. In this we have taken as the starting point the way in which attempts under a specialised statutory regime to recover damages for depreciation in value of land consequent upon contamination of a radioactive kind have fared at the hands of the courts. Here the decisions in *Merlin* and *Blue Circle* favour the claimant only to the extent that he or she can show evidence of physical damage. In adopting this approach the courts appear to deploy what may be termed a negligence-orientated dichotomy of damages. In this perspective damages are referable as being either pure economic loss on the one hand or consequential physical damage on the other.

What then arises is the question of how far such a dichotomy should figure in determining actions brought in private nuisance and not under the terms of the Nuclear Installations Act 1965 or in the tort of negligence. It is our argument that this is a particularly pertinent line of enquiry in the wake of the House of Lords decisions in *Cambridge Water*, and even more so after *Hunter*. We have identified two alternative lines of response open to the courts. First, there is scope to consider whether and how far the murky concept of amenity might accommodate the notion of stigma damages. On this point there are mixed signals to be found contained within the language in the various speeches in *Hunter*. However on a generous reading it might be tenable to argue that both the post-remediation stigma in *Blue Circle* and the market stigma in *Merlin* might be interpreted as instances of damage to the amenity.

At the very least, whatever the answer to such claims might be in general or on the specific facts, it might be better to formulate the question of liability in terms of amenity rather than see the damage as physical or economic. Nonetheless it has to be admitted that the courts might well prefer a second and more radical way forward. This would entail a refusal to transfer into the resolution of nuisance suits the judicial partiality to regard stigma as economic loss which is beyond the pale unless there is a scintilla of physical damage. In which case a subsidiary line of argument in this chapter has been concerned to high-

---

[79] A point which finds support in the reasoning in *In Re Paoli, supra* n.6.

Stigma Damages, Amenity and the Margins of Economic Loss   199

light that private nuisance is not cluttered with authorities that necessarily rule out the possibility of allowing recovery for pure economic loss. On the contrary, while the judicial consideration of the point is nowhere as full or direct as has been the case in the tort of negligence, the courts might wish to develop the *obiter* views expressed in *Ryeford Homes* and *British Celanese Ltd* so as to allow recovery of stigma damages.

Recognising damages for stigma-induced depreciation presents interesting points of principle. Experience in the United States reveals as much and more besides. Within the transatlantic case law there are instances of claims succeeding either on the basis of a threat of (re-)contamination or because of the proximity of the land to the source of pollution alone. These examples have mapped out a variety of concerns and consequential issues to be addressed. These display some forthright and weighty considerations, a number of which may cause English courts to pause for thought in developing their response to such private nuisance disputes in which such damages are sought. There may need to be some checks and balances if the potential for liability is not to become too extensive. There may prove to be thorny issues of causation and equally contentious issues surrounding the calculation of the loss in value. In our view such difficulties do not warrant a blanket denial of all such claims. To reject all claims solely because of such logistic and policy concerns might undermine a valuable role that tort can serve in ensuring proper redress for contamination of ownership rights.

From an environmentalist standpoint there is likely to be a more overarching reluctance to find the recognition of stigma damages appealing. The purpose of the award is to compensate the owner for a loss which is financial. It does not ensure that there is remediation for the benefit of the environment. It is therefore questionable how far the legal system's willingness to recognise this head of damage will afford any higher degree of common law protection of the environment. In some respects any proliferation in such claims may well reduce the inclination and financial ability of those responsible for contamination to meet the costs of clean-up. As other chapters in this volume indicate, this may not be a criticism that is confined solely to stigma damages. In some senses it is closely allied to the growing concern to identify the proper roles (possibly amounting to demarcation) of regulatory control regimes and the common law protection.[80] Stigma damages are then seen as not simply diverting funds from remediation but duplicating or trespassing upon the terrain that is occupied by statutory control. Arguably the point has less force because stigma claims either flow from circumstances where either there has been some repair (post-remediation cases such as *Blue Circle*) or there is at most some threat of contamination (market stigma). In market stigma cases remediation is not in issue.

---

[80] See further Steele, "Private Law and the Environment: Nuisance in Context" (1995) 15 *LS* 236. See also D. McGillivray and J. Wightman, "Private Rights and Environmental Protection" in P. Ireland and P. Laleng (eds.), *The Critical Lawyers' Handbook 2* (London, Pluto Press, 1997); T. Jewell and J. Steele, *Law in Environmental Decision-Making* (Oxford, Clarendon Press, 1998).

200 John Lowry and Rod Edmunds

More broadly, one premise for tort yielding to statutory regulation is the assumption of the sufficiency of the control mechanisms and the willingness and availability of resources to ensure effective enforcement. In the real world, there is evidence that regulators such as the Environment Agency are not always financially equipped to take enforcement action in all cases, even if they deem it expedient so to do.[81] That apart, stigma induced depreciation may often occur where there has been some regulatory breakdown. This was true in each of the cases of *Merlin* and *Blue Circle* (and can also be seen in the context of the amenity claim in *Blackburn*). This also points to the continuing vitality and validity of common law protection in the context of environmental litigation.

---

[81] For a random example of comment on the uneven and opaque approach to enforcement by the Agency, see ENDS Report 295, 6.

10

Towards a European Tort Law on the Environment? European Union Initiatives and Developments on Civil Liability in Respect of Environmental Harm

MARTIN HEDEMANN-ROBINSON and MARK WILDE

INTRODUCTION

IT IS NOW some ten years since the European Commission first submitted a proposal for a Community directive on civil liability in respect of environmental damage. Notwithstanding promises laid down in the previous two European Union (EU) action programmes on the environment, two draft directives, three revisions[1] of the Treaty of Rome 1957 (EC Treaty) and various Commission discussion documents specifically on environmental liability, to this date no Community legislation has yet been passed in order to establish an EU-wide toxic tort regime. Progress has been slow, in large part due to considerable opposition from industry and the scepticism of certain Member States. However, with the very recent publication by the European Commission of its White Paper on Environmental Liability,[1A] the Community may finally be on the verge of legislating for change. Given the length of time that the Community has had to ponder over the options, it is perhaps time to re-evaluate whether EU intervention in this field is feasible or desirable, and in particular question whether any prospective legislation would in fact constitute a significant contribution to enhancing environmental protection.

[1A] COM(2000)66 final of 9.2.2000, published on the EU's website: http:www.europa.eu.int/comm/environment/liability/. See postscript.

[1] Namely, by virtue of the Single European Act 1986 (SEA), the Treaty on European Union 1992 (TEU) and the Treaty of Amsterdam 1997 (ToA). Unless otherwise indicated, EC Treaty Arts. will be cited according to their new (i.e. post-Amsterdam) numberings. In order to avoid confusion and ease understanding, references to old (i.e. pre-Amsterdam) treaty numberings will be provided alongside in brackets where appropriate.

202 *Martin Hedemann-Robinson and Mark Wilde*

The aim of this chapter is to consider political and legal developments which have taken place at Community level, particularly during the last decade, with a view to examining the difficulties and complexities that emerged in discussions on prospective Community legislation on civil liability in respect of environmental harm. Since the Single European Act 1986 (SEA) first inserted a common environmental policy into the EC Treaty, the Community's original core objective of securing ever closer market integration between Member States has increasingly had to be realigned to take account of ecological interests. For instance, included amongst the constitutional principles of the Community legal order enshrined in the EC Treaty is an obligation on the EU to achieve "a high level of protection and improvement of the quality of the environment"[2] and to ensure that "environmental protection requirements must be integrated into the definition and implementation of the Community policies and activities . . . , in particular with a view to promoting sustainable development".[3] Arguments in favour of creating a Community system of civil liability in respect of environmental harm have tended to rest upon those twin objectives of the EU, namely environmental protection and the realisation of single market conditions. The former goal is supposedly enhanced, in that private individuals and organisations will be able to assist in the enforcement of EU environmental norms alongside the European Commission, namely in being able to sue or use the threat of civil action against polluters in respect of breaches of Community environmental law. The latter aim is also purportedly served by the fact that compliance costs in respect of environmental standards are made more uniform across the entire territory of the single market, thus ensuring the avoidance of any possible protectionist or other competitive distortions that might arise in the face of differing civil liability regimes operating in EU Member States.

However, it is rather easy to overstate the significance that a prospective Community legislative instrument on civil liability might have, in terms both of furthering market integration and enhancing environmental protection. As far as environmental protection is concerned, the contribution made by Community law here will depend very much upon the extent to which it will enable and encourage the public to attain effective access to national courts with a view to securing remedies that are appropriate to rectifying ecological damage. The traditional procedural and substantive principles that accompany tortious liability throw up considerable obstacles in this regard: namely, the focus on a market conceptualisation of the relevant parties in litigation, loss, damage and remedies. The task facing the Community legislature, namely primarily the Commission, Council of Ministers and European Parliament, will therefore be to ensure that a Community framework of liability will be constructed upon the basis of defending its ecological values and standards, as opposed to simply facilitating the resolution of unwarranted interactions as between individuals and organisations operating within the context of a market-place. As far as fur-

[2] Art. 2 EC.
[3] Art. 6 EC (old Art. 130r(2) EC, last sentence).

thering European market integration is concerned, the link between the Community's aspiration to eliminate anti-competitive distortions within the single market and a EU-wide environmental civil liability regime is rather uncertain. It is not clear whether, if at all, the emergence of several different toxic tort laws within the various Member States will materially distort conditions of competition between manufacturers located in different national jurisdictions within the single market. As regards enhancing environmental protection through decentralising the enforcement of Community environmental law, it is by no means clear thus far that the Commission has managed to craft a legislative proposal capable of attracting private individuals and environmental pressure groups to bring civil proceedings against polluters. As is discussed in detail later in the chapter, existing draft civil liability directives would leave many significant legal and financial hurdles for private environmental law enforcers to overcome.

Therefore, beneath the rhetoric that has accompanied recent discussions at Community level with respect to the potential significance of a EU environmental liability law, there lies a very real danger. Unless it is framed appropriately, such a law will fail to aid the better enforcement of Community environmental standards and effectively tolerate incidents of violation of EU anti-pollution norms in all but the clearest cases. Admittedly, it is true from a technical legal standpoint that Member States will be able to introduce or maintain more stringent civil liability regimes subsequent to the adoption of any EU eco-liability legislation. However, given the considerable amount of collective political investment and credibility that will have been involved in agreeing upon the parameters and standards of any Community legislative instrument, it seems somewhat doubtful to conceive that many Member States would make use of this option, other than those with pre-existing higher ecological standards and traditions to defend. In particular, no Member State can easily ignore the political and economic pressures involved of being seen to impose costs on its domestic industry over and above those imposed by fellow countries in the EU.

Above all, it is far too easy to regard civil liability as having the potential of a magic wand in terms of safeguarding and enhancing the enforcement of environmental protection. Environmental civil liability must be placed in its proper context. In all cases, it is a resource of last rather than first resort. Its potency, if any, will lie far more in its deterrence value rather than in its use in litigation. One must always be wary of falling into the trap of assuming that enforcement of environmental protection standards is automatically served through tort, an assumption which underestimates the grim realities of expense and protraction in respect of the prosecution of civil litigation.

In summary, this chapter aims to address the key legal issues and problems that have confronted the Community in deciding whether to introduce Community legislation on civil liability in respect of environmental harm. As a means of placing the discussion into context, the first section examines how, in its evolution, the European Community has realigned its market integration aims in the light of the challenges raised by environmental politics; in particular, how

204 Martin Hedemann-Robinson and Mark Wilde

the EU has derived legal competence to promulgate environmental regulatory controls (including a civil liability law). The second part of the chapter considers in detail the various initiatives that the Community political institutions have examined so far in relation to environmental civil liability, in particular with a view to assessing how effectively these would accommodate public as well as private interests of needing to safeguard the environment. The final part considers the potential impact of the European Court of Justice's (ECJ) decision in *Francovich*[4] on Member State liability in respect of breaching Community law, in terms of furthering enforcement of EU environmental law through civil proceedings. The chapter ends with some concluding observations on the Community's involvement to date in the use of tort law as a mechanism for enforcing Community environmental norms.

DEVELOPMENTS TOWARDS A COMMUNITY POLICY ON CIVIL LIABILITY IN RESPECT OF ENVIRONMENTAL HARM

Discussion of the recent proposals on environmental civil liability at Community level would be considerably impoverished without reference to the political and legal contexts underlying these developments. It is important to bear in mind the long-standing inherent difficulties that the legal and political order of the European Community faces in attempting to accommodate an environmental protection dimension in terms of regulating the operation of the single market.[5] However, as discussion of the evolution of Community environmental law and policy is not the chief concern of this chapter, it will therefore be addressed only briefly. More detailed and authoritative commentaries can, of course, be readily located elsewhere.[6]

Until relatively recently, it was a moot point whether or not the Community had legal competence to enact any environmental protection legislation. At its inception, in 1957, the European Community (EC) had no environmental policy commitments enshrined in the Treaty of Rome (EC Treaty), and no clear legal basis upon which to frame policy initiatives.[7] In its early post-war years, the main objective championed by the EU was to link economies in a manner which would facilitate economic expansion and bring about increased prosperity, employment and better housing. It was hoped that this would create the stable social and economic conditions necessary to ensure a lasting peace in Europe. At this time there was little appreciation at institutional level of how, or indeed

[4] Case C–6 & 9/90 *Francovich and Bonifaci* v. *Italy* [1991] ECR I–5403.

[5] See, for instance, M. Hedemann-Robinson, "European Community Law, the Environment and Consumers: Addressing the Challenge of Incorporating an Environmental Protection Dimension to Consumer Protection at Community Level" (1997) 20 *Journal of Consumer Policy* 1.

[6] See, for instance: L. Krämer, *E.C. Treaty and Environmental Law* (3rd edn., London, Sweet & Maxwell, 1998); S. Elworthy and J. Holder, *Environmental Protection—Text and Materials* (London, Butterworths, 1997).

[7] A situation much criticised in the UK and other Member States. See House of Lords Select Committee on the EC, 22nd Report Session 1977–8.

Towards a European Tort Law on the Environment? 205

whether, environmental protection should be accommodated within this overall strategy. Although public health issues were recognised as being associated with the standard of living, the objectives of environmental protection and economic expansion were generally considered as being mutually irreconcilable; it was the latter objective which took priority.[8]

By the time of signature of the Treaty of Amsterdam (ToA) in October 1997, the legal and political situation had become wholly transformed. A growing awareness of the heavy price which the environment was having to pay as a result of the pursuit of market integration objectives had crystallised into specific EC Treaty obligations and mandates on environmental protection. The cumulative effect of the reforms and amendments made to the EC Treaty by virtue of the SEA, TEU and ToA have resulted in a transformation of Community law and policy on the environment, involving a fundamental re-evaluation of the *rationale* of the Community itself.

The core tasks of the Community in relation to environmental protection have been clarified and consolidated in a number of respects. Article 2 EC, the EC Treaty provision which defines the fundamental aims of the Community, has been revised to emphasise the need for the Community to adhere to the principle of "sustainable development" instead of "sustainable growth", in line with recent international commitments,[9] and a "high level of protection and improvement of the quality of the environment". Environmental protection is expressly listed as an activity of the Community.[10] Furthermore, the principle that environmental protection should be integrated into all other areas of Community of policy is now incorporated within Part One of the EC Treaty which houses the most fundamental principles pertaining to the EU.[11]

Since ratification of the SEA in 1987 the EC Treaty has contained a specific collection of provisions designed to act as the main legal framework for the promulgation of Community environmental policy measures (now housed in Title XIX on the Environment, Articles 174–176 EC (old Articles 130r–t EC)). A solid platform has been established from which to launch environmental initiatives. Over time, a number of key principles have been included within these provisions in order to provide political guidance as regards the crafting of environmental policy: namely, the precautionary principle, that preventive action

---

[8] This was exemplified by the original text of Art. 2 EC, the provision which sets out the goals of the Community. It focused exclusively on developing economic growth within the context of an emerging common market: "[t]he Community shall have as its task, by establishing a common market and progressively approximating the economic policies of member states, to promote throughout the Community a harmonious development of economic activities, a continuous and balanced expansion, an increase in stability, an accelerated raising of the standard of living and closer relations between the States belonging to it".

[9] See e.g. the Rio Convention on biological diversity of 5 June 1992, to which the Community is a party (EC Decision 93/626 [1993] OJ L309/1).

[10] Art. 3(l) EC.

[11] Specifically the "integration principle" is contained in Art. 6 EC (replacing the third sentence of old Art. 130r(2) EC) which states: "environmental protection requirements must be integrated into the definition and implementation the Community policies and activities referred to in Art. 3, in particular with a view to promoting sustainable development".

should be taken (prevention principle), that environmental damage should be rectified at source (proximity principle) and that the polluter should pay (PPP).[12] Moreover, measures designed to approximate Member State laws under Article 95 EC (old Article 100a EC) in order to aid completion of the single market, are required to accommodate the Community's ecological principles.

Earlier legal uncertainty surrounding the correct selection of legal basis of Community environmental protection legislation has been markedly reduced since the decision-making procedures of Articles 95 and 175 EC have been aligned and the possibility has been provided in Article 95 EC for Member States to be able to adopt stricter environmental protection standards subsequent to harmonisation.[13] However, the long-standing problem of having to choose the correct legal basis for Community environmental protection measures has not been fully resolved, given the fact that Member States must show the Commission that there is "new scientific evidence" to justify a unilateral deviation from a measure passed under Article 95 EC, but do not have to do so in relation to one passed under Article 175 EC.[14] Given that the legal effects of these provisions differ in a material respect, it would probably not be possible to cite Articles 95 and 175 EC as a joint legal basis for those Community environmental measures which aim to protect the environment as well as serve to eliminate distortions of competition within the single market.[15] A choice will have to be made, leaving such measures vulnerable to legal challenge through, for example, annulment proceedings brought under Article 230 EC, on the ground that a fundamental procedural rule has been breached by virtue of an incorrect selection of legal basis.[16] A Community directive on civil liability in respect of environ-

[12] See Art. 174(2) EC.

[13] For detailed discussion on this issue see e.g. L. Krämer, "The Single European Act and Environmental Protection: Reflections on Several New Provisions in Community Law" (1987) 24 *CMLRev*. 659; Bianchi, "The Harmonisation of Laws on Liability for Environmental Damage in Europe: An Italian Perspective" (1994) 6 *JEL* 37; D. Chalmers, "Environmental Protection and the Single Market: An Unsustainable Development. Does the EC Treaty need a Title on the Environment?" (1994) 1 *LIEI* 65; Schemmel and De Regt, "The European Court of Justice and the Environmental Protection Policy of the EC" (1994) *Boston College of International and Comparative Law Journal* 53; D. Wilkinson, "Maastricht and the Environment: The Implications for the EC's Environment Policy of the Treaty on European Union" (1992) 4 *JEL* 221; D.A. Demiray, "The Movement of Goods in a Green Market" (1994) 1 *LIEI* 73.

[14] Art. 95(5) EC. Moreover, under Art. 95(6) EC, the Commission has up to six months after notification to veto or approve the national provisions, according to whether they amount to arbitrary discrimination, a disguised trade restriction or constitute an obstacle to the functioning of the internal market. No such powers are granted to the Commission in relation to measures passed under Art. 175 EC (see Art. 176 EC).

[15] The ECJ has, for instance, made it clear that a joint legal basis is ruled out where the material content of legislation could differ due to the existence of distinctive decision-making procedures involved in each Treaty Art.: Case 45/86, *Commission* v. *Council (Generalised Tariff Preferences)* [1987] ECR 1493 at para. 12 of the judgment; Case C–300/89, *Commission* v. *Council (Titanium Dioxide)* [1991] ECR I–2867, at paras. 19–20 of the judgment.

[16] For instance, a future Member State government keen to adopt stricter civil liability norms than those agreed at EU level might well object or ignore to the legal hurdles placed in its way by Art. 95(5)–(6) EC. Alternatively, from the perspective of the internal market, the Commission might object to the Council applying Art. 175 EC as a legal basis, on the grounds that Arts. 95(5)–(6) EC

mental harm might well be affected by the continuation of this legal problem, given its dual function of environmental protection and facilitating competition goals. On the other hand, recent case law of the ECJ would appear to offer some guidance on the point. This seems to favour Article 175 EC as a legal basis where single market considerations are merely ancillary or incidental to the legislative aims at hand.[17] The Commission, in the light of this jurisprudence, appears at the moment to favour resort to Article 175 EC for prospective EU environmental civil liability legislation.[18] However, this remains a moot point, not least because the Court has demonstrated that it may come to a different conclusion where it considers that the aims of the Community are equally weighted.[19] This level of legal uncertainty does not augur well in terms of facilitating a smooth decision-making and implementation process.

Development of an EU Environmental Liability Policy

Since its first action programme on the environment in 1973, the Community has accumulated a substantial body of environmental legislation. However, most environmental measures take the form of directives which are designed to achieve an overall reduction in the level of pollutants released into the environment during the normal course of industrial processes.[20] This approach does not deal with the consequences of abnormal, unintentional pollution either resulting from sudden, large-scale escapes of noxious substances or gradual accumulations. Such incidents often result in the release of high concentrations of pollutants capable of causing damage to both real and personal property and, in the most extreme cases, personal injury and even death. Thus, in terms of the pressures placed on the environment the effects of such incidents differ considerably from escapes resulting from routine operations. In these circumstances there is a need for a mechanism which is capable of securing the clean-up of the contamination and reducing the chances of such incidents occurring in future.

This gap in the EU's environmental strategy was highlighted during the 1970s and 1980s by a number of highly publicised disasters involving the release of

---

would provide a more effective mechanism for safeguarding the elimination of internal trading barriers. See comments by L. Krämer, *supra*, n.6, at 86–7.

[17] Case C–155/91 *Commission* v. *Council (Waste Management)* [1993] ECR I–939; Case C–187/93, *European Parliament* v. *Council (Shipment of Waste)* [1994] ECR I–2874. See De Sadeleer, "Casenote on C–155/91 *Commission* v. *Council*" (1993) 7 *JEL* 291.

[18] See para. III of the 1997 Working Paper on Environmental Liability of 17 November 1997 (obtainable from DGXI of the Commission, Brussels). See also the preference for Art. 175 EC (old Art. 130s EC) by the Commission as the basis for its most recent proposed dir. on landfill waste (COM(97)105fin), which contrasts with its approach in the earlier drafts where Art. 95 (old Art. 100a EC) was cited (see COM(91)102 SYN 335 and COM(93)275fin).

[19] Case C–300/89 *Commission* v. *Council (Titanium Dioxide)*, *supra* n.15. For a detailed assessment of this case, see J. Robinson, "Casenote on Titanium Dioxide" (1992) 4 *JEL* 109.

[20] E.g. the Drinking Water Dir. 80/778/EEC ([1980] OJ L229/11) sets a maximum concentration level for nitrates of 50 mg/l and a guide value of 25 mg/l.

208   *Martin Hedemann-Robinson and Mark Wilde*

extremely harmful agents. For example, in 1976, in Seveso, Italy, there was an extremely large-scale release of one of the most hazardous toxins, tetrachlorodibenzo-p-dioxin (TCDD) from the ICMESA plant. Many people suffered skin damage in the form of dermal lesions known as chloracne as a result of exposure to the toxin. Plants and crops were damaged and 77,000 livestock had to be slaughtered. In order to monitor the long-term effects of the accident a health monitoring programme was introduced which was not concluded until as recently as 1996.

The immediate response to these disasters focused on improving plant safety and emergency procedures. To this end Council Directive 82/501/EEC (the "Seveso" Directive)[21] was passed which obliges operators of plants engaged in specified hazardous production processes to take "all measures necessary" to prevent major accidents and limit their consequences. In short the Directive requires the implementation of schemes designed to ensure that operators identify major accident hazards, adopt all necessary safety procedures and provide appropriate training and information for persons present on site. In the case of certain specified high risk activities, the Directive requires the establishment of a complex notification procedure which must make the "competent authority" aware of the exact nature of the activities being carried out, the technical processes involved and the safety procedures followed so that emergency contingency plans can be drawn up.

Whilst it was hoped that the above approach would reduce the risk of major disasters occurring, it was recognised that it provided only a partial response to the problem. Left unaddressed are the issues of apportionment of liability following an accidental escape and the compensation of victims. It was not until after the Rhine pollution disaster in 1986, caused by the chemical leaks at the Sandoz plant in Basle, that the Council called upon the Commission to review all existing measures relating to the prevention and remediation of environmental damage and asserted that new measures should be considered which would ensure "prompt clean-up and restoration, coupled with equitable arrangements for liability and compensation by the polluters for any damage caused".[22] These statements focused attention on the possible use of civil liability as a component of the EU's environmental strategy. Such an approach has now been formally recognised as a result of the Fifth Community Environmental Action Programme (1993–2000).[23]

---

[21] [1982] OJ L230/1.

[22] [1986] EC Bull 11, point 2 1 146.

[23] [1993] OJ C138. The action programme specifically includes a commitment to establishing civil liability in respect of environmental harm, in stating that "an integrated Community approach to environmental liability will be established . . . making sure that, if damage to the environment does occur, it is properly remedied through restoration. Liability will be an essential tool of last resort to punish despoliation of the environment. In addition—and in line with the objective of prevention at source—it will provide a very clear economic incentive for management and control of risk, pollution and waste".

Towards a European Tort Law on the Environment? 209

Even before the Fifth Action Programme, the Commission had already started to develop a civil liability framework in the waste sector. In 1989, a formal proposal on civil liability for damage caused by waste was published in the form of a draft directive[24] which concentrated on the establishment of a strict liability regime. Following consultation with the Parliament,[25] a new, more far-reaching, proposal was published in 1991[26] which also included proposals for the establishment of clean-up funds and increased standing for non-governmental organisations (NGOs) such as environmental pressure groups.

The debate was widened following the publication of a Commission Green Paper on Remedying Environmental Damage 1993 (hereinafter referred to as the 1993 Green Paper).[27] The 1993 Green Paper was designed to stimulate debate on the possibility of establishing a civil liability regime in respect of damage to all environmental media resulting from a broader range of activities. The Paper, designed to trigger public discussion on the subject, addresses all major legal issues including: strict liability; the difficulty of establishing causation in environmental damage cases; whether normal civil remedies are adequate to compensate for environmental damage; and whether adequate insurance cover could be provided for increased civil liability. In addition, it considers in more detail than the waste proposals means by which central clean up funds could be established for use in circumstances where civil liability cannot be established. Following the publication of the 1993 Green Paper a joint public hearing on the subject was held by the European Parliament and the Commission, at which interested parties including industry and environmental organisations had the opportunity to put their points of view.[28] Shortly after the hearing, the Parliament exercised its powers under Article 192(2) EC (old Article 138b(2) EC) to call upon the Commission to submit a proposal for a directive on civil liability in respect of environmental damage.

The Commission then instigated two independent detailed reports on the subject, including, first, a comparative analysis of civil liability for environmental damage in each Member State,[29] the United States, Iceland, Norway and

---

[24] COM89(282)fin Commission Proposal for a Council Dir. on Civil Liability for Damage Caused by Waste [1989] OJ C251/3 (hereinafter referred to as the 1989 draft dir.).

[25] In accordance with the "consultation" procedure which was, at that time, applicable for legislation based upon Art. 95 EC (old Art. 100a EC). Parliament submitted its findings in a Resolution on the Commission Proposal for a Council Dir. on Civil Liability for Damage Caused by Waste [1990] OJ C324/248.

[26] COM(91)219fin—Amended Commission Proposal for a Council Dir. on Civil Liability for Damage Caused by Waste [1991] OJ C192 (hereinafter referred to as the 1991 draft directive).

[27] COM(93)47fin Commission Communication to the Council and European Parliament on remedying environmental damage.

[28] Joint Public Hearing of the European Parliament (Committee on the Environment, Public Health and Consumer Protection) and the Commission (DG XI Environment, Nuclear Safety and Civil Protection) on "Preventing and Remedying Environmental Damage" (Brussels, 3 and 4 Nov. 1993).

[29] McKenna & Co., "Study of Civil Liability Systems for Remedying Environmental Damage", Contract B4/3040/94/00065/MAR/H1, June 1996 (copies available from European Commission DG XI).

210   *Martin Hedemann-Robinson and Mark Wilde*

Switzerland and, secondly, an economic feasibility study.[30] The 1993 Green Paper does not specifically supersede the 1991 draft directive on waste.[31] However, Community legislative action does appear to be on hold whilst the debate generated by the 1993 Green Paper runs its course. However, it is entirely possible that the 1991 draft directive on waste would be shelved if a new, all-encompassing proposal on civil liability for environmental damage were published.

Running in parallel with the discussions at Community level on environmental civil liability were the initiatives produced by the Council of Europe which resulted in the Council of Europe Convention on Civil Liability for Damage resulting from Activities Dangerous to the Environment (the Lugano Convention).[32] Although the Council of Europe is an international organisation separate and distinct from the EU, the Convention is important in that the Community may decide to accede to the Convention as opposed to drafting its own proposal.[33] The Environment Commissioner has expressed support for this approach,[34] because of the length of time it would take the Community to pass its own free-standing directive. However, the Lugano Convention has been subject to considerable criticism as being too limited in scope[35] and containing some highly controversial provisions.[36] In short, the Convention requires signatories to adopt strict liability regimes for environmental damage, albeit subject to certain defences, and affords considerable standing to non-governmental organisations to pursue claims. A novel feature of the Convention is that it covers genetically modified organisms (GMOs). This could present an obstacle to

---

[30] ERM Economics, "Economic Aspects of Liability and Joint Compensation Systems for Remedying Environmental Damage", Ref. 3066, Mar. 1996 (copies available from European Commission DG XI).

[31] When the first draft of the 1993 Green Paper, *supra* n.27, was published in 1991, Dr. Karl von Kempis of the EC Commission stated at the European Liability Insurance Congress in Berlin that the Green Paper was not designed to replace the draft Waste Liability Dir. and that it would "not contain detailed legislative proposals, but rather state the situation in the member countries and show the Commission's position in the discussion with the Council of Ministers and the Parliament": reported in *World Insurance Report*, 8 May 1992, at 7–8.

[32] The Council of Europe's Convention on civil liability for damage resulting from activities dangerous to the environment was agreed in Mar. 1993 and opened for signature at Lugano, Switzerland, on 21 June 1993. To date, the Convention has been signed by Cyprus, Finland, Greece, Iceland, Ireland, Italy, Liechtenstein, Luxembourg and the Netherlands. However, it will not come into force until it has been ratified by three states. (The full text of Lugano is reproduced in [1993] Yearbook of International Environmental Law 691).

[33] See Art. 174(4) in conjunction with Art. 300 EC (old Arts. 130r(4) and 228 EC respectively) which provide Community with the capacity to enter into international agreements in the environmental field.

[34] According to Mr Chris Clark, an official of the Environmental Directorate of the Commission, DG XI), addressing a seminar on environmental liability held by Simmonds & Simmonds on 27 Sept. 1996. Reported as "Bjerregaard Poised for Fresh Move on Environmental Liability", *ENDS Report* 260, Sept. 1996, 38.

[35] The Convention, *supra* n.32, focuses on a limited number of hazardous activities which do not include the nuclear and transport industries.

[36] Including, e.g., affording non-governmental organisations wide standing and the inclusion of a developments risk defence (Art. 35(1)(b)).

Towards a European Tort Law on the Environment? 211

the signing of the Convention by the EU because the EU has yet to determine its position regarding the status of GMOs.

On 29 January 1997, the Commission held an orientation debate to consider its future policy on the subject of environmental liability. It resolved to respond to the European Parliament's resolution of April 1994,[37] by issuing a White Paper setting out the various options and the issues raised.[38] To this end, the views of interested parties (such as industry, insurance companies and environmental interest groups) were canvassed by the Commission's 1997 Working Paper on Environmental Liability (hereinafter the 1997 Working Paper) which identifies the key issues.[39] The White Paper has only just been published on 9 February 2000.[40] The 1997 Working Paper indicates the types of measures which the Commission is considering. For example, it refers to the possibility of easing the burden of proof on causation and increasing standing for environmental pressure groups.[41] The next section of this chapter will discuss the various components of a prospective environmental liability regime that have been considered by the Commission and in the Lugano Convention.

EUROPEAN UNION INITIATIVES ON CIVIL LIABILITY IN RESPECT OF ENVIRONMENTAL HARM

An examination of the various legislative drafts and other official policy documents that have emanated at EU institutional level on civil liability in respect of environmental harm clearly and crucially reveals a lack of political resolution on the part of Member States as regards enhancing environmental law enforcement at the horizontal level (i.e. as between private entities/individuals) through the mechanism of tort law controls. Behind the Commission's rhetoric of strict liability which has accompanied its proposals on civil liability in respect of environmental harm lies a host of caveats and compromises that raises question

[37] European Parliament Resolution A3–0232/94 on preventing and remedying environmental damage [1994] OJ C128/165 which requested the Council to propose a dir. "on civil liability in respect of (future) environmental damage".

[38] Mr Clark of DG XI of the Commission stated that failure to respond to the resolution "may" have legal consequences; see *supra* n.36. Not surprisingly the Commission and the Parliament disagree on the effect of Art. 192(2) EC (old Art. 138b(2) EC). The Parliament considers that this right to request the Commission to generate proposals represents a sharing of the Commission's right of initiative; see Rules of Procedure, Rule 36B, entitled "Legislative initiative". However, the Commission is of the opinion that the Treaty confers sole legal and political responsibility for any proposals submitted on the Commission, irrespective of whether they were drawn up at the request of another body. See answer to written question No 3471/92 [1993] OJ C292/22.

[39] European Commission 1997 Working Paper on Environmental Liability of 17 Nov. 1997 (obtainable from DG XI of the Commission, Brussels).

[40] For some very recent comments on an unpublished version of the draft White Paper, see R.G. Lee, "Draft White Paper on Environmental Liability" (1999) 8 *Environmental Liability* 1. See Postscript below for further details.

[41] This latter proposal represents a departure from the position adopted in the Green Paper. *supra* n.27, where the need for more liberal standing requirements appeared to be firmly rejected.

212   *Martin Hedemann-Robinson and Mark Wilde*

marks over whether a European Community-inspired toxic tort law would be able to make a significant contribution in terms of environmental protection. This is all the more concerning, as so much political effort and hyperbole has been invested in this long-awaited addition to the body of Community environmental law. Apart from the not inconsiderable lack of political will which has dogged the development of legislation in this field, another significant factor which has created stumbling blocks has been the Commission's choice to attempt to craft law enforcement at the horizontal level (i.e. as between private persons) in the form of tort as opposed to public law. Conceptualising environmental harm as being part of a bargaining process on the basis of an individualistic private rights discourse between two competing and equal parties in a market, as opposed to constituting an infringement of group rights defended under public law, necessarily prepares the ground for compromise and relativism built upon competing values of "right", of which environmental protection is only one amongst many. The Commission has, in some respects, tried to steer the discourse of toxic civil liability towards securing pre-eminence of environmental protection over competing economic concerns. However, so far the various EU initiatives on civil liability have failed to manipulate the tort law model to secure respect ultimately for public over private interests.

This section of the chapter aims to analyse key elements of a prospective EU framework regime for strict liability in respect of ecological harm. In particular, attention will be drawn to the evolution of the Commission's thinking and strategies in terms of reconciling the EU's environmental policy commitments and internal free market philosophy, with a view to pinpointing the fault-lines of discussion in this area.

Strict Liability

The central plank upon which draft EU directives on civil liability in respect of damage caused by waste have been based has been the concept of strict liability. Both the 1989[42] and 1991,[43] Commission draft directives on civil liability for damage caused by waste, make it clear that waste producers are to be made liable in respect of environmental harm irrespective of fault on their part.[44] Justification for this focus on remedying environmental harm, as opposed to allocation of blame, has rested on accommodating the guiding principles laid

---

[42] COM(89)282fin, *supra* n.24.

[43] COM(91)219fin, *supra* n.26.

[44] See Art. 3 of COM(89)282fin and COM(92)219fin, *supra* nn.24 and 26. See also the early Commission 1991 and 1993 proposals for a Council dir. on the landfill of waste, which expressly stipulated that waste disposal operators would be liable "under the civil law for the damage and impairment of the environment caused by the landfilled waste, irrespective of fault on his part" (Art. 14 of COM(91)102 and COM(93)275fin). Reference to strict liability has been dropped in the most recent version of the proposed landfill dir., presumably on the ground that this element would be covered under the proposed general civil liability dir. on waste (see COM(97)105fin).

down in Articles 174–176 EC for EU environmental policy development, including in particular the polluter pays and prevention principles as well the need to attain a high level of environmental protection throughout the Union.[45] The Commission's Explanatory Memorandum accompanying the initial 1989 proposal rather optimistically emphasises that its ambition underlying the introduction of no-fault liability is to ensure: that the victims will receive compensation; the recovery of the environment; and that economic agents of ecological harm will be held to account.[46] In its 1993 Green Paper (on remedying environmental damage),[47] the Commission duly notes that incorporation of fault into the liability equation would place an undue evidentiary burden on the plaintiff as well as invite the defendant to plead compliance with statutory norms and permits as a defence to allegations of negligence or recklessness.[48] Retaining a fault-based notion of civil liability would also divert remediation costs from being placed at the door of the polluter instead of the general taxpayer.[49] Such concerns have also served to promote moves towards greater reliance on strict liability frameworks both at national and public international law levels,[50] in respect of environmental harm.[51] Nevertheless, as will be explained further below, it is clear that the EU proposals so far envisage a number of ways in which defendant polluters would be able to evade liability for environmental harm, on grounds either directly or indirectly related to a reasonableness test. As has been aptly commented elsewhere, it is salient to remember in this context that strict liability does not mean absolute liability.[52]

Scope of Environmental Liability and Definition of Environmental Harm

Two important, if obvious, factors which qualify the impact of a strict liability regime are the range of industrial activities and actors subjected to a no-fault based approach to culpability. In keeping with a general trend at national and public international levels towards introducing strict liability into specific industrial sectors, as opposed to imposing generic, industry-wide civil law obligations, the EC legislative proposals of 1989 and 1991 focus exclusively upon targeting environmental harm caused by waste generated on a commercial basis,[53]

[45] See, for instance, the 5th and 10th recitals of the proposed 1989 and 1991 dirs., *supra* nn.24 and 26.

[46] COM(89)282fin. at point 4 of the Explanatory Memorandum annexed to the draft dir.

[47] COM(93)47 fin., *supra* n.27.

[48] *Ibid.*, at point 2.1.1.

[49] *Ibid.*, at 8.

[50] For instance, the 1993 Council of Europe Convention on civil liability for damage resulting from activities dangerous to the environment (Lugano), *supra* n.32, in principle denies a "reasonable care" defence.

[51] This has been a notable influence on the Commission's work on civil liability throughout: see e.g. its Green Paper on Remedying Environmental Damage COM(93)47fin., *supra* n.27, at point 2.2.1 and 1997 Working Paper on Environmental Liability, *supra* n.39, at point IV.1.

[52] See comment by the House of Lords Select Committee on the 1993 Green Paper "Remedying Environmental Damage" (Session 1993–4, 3rd Report (HL Paper 10)) at para. 55.

[53] See Art. 1 of COM(89)282fin. and COM(91)219fin., *supra* nn.24 and 26.

214   *Martin Hedemann-Robinson and Mark Wilde*

whilst in addition excluding nuclear and mineral oil sectors.[54] Thus, although the commercial producer and, in default, the importer and disposers of waste would be potentially liable parties under these draft civil liability regimes,[55] other forms of procuration of ecological damage which do not emanate from the generation of waste (for example, wildlife contamination through agricultural crop spraying), as well as activities emanating from non-commercial actors (for example, public agencies or non-commercial actors) would escape liability. The 1993 Council of Europe Convention on Civil Liability for damage resulting from activities dangerous to the environment (Lugano Convention) has followed in similar vein, specifically restricting liability to damage resulting from activities recognised to be inherently dangerous to the environment,[56] whilst excluding the fields of nuclear energy and carriage of goods.[57]

Since its 1993 Green Paper, the Commission has indicated an interest in broadening the remit of a Community-wide civil liability framework, in particular to target those industrial sectors engaging in particularly environmentally risky activities.[58] This change of attitude has been crystallised further in the shape of the Commission's recent 1997 Working Paper (on environmental liability), in which it sketched out how strict liability was intended to cover areas of EU environmental legislation which deal with inherently risky industrial activities[59] as well as those which are designed to protect natural resources (for example, flora and fauna protected under the Birds[60] and Habitats[61] Directives).

---

[54] See Art. 1(2), *ibid*.

[55] See Arts. 1,2(1)(a) and (2) of COM(89)282fin and COM(91)219fin., *supra* nn.24 and 26. Originally, commercial carriers of waste were outside the net of liability under the 1989 proposal, before being reigned in under the subsequent umbrella definition of "eliminator" of waste as defined in Art. 2(2)(f) of the 1991 draft. See the criticism of this liability gap and the narrowness of the definition of potentially liable parties made by the Economic and Social Committee in its Opinion CES(90)215 at points 4.3–4.4.

[56] Art. 6 of the Lugano Convention, *supra* n.32, stipulates that operators in respect of a "dangerous activity" shall be liable for damage caused "as a result of incidents at the time or during the period when he was exercising control of that activity". A "dangerous activity" is defined in Art. 2(1) as including one either performed professionally or by a public authority involving: "dangerous substances", "genetically modified organisms" or "micro-organisms" posing a significant risk to man, environment or property; waste disposal plants and deposit sites. (Each of these specific terms is defined with further precision in Art. 2.)

[57] See Art. 4, *ibid*.

[58] COM(93)47fin., *supra* n.27, at point 2.1.4. where the Commission considered the following factors for weighing up the introduction of strict liability into an industrial sector: type of hazard; likelihood and possible extent of damage; incentives for better risk management; feasibility and cost of remediation of damage; potential financial burden involved and need and availability of insurance.

[59] See point IV.2 of the 1997 Working Paper, *supra* n.39. The industrial activities referred to by the Commission covered by EU legislation are those: (i) which contain discharge or emission limits for hazardous substances into water or air, or dealing with dangerous substances and preparations with a view to environmental protection; (ii) concerned with the objective to prevent and control risks of accidents and pollution; (iii) on the handling, carriage and disposal of hazardous and other waste; (iv) in the field of biotechnology; (v) in the field of transport of dangerous substances.

[60] EC Dir. 79/409 on the conservation of birds [1979] OJ L103/1.

[61] EC Dir. 92/43 on the conservation of natural habitats and of flora and fauna [1992] OJ L206/7.

The Commission has justified its preference for extending strict liability here by reason of the special environmental value involved.[62] It has also indicated a preference for broadening out the scope of personal liability to include those in charge of operational control of the polluting activity or waste (potentially also to embrace lenders where directly involved in managerial functions). These proposed changes would provide encouragement for a more comprehensive involvement of private environmental law enforcement and constitute a significant departure from the earlier stages of the Commission's rather narrow train of thought, which appeared to be confined to focusing on targeting commercial strategies on waste (i.e. end of pipe scenarios).

Another crucial qualification to the impact of the EU strict liability regime being proposed is the extent to which the environment must be harmed before culpability is triggered. Initially, the Commission was rather tentative in defining the existence of unlawful ecological damage. In its 1989 draft directive, "injury to the environment" was defined as requiring a "significant and persistent interference in the environment caused by a modification of the physical, chemical or biological conditions of water, soil and/or air".[63] Taking account of the criticism directed at this rather vague definition,[64] the 1991 draft defined an "impairment to the environment" as being in existence where the activity caused "significant physical, chemical or biological deterioration of the environment".[65] Rather surprisingly, the Commission failed to clarify its understanding of the term "environment". The European Parliament in its 1990 Resolution had suggested a reference to the "sum of the earth's biotic and abiotic natural resources".[66] This would have fallen short of the broad definition included in the Lugano Convention,[67] which incorporates cultural as well as biological heritage. The Commission's 1993 Green Paper recognises the "fundamental importance" of securing a legal definition of environmental damage without, however, actually favouring any particular model description.[68] It also points out the difficulty of delineating an appropriate cut-off point between significant and insignificant ecological damage. Whilst the 1997 Working Paper is silent on defining ecological harm, it does reveal that the Commission is keen to provide a workable list of "weighing factors" in order for the courts and parties alike to

---

[62] *Ibid.*

[63] Art. 2(1)(d) of COM(89)282fin., *supra* n.24.

[64] For instance, the Economic and Social Committee pointed out the considerable difficulties which would be faced by plaintiffs in proving objectively the occurrence of a modification to the environment (CES(90)215 at point 6.4). See also the European Parliament's resolution [1990] OJ C324/251.

[65] See Art. 2(1)(d) of COM(91)219fin., *supra* n.26.

[66] EP Resolution, *supra* n.25: (Art. 2(1)(d)).

[67] Art. 2(10) of the Lugano Convention, *supra* n.32, states: " '[e]nvironment' includes:—natural resources both abiotic and biotic, such as air ,water, soil, fauna and flora and the interaction between the same factors;—property which forms part of the cultural heritage; and—the characteristic aspects of the landscape."

[68] COM(93)47fin., *supra* n.27, at point 2.1.7.

216   Martin Hedemann-Robinson and Mark Wilde

be able to make sense of understanding when the minimum threshold of damage has been reached in order to trigger liability.[69]

Determining the temporal extent of liability for ecological harm has not raised any deeply controversial issues for the EU, principally because of the widespread concern with the US system of corporate environmental liability under CERCLA (Comprehensive Environmental Response, Compensation and Liability Act 1980 and subsequent amendments in 1986). As is well known, CERCLA imposes a form of strict liability which incorporates a strong retroactive element, so that, for instance, current owners may become entangled within the web of PRPs (potentially responsible parties) in respect of predecessor (lawful) commercial activity.[70] Little support has been shown for introducing retroactivity in a EU strict liability regime. Reasons for this lack of enthusiasm lie with the uncertain implications for insurance coverage, the sense of injustice and the potential drain on public resources in terms of supporting lengthy litigation against the business community. These anxieties are linked with the experience of CERCLA in the USA. Hence, retroactive liability has never been on the agenda as far as the Commission is concerned.[71] In its 1997 Working Paper, the Commission suggests liability should arise in respect of ecological damage that becomes known[72] to a defendant after the EU regime enters into force, unless the latter is able to prove that all or part of the damage was caused prior to that date, in which case liability will be reduced or eliminated accordingly.[73] Attention from most quarters has been focused instead on the viability of non-litigious routes to eradicating historic pollution (such as taxation or joint compensation mechanisms).[74] Fairly durable status seems to have attached itself to the proposed limitation period of three years when the plaintiff is deemed to

---

[69] See the Economic and Social Committee's Opinion CES226/94 (at point 4.1.3) which favours grading liability thresholds according to factors surrounding the individual circumstances of each case, namely according to type of damage, ecological effects and site value from an environmental perspective. See also the Institute for European Environmental Policy's Report on the Commission's Green Paper, *supra* n.35 at 15, which, in disputing the workability of such ecological damage definitions, favours leaving legislation open-ended in order for courts to be able to adopt a pragmatic case-by-case approach.

[70] For further details on CERCLA, see Jacoby and Eremich, "Environmental Liability in the USA" in *Environmental Liability* (IBA Section on Business Law—Committee F (International Environmental Law) 7th Residential Seminar on Environmental Law) (London, Graham and Trotman, 1990); R. Revesz, *Foundations of Environmental Law and Policy* (Oxford, Oxford University Press, 1997); G. Goldenman *et al.* (eds.), *Environmental Liability in Central and Eastern Europe* (London, Graham and Trotman/Martinus Nijhoff, 1994), ch. 5.

[71] Both the 1989 and 1991 draft dirs. on waste liability, *supra* nn.24 and 26, expressly exclude liability in respect of historic pollution defined as being damage or environmental harm "arising from an incident which occurred before the date on which [the Directive's] provisions are implemented" (see Art. 13). The Commission also impliedly rules out retroactive liability in its 1993 Green Paper (COM(93)47fin., *supra* n.27) at point 2.1.5(iii) and explicitly in its 1997 Working Paper, *supra* n.39, at point V.4. The Lugano Convention, *supra* n.32, also rules out retroactive liability (Art. 5).

[72] Presumably this will include constructive as well as actual knowledge.

[73] See point V.4 (transitional regime).

[74] See, for instance: C. Connell, *Civil Liability for Damage of the Environment* (Bonn, Institute for European Environmental Policy, 1993) commissioned for the World Wide Fund for Nature, at 16.

Towards a European Tort Law on the Environment? 217

have notice of the ecological harm, with a cap of 30 years placed after the actual occurrence of the incident giving rise to environmental harm.[75]

Causation

One of the most onerous procedural hurdles for a plaintiff to overcome in any civil liability regime is to prove, to the requisite standard, that the defendant is responsible for the acts or omissions that have given rise to harm. As testified to by its 1989 and 1991 draft proposals, the Commission has so far been content to place the burden of proof squarely on the plaintiff's shoulders. Initially, in the 1989 draft directive, the Commission proposed that the plaintiff would have to "show the overwhelming probability of the causal relationship" between the producer's waste and the environmental harm sustained.[76] After widespread criticism of this onerous standard of proof,[77] the Commission modified its position in the 1991 draft directive, proposing instead that Member States would not be able to set the evidential burden higher than the standard of proof in civil law (i.e. balance of probabilities).[78] In its 1993 Green Paper, the Commission highlights the problems commonly associated with proving causation in environmental harm suits, such as pinpointing responsibility where there are potentially multiple sources, scientific uncertainty, or long-term chronic pollution.[79]

One possible solution in alleviating the evidentiary burden for plaintiffs, which did not appear to be taken up in the 1993 Green Paper, would be to shift the burden of proof in cases where defendants have engaged in commercial activities which entail inherently dangerous risks. This suggestion has been taken on board, for instance, in the Lugano Convention, under which courts are obliged to take due account of "the increased danger of causing damage inherent in the dangerous activity".[80] Under the German Environmental Liability Act 1990, plaintiffs need only establish a well-founded assumption of causation (*prima facie* case) in order to require the onus of proof to shift to the

---

[75] See Art. 9 of the 1989 and 1991 draft directives (*supra* nn.24 and 26). The Lugano Convention, *supra* n.32, mirrors these limitation periods (Art. 17). Admittedly, the cap on 30 years has been perceived as being arbitrary, given the fact that environmental pollution can often take a chronic form (i.e. very lengthy build-up phase such as in groundwater contamination scenarios as was made, for example, by the European Parliament in its 1990 Resolution, *supra* n.25). However, in practice, this may not pose such an acute problem in practice, as Member States will retain the right to provide for more generous time limits if the EU regime is promulgated on the legal basis of Art. 175 EC (old Art. 130s EC) by virtue of the impact of Art. 176 EC (old Art. 130t EC).

[76] Art. 4(6), *supra* n.24. This seems all the more surprising, given that the Commission acknowledges in its Explanatory Memorandum the difficulties often faced by plaintiffs in securing information regarding industrial activities (COM(89)282fin., *supra* n.24, at point 12).

[77] See e.g. Opinion of the Economic and Social Committee CES(90)215, at 3.2; Opinion of the European Parliament [1990] OJ C324/253.

[78] See Art. 4(1)(c).

[79] COM(93)47fin., *supra* n.27, at point 2.1.8.

[80] Art. 10. Such an approach has been given a favourable reception from the Economic and Social Committee in its Opinion CES226/94 I/CAT/CH/ss at point 4.3.3.

218 *Martin Hedemann-Robinson and Mark Wilde*

defendant.[81] Any such steps taken at EU level would be expected to be heavily resisted by industry. It would be seen as encroaching upon the traditional legal principles and cultures associated with the notion of equality of arms between litigants in the courtroom and regarded as tainted by the dangers inherent in having to prove a negative. Where the discourse of the dispute is to take place in the civil courts it becomes easy to ignore the informational asymmetries involved, as well as the magnitude of ecological risk. A predominant focus is placed instead on safeguarding the procedural rights of disputants perceived to be in equal positions of strength.[82]

Recently, as evidenced in its 1997 Working Paper, the Commission has indicated a willingness to be receptive to a more flexible type of evidentiary framework. In the Working Paper, the Commission proposes to mould the scope of the strict liability regime so as to focus on five areas[83] of industrial activities regulated by EU legislation, as well as to cover natural resources protected under existing EU environmental law.[84] A rebuttable presumption of a chain of causation between defendant and harm is to arise in the plaintiff's favour, where an activity in dispute is specifically addressed by the civil liability instrument. This will be able to be rebutted only by evidence on the defendant's part which satisfies a standard of "prevailing probability".[85] Such an approach in dealing with the burden of proof issue would potentially be of valuable assistance to the plaintiff in bringing a claim before the courts, effectively requiring the defendant to account publicly and in detail for his industrial activities. It would also provide a significant incentive for producers to scrutinise and monitor their activities for environmental law compliance. An additional effect of the "rebuttable presumption" test would be to supplement the important informational assistance provided by the Community's 1990 Directive on access to environmental information,[86] which requires local authorities to disclose information on local industrial compliance with environmental norms. The extent to which there will be a change in the burden of proof in favour of the plaintiff is a key issue to be resolved in the forthcoming Commission White Paper on environmental lia-

---

[81] See, for further commentary here on Germany, G. Brueggemeier, "Enterprise Liability for Environmental Damage: German and European Law" in G. Teubner, L. Farmer and D. Murphy (eds.), *Environmental Law and Ecological Responsibility* (London, Wiley, 1994) at 77 ff.

[82] See e.g. the House of Lords Select Committee on the EC Report, "Remedying Environmental Damage" (Session 1993–4, 3rd Report (HL Paper 10) at para. 58; Bowden, "Citizen Suits—Can We Afford Them and do We Need Them Anyway?" in D. Robinson and J. Dunkley (eds.), *Public Interest Perspectives in Environmental Law* (London, Wiley, 1995), at 180.

[83] Listed in point IV.2 of the 1997 Working Paper (*supra* n.39) as including Community legislation: (i) containing discharge or emission limits for hazardous substances into water or air and dealing with dangerous substances and preparations with a view to protecting the environment; (ii) with the objective to prevent and control risks of accidents and pollution; (iii) on the handling, treatment, recovery, recycling, reduction, storage, transport, transfrontier shipment and disposal of hazardous and other waste; (iv) in the field of biotechnology and (v) in the areas of transport of dangerous substances.

[84] *Ibid.*, at point IV.2(vi).

[85] See point V.1, *ibid.*

[86] EC Dir. 90/313 on the freedom of access to environmental information [1990] OJ L158/56.

Towards a European Tort Law on the Environment? 219

bility. One of the core tasks faced by the Commission here will be to strike a workable and fair balance between the need to ensure more effective compliance with environmental law through the aid of private law enforcement, whilst at the same time avoiding accusations that vexatious and wholly unsupported litigation will be legitimised.

Joint and Several Liability

One means of mitigating the difficulties in the plaintiff's task in proving a causal link between the defendant's act or omission and ecological harm in the face of a multiplicity of potentially responsible parties and other sources is to frame liability on a joint and several basis. Under the system of joint and several liability, each defendant is liable fully in respect of the action, but may then proceed to seek contributions from other liable parties on an apportionment basis. Crucially, the onus is not on the plaintiff to prove to what extent each defendant has been responsible for the environmental harm. Both the 1989 and 1991 draft directives apply joint and several liability in relation to multiple defendant producers,[87] in order to ensure effective protection of the "injured party".[88] Liability is further channelled on a joint and several basis along the waste disposal chain, so as to include producers, importers, persons in control of the waste at the material time and waste disposal undertakings.[89] The Lugano Convention has also adopted a joint and several liability basis.[90]

In its 1993 Green Paper, the Commission has noted that adjudicating strict liability on a joint and several basis comes not without its own potentially serious problems. For instance, disputes over correct apportionment could congest courts, spiral litigation costs, delay judgments, encourage forum shopping and produce the inequity of the so-called deep pocket effect, whereby plaintiffs will sue those with the greatest and readiest purse rather than necessarily consider bringing all those culpable to account.[91] In recognising these difficulties, the Commission aims to steer plaintiffs to channel actions against defendants in the order of immediacy of causation (i.e. being obliged to sue polluters first).[92] However, this will be of no assistance when the plaintiff is confronted by a number of polluters, which may well often be the case where the ecological harm is produced in areas of intense pollution (hot spots). Far more effective would be to ensure that any third party proceedings initiated by defendants do not delay execution of judgments, and thus require defendants to undertake remedial

---

[87] Art. 5 of COM(89)282fin. and COM(91)219fin., *supra* nns.24 and 26.

[88] *Ibid.*, 13th and 15th recitals.

[89] *Ibid.*, Art. 2(2).

[90] See Art. 11 of the Lugano Convention, *supra* n.32, which places the onus on the defendant to show partial responsibility in order to satisfy the courts that liability should be apportioned.

[91] COM(93)47fin., *supra* n.27, at point 2.1.4. See also C. Connell, *supra* n.74, at 13.

[92] *Ibid.* See also the Commission's 1997 Working Paper, *supra* n.39, at point V.2.

220   Martin Hedemann-Robinson and Mark Wilde

action prior to completion of adjudication apportioning liability as between multiple defendants.

Defences

A key test in analysing the stringency of strict liability toxic tort regimes is to consider the range of defences open to defendants. Defences can often qualify or reduce liability to the extent of forcing the defendant to prove unreasonable behaviour on the part of the polluter before liability attaches. The danger is, though, that such escape routes can introduce fault liability through the back door. The 1989 draft directive contains a number of partial and full exemptions for the defendant in the following cases: *force majeure*[93] and contributory negligence on the part of the injured party.[94] However, various potential escape routes are deliberately blocked off in the draft in order to maintain a channel of liability to the producer irrespective of fault. Thus, contracting out clauses *vis-à-vis* injured parties are outlawed,[95] and evidence of the existence of a licence or permit in respect of the industrial activity in dispute is ruled out as a defence.[96] Furthermore, no state-of-the-art type defence was included to mitigate against the general no-fault principle.[97] The 1991 draft directive differed from its predecessor only in allowing the producer an additional defence to be exempt from liability in the event of an intervention by a third party intended to cause ecological harm.[98] Thus, to a large extent, the Commission's early initiatives on securing strict civil liability were not seriously compromised by the introduction of defences. On the other hand, in its 1993 Green Paper, the Commission notes the balance that it deems needs to be struck in pitching strict liability so as, on the one hand, to create incentives for better environmental risk management in industry, comply with PPP as well as the prevention principle, and, on the other hand, to maintain economic viability for business under the regime.[99] This effectively reopens the whole issue of whether defences should be available on a broad standard of reasonableness. The most serious compromise of strict liability status would arise from introducing a state-of-the-art defence or mitigation on the basis that the defendant has complied with statutory norms[100] (for

---

[93] Art. 6 of COM(89)282fin., *supra* n.24.

[94] Art. 7(2), *ibid.*

[95] Art. 8, *ibid.*

[96] Art. 6(2), *ibid.*

[97] As laid down in Art. 3, *ibid.* This constitutes a significant break from the EU's approach to product liability for manufacturers, who enjoy a "state of the art" defence in the context of defective products: see Art. 7(e) of EC Dir. 85/374 on the approximation of the laws, regs. and administrative provisions of the Member States concerning liability for defective products [1985] OJ L210/29.

[98] Art. 6(1)(a) of COM(91)219fin., *supra* n.26.

[99] See points 2.1.6 and 4.1.2 of COM(93)47fin., *supra* n.27.

[100] EC Dir. 85/374 on product liability, *supra* n.97, exonerates producers from liability where "the defect is due to compliance of the product with mandatory regulations issued by the public authorities" (Art. 7(d)).

example, the holding of a licence or permit in respect of the activity concerned). Both escape routes would undermine PPP which requires responsibility to be imposed upon those who bring ecological risks into the environment.[101]

The 1997 Working Paper indicates that the Commission will continue to draw a tight rein on the number of defences available.[102] However, it is probable that a continuation with this strategy might meet with stiffer resistance at Council of Ministers level. Already, the Lugano Convention has shown how difficult it can be to secure a watertight agreement at European inter-governmental level on strict liability. Lugano contains defences in respect of ecological damage caused either necessarily from compliance with "a specific order or compulsory measure of a public authority",[103] or from pollution "at tolerable levels under local relevant circumstances",[104] in addition to those featured in the EC draft directives.[105] The Convention also allows contracting parties to enter a reservation to the effect that a state of the art would be admissible.[106] Moreover, it is only to be expected that industrial lobbying will continue to try to use the inclusion of defences based on state of the art and statutory compliance in the field of product liability as precedent.[107]

Standing to Sue

One of the most controversial and crucial issues surrounding the development of EU civil liability legislation in relation to the environment has been the question of determining whether non-governmental organisations (NGOs) such as environmental pressure groups should be able to have standing to sue. Granting such a right would run contrary to the traditional approach of civil law in requiring an individual plaintiff to have suffered personal loss or damage as a prerequisite for filing an action. The orthodox view on standing represents an obvious and considerable limitation on the number of possibilities for environmental harm claims to be heard before the civil courts. NGOs would usually be denied the possibility of suing on behalf of the damaged environment, unless their members have suffered some personal physical or economic affliction a

[101] See Connell, *supra* n.74, at 8–9.

[102] The 1997 Working Paper, *supra* n.39, recommends retaining only what it terms to be "common" defences, such as a precisely formulated Act of God, contributory negligence on the part of the plaintiff and intervention by a third party (at point V.3).

[103] Art. 8(c).

[104] Art. 8(d).

[105] See Arts. 8–9 for an overview of the defences.

[106] Art. 35(1)(b) stipulates that no liability shall be incurred by the "operator" of a dangerous activity where "the state of scientific and technical knowledge at the time of the incident was not such as to enable the existence of the dangerous properties of the substance or the significant risk involved in the operation dealing with the organism to be discovered".

[107] A state-of-the-art defence has been favoured by the House of Lords Select Committee on the EC's Report, "Remedying Environmental Damage" (Session 1993–4 3rd Report (HL Paper 10)) at para. 56.

222   Martin Hedemann-Robinson and Mark Wilde

result of the contested act or omission. Such a position is not dissimilar to that in relation to judicial review proceedings in some jurisdictions, such as England and Wales.[108] It has been argued that denying NGOs access to the civil courts raises the problem that environmental protection must often have to coincide with private commercial interests,[109] or be safe from the political pressures of any sweetheart compromise deal between public enforcement agency and defendant[110] before civil actions can be expected to be brought. The Netherlands offers an interesting precedent for adopting a bold step in favour of conferring standing to ecological interest groups to bringing civil actions (*actio popularis*). Under Dutch law, such groups have been granted the right to bring civil claims on behalf of the unowned environment in order to be able to obtain injunctive relief against polluters and even receive compensation in respect of clean-up costs incurred, the damage to the environment being categorised by the courts as damage to the interests of the ecological group.[111]

This particular issue has become increasingly recognised by the Commission as being of central importance to ensuring viability of a civil liability regime as a means of significantly enhancing horizontal environmental law enforcement. Initially, the Commission fought shy of the issue of standing in its 1989 draft proposal for a waste liability directive, leaving it up to individual Member States to determine whether or not to grant the right to sue to "common interest groups".[112] Even though the Commission recognised that environmental harm could be more readily conceived of in terms of an infringement of public, as opposed to individual, rights and interests, it was content to decide to grant only public authorities standing to sue on behalf of the general public.[113] It preferred to remain neutral, as it saw it, on the issue of granting NGOs standing, given the divergence of Member State laws on the issue.[114] Such reasoning sat uneasily alongside its concerns to eliminate competitive distortions that might arise due to differing standards on liability within the EU and to ensure a high level of environmental protection throughout the Community in accordance with Articles 2 and 174 EC (old Article 130r EC).[115]

---

[108] See s. 31(3) of the Supreme Court Act 1981 and RSC Ord. 53 r.3(7), and *R.* v. *HMIP and MAFF, ex p. Greenpeace Ltd.* (1994) 6 JEL 273.

[109] See e.g. C. Connell, *supra* n.74, at 9.

[110] See D. Robinson's comments with respect to the United States in his chapter "Public Interest Environmental Law Firms in the US" in D. Robinson and J. Dunkley (eds.), *supra* n.82, 56.

[111] For detailed discussion and examination of Dutch environmental law on this point see: P. Klik, "Group Actions in Civil Lawsuits—the New Law in the Netherlands" (1995) *European Environmental Law Review* 14; Betlem, "Standing for Ecosystems—Going Dutch" [1995] *CLJ* 153; G. Betlem, *Civil Liability for Transfrontier Pollution* (London, Dordrecht, Boston, 1993). See also M. Fuehr, B. Gebers, T. Ormond and G. Roller, "Access to Justice—Legal Standing for Environmental Associations in the EU" in D. Robinson and J. Dunkley (eds.), *supra* n.82.

[112] Art. 4(4) of COM(89)282fin, *supra* n.24. Furthermore, the draft dir. restricted the range of remedies open to NGOs to include a "prohibition or cessation of the act giving rise to" environmental harm.

[113] Art. 4(3), *ibid.*

[114] See the Commission's Explanatory Memorandum to the 1989 draft dir., COM(89)282fin., *supra* n.24, at point 7.

[115] See the 3rd and 5th recitals to the 1989 draft dir., *supra* n.24.

Towards a European Tort Law on the Environment? 223

As a result of pressure from various quarters,[116] the Commission revised its initial thinking in the 1991 draft directive on waste liability. Although, in principle, Member States were to remain in charge of determining the persons able to bring actions in the event of environmental harm,[117] they would now be required to ensure that environmental NGOs had the right at least either to seek injunctive relief against the defendant or join in existing legal proceedings.[118] However, Member States would still be entitled to lay down conditions under which such NGOs would be able to file suits. Thus, this caveat would presumably enable Member States (in some cases to continue) to require the NGO to undergo a minimum length of presence or registration within the domestic jurisdiction.[119] The Commission would have to make sure that any new proposal on civil liability emanating from the imminent White Paper would prevent these and other techniques of filtering out vexatious litigation from becoming overly restrictive. To its credit, in its 1993 Green Paper, the Commission notes the potentially adverse effects that arise in limiting the right to sue only to those who have a legally defined interest to protect, in particular where the unowned environment has been harmed.[120] These concerns need to be addressed in the Community civil liability legislation.

In its more recent 1997 Working Paper, the Commission restated its commitment to ensuring NGO access to the civil courts, as a means of ensuring appropriate state intervention to protect the environment in the context of natural resource damage and contaminated land. The proposed rights of standing appear akin in some respects to US citizen suit measures,[121] designed to empower NGOs either to challenge Member States which fail to take protective steps against polluters or, in urgent cases, to seek injunctive relief from the civil courts directly against the alleged polluter.[122] Significantly, for the first time it seems that the Commission is seeking to address the related issue of legal costs, by aiming to require that Member States organise civil procedural rules so that they are not prohibitively expensive for NGOs. The actual and potential magnitude of legal costs in environmental suits have been a major force in deterring NGOs from bringing actions in several jurisdictions. The threat of civil procedural rules such as costs following the event, as applied normally in English civil proceedings, or even simply the financial burden imposed on parties in having

---

[116] See the Economic and Social Committee's Opinion CES(90)215 at point 7.3 and the European Parliament's Resolution [1990] OJ C324/253.

[117] See Art. 4(1)(a) of COM(91)219fin., *supra* n.26.

[118] See Art. 4(3), *ibid*.

[119] Such as is the case in Belgium and to some extent in Switzerland. For details on the various Member States which set particular requirements for NGO standing, see M. Fuehr, B. Gebers, T. Ormond and G. Roller, *supra* n.111.

[120] COM(93)47fin., *supra* n.27 at point 2.1.9. See also the Economic and Social Committee's Opinion on the Green Paper CES 226/94, *supra* n.69, making a concurring note at point 4.2.1.

[121] For overviews, see D.H. Robbins, "Public Interest environmental litigation in the US", in D. Robinson and J. Dunkley (eds.), *supra* n.82, at 9.

[122] See point V.5 of the 1997 Working Paper, *supra* n.39.

224   *Martin Hedemann-Robinson and Mark Wilde*

to meet their own legal costs[123] can easily deter an NGO, whose sources of finance often rest on not unlimited charitable funding, from embarking upon litigation which might lead to its insolvency.[124] Such a deterrence factor might be reasonably mitigated by empowering the courts to ensure that Member States underwrite NGO legal costs unless the court deems the action to have been brought without any substantial justification. Steps have been taken with this aim in mind in the USA under the Equal Access to Justice Act 1980 with regard to NGOs' attorney fees.[125]

That the Commission will face serious resistance from industrial lobby groups and certain Member States on this point is, of course, clear. The Lugano Convention reflects this in having been able to secure only a meek and rather vague compromise in conferring upon environmental NGOs the right to "request" action to be taken in respect of environmental harm, the Contracting Parties remaining competent to determine issues of admissibility, forum and legal effects of such review procedures.[126]

Remedies

Without the availability of a sufficient range of remedies suited to the task of achieving a high level of environmental protection, any EU-wide strict liability regime on ecological harm would probably be meaningless. Liability which does not result in adequate remediation of environmental conditions according to ecological standards falls into the trap of turning effectively into a licence or tax to pollute.[127] Given that the traditional view of tort law on remedies has focused on usually permitting the payment of damages as a means of recompensing victims of loss and/or injury to property or person, it is not difficult to see how ineffective, indeed positively harmful, this approach would be in the environmental pollution context. As Steele has pointed out, the rhetoric of rectification of a wrong in tort law, which centres on compensating for market losses, should not be equated with physical rectification of environmental harm.[128]

It is therefore significant to note that the Commission throughout has rightly sought to introduce remedies which are suited to serve environmental goals as opposed to merely short-term economic interest. The 1989 draft directive pro-

[123] See e.g. the comments in relation to the lack of NGO actions in view of the requirement to be represented by counsel in E. Fernandes, "Collective interests in Brazilian Environmental Law" in D. Robinson and J. Dunkley (eds.), *supra* n.82, 126.

[124] See the comments by M. Day, "Shifting the Balance" in D. Robinson and J. Dunkley (eds.), *supra* n.82, at 184 ff.

[125] See, for commentary, D.H. Robbins, *supra* n.121, at 25.

[126] Art. 18.

[127] See A. Murdie, *Environmental Law and the Citizen in Action* (London, Earthscan, 1993) at 122, who makes similar and related arguments on the implications of civil damages in relation to environmental protection.

[128] J. Steele, "Remedies and Remediation—Foundational Issues in Environmental Liability" (1995) 58 *MLR* 615, at 619.

Towards a European Tort Law on the Environment? 225

vides plaintiffs with the traditional market-value options of requiring indemni-
fication, whether in respect,of damage done to property, physical injury or of
clean-up measures already taken. In addition the 1989 draft directive seeks to
address environmental damage,[129] through the possibility of securing injunctive
relief or reimbursement in respect of clean-up measures in relation to ecological
harm. Specifically, it envisages plaintiffs being able to bring legal proceedings in
order to obtain a "prohibition or cessation" of the activity in question, reimbursement of measures taken to prevent ecological harm, restoration of the
environment to its state prior to ecological harm and reimbursement in respect
of expenditure incurred in connection with steps taken with this restorative purpose in mind.[130] As regards remedies available to what the draft directive refers
to as "common interest groups", the draft text restricts these to include prohibition or cessation of the activity concerned as well as reimbursement in respect
of expenditure incurred with a view to preventing ecological harm or securing
its restoration.[131] The 1991 draft proposal made a few important refinements to
these provisions. Injunctive relief would be available in respect of omissions as
well as activities, and the uncompromising rhetoric of restoration in relation to
the environment was replaced with the more subjective and malleable term
"reinstatement".[132] Furthermore, ecological NGOs would be entitled to seek
the full range of injunctive relief on offer as well as reimbursement for clean-up
or preventive action.[133]

However, it is significant to note that underlying the wide range of remedies
foreseen by the 1989 and 1991 draft texts there exists an important qualification.
Applications to court to "restore" or "reinstate" the environment to the condition it was in prior to its impairment, or the claim for reimbursement in respect
of expenditure incurred to this end, is made subject to a cost-benefit analysis.[134]
Thus, where the costs substantially exceed the benefit arising for the environment from such reinstatement or restoration and other alternative measures to
these ends "may be undertaken at a substantially lower cost", then the plaintiff's
range of remedies is amended to fit these alternative strategies. In this sense, the
range of remedies open to plaintiffs is narrowed according to an indeterminate
scale of reasonableness, whereby the economic interests of the defendant (and
perhaps wider community) are pitched against ecological principles. To what
extent this formula is compatible with the EU environmental policy goals under
Articles 174–176 EC remains an open question, and will be dependent largely on
Member States' court reactions. In a similar way, the Lugano Convention also
heavily qualifies the extent of its commitment to compensate plaintiffs for
having undertaken "measures of reinstatement" and "preventive measures" in

---

[129] See Art. 4(1)(c) and (e) of COM(89)282fin., *supra* n.24.
[130] See Art. 4(1)(a), (b) and (d) respectively, *ibid.*
[131] Art. 4(4), *ibid.*
[132] See Art. 4(1)(b) of COM(91)219fin., *supra* n.26.
[133] Art. 4(3), *ibid.*
[134] Art. 4(2) of COM(89)282fin. and COM(91)219fin, *supra* nn.24 and 26.

defence of the environment.[135] The Commission has indicated that it is keen to retain this balancing process, despite the difficulties and dangers in assessing ecological damage, in terms of, or alongside economic loss.[136] To what extent such weighing up of competing interests will lean towards accommodating industrial over ecological interests will depend greatly on how strictly and precisely the Commission will propose to frame for the national courts the parameters regarding remedies pertaining to reinstatement of the environment. The 1989 and 1991 draft directives simply shelve this difficult political issue for the national courts to resolve.

Insurance and Joint Compensation Systems

It is not without good reason that litigation is often described as being a weapon of last resort. For even a strict liability regime will not be able to secure remedial action in respect of all incidents of ecological harm. For instance, where the defendant is insolvent, untraceable or immune from culpability due to the absence of retroactive liability, the option of civil action is either unavailable or worthless.[137] Insurance schemes constitute a potentially effective means of combating the problem of financial inability of a polluter to remedy ecological harm. Joint compensation schemes (JCS) feature as a potential back-up to situations of untraceability, coming closer to accommodating PPP than the alternative of general taxation. These systems are designed to pool funding from those sectors of industry most likely to generate ecological harm. They aim to provide a collective source of finance to meet the costs of environmental litigation sustained by a particular individual member of the group or where pollution can only be traced to an activity associated with the sector as opposed to particular parties. Within Europe, the evolution of these systems, both environmental insurance and JCS, is at a relatively early stage in terms of commercial availability and in terms of public regulation. Nevertheless, the Commission has increasingly recognised their importance in underpinning a prospective EU strict liability regime.

In the earlier stages of crafting civil liability initiatives, the Commission remained tentative in coming forward with concrete suggestions as regards insurance cover and JCS. The 1989 draft directive effectively avoided the issue

---

[135] Art. 2(8) of the Lugano Convention, *supra* n.32, defines measures of reinstatement to mean "any *reasonable* measures aiming to reinstate or restore damaged or destroyed components of the environment, or to introduce, where *reasonable*, the equivalent of these components into the environment". Art. 2(9) describes preventive measures as including "any *reasonable* measures taken by any person, after an incident has occurred to prevent or minimise loss or damage." (emphasis supplied).

[136] See COM(93)47fin., *supra* n.27, at point 2.1.10. See also the 1997 Working Paper, *supra* n.39, at para. IV.4.a, in which the Commission favours applying a "cost-benefit" test in order to keep restoration costs "reasonable" and setting minimum "baseline" conditions in respect of natural resources, below which restoration becomes mandatory.

[137] See C. Connell, *supra* n.74, at 16.

of compensation in respect of damage to the environment in cases of insolvency and non-traceability. Instead, it kicked the issue into the long grass, stipulating that it would be dealt with by a separate regulation.[138] The Commission preferred to remain cautious in deciding how to tackle non-recoverable ecological damage and injury to the environment, aiming to postpone a decision until the end of 1992.[139] In its Explanatory Memorandum to the 1989 proposal, the Commission recognised that failure to harmonise rules on apportionment of costs could lead to competitive distortions in terms of transaction costs for business within the EU as well as an undermining principle set out in Articles 2 and 174 EC (such as the principle of securing a high level of environmental protection throughout the Community).[140] Nevertheless, in view of the resistance of industry to being obliged to organise even limited insurance cover and the rapidly evolving state of this market, the Commission preferred to bide its time. The European Parliament's reaction was less abstentionist,[141] proposing that a residual duty of intervention be placed on Member States in the event of non-traceability of culpable polluters,[142] the introduction of minimum levels of compulsory insurance on producers[143] as well as the introduction of a centrally organised JCS.[144] The Commission's 1991 amended draft directive responded in part to these counter-proposals, requiring that producers and eliminators of waste would be obliged to be "covered by insurance or any other financial security". However, it abstained from providing guidance on or definitions of minimum coverage,[145] whilst agreeing to study the feasibility of a JCS arrangement along the lines suggested by the European Parliament.[146]

Whilst both the subjects of insurance and JCS have received greater prominence in the Commission's subsequent publicised deliberations on horizontal enforcement of EU environmental law, it is not yet clear to what extent they will feature as a complement to a prospective strict liability regime. The 1997 Working Paper is noticeably silent on the point. In its 1993 Green Paper, the Commission discussed the relative merits and pitfalls involved. It noted, for

[138] See Art. 11 of COM(89)282fin., *supra* n.24.

[139] *Ibid.*

[140] See point 10 of the Explanatory Memorandum, COM(89)282fin., *supra* n.24.

[141] See also the Opinion of the Economic and Social Committee (CES(90)215, *supra* n.116, at point 10.1 where it argues that delay in addressing non-recoverability through strict liability would simply encourage Member States to develop their own rules, thereby jeopardising chances of EU harmonisation.

[142] See Art. 8a of the draft modified text of a civil liability dir. on waste proposed by the European Parliament in its Resolution A3–272/90 [1990] OJ C324/255.

[143] Art. 11 of the EP's amended draft text (as cited in *ibid.*) would require minimum cover of Euro 70m in respect of damage property and person, and Euro 50m in respect to environmental impairment (Euro 100m for radioactive waste).

[144] Art. 11(5) of the EP's draft text suggested the Commission examine the feasibility of setting up a "European Fund for Compensation for Damage and Impairment of the Environment caused by waste", in the context of requiring the Council to decide upon common rules regarding limitation of liability, insolvency or non-traceability.

[145] See Art. 11(1) of COM(91)219fin., *supra* n.26.

[146] Art. 11(2), *ibid.*

228 *Martin Hedemann-Robinson and Mark Wilde*

instance, the attraction of insurance as a lever for ensuring an enhancement of environmental risk management although the extent (or indeed availability) of cover would depend on satisfying the insurer of sufficient quality controls. However, it also observed how this had to take into account the technical difficulties faced by the insurer in assessing probability and extent of ecological damage. Such uncertainty affects the degree of availability as well as terms and conditions of insurance policies (for example, the inclusion of large deductibles in the event of loss, or stipulations to the effect that cover is limited to sudden events only). Compulsory insurance runs the risk of industry being captive to very high premiums. The Commission, however, appeared to indicate that it was receptive to introducing mandatory insurance, coupled with an assurance that Member States provide sufficient top-up cover for bad risks and allowances for small and medium-sized enterprises (SMEs).[147]

Likewise, as far as JCS systems are concerned, the Commission appears to favour their development as a complement to strict liability. The 1997 Working Paper recognises that, in the event of non-traceability of ecological harm to any particular polluter, JCS offers itself as a quick and relatively non-punitive option to financing the costs of ecological restoration. Whilst acknowledging that such a shared form of responsibility deviates somewhat from the ideals of PPP, in burdening a particular industrial sector with the responsibility of rectifying ecological harm, the Commission accepts that this comes as close as possible to ensuring that the polluter pays rather than the general taxpayer.[148] It is not clear whether the Commission continues to contemplate developing a regulated and centralised JCS system along the lines outlined in its 1989 and 1991 proposals. In the 1993 Green Paper it has shown favour for alternative decentralised forms of JCS.[149] Moreover, it may perhaps be significant that the most recent draft of the proposed directive on landfill waste[150] has abandoned providing for any publicly regulated landfill aftercare funds, as was proposed in earlier draft versions,[151] in favour of focusing on augmenting pricing to cover aftercare (i.e. up to 50 years after closure of landfill sites).[152] However they evolve in practice, it is clear that the Commission must ensure that JCS are used as a back-up measure rather than as an alternative to strict liability and insur-

---

[147] COM(93)47fin., *supra* n.27, at point 2.1.11. This approach perhaps contemplates a partnership between government and industry in insurance, akin possibly to that applied in export credit guarantee schemes.

[148] See point 3.0 of the Explanatory Memorandum annexed to the 1991 draft proposal, *supra* n.26.

[149] See COM(93)47fin., *supra* n.27, at 28.

[150] See COM(97)105fin. Draft proposal for a Council dir. on the landfill of waste (published on 5 Mar. 1997).

[151] See Art. 18 of COM(91)102 SYN Proposal for a Council dir. on the landfill of waste of 23 Apr. 1991 [1991] OJ C190/1) and COM(93)275fin. Amended proposal for a Council dir. on the landfill of waste of 10 June 1993.

[152] See Art. 10 of COM(97)105fin., *supra* n.44. See also the Opinion of the Economic and Social Committee CES 226/94, *supra* n.69, at para. 4.5.3 which criticises a single European JCS Fund for being inflexible and weakening the principle of individual liability.

Towards a European Tort Law on the Environment? 229

ance, so that PPP is not unduly compromised.[153] Although the position has not yet been made clear, as the White Paper is still pending, it appears that the Commission may well be leaning towards giving the markets and Member States, at least for an interim period, a free rein to decide upon the parameters of insurance and JCS.[154]

STATE LIABILITY FOR ENVIRONMENTAL HARM—*FRANCOVICH* AND TORTIOUS LIABILITY OF GOVERNMENTAL ACTIONS AND OMISSIONS

Parallel to the discussions and deliberations outlined above about creating an EU-wide civil liability regime to aid horizontal enforcement of Community environmental norms (i.e. actions as between private persons), the ECJ has since the beginning of the 1990s begun to develop an important body of jurisprudence establishing a Member State liability regime capable of enhancing vertical enforcement of Community norms (i.e. actions between private individual plaintiffs and Member State defendants).[155] This body of case law, which commenced with the well-known case of *Francovich*,[156] opened up the possibility for private individuals, under certain conditions, being able to sue Member States for compensation where the latter fail to carry out their duties to implement Community law. The possibilities and ramifications of this development towards a European tort of breach of statutory duty in terms of Community environmental law have only just begun to be evaluated.[157] Given the fact that the responsibility for implementing EU environmental law almost exclusively rests with Member States, the Commission having only limited powers and resources to enforce their proper execution through the protracted route of taking infraction proceedings under Article 226 EC (old Article 169 EC), legal redress open to private individuals against Member States assumes particular importance. The ECJ has so far shied away from developing a horizontal dimension to *Francovich*, so as to create a cause of action for private individuals against other private persons in respect of breaches of Community law,

---

[153] See the comments made by C. Connell, *supra* n.74, at 16; House of Lords Select Committee on the EC Report, *supra* n.52, at 61.

[154] Such a stance would mirror the position taken as regards the Lugano Convention, *supra* n.32, which simply provides that "where appropriate" contracting parties shall ensure operators be required to "participate in a financial security scheme or to have and maintain a financial guarantee up to a certain limit, of such type and terms as specified by internal law, to cover the liability under this Convention" (Art. 12).

[155] For a useful overview of the area see R. D'Sa, *European Community Law and Civil Remedies in England and Wales* (London, Sweet & Maxwell, 1994) at 150–74.

[156] Case C–6 & 9/90 *Francovich and Bonifaci* v. *Italy* [1991] ECR I–5403.

[157] See e.g. S. Elworthy and J. Holder, *Environmental Protection—Text and Materials* (London, Butterworths, 1997) at 201 ff.; Lefevere, "State Liability for Breaches of Community Law" (1996) *European Environmental Law Review* 237; K. Macrory, "Environmental Citizenship and the Law: Repairing the European Road" (1996) 8 *JEL* 219; R. Gray, "Equitable Property" (1994) 47(2) *CLP* 157.

230 *Martin Hedemann-Robinson and Mark Wilde*

although such a development has been recently mooted by Advocate General van Gerven in the *Banks*[158] case.

The contours of the conditions for state liability in respect of contraventions of Community law have been set out in a series of cases by the ECJ. The Court essentially created this new unwritten[159] cause of action in order to ensure that Member States would not be able to evade their Community obligations to establish new rights for the benefit of private individuals. It was principally designed to bolster the legal position of the individual where the doctrines of direct effect[160] and indirect effect[161] might not be able to assist individual litigants in ensuring that Member States adhered to their Community obligations. In *Francovich* itself the plaintiff sought to rely upon Council Directive 80/987[162] which harmonised the protection of workers in the event of insolvency of the employer. Under the instrument, Member States are required to guarantee workers a minimum amount of unpaid wages owed by the insolvent employer. As the Italian government had failed to implement the directive into national law within the specified deadline, Andrea Francovich sued the Italian state for compensation in respect of the economic loss he incurred in being unable to reclaim outstanding wages. The ECJ first confirmed that the directive was not directly effective, in that its terms were not sufficiently precise and unconditional to be capable of being relied upon by the plaintiff before the Italian courts.[163] Neither would the doctrine of indirect effect have been any use to Mr Francovich because no relevant national legislation covering the area of insolvency protection had been passed whose interpretation could have been made to conform with the terms of the directive. The ECJ then held that, subject to three conditions, the plaintiff would be able to recover compensation from the

---

[158] Case C–128/92, *Banks* v. *British Coal* [1994] ECR I–1209.

[159] There is no express provision in the Treaty of Rome providing for non-contractual state liability in respect of failure to carry out Community obligations. The ECJ has derived it from basic tenets of Community law, including in particular the general obligations imposed on Member States under Art. 10 EC (old Art. 5 EC) "to take all appropriate measures . . . to ensure the fulfillment of obligations arising out of [the] EC Treaty" as well to "abstain from any measure which could jeopardise the attainment on the objectives of [the EC] Treaty".

[160] The doctrine of direct effect as laid down by the ECJ (e.g. in Case 26/62, *Van Gend en Loos* v. *Netherlands* [1963] ECR 1) confers on private persons the right to enforce Community norms directly before the national courts where the Community norm is sufficiently precise and unconditional. The ECJ has confirmed that, subject to the above qualification, certain EC Treaty Arts. (e.g. most notably Arts. 28, 39, 43, 49, 81, 82 and 141 EC (old Arts. 30, 48, 52, 59, 85, 86 and 119 EC respectively) as well as regulations may be enforced against Member States (vertical direct effect) as well as against other private individuals (horizontal direct effect). The ECJ has, however, confirmed that Community dirs. cannot have horizontal direct effect: see Case 152/84, *Marshall* v. *Southampton and South-West Hampshire Area Health Authority* [1986] ECR 723.

[161] Indirect effect relates to the body of jurisprudence developed by the ECJ which requires Member State courts, "in so far as is possible" in accordance with domestic constitutional law, to interpret national legislation to be in conformity with Community dirs.: see e.g. Cases 14/83, *Von Colson and Kamann* v. *Land Nordrhein Westfalen* [1984] ECR 1891 and C–106/89, *Marleasing SA* v. *La Comercial Internacional de Alimentacion SA* [1992] ECR I–4135.

[162] [1980] OJ L283/23.

[163] The dir. left Member States discretion in determining the identity of the entity which would be responsible to make payment such payments (Art. 5).

Towards a European Tort Law on the Environment? 231

Italian state in having failed to meet its Community obligations: namely, that the directive had to entail the granting of individual rights, it being possible to identify the content of those rights from the directive's provisions and that there existed a causal link between the breach of the Member State's obligations and the loss and/or damage sustained by the plaintiff.[164]

In subsequent cases, the ECJ has further refined the parameters of state liability. In *Brasserie du Pêcheur*,[165] the ECJ clarified that Member States would be liable to pay compensation in respect of any binding Community norm where the EU source of law in question was intended to confer individual rights, the breach of this norm was "sufficiently serious" and there existed a causal link between the breach and the damage suffered by the plaintiff.[166] According to the Court, "sufficiently serious" meant that a Member State had to have "manifestly and gravely disregarded the limits on its discretion". The ECJ indicated that the national courts would have to evaluate this from a range of factors, including whether the Community norm was ambiguous or otherwise unclear, the breach was intentional or involuntary, any error of law was excusable, any Community institution had contributed to inducing the Member State to commit an infringement or whether the defendant state had adopted or retained any national measures contrary to Community law.[167] Thus, the ECJ confirmed that Member State liability for Community law violations was subject to a concept of fault commensurate with that adopted in relation to non-contractual liability of Community institutions.[168] In that sense, liability cannot in principle be characterised as being strict. However, the Court has also confirmed that where Community norms leave Member States with no discretion as regards implementation of EU policy, then mere infringement of the norm may be sufficient to constitute a sufficiently serious breach.[169] Thus, for instance, in the cases of *Dillenkofer*[170] and *Francovich* the Court confirmed that a failure to implement unambiguous obligations of directives by the set deadline would be sufficiently serious infringement of EU law.

Notwithstanding the possibilities seemingly opened up by virtue of the *Francovich* jurisprudence in terms of enhancing environmental law enforcement through a civil liability mechanism, there are serious limitations which so far the

[164] See para. 40 of the judgment.

[165] Cases C–46,48/93, *Brasserie de Pêcheur SA* v. *Germany and R.* v. *Sec State for Transport, ex p. Factortame* [1996] ECR I–1029.

[166] See para. 51 of the judgment. Germany and the UK had breached EC Treaty Arts. in these cases (Arts. 28 and 43 EC (old Arts. 30 and 52 EC) respectively).

[167] See para. 56 of the judgment.

[168] See Arts. 235 and 288 EC (old Arts. 178 and 215(2) EC respectively). The ECJ has confirmed that Community institutions will not be liable for any private losses incurred as a result of unlawful Community legislation, unless there has been a "sufficiently flagrant violation of a superior rule of law for the protection of the individual": see e.g. Case 5/71, *Aktien-Zuckerfabrik Schöppenstedt* v. *Council* [1971] ECR 975, at para. 11 of the judgment.

[169] See e.g. Case C–392/93, *R.* v. *HM Treasury, ex p. BT plc* [1996] 2 CMLR 217; Cases C–178–179, 188–190/94 *Dillenkofer et al.* v. *Germany* [1996] 3 CMLR 469.

[170] *Ibid.*

232 Martin Hedemann-Robinson and Mark Wilde

ECJ has been willing to attach to this jurisprudential development. First, there is the issue of standing. Currently, the case law requires that plaintiffs demonstrate that they have suffered personal damage or loss as a result of the breach of Community law in order to be able to bring proceedings. This limitation can be traced back to the ECJ's anthropogenic conception of the Community legal order, namely as one which "not only imposes obligations on individuals but is also intended to confer upon them rights which become part of their legal heritage".[171] Continued insistence upon there being personal loss will severely limit the range of actions that might be brought in order to ensure Member State compliance with EU environmental legislation, as many types of environmental harm have either no, or too tenuous a, link with an abrogation of private rights, such as a failure to adhere to Community measures designed to protect nature and wildlife.

So far the ECJ has not specifically ruled whether it would accept the possibility of individuals or NGOs suing Member States on behalf of the environment itself. Although the Court has indicated that individuals should be able to rely on the doctrine of direct effect in order to enforce certain Community environmental directives, this appears to be only where public (i.e. human) health and welfare are at stake.[172] For instance, in the *Groundwater* case,[173] the ECJ stated that Member States were obliged to implement into the national laws sufficiently clear and precise provisions enabling individuals to be in a position to enforce their rights in terms of the discharge limits and controls imposed by Directive 80/68, concerned with protecting the quality of groundwater. It was no defence for Member States to argue that there was no need for implementation, given that the directive contained directly effective provisions.[174] Where, however, the object of the Community environmental norm is to protect the environment as distinct from immediate human health and welfare issues, such as in the case of the Wild Birds and Habitat Directives,[175] the requisite private (material or economic) interest of the individual appears to be missing. Moreover, it appears doubtful, on reading the current case law, to expect that the ECJ will accept the possibility of NGOs being able to sue on behalf of the environment or to construe ecological harm to be damage sustained by the organisation itself.[176] As has been pointed out elsewhere, the development of state liability under *Francovich* has firm anthropogenic roots.[177] It has been

---

[171] See Case 26/62, *Van Gend en Loos* [1962] ECR 1 at 12.

[172] See for instance the following cases illustrating this point: Case C–58/89 *Commission* v. *Germany* [1991] ECR I–4983; Case 361/88, *Commission* v. *Germany* [1991] ECR I–2567.

[173] Case C–131/88, *Commission* v. *Germany* [1991] ECR I–825.

[174] See paras. 8–9 of the judgment, *ibid*.

[175] EC Council Dir. 79/409 on the conservation of birds, *supra* n.60, and EC Council Dir. 92/43 on the conservation of natural habitats and of fauna and flora, *supra* n.61.

[176] See Van Gerven AG's comments linking "environmental groups" with the task of enforcing dirs. in Case C–131/88, *Commission* v. *Germany* [1991] ECR I–825, at 850.

[177] See R. Macrory, *supra* n.157 at 222 ff.; S. Elworthy and J. Holder, *supra* n.157, at 332; and S. Grosz, "Access to Environmental Justice in Public Law" in D. Robinson and J. Dunkley (eds.), *supra* n.82, at 201.

Other problems also seriously qualify the impact of *Francovich* in terms of being a potential basis for pursuing civil environmental litigation. At the moment the Court has not indicated that it will contemplate requiring national courts to afford any remedy other than monetary compensation to victims. Yet, as has already been discussed earlier, injunctive relief is perhaps the most effective civil remedy for stemming or preventing environmental harm. Furthermore, where EU legislation provides Member States with a range of implementation options, or at least refrains from obliging them to adopt any concrete control standards, this will make it far more difficult for the individual plaintiff to argue that the defendant Member State has committed a sufficiently serious breach of the Community environmental norm in issue.[178] This trend is likely to continue in relation to the development of the Community's environmental policy for a number of reasons: the continuing entrenchment of the doctrine of subsidiarity,[179] under which Member States will expect a range of options for policy implementation; the availability of temporary and indefinite derogations for Member States under the auspices of Title XIX on the Environment (Articles 174–176 EC);[180] and moves toward incorporating a more economically and environmentally disparate membership of the EU under the Agenda 2000 Programme. In addition, the issue of causation is likely to pose a familiar substantial obstacle in the way of proving state liability claims. This will be so, especially as environmental principles contained in Articles 6 and 174 EC pertaining to the precautionary approach, preventive action and attainment of a high level of environmental protection, are, in contrast with key market freedoms such as the free movement of goods and services, not directly effective.[181]

---

[178] For similar comments, see J.G.J. Lefevere, *supra* n.157, at 240; S. Elworthy and J. Holder, *supra* n.157 at 204. See also J. Holder, "A Dead End for Direct Effect? Prospects for Enforcement of EC Environmental Law by Individuals" (1996) 8 *JEL* 313.

[179] The doctrine of subsidiarity, incorporated as a general principle in the Treaty of Rome by virtue of the TEU, is housed in Art. 5(2) EC (old Art. 3b(2) EC). The ToA attached a Protocol on the Application of the Principle of Subsidiarity and Proportionality to the EC Treaty, in order to flesh out the doctrine in more detail. The seventh paragraph of the Protocol specifically calls for a decentralised approach to implementation: "(7) Regarding the nature and extent of Community action, Community measures should leave as much scope for national decision as possible, consistent with securing the aim of the measure and observing the requirements of the [EC] Treaty. While respecting Community law, care should be taken to respect well-established national arrangements and the organization and working of member states legal systems. *Where appropriate and subject to the need for proper enforcement, Community measures should provide member states with alternative ways to achieve the objectives of the measures*" (emphasis supplied).

[180] See comments made by D. Chalmers, *supra* n.13, at 91–3.

[181] See J. Holder, *supra* n.178, at 334; R. Macrory, *supra* n.157, at 231.

234 Martin Hedemann-Robinson and Mark Wilde

These limitations were recently highlighted by the English High Court in the *Bowden*[182] case. In that case Carnwath J struck out a claim by Bowden, a mussel fisherman from the south coast of England, for damages in respect of alleged breaches of Community legislation on marine pollution and shellfish protection. An integral part of the judge's reasoning was his conclusion that none of the EU legislation specifically granted rights to individuals. He refused to accept that such rights could be implied from the fact that the Community measures were designed to protect the environment or public in general (for example, as consumers or bathers). As regards the plaintiff's allegations that the defendants had failed to secure the implementation of the Shellfish Waters Directive,[183] in not having designated protected shellfish waters, including the area off the Devon coast fished by Bowden, the judge opined:

> However, even if it were established that failure to designate the relevant area was a breach of the Directive, it would be a breach of an obligation owed to the public in general. There is nothing which could tie it to the specific rights of individuals, or which would enable the content of those rights to be ascertained. Accordingly, there is no basis for a claim in damages under that Directive.[184]

It is to be regretted that the judge was prepared to make such a bold assertion without referring first to the ECJ for a preliminary ruling under Article 234 EC on the issue, not least because there is a lack of case law from Luxembourg so far on the extent of state liability for non-implementation of Community environmental legislation.[185]

Most commentators have thus far remained rightly sceptical of the potential impact that the so-called *Francovich* jurisprudence may have in terms of advancing ecological protection. Much will depend upon the ECJ's preparedness in future to accommodate and develop an environmental protection dimension to its existing case law. Hitherto, the Court has been keen to enhance private individual involvement through the creation of rights and remedies in order to develop the liberal ideals underpinning the Community. Yet times have changed, in constitutional terms, for the EU. Under the new Articles 2 and 6 of

---

[182] *Bowden v. South West Water Services Limited, Secretary of State for the Environment and Director General of Water Services* [1998] 3 CMLR 330.

[183] Dir. 79/923 [1979] OJ L281/47.

[184] *Ibid.*, at para. 58 of the judgment.

[185] It is, for instance, well-established by the ECJ that where a national court considers that Community law is relevant to litigation at hand, and that the correct interpretation and/or application of that law is unclear, the national court is obliged to refer the matter to the ECJ for a preliminary ruling under Art. 234 EC, notwithstanding that it is not a final court of appeal: Case 166/73 *Rheinmühlen-Düsseldorf v. Einfuhrh und Vorratsstelle für Getreide* [1974] ECR 33. A reference to the ECJ will not be required only where the correct interpretation of Community law is, in the absence of existing ECJ precedent, "so obvious as to leave no scope for any reasonable doubt as to the manner in which the question raised is to be resolved. Before it comes to [that] conclusion, [it] must be convinced that the matter is equally obvious to the courts of the other member states and the Court of Justice": Case 283/81 *Srl CILFIT and Lanificio di Gavardo SpA* v. *Ministry of Health* [1982] ECR 472 at para. 16 of the judgment. The legal effects of the *Francovich* jurisprudence in relation to *Bowden* could hardly be said to be at all obvious.

the EC Treaty, as amended by the ToA, there is to be a stronger commitment placed on the EU towards ensuring greater ecological responsibility.[186] Indeed, it can now be argued with increasing credibility that the amendments made to the EC Treaty by virtue of the ToA place environmental protection on a par with traditional single market goals. Bearing in mind this change of emphasis in the Community's list of priorities, it will be interesting to see whether the ECJ will develop its jurisprudence on state liability, direct and indirect effect to accommodate the new ecological dimension or *telos* inherent within the Community's constitutional framework. Much will depend on the Court's preparedness to alter its baseline perceptions about the proper functions of its rights jurisprudence, and to concede that the search for environmental protection is as much an integral part of the individual's legal heritage in the Community legal order as is the human construct of market integration and freedoms.[187] It is only then that, in the words of Kevin Gray, the ECJ will "come close to conceding the existence of and individual right to the effective and structured management of the ecosystem on behalf of all citizens".[188]

CONCLUSIONS

Many political and legal problems that have accompanied the tentative developments at Community level towards initiating a collective approach to civil liability in respect of environmental harm remain to a large extent unresolved. Notwithstanding the wealth of discussion and argument that has abounded in Brussels on this topic, it remains the case that the public is largely in the dark as regards whether and what sort of civil liability regime may now be framed at Community level.

In terms of political will obstacles, the Council has fought shy of introducing legislation on a qualified majority voting basis, remaining sensitive to the subsidiarity concerns of certain Member States, notably the UK, that strategies in respect of ensuring compliance with environmental standards should be developed and implemented by the Member States themselves in the absence of any clear competition-based reasons for harmonisation.[189] It is not clear to what extent this factor has changed. Indeed, the reluctance of the Council to enact legislation may now be more entrenched than ever, given that since the first draft directive in 1989 several Member States have enacted toxic tort laws.[190]

---

[186] See *supra* at n.11.
[187] See, for a similar discussion, R. Macrory, *supra* n.157, at 233.
[188] K. Gray, *supra* n.157, at 205.
[189] See the Memorandum of the UK Government, *Response to the Communication from the Commission of the EC (COM(93)47fin) Green Paper on Remedying Environmental Damage* (Oct. 1993) at 1–2.
[190] Including Denmark (Act on Compensation for Environmental Damage 225/1994); Finland ((Environmental Damage Compensation Act 737/1994); Germany (Environmental Liability Act 1991); and Sweden (Environmental Protection Acts 1969:387 and 1986:225)

236   *Martin Hedemann-Robinson and Mark Wilde*

As far as outstanding legal issues are concerned, the Commission's draft directives and subsequent discussion papers indicate that much progress has been made on its part in recognising the importance of ensuring that a Community-inspired civil action will be readily accessible to the public (individuals and NGOs) and contain remedies suitable for ensuring immediate remedial action in respect of ecological damage. Thus, for instance, the Commission appears now to be contemplating a realignment of the burden of proof, the availability of injunctive relief, legal standing for environmental NGOs and affordable legal costs for plaintiffs. Cumulatively, these procedural innovations will go a long way to easing the legal and financial burdens faced by the environmental lobby when deciding whether to pursue environmental tort claims. One recent commentary on the draft White Paper has suggested that "this is a powerful legal cocktail indeed, and one which will radically alter the common law liability system".[191]

However, a variety of indications suggest that Community legislation on civil liability for environmental harm, when it finally emerges, may not be able to open up a second legal front against polluters. Many legal issues vital to securing the effectiveness of civil litigation have either remained untouched or insufficiently dealt with by the Commission so far. For instance, in its 1997 Working Paper, the Commission appears wedded to the concern that restoration costs imposed on defendants be kept to reasonable level (according to a cost-benefit test) and that liability should only be triggered when "significant or considerable" ecological damage has been done (according to a minimum threshold test).[192] This appears to be very close to a fault-based approach. In addition, the Commission has failed to secure clarification on insurance issues, an issue which in practice lies at the heart of most large-scale civil litigation. Without adequate insurance cover being in place, private environmental law enforcers will think twice about bringing civil actions, because the outcome may well be insolvency rather than clean-up. Thus, it is notable that the Commission remains sensitive to defendant producers' concerns. Moreover, so far the Commission has been unimaginative in addressing the issue of legal costs, a key issue in any civil litigation let alone toxic tort claims. Few NGOs will be able to muster the financial resources to swallow substantial legal costs. It is surprising and disappointing that the Commission has not at least floated the idea of Member State government financial support for private claims brought in good faith.

There is no doubt that, if and when Community legislation is passed, it will contribute in psychological terms (if not in terms of immediate tangible results) towards promoting the adherence of Community environmental norms. It is abundantly clear that, on its own, the Commission is unable to find the resources or means to ensure that Member States enforce Community environmental legislation *vis-à-vis* commercial and non-commercial actors. The overall

[191] R. Lee, "Draft White Paper on Environmental Liability" (1999) 8 *Environmental Liability* at 5.

[192] *Supra*, n.39, at 3 (Section IV.4.a).

success of a EU toxic tort regime will depend largely on its ability to harness the resources of the private enforcer (for example, NGOs or members of the public), so as to deter violations of and encourage detailed monitoring of compliance with EU environmental standards. In the absence of a directive on civil liability passed by the Community, and without radical changes made to the ECJ's existing *Francovich* jurisprudence on Member State liability for breaches of Community law, NGOs and individuals will not be equipped with the legal tools they need to assist the Commission in ensuring Member State implementation of binding EU environmental standards.

Defects aside, the Commission's strategy on eco-civil liability, when finally crystallised and if adopted by the Council of Ministers will blow a welcome draught of fresh air into the rather stagnant area of environmental law enforcement.

POSTSCRIPT

Subsequent to the completion of this chapter in 1999, the European Commission published its White Paper on Environmental Liability on 9 February 2000.[193] As expected, the White Paper draws on much of the previous arguments and ideas developed and adopted by the Commission in this field. Whilst it is not within the scope of this brief postscript to provide a comprehensive assessment of the White Paper, the authors wish to outline a few of its most important points. The Commission has invited all interested parties to submit comments on the White Paper by 1 July 2000,[194] after which it will proceed to draft a framework directive on environmental liability.

The Commission signals in the White Paper that it wishes to ensure that any prospective EC environmental liability regime will address the subject of bio-diversity damage. The overall structure of environmental liability will continue to be premised on a strict liability basis in respect of physical damage and personal injury. However, bio-diversity damage is to be assessed differently. Specifically, the White Paper proposes that polluters are to be held liable for damage caused to natural resources, namely at least those covered under the Community's wild birds and habitats directives in the areas designated under the auspices of the Natura 2000 network.[195] Liability is to be strict in the event of damage resulting from actually or potentially dangerous activities regulated by the Community. In other cases of bio-diversity damage, liability will be fault-based. On the one hand, this development is to be welcomed, in that it shows

---

[193] COM(2000)66 final, published on the EU's website: http:www.europa.eu.int/comm/environment/liability/

[194] Comments can be sent directly to the Commission's Directorate-General XI for Environment, Nuclear Safety and Civil Protection Legal Affairs Unit (DG ENV.B.3), rue de la Loi 200, 1049 Brussels or by email to: Carla.DEVRIES@cec.eu.int or Charlotta.COLLIANDER@cec.eu.int.

[195] Council Directives 79/409/EEC on the conservation of wild birds OJ 1979 L 103/1 and 92/43/EEC on the conservation of natural habitats and wild flora and fauna OJ 1992 L 206/7.

that the Commission is recognising the disadvantages of confining an environmental liability regime to have recourse to traditional tortious concepts of damage (ie. as being linked to property damage or personal injury). On the other hand, it is significant to note that the definition of 'dangerous' might well then become of major legal and political importance, given the difficult substantive and civil procedural hurdles noted above that litigants have to face in proving fault. From an environmental perspective, such a distinction may indeed prove to be arbitrary and a hindrance; much will depend upon the degree of political weight attached to the industrial lobbies in the final legislative settlement.

The Commission has laid down some other criteria in the White Paper with which it aims to use in order to craft a future framework directive. As far as strict liability is concerned, as expected the Commission effectively rules out any inclusion of a development risk defence, although it does accept that the scope and extent of liability may have been restricted in other ways: namely, through ensuring that the directive is not retroactive, taking into account the existence of trade permits in respect of the activities concerned, introducing a cost-benefit approach to the subject of restoration of damage and emphasising the existence of significant damage as a prerequisite to liability. In terms of access to justice issues, the Commission confirms in the White Paper that it wishes to vest interest groups with standing to take civil legal action against polluters in the event of no action being taken by the Member State authorities or in cases requiring immediate intervention. Disappointingly, the Commission fails to provide any detailed initial position on GMOs, insurance and burden of proof issues in the White Paper. No doubt these and other aspects of the environmental liability policy will be battled out in the inter-institutional negotiations and lobby meetings yet to come.

In essence, the White Paper reveals that, whilst some progress has been made on crystallizing various parts of Community policy in this field, the Commission is still far from reaching any firm conclusions on many of the key points relating to the establishment of a Community-wide environmental liability model. Taking this into account, it is an entirely open question as to whether or not the Commission will be able to deliver a proposal for a directive in the near future.

29 March 2000

11

Environmental Protection and the Role of the Common Law: A Scottish Perspective

JEREMY ROWAN-ROBINSON and
DONNA McKENZIE-SKENE

INTRODUCTION

THE COMMON LAW of Scotland has a long history of involvement in environmental protection. "Scots law", asserts Murray, "has always recognised the importance of certain matters which would, I think, be recognised as of critical importance by any environmental yardstick."[1] Today, there is a tendency to think of environmental protection as being achieved by a seemingly ever increasing volume of legislation, but this does not mean that the role of the common law in environmental protection has become obsolete. Furthermore, as Lyall observes, "in many instances the rules elaborated through legislation are developments and elaborations of the principles of the common law. That the fundamental concept of 'harm' is restrictive of 'right' has long roots".[2]

In the context of environmental protection, these roots are found mainly, but not wholly, in the law of property and, more particularly, in the law of neighbourhood. An early concern of the law of neighbourhood was with water quality. The position then, as now, was that riparian owners were entitled to use the water of a river flowing through their land but had to send it down to their neighbours undiminished in quantity and unimpaired in quality. There is a body of case law from the last century concerned with protecting the rights of downstream neighbours to clean water. The courts broadly operated what would today be recognised as a receptor standard and took account of the ability of a watercourse to absorb and neutralise pollution, although they were concerned with the effects on the downstream proprietors rather than with the capacity of

---

[1] J. Murray, "Environmental Law: A Scots Law Perspective", unpublished paper, Socio-Legal Seminar on Environmental Issues, University of Edinburgh, 1993.

[2] F. Lyall, *Air, Noise, Water and Waste: A Summary of the Law in Scotland* (Glasgow, Planning Exchange, 1982), at 3.

240   Jeremy Rowan-Robinson and Donna McKenzie-Skene

the receiving environment to absorb the pollution as such. The maintenance of water quality became a matter of particular concern in Scotland with the dramatic rise in the death rate in Glasgow in the 1820s and 1830s from typhus, cholera and other diseases caused by polluted water resulting from rapid industrialisation.[3] The law was also concerned, however, to protect landowners generally from nuisance caused by neighbours,[4] and Whitty notes that in the period from 1790 to 1820 the trickle of nuisance cases swelled to a flood under the impetus of industrial growth.[5] The law of nuisance was mobilised in the towns against polluting industrial processes,[6] and it has been suggested that this branch of the common law was the commonest way in which environmentally objectionable activities were treated in the past.[7]

Nuisance, despite its roots in the law of property, is now generally treated as part of the law of delict, at least in so far as it involves claims for damages for harm suffered as a result of a nuisance.[8] Thomson states that:

> the essence of the modern Scots law of delict is the obligation of a person to compensate another who has suffered loss as a result of the wrongful actions of that person. This obligation to pay compensation is called reparation. The obligation to make reparation where loss has been suffered as a result of a person's wrongful actions is obediential; it arises *ex lege* regardless of the will of the wrongdoer.[9]

The obligation to make reparation for loss caused by nuisance is one species of delictual liability.[10] The obligation to make reparation for loss caused by negligence[11] is, of course, another,[12] and, like nuisance, is an important part of the common law in the context of environmental protection. Cameron states that negligence is a useful part of the environmental armoury of the common law because the prospect of liability "may encourage safe behaviour in circumstances where activities are acknowledged to be hazardous".[13]

While obligations in nuisance and negligence arise as a matter of law and independently of the will of the parties concerned, environmental obligations may also arise by agreement between parties. An obvious example would be a contract for the sale of heritage where a seller undertakes to indemnify the purchaser for loss arising from the need to clean up contaminated land. Such

---

[3] See T.C. Smout, *A History of the Scottish People 1560–1830* (London, Fontana, 1972), at 398.

[4] J. Rankine, *The Law of Landownership* (4th edn., Edinburgh, W Green & Son Ltd, 1909), at 342–3.

[5] *Stair Memorial Encyclopaedia,* (Edinburgh, Law Society of Scotland, Butterworths, 1990) Vol 14, "Nuisance", para. 2011.

[6] G.D.L. Cameron, "Civil Liability for Environmental Harm" in C.T. Reid (ed.), *Environmental Law in Scotland* (2nd edn., Edinburgh, W. Green & Son Ltd/London, Sweet & Maxwell), at 169.

[7] Murray, *supra*, n.1.

[8] The primary remedy for nuisance, however, is interdict, which may be a very powerful weapon in environmental cases: see further below, at n.67 and associated text.

[9] J.M. Thomson, *Delictual Liability* (Edinburgh, Butterworths, 1994) at 1.

[10] See Lord President Hope in *Kennedy* v. *Glenbelle*, 1996 SLT 1186, at 1188 J–L.

[11] That is, a failure to take reasonable care to prevent foreseeable injury to someone else.

[12] *Ibid.*

[13] *Supra*, n.6 at 183.

Environmental Protection and the Role of the Common Law 241

contractual obligations are of increasing importance in the field of environmental protection, and the law of contract, which is mainly, although not wholly, common law, is therefore a third important part of the common law in this context.

This chapter will assess the role of these three areas of the common law, nuisance, negligence and contract, in promoting environmental protection in Scotland today.

NUISANCE

The origins of the law of nuisance are complex.[14] As indicated above, it was initially regarded as part of the law of property or neighbourhood; subsequently, during the nineteenth century, it came to be regarded as a category of delict.[15] The only institutional definition of nuisance is offered by Bell:

> The description of nuisance in Scotland is the same, whether the public or the individual be regarded. Whatever obstructs the public means of commerce and intercourse, whether in highways or navigable rivers; whatever is noxious or unsafe, or renders life uncomfortable to the public generally, or to the neighbourhood; whatever is intolerably offensive to individuals, in their dwelling-houses, or inconsistent with the comfort of life, whether by stench (as the boiling of whale blubber), by noise (as a smithy in an upper floor), or by indecency (as a brothel next door), is a nuisance.[16]

This definition is very wide and encompasses a public as well as a private role which has nothing to do with the law of neighbourhood. It is, however, the private role of nuisance which has been emphasised in Scots law. Rankine, for example, takes a narrower view than Bell of the nature of nuisance:

> [t]he natural rights incident to ownership may be described with sufficient exactness as resolving into a right to comfortable enjoyment. Conversely, the natural restrictions thereby entailed are imposed by law for the purpose of preventing any interference with this right.[17]

This focuses on the latter part of Bell's definition. Nuisance in this sense amounts to an unreasonable disturbance to the comfortable enjoyment of property. In *Watt* v. *Jamieson*,[18] Lord President Cooper referred to nuisance in terms of a person so using his property "as to occasion serious disturbance or substantial inconvenience to his neighbour or material damage to his neighbour's property", and it has been suggested that the law of nuisance is encapsulated in the Latin maxim *sic utere tuo ut alienum non laedas* (use your own property in a way that you do no harm to others).[19] It has been in this capacity, rather than

---

[14] *Supra* n.5, paras. 2001–33.
[15] *Ibid.*, para. 2017.
[16] Bell, *Principles*, § 974.
[17] Rankine, *supra* n.4, at 387.
[18] 1954 SC 56 at 58.
[19] W.J. Stewart, *Delict* (3rd edn., Edinburgh, W. Green, 1998) at 21.

242   *Jeremy Rowan-Robinson and Donna McKenzie-Skene*

in the capacity of what has been described as "the less well-developed law on nuisance affecting public places",[20] that nuisance has had such impact on environmental protection as it has had.[21]

The onus of proof in establishing that an activity amounts to a nuisance rests with the pursuer.[22] To establish nuisance, it is necessary to show that the activity complained of is *plus quam tolerabile*.[23] This is sometimes put in terms that the resulting harm to the defender must be material. In *Fleming* v. *Hislop*,[24] the Earl of Selborne said that the word material "excludes any sentimental, speculative, trivial discomfort or personal annoyance of that kind—a thing which the law may be said to take no notice of and have no care for . . . what causes material discomfort and annoyance for the ordinary purposes of life to a man's house or to his property is to be restrained". In *Cummnock & Doon Valley District Council* v. *Dance Energy Associates Ltd*,[25] the pursuer sought interim interdict to prevent a rave taking place on the ground that it would cause unreasonable disturbance. It was anticipated that the rave would be a one-off all-night dance with very loud music in an isolated location and attended by many thousands of people. Sheriff Gow refused interim interdict, holding that noise nuisance over a limited period was not such as to inconvenience beyond a reasonable level of tolerance where this was a one-off event and few people were likely to be disturbed. Similarly, in *Davidson* v. *Kerr*,[26] a householder complained of noise over a period of years from neighbours living in the other half of a semi-detached house. Sheriff Poole dismissed an action for interdict on the ground that, although the pursuer had been disturbed, the noises complained of were the result of the normal, domestic use of a family home and would not have seriously disturbed or substantially inconvenienced an average reasonable person in the locality. This has been referred to as the principle of reasonable user—"the principle of give and take as between neighbouring occupiers of land".[27]

[20]   *Supra* n.5, para. 2017.

[21]   In some ways, the failure to develop the public aspect of nuisance may be regarded as unfortunate from the point of view of environmental protection, because it would have given a much wider scope to nuisance as a tool of environmental protection: the emphasis on the protection of private rights by the law of nuisance may be seen as restricting its utility as an instrument of environmental protection. In England and Wales, public and private nuisance are two distinct categories.

[22]   *Central Motors (St Andrews) Ltd* v. *St Andrews Magistrates*, 1961 SLT 290, *per* Lord Migdale at 294; *Webster* v. *Lord Advocate*, 1984 SLT 13, *per* Lord Stott at 15.

[23]   *Watt* v. *Jamieson*, 1954 SC 56, *per* Lord President Cooper at 58. In *Kennedy* v. *Glenbelle, supra* n.10, Lord President Hope stated that the *plus quam tolerabile* test was peculiar to liability in damages for nuisance: F. McManus, "*Culpa* and the Law of Nuisance" [1997] *JR* 259, interprets this as meaning that Lord President Hope was stating that the test was confined to cases of physical damage and suggests that if that was so, his statement was unwarranted, the test applying generally in the law of nuisance. If McManus' interpretation of Lord President Hope's meaning is correct, the authors agree that it is unwarranted and that the authorities suggest rather that the test is of general application in nuisance cases (damages not being the only remedy available in a nuisance case). The circumstances in which an action for damages in nuisance may be brought is discussed further below.

[24]   13 R (HL) 43 at 45. See too Lord Bramwell at 47.

[25]   1992 GWD 25–1441.

[26]   1996 GWD 40–2296.

[27]   *Cambridge Water Co.* v. *Eastern Counties Leather plc* [1994] 2 WLR 53, *per* Lord Goff at 74; *Graham and Graham* v. *Re-Chem International Ltd* [1996] Env. LR 158.

Environmental Protection and the Role of the Common Law   243

There is some doubt about how far the determination of whether an activity is *plus quam tolerabile* involves a balancing of interests. In *Watt* v. *Jamieson*,[28] Lord President Cooper observed that:

> The balance in all cases has to be held between the freedom of a proprietor to use his property as he pleases, and the duty on a proprietor not to inflict material loss or inconvenience on adjoining proprietors or adjoining property; and in every case the answer depends on considerations of fact and degree.

However, the Lord President's remarks were prefaced with the statement that "the proper angle of approach to a case of alleged nuisance is rather from the standpoint of the victim of the loss or inconvenience than from the standpoint of the alleged offender".[29]

The suggestion that there should be a balancing of interests was roundly rejected in *Webster* v. *Lord Advocate*.[30] In that case the pursuer owned a flat overlooking and immediately adjacent to the esplanade at Edinburgh Castle. She raised an action for declarator and interdict in relation to alleged nuisance by noise from the Edinburgh Military Tattoo and from associated works. It was argued for the defenders, *inter alia,* that the public interest in the continuance of the Tattoo far outweighed any interest which neighbouring occupiers might have in its cessation. Lord Stott rejected this argument holding that "interest cannot overrule law". The question, however, is not whether the particular pursuer regards the level of disturbance as intolerable but whether reasonable people viewing the circumstances in an objective and impartial manner would so regard it.[31] It follows from the proposition that nuisance is judged from the standpoint of the victim that the fact that the activity giving rise to the alleged nuisance is a normal and natural use of property is not a defence to an action for nuisance.[32]

In an action for nuisance founding on disturbance to the comfortable enjoyment of property, the question also arises whether the activity complained of is out of place in the locality.[33] In *Maguire* v. *Charles McNeil Ltd*,[34] Lord President Clyde said:

> The doctrine of locality is a concession made by the law to that social necessity which (particularly in towns) drives people into close neighbourhood, not only with each other, but also with the work by which they earn their living . . . The [doctrine] operates more or less severely according to the particular character which is impressed on a locality by the operation, conscious or unconscious, of the economic methods or habits of the community.[35]

---

[28] 1954 SC 56 at 58.
[29] *Ibid.*, at 57 and 58.
[30] 1984 SLT 13.
[31] *Supra* n.5, para. 2041.
[32] *Watt* v. *Jamieson*, 1954 SC 56; *Lord Advocate* v. *Reo Stakis Organisation*, 1982 SLT 140.
[33] *Supra* n.5, para. 2056.
[34] 1922 SC 174.
[35] *Ibid.*, at 185.

244   *Jeremy Rowan-Robinson and Donna McKenzie-Skene*

In *Inglis* v. *Shotts Iron Co.*,[36] Lord Shand noted that "[t]hings which are forbidden in a crowded urban community may be tolerated in the country. What is prohibited in enclosed land may be tolerated in the open." It is easy to see, for example, that smells which are acceptable in the countryside may be quite unacceptable in urban areas. Even within urban areas, as the editors of *Gloag and Henderson* put it: "what is a nuisance in a residential neighbourhood would not necessarily be one in an industrial district".[37]

For some time, there was uncertainty about whether it was necessary to establish fault to succeed in a nuisance action. Nuisance generally involves conduct which is continuing rather than one-off, and the principal remedy is therefore an interdict restraining the offending conduct. In such cases, as Thomson observes, "whether or not the nuisance was caused by conduct which amounted to *culpa* on the part of the defender is largely irrelevant",[38] and it is now clearly established that it is not necessary to prove *culpa* where the remedy sought is interdict only.[39] However, where the action is one for damages, it is now equally clearly settled that the pursuer must prove fault on the part of the defender,[40] except, possibly, in a case involving interference with the course of a natural stream,[41] and this requirement is a separate and distinct requirement from the requirement to prove that the conduct is *plus quam tolerabile*.[42] As noted, a claim for damages for nuisance is classified as a delictual claim, and it is on this basis that the requirement for fault is imposed.[43] In *RHM Bakeries (Scotland) Ltd* v. *Strathclyde Regional Council*,[44] bakery premises were flooded following the collapse of a sewer. The sewer was operated and controlled by the local authority. The bakery raised an action for damages against the local authority on the ground, *inter alia,* that the flooding was a nuisance for which the authority was strictly liable. Giving the judgment of the court in the House of Lords, Lord Fraser of Tullybelton upheld the local authority's averment that the action at common law was irrelevant because it excluded

[36] (1881) 8 R 1006 at 1021.

[37] W.M. Gloag and C. Henderson, *The Law of Scotland* (10th edn., Edinburgh, W. Green, 1995), para. 31.10.

[38] J.M. Thomson, *Delictual Liability* (Edinburgh, Butterworths, 1994), at 160. The question of the foreseeability of harm will also generally be irrelevant where the proceedings are for interdict because the proceedings concern the continuance of present harm *supra* n.5, para. 2094.

[39] See *Logan* v. *Wang*, 1991 SLT 580. McManus, *supra* n.23, at 264, argues that this distinction is illogical because the conduct sought to be interdicted must amount to a wrong before it can be interdicted, and therefore *culpa* is relevant in a nuisance action even where the only remedy sought is interdict, but the decision in *Logan* v. *Wang* is quite clear in this respect.

[40] *RHM Bakeries (Scotland) Ltd* v. *Strathclyde Regional Council*, 1985 SC (HL) 17.

[41] In *Caledonian Railway Co.* v. *Greenock Corporation*, 1917 SC (HL) 56, strict liability for damage caused by the escape of water in such circumstances seems to have been imposed by the court. That case was discussed in *RHM Bakeries (Scotland) Ltd* v. *Strathclyde Regional Council*, where the court took the view that the basis for liability in that case was not entirely clear and that the decision should be regarded as being confined to its own special facts: *ibid.*, at 42. Lord President Hope in *Kennedy* v. *Glenbelle*, *supra* n.10, was also content to regard that case as forming a possible special exception to the rule that *culpa* was required in a nuisance action for damages (see 1188 G–H).

[42] *Kennedy* v. *Glenbelle*, *supra*, n. 10.

[43] See Lord President Hope in *ibid.*, at 1188 J–K.

[44] 1985 SC (HL) 17. See too *ibid.*

Environmental Protection and the Role of the Common Law   245

any reference to fault.[45] The doubt about whether *culpa* was an essential element in Scots law for the liability of a proprietor to a neighbour arose, he said, from the fact that the English decision in *Rylands* v. *Fletcher*[46] had sometimes been referred to as if it were authoritative in Scotland. He went on to say that, in his opinion, that decision "has no place in Scots law, and the suggestion that it has, is a heresy which ought to be extirpated".[47] In some cases, however, the result in Scots law, based on *culpa*, may be not much different in practice from that achieved in England and Wales under the rule in *Rylands* v. *Fletcher*. In *McLaughlan* v. *Craig*,[48] Lord Cooper said that there were cases "in which there is little difference in the result between the application of the English rule of absolute liability and the Scottish rule of *culpa*, where the facts raise a presumption of negligence so compelling as to be practically incapable of being displaced".[49]

In *Kennedy* v. *Glenbelle*, it was recognised that the necessary *culpa* may take various forms.[50] In outlining the different types of *culpa* which might be relevant in a nuisance action, Lord President Hope adopted the classification of the categories of *culpa* contained in Volume 14 of the *Stair Memorial Encyclopaedia*, *viz*, malice, intent, recklessness and negligence, and added to them a further category of "conduct causing a special risk of abnormal damage where it may be said that it is not necessary to prove a specific fault as fault is necessarily implied in the result".[51] As an example of the last category, Lord President Hope referred to, *inter alia*, the case of *Chalmers* v. *Dixon*,[52] in which Lord President Moncrieff had said:

> If a man puts upon his land a new combination of materials, which he knows or ought to know are of a dangerous nature, then either due care will prevent injury, in which case he is liable if injury occurs for not taking that due care, or else no precautions will prevent injury, in which case he is liable for his original act in placing the materials on the ground.[53]

Later in his speech, Lord President Hope suggested that this category of *culpa* might simply be another example of recklessness,[54] but whatever its classification,

---

[45] As to the different circumstances in which fault may be shown in a nuisance action see *ibid.*, *per* Lord Hope at 1189.

[46] (1868) LR 3 HL 330.

[47] *Rylands* v. *Fletcher* involved liability for the escape of dangerous substances from the defender's premises and appeared to impose strict liability for such an escape. The decision was discussed and explained in the subsequent case of *Cambridge Water Co. Ltd* v. *Eastern Counties Leather plc* [1994] 2 AC 264, which is discussed further below at n.61. There are, however, grounds for suggesting that strict liability applies in Scots law where damage results from the alteration of the channel of a stream: *Caledonian Railway* v. *Greenock Corporation*, *supra* n.41, and discussed above at n.41; see also *G & A Estates Ltd* v. *Caviapen Trustees Ltd (No.1)*, 1993 SLT 1037.

[48] 1948 SC 599.

[49] *Ibid.*, at 611.

[50] See particularly Lord President Hope, *supra* n.10, at 1188L and Lord Kirkwood at 1191A.

[51] *Ibid.*, at 1188L.

[52] (1876) 3R 461.

[53] *Ibid.*, at 464. See also *Edinburgh Railway Access and Property Co.* v. *John Ritchie and Co.* (1903) 5 F 299 and *Noble's Trs.* v. *Economic Forestry (Scotland) Ltd*, 1988 SLT 662.

[54] *Supra* n.10, at 1189 L.

246 *Jeremy Rowan-Robinson and Donna McKenzie-Skene*

it is one which may have an especial resonance in the field of environmental protection, since it appears to allow the fault necessary for the purposes of an action
of nuisance to be established simply by the bringing into existence of something
hazardous to the neighbour's property.[55]

Negligence as a category of *culpa* in a nuisance action raises some special
issues, in particular, whether the requirements for establishing negligence for
this purpose are the same as the requirements for establishing delictual liability
for negligence generally. The requirements for establishing negligence generally
are discussed below, together with the particular problems that they raise in the
context of environmental cases. In *Kennedy* v. *Glenbelle* itself, Lord President
Hope stated that *culpa* could be established by demonstrating negligence "in
which case the ordinary principles of the law of negligence will provide an
equivalent remedy".[56] McManus interprets this as meaning that negligence for
these purposes is "foursquare with liability in the law of negligence",[57] but
Thomson is more sceptical, and suggests that, in any event, "to insist on the full
panoply of the law of negligence is gilding the rose in this situation. Should it
not be enough to establish culpa for the purpose of a claim for damages in nuisance that the defender's conduct simply fell below the standard of reasonable
care?"[58] The answer to this question may have important consequences for
those contemplating bringing an action in nuisance, particularly in environmental cases, although of course negligence is, as already seen, only one of the
ways in which *culpa* can be established for this purpose.

It has been held that it is necessary to establish that the harm or damage
caused by the nuisance was foreseeable. In *Graham and Graham* v. *Re-Chem
International Ltd*,[59] the defendants operated a toxic waste incinerator near
Stirling. The plaintiffs carried on a dairy herd enterprise nearby. They sued the
defendants for damages in nuisance and negligence for harm to their cattle herd
caused by the ingestion of chemicals from the incinerator while grazing.
Although the events took place in Scotland, the case was heard before the
Queen's Bench Division and it was agreed between the parties that the relevant
law was the law of Scotland, and that for this purpose there was no material difference between the law of Scotland and that of England and Wales.[60] The
plaintiffs submitted, with regard to the action in nuisance, that unless the defendants could bring themselves within the principle of "reasonable user" they
would be liable for foreseeable damage caused by emissions from the incinerator. Forbes J, following the judgment of Lord Goff in the House of Lords in

---

[55] See, however, F. McManus, "Liability for *Opera Manufacta* (New Works) in Scots Law"
[1998] JR 281.

[56] *Supra*, n.10 1189K.

[57] *Supra*, n.23, at 272.

[58] J.M. Thomson, "Damages for Nuisance", 1997 *SLT (News)* 177 at 178.

[59] [1996] Env. LR 158.

[60] It will be obvious from the discussion in this chapter that the accuracy of that assumption may
be questioned to at least some extent, although broadly speaking the principles applicable, at least
in negligence, are the same.

Cambridge Water Co. v. *Eastern Counties Leather plc*,[61] accepted that the plaintiff's right to recover damages in nuisance was limited to the right to recover damages for harm or damage which the defendants could reasonably foresee might be caused by the nuisance in question. He went on to add, however, that it was not necessary, in order to satisfy the foreseeability test for the purposes of an action in nuisance, that the defendants should be precisely aware of how their operations could cause the harm complained of. In the event, it was held that the damage complained of was a foreseeable consequence of the defendant's actions, but the action failed on other grounds.[62]

It is a defence to an action for nuisance to show that the right to object has been extinguished by negative prescription in accordance with the provisions of sections 7 and 8 of the Prescription and Limitation (Scotland) Act 1973. To succeed with this defence it will be necessary to show that the right to object has existed continuously for a period of 20 years without being exercised. It is also a defence to show that statutory authority exists for the activity.[63] For example, section 40 of the Civil Aviation Act 1949 provides immunity from liability for technical nuisance (although not for material injury) resulting from the flight of an aircraft at a reasonable height or the ordinary incidents of such flight or resulting from noise and vibration at take-off and landing.[64] However, statutory authority will not be a defence if the activity complained of could have been carried out in a way which is not a nuisance.[65]

An action for nuisance may be brought only by those with a recognised interest in the land affected by the nuisance,[66] and this may be a major factor limiting its utility in the field of environmental protection in some cases. The principal remedy for nuisance in the context of environmental harm will tend to be interdict, which is directed towards preventing the continuance of a nuisance. Interdict may be also be sought against anticipated nuisances, although it may be difficult to establish that the activity will be *plus quam tolerabile*.[67] Although interdict is essentially a negative remedy, Smith *et al.* show that it can, in the field of environmental protection, be a technology forcing instrument.[68] For example, in *Shotts Iron Co.* v. *Inglis*,[69] the interdict was framed so as to prevent the defenders from carrying on their industrial activity in a way that would continue to cause an unacceptable level of air pollution; and in *Webster* v. *Lord*

---

[61] *Supra* n.47.

[62] See further below, at 252.

[63] See generally on this *Department of Transport* v. *North West Water Authority* [1984] AC 336.

[64] See the discussion in *Steel-Maitland* v. *British Airways Board*, 1981 SLT 110.

[65] *Lord Advocate* v. *North British Railway*, 1894 2 SLT 71.

[66] *Hunter* v. *Canary Wharf Ltd* [1997] 2 WLR 684. The case is an English case, but it is thought that the position in Scotland would be the same, given the foundation of nuisance in the law of property.

[67] *Gavin* v. *Ayrshire County Council*, 1950 SC 197, *per* Lord Cooper at 207.

[68] C. Smith, N. Collar and M. Poustie, *Pollution Control: The Law in Scotland* (Edinburgh, T. & T. Clark, 1997), at 29.

[69] (1882) 9 R (HL) 78.

Advocate,[70] the Edinburgh Tattoo was prevented from erecting the grandstand in a way which would continue to cause a noise nuisance. The court may make a declaratory finding of nuisance and suspend interdict pending remedial measures. At this point, the public interest in the interim continuance of the activity may be a factor.[71] For example, in *Webster* the interdict was suspended for six months so that the Tattoo could go ahead that year.[72] The other remedy is damages, which may be awarded as well as, or instead of, interdict. Damages may be awarded in nuisance, however, only for injury to the land affected by the nuisance, and not for personal injury or damage to moveable property.[73] Such injury, however, includes not only physical injury to the land, for example, that caused by flood, but the discomfort and inconvenience caused by nuisances such as smells, smoke or noise: in *Hunter* v. *Canary Wharf Ltd*,[74] damages for discomfort and inconvenience suffered as a result of a nuisance were classified along with physical damage to land as damages affecting the land rather than personal injury claims, on the basis that the amenity and utility of the land were affected by the nuisance precisely because persons were liable to suffer inconvenience, annoyance and illness. Any claim for damages for personal injury "proper" or for damage to moveable property which is not consequential on physical damage to the land will, however, require to be brought as a claim in negligence rather than in nuisance.[75] It has already been noted that where a nuisance has resulted in physical damage to property, an award of damages depends on the pursuer being able to establish *culpa* on the part of the defender.[76] McManus notes that there is little authority on whether *culpa* is relevant where the nuisance has not caused physical damage to the property, but takes the view that, logically, it must be,[77] a view shared by the authors. The court does not have power to award prospective damages in lieu of interdict,[78] although it may award damages for the cost of measures taken to prevent a recurrence of the nuisance.[79]

---

[70] 1984 SLT 13.

[71] See *Clippens Oil Co.* v. *Edinburgh and District Water Trustees* (1897) 25 R 373, *per* Lord McLaren at 383.

[72] See also *Ben Nevis Distillery (Fort William) Ltd* v. *The North British Aluminium Co. Ltd*, 1948 SC 592.

[73] *Hunter* v. *Canary Wharf Ltd*, *supra*, n.66. It should be noted, however, that it was stated in that case that damage to moveable property consequential on (physical) damage to land could be recovered, which seems correct. See also Thomson, *supra*, n.58.

[74] *Supra*, n.66.

[75] Negligence is discussed further below.

[76] See above.

[77] *Supra*, n.23, at 275.

[78] *Supra* n.5, para. 2150.

[79] *G & A Estates Ltd* v. *Caviapen Trustees Ltd (No 1)*, *supra*, n.47.

NEGLIGENCE

The law of negligence is concerned with harm which is caused unintentionally but carelessly: liability in negligence arises where the defender has failed to take reasonable care where there is a foreseeable risk of injury. In order to succeed in an action based on negligence, a pursuer must be able to show that the defender owed him or her a duty of care, that the defender breached that duty and that that breach of duty has caused, in both a factual and a legal sense, the loss, injury and damage sustained by the pursuer. Each of these requirements may raise special problems in the context of environmental protection.

With respect to the duty of care, the starting point is the celebrated case of *Donoghue* v. *Stevenson*,[80] and in particular Lord Atkin's famous dictum:

> The rule that you are to love your neighbour becomes in law, you must not injure your neighbour; and the lawyer's question, Who is my neighbour? receives a restricted reply. You must take reasonable care to avoid acts or omissions which you can reasonably foresee would be likely to injure your neighbour. Who, then, in law is my neighbour? The answer seems to be—persons who are so closely and directly affected by my act that I ought reasonably to have them in contemplation as being so affected when I am directing my mind to the acts or omissions which are called into question.[81]

In other words, a duty of care is owed to persons whom the defender can reasonably foresee as being potentially affected by his actions. This requirement is sometimes expressed as a requirement that there be sufficient proximity between the parties. This need not necessarily be physical proximity, although in some cases this may be an important element.[82] In the context of environmental protection, there may be difficulty in establishing a duty of care because in some cases it may be difficult to establish the requisite degree of proximity.

With regard to the breach of any duty of care which is owed to the pursuer, the actual harm which was suffered by the pursuer must have been a reasonable and probable consequence of the defender's act or omission.[83] One consequence of this is that, as Thomson states, "the scientific knowledge available to the hypothetical reasonable person at that time can be crucial".[84] This is illustrated by the case of *Roe* v. *Minister of Health*,[85] where a patient was paralysed as a

---

[80] 1932 SC (HL) 31.

[81] *Ibid.*, at 44. It should be noted that although the concept of "neighbourhood" invoked here may suggest an affinity with the law of nuisance, with its roots in the law of neighbourhood, there is in fact no connection between the two.

[82] See, for example, the well known case of *Bourhill* v. *Young*, 1942 SC (HL) 78, where a pursuer who suffered nervous shock as a result of seeing the aftermath of an accident was held not to be owed a duty of care by the motorcyclist involved as she was outwith the area in which she could have been at risk of physical injury and could not therefore have been within his contemplation as being potentially affected by his actions. The law relating to nervous shock has, of course, developed since that case, but the point remains valid.

[83] *Muir* v. *Glasgow Corporation*, 1934 SC (HL) 3.

[84] *Supra* n.9, at 98.

[85] [1954] 2 QB 56.

250 *Jeremy Rowan-Robinson and Donna McKenzie-Skene*

result of phenol in an anaesthetic. The vials of anaesthetic in question had been stored in phenol, which had leaked into the vials through invisible cracks. It was held that given the state of scientific knowledge at the time, the paralysis of a patient could not have been foreseen as a reasonable and probable consequence of storing the vials in phenol. This may be a particularly important issue in environmental cases, where the environmentally harmful consequences of an activity may become known only after a lapse of time. This issue arose in *Graham and Graham* v. *Re-Chem International Ltd*. There, the point at issue was the harmful effects of organic pollutants emitted from the defender's incinerator. Forbes J said that, at the time the incinerator was in operation, "it had been known for some time that the destruction of waste by incineration resulted in the emission of organic pollutants such as dioxins and furans in fly ash carried in the flue gasses. It was also well known that some of these compounds are very toxic".[86] On that basis, he was prepared to hold that it was foreseeable that such compounds could cause damage of the type complained of by the pursuers, even though the defenders did not know at the relevant time exactly how, when and where such compounds were formed. The issue was discussed initially in the context of the claim in nuisance rather than negligence, but it was also discussed in the context of the claim in negligence, where the pursuers argued that no question of foreseeability arose for the same reasons as discussed in connection with the claim in nuisance. This does not seem to have been disputed by the defenders and Forbes J expressed himself in agreement generally with the pursuer's arguments. He also said, however:

> [The defender's] knowledge at the relevant time as to how, when and where dioxins and furans might be formed in a waste incinerator during its operation would clearly be material to any determination as to what Re-Chem then knew and understood about the full nature of the chemical processes involved . . . *In certain circumstances, such a determination might be of considerable importance in deciding whether the emission of such substances constituted breach of a common law duty of care.*[87]

Clearly, therefore, although the test of foreseeability had been satisfied in the context of both nuisance and negligence in this case, it may still be a potentially difficult issue in other environmental cases. It should be noted, however, that if injury of the type sustained by a pursuer is reasonably foreseeable, every link in the chain which produced it need not be foreseeable, and the fact that the harm suffered by the pursuer was much greater than could have been foreseen is also irrelevant.[88] Again, this may be important in environmental cases where the effects of, for example, a polluting incident may be much worse than could have been predicted.

Even where damage of the type sustained by the pursuer is reasonably foreseeable, the defender will be in breach of his duty of care only if he is at fault.

---

[86] *Supra*, n.59, at 166.
[87] *Ibid.*, at 169, emphasis supplied.
[88] *Hughes* v. *Lord Advocate*, 1963 SC (HL) 31.

Environmental Protection and the Role of the Common Law   251

Culpa in this context consists of a failure to reach the necessary standard of care, that is, the standard of the reasonable person in the position of the defender. What is reasonable in any particular case will depend on the circumstances of that case, and effectively involves a balancing process: "[t]he relevant factors to be considered include the probability of injury, the seriousness of the injury, the practicability of precautions, the cost of the precautions and the utility of the defender's activities".[89] Evidence of the practice of others in the same position as the defender, for example, other operators in the same industry, is also important but not conclusive.[90] An example of such a balancing exercise in an environmental context can be seen in the English case of *Tutton* v. *A.D. Walter Ltd*.[91] A farmer used a pesticide which was known to be harmful to bees on his crop of oil seed rape. As a result, bees belonging to a number of beekeepers in the area, of whom the farmer was aware, were killed in large numbers. It was established that the harm to the bees could have been minimised by spraying at a different time and/or by giving sufficient notice to the beekeepers to allow them to remove the bees from the danger area. Furthermore, the use of the pesticide was most efficacious at the time that its use was least harmful to bees, and all of these matters were well known. The court said:

> In the circumstances . . . the risk to bees was high and the likelihood of their loss great. However . . . it cannot be said that the consequences of failure to take such care, ie the loss of some or all of the bee colonies, is, in context, of the kind of cases with which this court has to deal—a matter of such gravity as to attract the very highest standards of care—but of course it is far from trivial. In financial terms this is a comparatively small claim, and colonies of bees are replaceable. This must be balanced against the cost and practicability, from the farmer's point of view, of overcoming the risk to the bees.[92]

The court went on to stress that the essential point was that the interests of the farmer and the beekeepers were almost entirely compatible, and it was held that the farmer had fallen short of the necessary standard of care. In environmental cases generally, however, it is almost axiomatic that the interests of those involved are likely not be compatible at all, and environmental cases may therefore raise particular difficulties in the context of such a balancing exercise: often, activities which are environmentally very hazardous also have potentially very serious consequences for individuals or property, suggesting high standards of care, but at the same time have high costs involved in taking preventive measures and are regarded as having a high social utility, for example, nuclear power generation or waste disposal. Furthermore, the defender need only do what is reasonable, even if he could have done more with little or no further cost or effort, and where a defender has acted reasonably, there will be no breach of

---

[89] Thomson, *supra* n.9, at 103.

[90] *Morton* v. *William Dixon Ltd*, 1909 SC 807; *Cavanagh* v. *Ulster Weaving Co.* [1960] AC 145; *Brown* v. *Rolls Royce Ltd*, 1960 SC (HL) 22.

[91] [1985] 3 WLR 797.

[92] *Ibid.*, at 810.

duty. An important factor here may be the existence of guidelines, for example as to safe levels of emissions or chemicals in a water supply. It has been held that there could be no breach of a duty of care where defenders had complied with statutory guidelines as to emissions.[93]

With respect to the issue of causation, the pursuer must show that the loss complained of was caused, in both a factual and a legal sense, by the negligent act or omission of the defender, and this may be particularly difficult in environmental cases. In *Graham and Graham* v. *Re-Chem International Ltd,*[94] the plaintiffs alleged that their cattle had become ill as a result of the toxic chemicals emitted from the defender's incinerator. It was accepted that it was not necessary to show that the emissions from the incinerator were the sole or even the dominant cause of the loss complained of: "it would be sufficient to establish that the alleged emissions . . . caused or materially contributed to the ill-health of [the pursuers'] cattle".[95] It was held on the evidence, however, that the pursuers had failed to establish this, and the action therefore failed. In fact, there was evidence of various other possible causes of the ill-health of the cattle, and it was accepted that, on the balance of probabilities, these were the real causes of that ill-health. Where there is no other explanation for the damage complained of, therefore, it may be easier for the pursuer to establish the necessary causal link between the defender's negligent act or omission and the loss sustained, but again the state of scientific knowledge may be crucial in establishing whether the thing complained of could be a possible cause of the injury sustained. This is particularly so in cases involving illness caused by alleged negligent acts or omissions, for example, where the pursuer alleges that he is suffering from cancer as a result of harmful emissions: since such an illness can occur naturally, it may be extremely difficult to show even on the balance of probabilities that the pursuer's illness was in fact caused or materially contributed to by the emissions rather than having occurred naturally. The matter will not, however, necessarily be determined wholly on the basis of scientific evidence, or lack of it. It has been said that "[t]he fact that experts cannot identify the process of causation scientifically does not preclude the court from making the inference, on all the facts, that the defendant's negligence materially contributed to the plaintiff's injury".[96] In this context, Pugh and Day refer to the unreported Irish case of *Hanrahan* v. *Merck Sharp and Dhome (Ireland) Ltd,*[97] which also involved farmers claiming for personal injury and damage to livestock allegedly caused by toxic emissions from the defenders' chemical plant. They report that the Supreme Court, reversing the decision of the court at first instance, found that on the basis of the direct evidence of the witnesses as to how

[93] *Budden* v. *BP Oil Ltd and Shell Oil Ltd; Albery-Speyer* v. *BP Oil Ltd and Shell Oil Ltd,* 1980 PCR 586.

[94] *Supra,* n.59.

[95] *Ibid.,* at 172. It was accepted that this was the appropriate approach in respect of the claims in both nuisance and negligence.

[96] C. Pugh and M. Day, "Toxic Torts" (1991) *NLJ* 1549, 1596 at 1597.

[97] Dublin Supreme Court, 5 July 1988.

Environmental Protection and the Role of the Common Law   253

they felt and what they observed at the time, it was a legitimate inference that the toxic emissions caused the damage.[98] This case is not necessarily inconsistent with the approach of Scots law to causation or even with the *Graham* case, since, as noted, there was other evidence in that case which showed a more likely cause of the damage complained of. Pugh and Day suggest that the courts will look at five factors in determining the question of causation in cases where a pursuer has sustained personal injury: evidence that the substance can cause the disease or injury suffered; evidence of temporal association; evidence that the victim was not exposed to some other substance equally or more likely to have caused the disease or injury; evidence that the victim was not subject to the disease naturally and epidemiological evidence.[99] The burden of proving causation may therefore be lessened if the courts prove to be prepared to take a broad view of the matter in the light of such evidence, but it will still remain one of the most difficult hurdles.

There are a variety of defences to a claim in negligence. The defender may, of course, establish that he owed no duty of care to the pursuer, or that he did not breach his duty of care, or that the cause of the loss sustained by the pursuer was something else and his breach of duty did not cause or materially contribute to it. Justification, necessity, *damnum fatale,* consent, criminality of the pursuer and statutory authority are all defences to a claim in negligence and may have particular relevance in certain types of environmental claim. Contributory negligence on the part of the pursuer is also a defence, and a finding of contributory negligence will reduce the pursuer's damages by the proportion that the pursuer was himself to blame for his loss.[100]

An obligation to make reparation for a delictual act generally prescribes after five years,[101] but there are various exceptions to this rule. Importantly in this context, an obligation to make reparation for personal injury or death resulting from a delictual act prescribes only after 20 years,[102] but there is a three-year limitation period: the pursuer must commence an action for reparation within three years or the defender will be able to plead that the action is time barred.[103] In the case of a claim for personal injury, the three-year period runs from the date on which the injuries were sustained *or*, where the act or omission which caused the injury is continuing (which may often be the case in environmental cases, for example, cases involving pollution), from the date on which the injuries were sustained or the date on which the act or omission ceased, whichever is the later.[104] However, the limitation period will not commence from that date unless the pursuer was aware, or it was reasonably practicable

---

[98] *Ibid.*

[99] *Ibid.* Not all of these categories will, of course, be relevant in other types of claim, but the same general principles will apply.

[100] Law Reform (Contributory Negligence) Act 1945.

[101] Prescription and Limitation (Scotland) Act 1973, s. 6.

[102] *Ibid.*, sch. 1(2)(g).

[103] *Ibid.*, s. 17.

[104] *Ibid.*

254 *Jeremy Rowan-Robinson and Donna McKenzie-Skene*

for him to be aware, that the injuries were sufficiently serious for him to bring an action, that they were caused by an act or omission and that that act or omission was the responsibility of the defender, and in these cases the period will start to run only when the pursuer becomes aware of the necessary fact or could reasonably have become aware of it. This may be important in environmental cases where, for example, an illness caused by pollution which has long since ceased may take time to manifest itself, it becomes apparent only after a lapse of time that a state of affairs which has caused injury was the result of an act or omission of the defender or a connection between that act or omission and the damage sustained becomes known, perhaps through scientific investigation, only after a lapse of time. At the same time, the fact that the time period begins to run from the time when it was reasonably practicable to discover the relevant information may work against the pursuer in environmental cases: for example, Pugh and Day point out that a pursuer may have had suspicions for a long time that his illness was linked to pollution, and that in such a case the question may turn on the degree to which that suspicion is supported by the scientific community.[105] In the case of death, where a person dies from injuries sustained as a result of a delictual act within three years, the three-year limitation period runs from the date of death.[106] However, none of the limitation periods described runs while one of the statutory exemptions applies, for example where the pursuer is under a legal disability such as non-age or mental disability,[107] and in the case of a claim for personal injuries or death, the court has a discretion to allow the pursuer to commence an action outwith the limitation period if it seems equitable to do so,[108] although in practice it is exercised only in exceptional cases.

It should be noted that the only remedy available for negligence is damages. It is not possible, for example, to obtain an interdict in the context of an action based on negligence. The purpose of an award of damages is to compensate the pursuer for his or her losses and to put him or her in the same position, so far as money can, as he or she would have been in if the negligent act or omission had not occurred.[109] However, the pursuer will not necessarily be able to recover every loss which he or she has sustained: losses which are too remote are irrecoverable. Remoteness is a problematic concept. The classic statement of the rule on remoteness of damage in Scots law is that of Lord Kinloch in the case of *Allan v. Barclay*,[110] where he said:

> The grand rule on the subject of damages is, that none can be claimed except such as naturally and directly arise out of the wrong done; and such, therefore, as may reasonably supposed to have been in the contemplation of the wrongdoer.[111]

[105] *Supra*, n.96 at 1597.
[106] Prescription and Limitation (Scotland) Act 1973, s. 18.
[107] *Ibid.*, ss. 17(3), 18(3), 22B and 22C.
[108] *Ibid.*, s. 19A.
[109] See e.g. *O'Brien's Curator Bonis v. British Steel plc*, 1991 SCLR 931.
[110] (1864) 2 M 874.
[111] *Ibid.*, at 876.

Environmental Protection and the Role of the Common Law 255

This formulation contains two elements: whether the loss arises naturally and directly from the wrong done and whether it was reasonably foreseeable on the part of the wrongdoer. The difficulty is that they are not contiguent: a loss may arise naturally and directly from the wrong but not be reasonably foreseeable, or it may be reasonably foreseeable but not arise directly and naturally from the wrong. Furthermore, it may sometimes be difficult to distinguish situations which raise an issue of remoteness of damage from those which raise an issue of the existence of a duty of care and/or causation. The applicable test for remoteness of damage has caused difficulty in England,[112] and the position is generally regarded as unsettled in Scotland,[113] although it has been said that it is too simplistic to see the question of remoteness of damages in Scots law in terms of reasonable foreseeability on one hand and direct consequences on the other, the courts in fact applying a combination of both tests with recovery of loss only being denied if it is utterly speculative.[114] Remoteness of damage may be particularly problematic in environmental cases where some or all of the losses sustained as a result of an environmental incident may not be reasonably foreseeable at the time or may be reasonably foreseeable but could not be classified as a natural and direct consequence of the wrong. It should be noted, however, that a defender must take his victim as he finds him, so that he will be liable in negligence notwithstanding that the harm which results is much greater than could have been expected, for example, where an escaped chemical which would normally cause only skin irritation causes a particularly sensitive person to suffer a fatal asthma attack.[115]

CONTRACT

The law of contract is concerned with obligations undertaken by parties voluntarily and Cameron notes that "there is great scope for creating civil liability for environmental harm through the use of contractual terms".[116]

Until recently, the role of contracts in environmental law has been limited, with two exceptions. The first is conditions of tenure contained in feudal grants and dispositions of heritage, some of which have long had an association with

---

[112] See, in particular, *Re Polemis and Furness, Withy and Co. Ltd* [1921] 3 KB 560; cf. *Overseas Tankship (UK) Ltd* v. *Morts Dock and Engineering Co.* [1961] AC 388. It has been questioned whether the latter case is truly a remoteness of damage case at all: see e.g. Thomson, *supra* n. 38 at 227. See also *Koufos* v. *Czarnikov* [1969] 1 AC 350.

[113] See e.g. Thomson, *supra* n.38, at 227–8; Stewart, *supra* n.19, at 73. See *Kelvin Shipping Co.* v. *Canadian Pacific Railway Co.*, 1928 SC (HL) 21; *Cowan* v. *National Coal Board*, 1958 SLT (Notes) 19; *Campbell* v. *F & F Moffat (Transport) Ltd*, 1992 SCLR 551.

[114] Thomson, *supra* n.38, at 228.

[115] This rule is sometimes referred to as the "thin skull rule": see *McKillen* v. *Barclay Curle and Co.*, 1967 SLT 41.

[116] G.D.L. Cameron, *supra* n.6, at 185. It should be noted that although Scots law, unlike English law, recognises as enforceable a gratuitous promise, in this context one is more likely to be concerned with mutual contracts agreed between two or more parties.

the environment. Such conditions may, *inter alia*, be directed at restricting development so as to safeguard amenity, at ensuring that certain standards are observed in building with regard to density, design or materials, at the prevention of activities that may constitute a nuisance and at the provision of landscaping.[117] While the intention in imposing such conditions will in many instances have been to maintain the value of the feu duty or to protect the value of neighbouring property rather than to benefit the environment, the effect has quite often been of benefit to the wider environment, and the development of Edinburgh's New Town in the late eighteenth and early nineteenth centuries in accordance with standards laid down in feudal grants is generally regarded as an outstanding example of what was, in effect, an early form of private planning control.[118] One feature of such conditions is that, unlike other contractual obligations, they may, if they satisfy certain requirements, run with the land.[119] This means that they are enforceable not only against the original parties, but against singular successors: in other words, they bind those who were not parties to the original contract. The requirements which must be satisfied before condition(s) will run with the land in this way were laid down in *Tailors of Aberdeen* v. *Coutts*.[120] In essence, the condition(s) in question must show an intention to bind the land (although no technical words are required); they must not be useless, vexatious or contrary to law or public policy; they must be clear in their terms in order to avoid the presumption in favour of freedom,[121] and they must be recorded in the Register of Sasines or in the Land Register for Scotland. Where conditions do run with the land, they may continue to deliver environmental benefits long after the original contractual relationship has come to an end. Feudal real burdens will disappear if the feudal system is abolished as is currently being proposed,[122] but the Scottish Law Commission has recommended a mechanism for converting conservation obligations which currently operate within the feudal system into "conservation burdens",[123] a new type of

---

[117] See J.M. Halliday, *Conveyancing Law and Practice* (Edinburgh, W. Green & Son Ltd, 1986), paras. 19–33; and W.M. Gordon, *Scottish Land Law* (2nd edn., Edinburgh, W. Green & Son Ltd, 1999), paras. 22–44.

[118] Indeed, it has been suggested on the strength of this example that planning would be radically improved in Scotland if the current statutory system was swept away and replaced by a "modernised system of feu charters": see *Omega Report: Scottish Policy*, (London, Adam Smith Institute, 1983), ch 3.

[119] Conditions which run with the land are known as real burdens.

[120] (1840) 1 Rob. App. 296. The Scottish Law Commission has, however, recommended some changes in the requirements: see Scottish Law Commission Discussion Paper on Real Burdens (Discussion Paper No. 106) 1998.

[121] *Anderson* v. *Dickie* 1915 SC (HL) 79, 1915 1 SLT 393.

[122] The Scottish Law Commission has recommended abolition of the feudal system (see its Report on Abolition of the Feudal System, Scot Law Com No , 1999) and the present government is committed to abolition of the feudal system as part of its wider proposals for land reform in Scotland (see Land Reform Policy Group Recommendations for Change, Scottish Office, January 1999). The matter will be one for the Scottish Parliament.

[123] Report on Abolition of the Feudal System, *ibid,*; see also Scottish Law Commission Discussion Paper on Real Burdens (Discussion Paper No 106), 1998, at para. 2.59.

Environmental Protection and the Role of the Common Law 257

burden which it has proposed be introduced.[124] The Scottish Law Commission has also proposed that existing neighbour burdens,[125] and community burdens,[126] which may have positive environmental effects, should remain and that it should continue to be possible to create new neighbour and community burdens.[127] However, some of its proposals for changes to the law relating to the creation, variation and extinction of real burdens may adversely affect the usefulness of such burdens as a tool of environmental protection. The Discussion Paper proposes that a "sunset" rule be introduced whereby existing burdens would cease to have effect after a specified period of time, to be prescribed by statute, which could be extended once (on an application to the Lands Tribunal) but not subsequently.[128] It also proposes that where new burdens are created, it should be a condition of their validity that the length of time for which they are to endure is stipulated in the constitutive deed, a maximum duration being prescribed by statute, and that such burdens should not be renewable.[129] If these recommendations are ultimately accepted and apply to burdens which either intentionally or incidentally have the result of protecting the environment, valuable environmental protection secured by such burdens could be lost on their extinction.

The second exception is statutory agreements. Such agreements have a well-established role in environmental protection: for example, the statutory power to negotiate agreements for planning purposes was first introduced in 1909,[130] and for nature conservation in 1949.[131] Planning agreements entered into under what is now section 75 of the Town and Country Planning (Scotland) Act 1997 operate concurrently with conventional regulation. They are used quite extensively in Scotland as an aid to development control and quite often have an environmental objective.[132] Such agreements enable planning authorities to achieve greater flexibility in the regulation of large, complex developments and to secure certainty of control where there are limits to the use of conventional regulation. There are several statutory provisions directed at the use of agreements to promote nature conservation objectives. For example, section 16 of the National Parks and Access to the Countryside Act 1949 provides for management

---

[124] Discussion Paper on Real Burdens, *supra*. The proposed new conservation burdens are discussed further below.

[125] That is, burdens imposed on neighbouring property for the benefit of the property in the title of which they are imposed.

[126] That is, burdens which benefit a defined community, for example, the proprietors on a particular housing estate.

[127] Discussion Paper on Real Burdens, *supra* n.120.

[128] Views are sought on the appropriate length of the specified period and also on possible exceptions to the general rule.

[129] Again, views are sought on the appropriate length of the specified period and also on possible exceptions to the general rule.

[130] Housing, Town Planning etc. Act 1909, Sch. 4, para. 13.

[131] National Parks and Access to the Countryside Act 1949, s. 16.

[132] *Section 50 Agreements*, consultants' report by J. Rowan-Robinson and R. Durman, (Edinburgh, Scottish Office Central Research Unit, 1992).

agreements for national nature reserves,[133] section 49A of the Countryside (Scotland) Act 1967 provides that a planning authority or Scottish Natural Heritage (SNH) may enter into an agreement with a landowner for the purpose of preserving or enhancing the natural beauty of the countryside or promoting its enjoyment by the public,[134] and section 15 of the Countryside Act 1968 empowers SNH to seek an agreement with a landowner who is threatening to damage the nature conservation interest in a site of special scientific interest.[135] Although such agreements are creatures of statute, they appear to be enforceable in the same way as an ordinary contract. In *Blair* v. *Lochaber District Council*,[136] which concerned a contract of employment, Lord Clyde said that "there is no reason for judicial review where there are contractual rights or obligations which can be enforced, at least as a matter of general principle", and in *McIntosh* v. *Aberdeenshire Council*,[137] Lord MacLean, dismissing a petition for judicial review, said of a planning agreement that:

> whether all the obligations under the Agreement have been fulfilled is primarily a matter for the parties to it, and, in the event of disagreement, resolution according to the private law and the contractual principles which are part of it.[138]

In addition, the provisions governing some of the statutory agreements referred to above provide for their recording so that they may be enforceable not only between the original parties, but against singular successors. Section 75(3) of the Town and Country Planning (Scotland) Act 1997, for example, provides that if a planning agreement has been recorded in the Register of Sasines or in the Land Register of Scotland, it may be enforceable at the instance of the planning authority against persons deriving title to the land from the person with whom the agreement was entered into. The Scottish Law Commission, on considering these types of statutory agreement, thought they appeared random and should be replaced, or at least supplemented, by a general provision allowing categories of public bodies to enter into conservation agreements and has therefore proposed the introduction of "conservation burdens". Such burdens would be subject to the same proposed new rules for creation, variation and extinction discussed above in relation to neighbour and community burdens, and the points made there apply *mutatis mutandis*: in fact, given the expressed purpose of conservation burdens, they apply even more strongly.

---

[133] There are currently 47 such agreements in Scotland covering in all 75,517 ha (*Facts and Figures 1997–98*, SNH, Edinburgh, 1998).

[134] There are currently 54 such agreements in Scotland covering 363,200 ha (*ibid.*).

[135] There are currently 545 such agreements in Scotland covering 74,127 ha (*ibid.*).

[136] 1995 SLT 407.

[137] 1998 SCLR 435. See too *Avon County Council* v. *Millard* [1985] 274 EG 1025 in which Fox LJ said of the corresponding provision in the English planning Act then in force: "Parliament, by section 52, gave power to local authorities to enter into such a contract as this. There is nothing in section 52 which indicates that ordinary civil remedies for breach of such contract were not available". The Court of Appeal in that case granted an interlocutory injunction to restrain mineral operations being carried on in contravention of the terms of an agreement.

[138] *Ibid.*, at 439.

Environmental Protection and the Role of the Common Law   259

The role of contract in environmental protection is expanding, however, principally as a result of controversy created by a government proposal to require local authorities to establish a register of land which was, or had been, subject to a contaminative use.[139] The definition initially proposed for contaminative use was so wide-ranging that a great deal of land in the UK would have been registered,[140] and the proposal caused widespread concern in the property market. This was partly because of the likely blighting effect of the register and partly because of fears, fuelled by experience in the United States, about the distribution of liability for the cost of cleaning up contamination, a cost which in some cases could be very substantial. The proposal for such registers was subsequently withdrawn, but by then the business community had become more aware of the potential for environmental liability. The consequence has been that contracts for company acquisitions and sales with assets which may include contaminated land, and contracts for the purchase, sale, leasing, insuring and lending on the security of property which may be or may become contaminated, now commonly incorporate obligations of an environmental nature. Recent research into the reaction of lending banks to the controversy, for example, found that loan documentation in such cases is now likely to require borrowers to fund a site survey and any necessary remedial work at the outset and to observe good environmental management practices during the lifetime of the loan.[141]

Furthermore, concern about the distribution of liability for cleaning up contaminated land has now grown into a more general concern about liability for pollution. That concern is reflected in contractual obligations, whether between vendor and purchaser, landlord and tenant or employer and contractor, which have as their objective the management of the risk. In some cases environmental obligations may also be implied in a contract. In *Golden Sea Produce Ltd* v. *Scottish Nuclear plc*,[142] for example, the proprietors of a fish hatchery business took a lease of a site from the owners of Hunterston A power station. The lessees were allowed, *inter alia*, to use the heated cooling water effluent from the power station. A large part of the lessees' stock of fish subsequently died as a result of an excessive level of chlorine accidentally pumped from the power station. The lessees claimed damages against the lessor averring that the lessors were liable under the lease. In the Outer House Lord MacLean held that, although the lease imposed no express obligation as to the quality of the heating water, a lessor who conducts operations on his property is under an implied obligation not to derogate from the grant.

The role of contracts is not, however, limited to distributing liability for environmental harm through warranties and indemnities. There are indications that

---

[139] Environmental Protection Act 1990, s. 143, since repealed.

[140] See "Public Registers of Land which may be Contaminated", Department of the Environment consultation paper, 1991.

[141] J. Rowan-Robinson, C. Theron and A. Ross, "Policing the Environment: Private Regulation and the Role of Lenders" (1996) 4(6) *Env. Liability* at 114–18.

[142] 1992 SLT 942.

260   *Jeremy Rowan-Robinson and Donna McKenzie-Skene*

a number of large firms have taken steps to improve their environmental image by seeking to reduce the environmental impact of goods, components and services which they provide. For example, several large retailers now incorporate provisions in contracts with their suppliers requiring the supply of "green" products,[143] and a number of companies, with an eye to the conservation of fish stocks, have moved, through contractual arrangements with suppliers, to phase out the use of fish oil from food production.[144] It is clear, therefore, that terms relating to a variety of environmental issues are increasingly being incorporated into commercial contracts in practice.

Where such terms are subsequently breached by one party, the other party or parties may have a variety of remedies, and where a party makes clear in advance that he does not intend to fulfil his obligations under the contract (anticipatory breach), the other party or parties may treat that as an actual breach of contract and elect to exercise any remedies open to them at once rather than waiting for the time of performance to arrive.[145] Remedies may include enforcing payment (for example, where the contract provides for a payment to be made towards the cost of cleaning contaminated land), specific implement[146] (in the form of a decree *ad factum praestandum* where the obligation is a positive obligation to do something other than pay money, for example, to carry out works to clean up contaminated land, or in the form of an interdict where the obligation is to refrain from doing something, for example, to refrain from polluting a stream), withholding performance until the party in breach performs or agrees to perform[147] (for example, refusing payment until a certificate stipulated for in the contract confirming that the produce supplied is organic is produced), breaking off contractual relations altogether and treating the contract as being at an end, damages (calculated either in accordance with the provisions of the contract, if applicable,[148] or in accordance with the normal common law rules[149]) and any other remedies specifically stipulated for in the contract (for

---

[143] ENDS, 1993, No.221 at 18, "B & Q: Lessons learned in supplier auditing".

[144] ENDS, 1996, No.256 at 26, "Companies move to phase out fish oil from food production".

[145] See *Hochester* v. *De La Tour* (1853) 2 E & B 678. The Scottish Law Commission is currently considering the whole area of remedies for breach of contract, and has made a number of important recommendations: see Scottish Law Commission Report on Remedies for Breach of Contract (No 174) 1999.

[146] It is a general rule in Scots law that the aggrieved party may demand specific implement: see *Stewart* v. *Kennedy* (1890) 17 R (HL) 1. There are, however, a number of exceptions to the rule: a full discussion of these is beyond the scope of this work, but see W. McBryde, *The Law of Contract in Scotland* (Edinburgh, W. Green/Sweet and Maxwell, 1987), ch. 2.

[147] Where the withholding of performance takes the form of withholding payment, it is known as retention; where it takes the form of refusal to perform some other type of obligation, it is more commonly referred to as a lien, although the terms are often used interchangeably.

[148] It should be noted, however, that (in broad terms) contractual provisions governing damages, however designed in the contract, will be enforceable only if they are a genuine pre-estimate of loss and such provisions which are in effect a penalty will not be enforceable: see generally McBryde, *supra* n.146, at para. 20–125. The Scottish Law Commission is currently considering remedies for breach of contract generally and has issued and has issued a specific Report on Penalty Clauses (Scot Law Com (No 171) 1999.

[149] See further below.

Environmental Protection and the Role of the Common Law 261

example, interest, irritancy). A party will be entitled to break off contractual relations altogether and treat the contract as at an end, however, only if the breach by the other party is material, at least where the obligations of the parties are mutual or interdependent: what is material may be specified in the contract itself (for example, a condition that the products supplied comply with certain environmental criteria may be specifically stated to be material) or, in the absence of any such contractual provision, determined from the circumstances.[150] Where more than one remedy is available, a party may choose to pursue one remedy rather than another, for example, claiming damages rather than seeking specific implement, and this may have an impact on the effectiveness of the term as an instrument of environmental protection: if damages are sought rather than specific implement, for example, although the party in breach has been made to pay for the breach, environmental damage may have occurred but ultimately be left unremedied. Furthermore, the quantum of any damages may in itself be problematic. Where the quantum of damages is not determined by the contract itself, the rule at common law is that damages:

> should be either such as may fairly and reasonably be considered arising naturally, *ie*, according to the usual course of things, from such breach of contract itself, or such as may reasonably be supposed to have been in the contemplation of both parties at the time they made the contract as the probable result of the breach of it.[151]

In *Victoria Laundry (Windsor) Ltd* v. *Newman Industries Ltd*,[152] Asquith LJ distinguished the two heads in *Hadley* v. *Baxendale* as imputed knowledge (arising naturally) and actual knowledge (in the contemplation of the parties). Broadly, this means that the defender may be liable in breach of contract not only for loss arising naturally in the usual course of things from the breach but also for losses arising from special circumstances of which the defender had actual knowledge.[153] However, the scope of the second head of claim in *Hadley* v. *Baxendale* is unclear in practice and, as McBryde observes, "[i]n truth it is sometimes difficult to distinguish imputed and actual knowledge".[154] The calculation of damages may therefore raise difficult issues in cases involving environmental issues where there may be dispute not only about whether a particular loss arose directly from the defender's breach of contract but whether it was within the contemplation of the parties.

A related matter is that of enforcement. The general rule is that, in the absence of any indication to the contrary, only the parties to a contract acquire rights and obligations under it, which may be a serious restriction on the effectiveness of contractual conditions as a means of environmental protection. There are a

---

[150] See e.g. *Wade* v. *Waldon*, 1909 SC 571; *Graham* v. *United Turkey Red Co.*, 1922 SC 533.

[151] *Hadley* v. *Baxendale* (1854) 9 Exch. 341, *per* Alderson B at 354. See too *Karlshamns Oljefabriker A/B* v. *Monarch Steamship Co.*, 1949 SC (HL) 1, 1949 SLT 51.

[152] [1949] 2 KB 528.

[153] See e.g. *Strachan and Gavin* v. *Paton* (1826) 3 W & S 19 (HL); and see generally "Obligations" in *Stair Memorial Encyclopaedia*, Vol. 15, para. 906

[154] McBryde, *supra* n.146, para. 20–62.

number of exceptions to this rule. It has already been noted that some conditions of tenure and some statutory agreements may, in specified circumstances, create obligations which are enforceable not only between the original parties to the contract but against singular successors. In addition, under the Leases Act 1449 certain tenants have a real right enforceable against the landlords' singular successors and a real right is also conferred on a tenant in a case where a long lease is recorded in the Register of Sasines or the Land Register of Scotland. The most important exception in this context, however, is where a *jus quaesitum tertio* is created. In Scotland, it is possible for a third party to acquire enforceable rights under a contract to which he is not a party.[155] Such rights may be conferred explicitly in the contract or they may arise by implication from the terms of the contract where these show that the contracting parties intended that the third party should have a direct right of enforcement. The right of reciprocal enforcement of feudal conditions between co-feuars on residential estates is sometimes referred to as a good example of a *jus quaesitum tertio* and provides an illustration in an environmental context.[156] Proprietors of houses on residential estates are generally concerned to see that their neighbours do not engage in activities, for example the introduction of a business use, which will damage their amenity and McDonald notes that:

> The problem of reciprocal enforcement as amongst co-feuars first came to the notice of the courts early in the nineteenth century, when landowners started to use building conditions as a mechanism for promoting and controlling urban development.[157]

The decision in *Hislop* v. *MacRitchie's Trs.*[158] provides that, for a *jus quaesitum tertio* to arise, both co-feuars must have derived their title from a common author, whether as superior or disponer, and be subject to the same condition and, in addition, the title must disclose "clear evidence of an intention to create mutuality and community of rights and obligations as between the respective co-feuars".[159] It is important to note, however, that a *jus quaesitum tertio* will not arise merely because a third party has an interest in a contract. It has been argued, for example, that a *jus quaesitum tertio* exists between an employer and

---

[155] The same is now true in England and Wales in defined circumstances: see the Contracts (Rights of Third Parties) Act 1999.

[156] Reid argues that the classification of a co-feuar's right as a *jus quaesitum tertio* is misleading because it implies a connection with the law of contract which hardly exists. There is, he says, no perpetual feudal contract between superior and vassal; the liability of the vassal to the superior is primarily a matter of property law: K. Reid, *The Law of Property in Scotland* (Edinburgh, The Law Society of Scotland/ Butterworths, 1996), para. 402.

[157] A.J. McDonald, "The Enforcement of Title Conditions by Neighbouring Proprietors" in D.J. Cusine (ed.), *A Scots Conveyancing Miscellany: Essays in Honour of Professor J M Halliday* (Edinburgh, W. Green & Son Ltd, 1987), at 9.

[158] (1881) 8 R (HL) 95.

[159] McDonald, *supra* n.157, at 11. As noted above, this requirement may be satisfied by express stipulation in the titles derived from the common author: in the absence of such a stipulation, it would be necessary to establish the necessary mutuality of rights and obligations by reasonable implication, perhaps from a reference in the titles to a common feuing plan or building scheme, or alternatively by mutual agreement between the feuars themselves.

Environmental Protection and the Role of the Common Law   263

a sub-contractor under a building contract so that contractual remedies might be invoked by one against the other, for example, for loss resulting from bad environmental management practice, but in *J.B. Mackenzie (Edinburgh) Ltd* v. *Lord Advocate*,[160] it was held that the relationship between an employer and a sub-contractor will not normally satisfy the requirements for establishing such a right. The circumstances in which anyone other than the parties to the contract may enforce it are therefore, in practice, very limited.

THE INTER-RELATIONSHIP OF NUISANCE, NEGLIGENCE AND CONTRACT

The circumstances in which environmental protection issues may arise are almost infinitely varied, and the precise circumstances of the case may determine, or at least influence, the basis of any action to be taken by the pursuer. There is a large overlap between the requirements for establishing a case in nuisance and those for establishing a case in negligence, and indeed the pursuer may advance alternative claims under both heads,[161] but there are differences which may mean that the case may be pled on one of these grounds only: for example, as previously noted, only a person with a relevant interest in land may bring an action in nuisance, so if the pursuer does not have such an interest, an action in nuisance will be precluded. Where there is a contract between the parties, it may also be possible in certain circumstances to found a claim in delict:

> A contract may place persons in a relation of proximity so that one owes the other a duty not to cause him harm. Conduct may both amount to a delict to a person and have consequences in the law of contract.[162]

Where such a situation arises, it will be necessary to consider the potential advantages and disadvantages of each type of action in the particular circumstances: for example, a claim founded on breach of contract may be advantageous because of the lack of any requirement to prove fault or because it can open the door to a wider variety of remedies.[163]

CONCLUSION

Three areas of the common law of Scotland have been identified as being of particular relevance to environmental protection: nuisance, negligence and contract. Each has different requirements and each may have a slightly different role

---

[160] 1972 SC 231, 1972 SLT 204.

[161] See e.g. *Graham and Graham* v. *Re-Chem International Ltd, supra,* n.59.

[162] D.M. Walker, *The Law of Contracts and Related Obligations in Scotland* (Edinburgh, T. & T. Clark, 1995), para. 1.12. See also M. Hogg, "Concurrent Liability in the Scots Law of Contract and Delict" [1998] *JR* 1.

[163] See above. There may also be differences in what may claimed as damages: e.g. the precise rules on remoteness are different in each case (see above and *Koufos* v. *Czarnikov, supra,* n.112).

to play in environmental protection. It is important, however, not to overstate their contribution. Although, as was observed at the outset, the common law has a long history of involvement in environmental protection, its response to environmental problems has been slow and patchy. Neither the law of nuisance nor that of negligence is directly concerned with environmental protection *per se*: its contribution to environmental protection is seen rather as incidental, through the deterrent effect of potential liability. It may be questioned, however, to what extent potential liability in nuisance or negligence does in practice deter environmentally damaging behaviour, particularly given the various difficulties, discussed above, which arise in "environmental" cases brought under these heads. As indicated above, the law of nuisance focuses on the protection of proprietary, rather than environmental, rights, and even where proprietary rights touch on the environment, there are hurdles which must be overcome in bringing an action: there are important limitations on who may bring an action; it is not possible to bring an action for personal injury per se or for damage to property other than land itself (except where that damage is consequential on physical damage to the land); it is necessary to prove *culpa* where damages are sought and foreseeability of harm must be established. A negligence action, unlike a nuisance action, is not confined to those with an interest in land, but it is necessary to establish that the defender owed the pursuer a duty of care, that that duty was breached and that the breach of duty caused the pursuer's loss, all of which may be particularly problematic in environmental cases, and the only remedy in a negligence action is damages, the quantification of which may raise difficult issues in environmental cases. While it is, therefore, possible to agree with McManus that nuisance is the most important delict employed in an environmental context,[164] it is also impossible not to agree with Ogus and Richardson when they state, in their evaluation of the role of private nuisance in environmental protection in England, that "the nuisance action can play at best a subsidiary role in any system of pollution control having as its objective general social welfare",[165] and indeed, not to conclude that the law of negligence also can play, at best, a subsidiary role in environmental protection.

In contrast, the law of contract, at least in the commercial world, is beginning to play a more important role in environmental protection than nuisance and negligence and may have less of a subsidiary role to play than those other areas of law. Of course, contracts are essentially a private matter between the parties: the parties must choose to enter them in the first place; generally, only the parties may enforce them and, even where action is taken as a result of a breach of the contract, this may not result in environmental damage being prevented or remedied. Furthermore, environmental maters will often be only incidental to the main purpose of the contract. Nonetheless, business relationships occur within and are given shape by a wider framework of public regulation, a frame-

[164] McManus, *supra*, n.23.
[165] A.I. Ogus and G.M. Richardson, "Economics and the Environment: A Study of Private Nuisance" (1977) 36 *CLJ* at 284.

work which in the field of environmental protection is becoming ever more extensive and sophisticated. Contractual obligations of an environmental nature are to quite a large extent entered into with a view to anticipating and preventing environmental liability arising under this framework,[166] they are concerned with promoting environmentally responsible behaviour so as to avoid statutory liability. Private regulation in the form of contractual provisions, may therefore be seen to operate under the shadow of, and as a complement to, the wider framework of public regulation, and although the objective of a contractual arrangement is the achievement of the private welfare goals of the parties, it is no coincidence that the outcome may be the achievement of public interest goals, in this case protection of the environment from unsociable business activity. It is not, therefore, unreasonable to suggest that the role of the common law in the form of contractual obligations is of growing importance to environmental regulation within the wider statutory framework.

As Lyall comments, however: "[s]peed, certainty, comprehensiveness and an ability to deal with the apparently novel problems of industrialisation, urban growth, public health and recreation, both substantively and through the creation and empowering of agencies, justified and justify legislative action".[167] There is, therefore, no doubt that in Scotland, as in England and Wales, public regulation is, and will remain for the foreseeable future, at the heart of environmental protection, and the role of the common law will remain a more or less subsidiary one.

---

[166] See Rowan-Robinson, Theron and Ross, *supra* n.141.
[167] Lyall, *supra* n.2, at 3.

Index

Access to environmental information, freedom
of:
European law, 218
Air pollution, *see* Atmospheric pollution
Amenity:
nuisance, 41
scope of protection of, 179
stigma damages and, 179, 187–95
enigma in English law, whether, 187–9
narrow and tangible terms, perception in,
189–92
United States, broader approach in, 192–5
Atmospheric pollution:
authorisations, 55, 56
BATNEEC, 56
comparative efficiency of common law's
environmental protection, 71–4
conclusions, 74–5
controlling, 51–76
factory emissions, 55
growth in law to control, 51–2
Integrated Pollution Control (IPC), 54, 55–7
authorisations, 55, 56
BATNEEC, 56
defects in system, 55
directive, 75–6
enforcement, 56–7
Agency enforcement, 56
Integrated Pollution Prevention and
Control Directive, 75–6
offences, 55
operation, 55
penalties, 56
prescribed processes, 55
judicial review, 57–62
availability of review, 57–8
Environment Agency, 58
local authorities, 58
locus standi, 57–62
problems, 58–9
standing, 58–62
less polluting processes, 54
Local Authority Air Pollution Control
(LAAPC), 54, 55–7
authorisations, 55, 56
defects in system, 55
enforcement, 56–7
operation, 55
penalties, 56
prescribed processes, 55

more polluting processes, 54
non-natural use, 52
nuisance, 52
strict liability in, 62–6
prescribed processes, 55
range of issues affecting, 52
reasonable user, 52
Rylands v Fletcher, 52, 53, 62–6
Smoke Control Areas, designation of, 54
statutory nuisance, 54, 57
strict liability in nuisance, 62–6
tort action:
comparative efficiency of common
law's environmental protection,
71–4
conditional fee arrangements, 67–8
distinctive features of action, 67–74
exemplary damages, 69–71
public interest litigation, 68–9
punitive damages, 69–71
waste management, 56
Australia:
nuisance, 172

BATNEEC, 56
Birds, protection of,
European law, 214, 232

Causation:
European law, 217–19
nuisance, *see under* Nuisance
Scotland, environmental protection and
common law in, 252–3
stigma damages, 197
Cemeteries:
victorian foundations of law, 19
Commissioners:
victorian foundations of law, 19
Common law:
comparative efficiency environmental
protection, 71–4
contaminated land,
deficiencies in control of, 115–20
future of, 134–7
development, 1–2
environmental disputes, use in, 115–20
transaction costs, 119
trespass, 116
victorian foundations, 1–2
Conditional fee arrangements, 67–8

268 Index

Contaminated land, statutory liability for, 115–37
  appropriate person, 131–4
  blighted land, 121–2
  closed landfill sites, inspection of, 122
  Commission Green Paper, 122–3
  common law,
    deficiencies, 115–20
    future of, 134–7
  cost/benefit, 130–1
  definition of contaminated land, 123, 124–8
    generally, 124–5
    pollution of controlled waters, 126–7
    significant harm, 126
    suitable for use approach, 128
  derelict land, 125
  duty to identify sites, 123
  Environmental Protection Act 1990, Part IIA, 120–34
  function of provisions, 121
  generally, 115
  guidance notes, 121
  high profile cases, 120–1
  identification of sites by risk posed, 123
  inspection, 121, 129
  liability, 123
  market forces, use of, 121, 123–4
  need for, 120–1
  new provisions, 123
  objectives of law, 123
  outline of provisions, 121
  pollution of controlled waters, 126–7
  register, 123
  registers, 121–2
  remediation, 129–31
  retrospective liability, 122
  significant harm, 126
  special site, 123
  suitable for use approach, 128
Contract:
  Scotland, environmental protection and common law in, 255–63
  conditions of tenure, 255–7
  contaminated land, 259
  inter-relationship with negligence and nuisance, 263
  planning, 257–8
  role of law, 255–6, 259
  statutory agreements, 257–8
  terms in commercial contracts, 259–61
Contributory negligence:
  European law, 220
Controlled waters, pollution of, 126–7
Corrective justice:
  tort, 78–80
Council of Europe:
  Lugano Convention, 210, 211

Damages, 119–20
  nuisance, 34, 43–4, 46
    forseeability, 34, 43–4, 118, 152–7
  punitive, *see* Punitive damages
  Scotland, environmental protection and common law in, 254–5
  stigma, *see* Stigma damages
Defences:
  European law, 220–1
Dicey:
  victorian foundations of law, 23, 24
Disseisin:
  nuisance and, 30, 42
Drinking water:
  European law, 207
Dust:
  nuisance, 30

Economic loss:
  pure, 99, 195–6
  stigma damages, 179
Enterprise zones:
  nuisance, 43
Environment Agency:
  functions, 56
  information available to, 56
  inspectors, 56
  Integrated Pollution Control (IPC) enforcement, 56
  judicial review, 58
Environmental damage:
  European law, 77
  meaning, 77
Environmental pollution, 139
Environmental protection:
  growth of law on, 51–2
  nuisance and, *see under* Nuisance
  private law, role of, 52
  torts and, 141–3
Environmental torts:
  classification as, 140
European Convention on Human Rights:
  television reception, interruption of, 87
European law:
  access to environmental information, freedom of, 218
  birds, protection of, 214, 232
  causation, 217–19
  civil liability:
    access to environmental information, freedom of, 218
    aims of system, 202
    arguments in favour of system, 202
    birds, protection of, 214, 232
    causation, 217–19
    community policy, development of, 204–11
    competition and, 203

Index 269

conclusions, 235–7
contributory negligence, 220
defences, 220–1
developments, 201–37
disasters, 207–11
EU initiatives, 211–29
force majeure, 220
Francovich, 229–35
generally, 201–4
governmental acts and omissions, 229–35
habitats, protection of, 214, 232
harm, definition of environmental, 215–17
industrial processes, 207
initiatives in, 201–37
injury to the environment, definition of,
215–17
insurance, 226–9
joint compensation systems, 226–9
joint and several liability, 219–20
large scale disasters, 207–11
liability policy, development of, 207–11
limitation period, 216–17
NGOs, standing of, 221–24
rationale of proposed system, 202–3
remedies, 224–6
scope of environmental liability, 213–17
significance, 202, 203
standing, 221–4
State liability for environmental harm,
229–35
state-of-the-art defence, 220
strict liability, 212–13
waste, 213–14
community policy on environmental harm,
development of, 204–11
activity of Community, environmental
protection as, 205
case law, 207
competence to legislate, 204
core tasks, 205
drinking water, 207
harmonisation, 206
legal context, 204
legal framework, 205
objectives, 204–5
political context, 204
principles, 205–6
specific obligations, 205
sustainable development, 205
contributory negligence, 220
defences, 220–1
drinking water, 207
environmental damage, 77, 215–17
habitats, protection of, 214, 232
harm, definition of environmental, 213–17
initiatives in liability for environmental
harm, 201–37
insurance, 226–9

joint and several liability, 219–20
state-of-the-art defence, 220
remedies, 224–6
scope of environmental liability, 213–17
standing, 221–4
State liability for environmental harm,
229–35
strict liability, 212–13
waste, 213–14
see also White Paper on Environmental
Liability
Exemplary damages, *see* Punitive damages

Factory emissions:
atmospheric pollution, 55
Force majeure, 220

Getzler:
victorian foundations of law, 2–3

Habitats, protection of:
European law, 214, 232
Housing:
victorian foundations of law, 18

Injunctions:
nuisance, 101–2
Inspection:
contaminated land, 121
contaminated land, statutory liability for,
121, 129
landfill sites, 122
Inspectorates:
victorian foundations of law, 19
Insurance:
European law, 226–9
joint compensation systems, 226–9
Integrated Pollution Control (IPC):
atmospheric pollution, 54, 55–7
authorisations, 55, 56
BATNEEC, 56
defects in system, 55
enforcement, 56–7
Environment Agency, enforcement by, 56
Integrated Pollution Prevention and Control
Directive, 75–6
offences, 55
operation, 55
penalties, 56
prescribed processes, 55

Joint compensation systems, 226–9
Joint and several liability:
European law, 219–20
Judicial review:
atmospheric pollution, 57–62
availability of review, 57–8
Environment Agency, 58

270   *Index*

Judicial review (*cont.*):
  local authorities, 58
  locus standi, 57–62
  problems, 58–9
  standing, 57–62
  Environment Agency, 58
  local authorities, 58
  locus standi, 57–62

Landfill sites:
  inspection, 122
Landfill tax, 86
Licensees:
  nuisance and occupation by, 46–7, 87–8
Limitation period:
  environmental harm, liability for, 216–17
  negligence, 253–4
Local authorities:
  contaminated land inspection, 129
  judicial review, 58
Local Authority Air Pollution Control
  (LAAPC):
  atmospheric pollution, 54, 55–7
  authorisations, 55, 56
  defects in system, 55
  enforcement, 56–7
  operation, 55
  penalties, 56
  prescribed processes, 55
Local Government Board:
  creation, 19
Local regulations:
  victorian foundations of law, 19
Locus standi:
  judicial review, 57–62
Lugano Convention, 210, 211, 214, 217, 221

Maine, Henry:
  victorian foundations of law, 20–1
Art-of-the-art defence:
  European law, 220

Negligence:
  adaptability, 139
  contaminated land, 116
  development of law, 161–2, 163
  limitation period, 253–4
  nuisance and 152–7, 161–78, *see also under*
    Nuisance
  reasonable care, 164
  Scotland, environmental protection and
    common law in, 240, 249–55
  breach of duty, 251–2
  causation, 252–3
  damages, 254–5
  defences, 253–4
  duty of care, 249–50
  forseeability, 250–1

inter-relationship with contract and
  negligence, 263
limitation period, 253–4
remedies, 254–5
remoteness of damage, 255
standard of care, 251
Noise:
  nuisance, 30, 35–6, 46
Nuclear installations:
  stigma damages, 182–3
Nuisance:
  actual damage, 37
  adoption of nuisance, liability for, 167–8
  amenity, interference with, 41
  atmospheric pollution, *see* Atmospheric
    pollution
  Australia, 172
  balancing test, 36
  builders, 41–3
  case law, importance of, 27
  causation, 143–51
    burden of proof, 143–4
    complexity of evidence, 148
    contribution by plaintiff, 148
    expert evidence, 146–8
    general principles of tortious liability, 148
    "hard" versus "soft" causation, 144–9
    holistic approach, 149–51
    "justly ascribing" causes, 144
    material increase in risk, 144
    medical knowledge, prevailing, 143–4
    scientific evidence, 144–8
  character of law, 28, 29–34
  character of neighbourhood, 37, 38
    planning permission, 38–9
  classification of interference with rights,
    29–30
  cognitive explanation of law, 28
  common law,
    advantages, 139
  cognitive explanation of law, 28
  development of, 27
  locality of case law, 28
  moral knowledge, 28–9
  nature of nuisance, 27–8
  theoretical explanations, 27–8
    conclusions, 47–8
    conflicts within law, 27–8
    construction materials, use of, 42
    contaminated land, 117–18
    continuation of nuisance, liability for,
     167–8
    creating nuisance, liability for, 164–7
    damages, 34, 43–4, 46
    forseeability, 34, 43–4, 118, 152–7
    punitive, 69–71
  definition, 27–9, 100
  development of common law, as, 27

Index 271

development of law, 100
discomfort not actual damage caused, 41
disseisin and, 30, 42
duration:
 annoyance, 31
 work, 33
dust, 30
enterprise zones, 43
environmental protection and:
 boundaries between private nuisance,
  negligence and fault, 161–78
 causation, 143–51
 central question, 157
 conclusion, 157–9
 forseeability and fault, 152–7
 generally, 139–41
 Graham case, 142–3
 Hanrahan case, 142
 Sharp & Dohme case, 142
 torts, role of law of, 141–3
examples, 29
explanation of law, 27
fault, 152–7, 163
forseeability, 34, 43–4, 118, 152–7
glare from glass, 42
health and wealth, protection of, 96–103
height of building, effect of, 40, 41, 42
incompatible used of neighbours land, 32,
 118
injunctions, 101–2
interest in land, parties with, 40, 45–6
interference with land,
 classification, 29–30
 moral questions, 31
invasion, 30
liability, 152–3
 adoption of nuisance, 167–8
 continuation of nuisance, 167–8
 creating nuisance, 164–7
licensees, occupation by, 46–7, 87
locality doctrine, 118
malice, 33, 40
measure of damages, 46
moral question, basic, 31, 33–4
natural hazards, 35
negligence and, 152–7, 161–78
 adoption of nuisance, 167–8
 continuation of nuisance, 167–8
 creation of nuisance, 164–7
 different approaches, 173–8
 Hunter v Canary Wharf, impact of, 171–3
 injury, type of, 171–2
 not required, 164–7
 reasonable care, 164
 remedies, 172
 Sedleigh-Denfield, response to, 168–71
 stepping back from problem, 174
 suppression of problem, 173–4

surgery, 174–8
 techniques of dealing with problem, 173–8
neighbourhood character rule, 31–2, 33–4
noise, 30, 35–6, 46
non-natural user, 35–6, 37, 38
occasional annoyance, 33
occupier, special position of, 35
parties, interested, 40, 45–6
planning permission, 38–40
poisonous gas escapes, 36
preventing harmful conduct, 101–3
private:
 Australia, 172
 claimants, 172
 definition, 161
 negligence, relationship with, 161–78
 overwhelmed by negligence, whether,
  163–71
 personal interests, 171–2
 public nuisance distinguished, 100–1
 type of injury, 172
proprietary concept, 29
public and private nuisance distinguished,
 100–1
public utility, 33
punitive damages, 69–71
reasonable user, 31, 35–8, 40, 41, 242
 atmospheric pollution, 52
 creation of nuisance, 164
 reasonable care in negligence distinguished, 164
reasonableness of conduct, 32
recent cases, 34–49
reciprocality, principle of, 32
relationship with other branches of law, 28
resources available to abate nuisance, 44–5
Rylands v Fletcher, relationship with, 34
Scotland, environmental protection and
  common law in, 240, 241–8
 balancing of interests, 243
 comfortable enjoyment of property, 243–4
 definition, 241–2
 fault, 244–6
 inter-relationship with contract and
  negligence, 263
 material harm, 242
 onus of proof, 242
 origins of law, 241–2
 plus quam tolerabile, activity being, 242–3
 reasonable user, 242
 smoke, 30
 statutory authority, defence of, 38–9, 43
 statutory, *see* Statutory nuisance
 steam engines, 18
 strangers, activities of, 35
 strict liability in, 62–6
 structural features of building causing, 42
 subject matter of law, 27

272 Index

Nuisance (*cont.*):
  Scotland (*cont.*):
    systematic annoyance, 33
    television reception, interference with,
      40–1, 43, 44, 45, 87
    temporary, 33
   theoretical explanation, 27
   threshold, 35, 37
   timing of annoyance, 31
   trespass and, 30
   trivial interferences, 34
   use of land, reasonable, 31
   wanton conduct, 33
   water contamination, 34–5, 44

Offences:
  Integrated Pollution Control (IPC), 55

Packaging, 86
Penalties:
  Integrated Pollution Control (IPC), 56
  Local Authority Air Pollution Control
   (LAAPC), 56
Planning permission:
  challenging, 39
  character of neighbourhood, change in, 38–9
  nuisance, 38–40
Poisonous gas escapes:
  nuisance, 36
Polluter pays principle, 140
Pollution:
  atmospheric, *see* Atmospheric pollution
  controlled waters, 126–7
Product liability, 89
Public interest litigation:
  tort, 68–9
Punitive damages:
  Rylands v Fletcher, 69–71
Pure economic loss, 99, 195–6

Quia timet injunctions, 101–2

Railways:
  victorian foundations of law, 17
Registers:
  contaminated land, 121–2, 123
Regulation:
  dominance in modern law, 86–7
Regulators:
  regulating the, 108–11
Remediation of contaminated land, 129–31
Remedies:
  European law, 224–6
Reservoirs:
  bursting, 9–12, 17
Riparian law:
  importance, 3
  victorian foundations of law, 3

Rylands v Fletcher:
  atmospheric pollution, 52, 53
  atmospheric pollution, 52, 53, 62–6
  contaminated land, 119–20, 135–6
  continuing interferences, 34
  development of rule, 139
  forseeability of damage, 80
  future of rule, 98
  non-natural user, 35, 37, 38, 119
  nuisance and, 34
  plaintiffs, 119
  punitive damages, 69–71
  strict liability, 34, 35, 38

Scotland, environmental protection and
    common law in, 239–65
  conclusion, 263–5
  contract, 255–63
   conditions of tenure, 255–7
   contaminated land, 259
   enforcement of terms, 261–2
   inter-relationship with negligence and
    nuisance, 263
   planning, 257–8
   role of law, 255–6, 259
   statutory agreements, 257–8
   terms in commercial contracts, 259–61
  generally, 239–41
  history, 239–41
   negligence, 240, 249–55
   breach of duty, 251–2
   causation, 252–3
   damages, 254–5
   defences, 253–4
   duty of care, 249–50
   forseeability, 250–1
   inter-relationship with contract and
    negligence, 263
   limitation period, 253–4
   remedies, 254–5
   remoteness of damage, 255
   standard of care, 251
  nuisance, 240, 241–8
   balancing of interests, 243
   comfortable enjoyment of property, 243–4
   definition, 241–2
   fault, 244–6
   inter-relationship with contract and
    negligence, 263
   material harm, 242
   onus of proof, 242
   origins of law, 241–2
   plus quam tolerabile, activity being,
    242–3
   reasonable user, 242
Smallpox hospitals, 103–4
Smelting works:
  victorian foundations of law, 5–9

Smoke:
 nuisance, 30
Smoke Control Areas:
 designation, 54
Standing:
 European law, 221–4
 judicial review, 57–62
State liability for environmental harm, 229–35
Statutory authority, defence of,
 nuisance, 38–9, 43
Statutory nuisance:
 atmospheric pollution, 54, 57
 limits to scope, 57
 prejudicial to health or a nuisance, 57
Steam engines:
 nuisance from, 18
Stigma damages, 179–200
 amenity, 179, 187–95
  enigma in English law, whether, 187–9
  narrow and tangible terms, perception in,
   189–92
  United States, broader approach in, 192–5
 causation, 197
 conclusion, 198–200
 damage, legally recognisable, 181
 delineating terrain, 180–2
 desirability of recovery, 196–8
 economic loss from, 179, 195–6
 English Courts, in, 182–3
 fear of contamination, 181
 market stigma, 181
 meaning, 180
 meaning of stigma, 180–1
 nuclear installations, 182–3
 perception of damage, 180
 permissible losses, 185–7
 physical damage,
  establishing, 183–5
  expert evidence, 183
  factual view, 183–5
  precondition, 182–3
 post-remediation stigma, 181
 precondition of physical damage, 182–3
 problem of, 179
 United States, 179, 181–2
Strict liability:
 atmospheric pollution, 62–6
 European law, 212–13
 nuisance and, 62–6
 Rylands v Fletcher, 34, 35, 38
 victorian foundations of law, 9–12
Sulphuric acid control:
 victorian foundations of law, 5–9

Television reception, interference with:
 nuisance, 40–1, 43, 44, 45, 87
Tort:
 challenge facing law, 89–91

conditional fee arrangements, 67–8
corrective justice, 78–80
distinctive features of action, 67–74
environmental pluralism and, 93–113
 Canada, 113
 conclusion, 111–13
 differences of view about science and risk,
  103–8
 generally, 93–4
 individual health and wealth, protection
  of, 96–103
 land use planning, 110
 negligence, 98–9
 nuisance, 100–1
 procedural barriers, 105–6
 pure economic loss, 99, 179, 195–6
 quia timet injunctions, 101–2
 regulating the regulators, 108–11
 risk, tackling, 101–3
 roles for tort action, 93–6
 Rylands v Fletcher, 98
 smallpox hospitals, 103–4
 statutory schemes and, 99–100
 structural malaise, 96–101
 substantive barriers to action, 106–8
 testing orthodoxy, 103–8
environmental protection and, 141–3
environmental torts, 140
 role of, 94–6
forseeability:
 damage, 80
 risk, 80
individual to the environment, from,
 77–91
negligence, 98–9
nuisance:
 standing, 101
nuisance, *see* Nuisance
procedural barriers to action, 105–6
public interest litigation, 68–9
risk:
 regulation and, 85–9
 science and, 82–5
 science, law and risk, 82–5
 substantive barriers to action, 106–8
 toxic torts, 80–2, 151
 White Paper on Environmental Liability,
  77
 workplace injuries, 78–9
Town planning:
 victorian foundations of law, 18
Toxic torts, 80–2, 151
Trespass:
 contaminated land, 116
 nuisance and, 30

United States:
 stigma damages, 179, 181–2

274 *Index*

Victorian foundations of law, 1–25
1840–80, 12–24
administrative law, growth in, 19
cemeteries, 19
commissioners, 19
common law,
development, 1–2
resilience, 23
statute law, relationship with, 24
conclusion, 24–5
defence, 14
Dicey, 23, 24
disruptive statutes, 16–21
drafting of legislation, 17
efficiency, 16
evidence, 14
facts of case, importance of, 4–5
forms of action, 14–15
generally, 1–4
Getzler, 2–3
growth in legislation, 17–21
harbours, 17
housing, 18
inspectorates, 19
judges, role of, 12–16
Judicature Commissions, 14
judicial response to problems with law, 21–4
jury, role of, 7–8
decline in, 12–13
land-use law, 3
law and equity, relationship between, 14
law reports, 5
law text books, 15–16
Local Government Board, 19
local regulations, 19
Maine, Henry, 20–1
medieval precedents, 1
mid-century, 12–16
nuisance, 17
Parliament, significance of, 2–3
pleadings, 13–14
precedents, 15
private Acts, 17
professionals, 16
progressive society, demands of, 21
railways, 17
reform, 14
reservoirs:
bursting, 9–12, 17
"reservoir bills", 17
riparian law, 3
Rylands v Fletcher, 9–11
significance, 11–12
Select Committee on Noxious Vapours, 5
smelting works, 5–9
statement of claim, 14
steam engines, nuisance from, 18
strict liability, 9–12
sulphuric acid control, 5–9
Tipping v St. Helen's Smelting Co., 4–9
significance, 11–12
town planning, 18
transcripts of cases, 5

Waste management:
atmospheric pollution, 56
European law, 213–14
Waste Regulation Authorities:
landfill site inspection, 122
Water contamination:
nuisance, 34–5, 44
Water law, *see* Riparian law
White Paper on Environmental Liability, 77–8
consequences, 201
effect, 77
publication, 201
tort law, impact on, 77
see also European law